THE COMPLETE
Watercolor Course

The Ultimate Step-by-Step Guide to Painting Landscapes, Still Lifes, and Portraits

THE COMPLETE
Watercolor Course
The Ultimate Step-by-Step Guide to Painting Landscapes, Still Lifes, and Portraits

amber
BOOKS

This edition first published in 2010

Published by
Amber Books Ltd
Bradley's Close
74–77 White Lion Street
London N1 9PF
United Kingdom
www.amberbooks.co.uk

Material previously published in the part-work *Step-by-Step Art-Course*

ISBN: 978-1-906626-78-5

Contributing Artists:
Harold Bartram, Chris Bramley, Ken Cox, Sharon Finmark, Michael Grimsdale,
Lavinia Hamer, Xiaoeng Huang, Wendy Jelbert, John Raynes, Tom Robb, Ian Sidaway,
Adrian Smith, Hazel Soan, Tig Sutton, Richard Taylor

Printed in China

Contents

Equipment & Techniques

Getting started with choosing the correct easel, paper and brushes, keeping a sketchbook, making washes, basic composition and mixing colours.

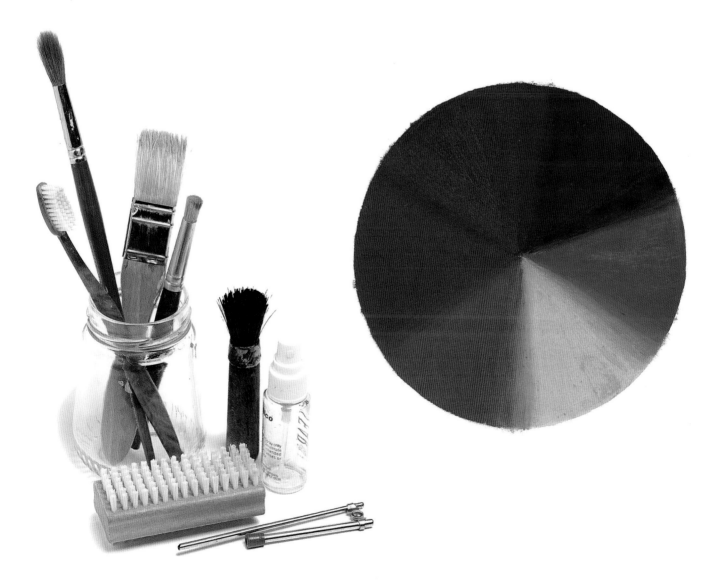

Blueprint for a painting

Like a play or film, a picture must be put together so that its component parts make a balanced, harmonious whole to hold the attention of the viewer. This important skill is called 'composition'.

Traditionally, artists have used the rectangle as the framework for paintings. When used horizontally, it is referred to as having a 'landscape' format, and when used upright as having a 'portrait' format.

Getting the right fit

The shape and size of the rectangle has to be right for what you want to fit into it. If it is too small, the image looks squashed and this makes the viewer want to see past the edges; too large, and the eye wanders about trying to find something to hold its interest. Good composition is achieved when all the elements of the picture (colours, shapes, tones, textures and, vitally, the spaces between them) relate to each other in a balanced way.

The focal point

Imagine that you have just moved into an empty house and you are arranging the furniture in the living room. You will probably set out the armchairs and sofa so that they face the television, or perhaps a fireplace. These are 'focal points', and the angles and relative distances that you create in positioning the furniture is an important consideration.

Alternatively, the chairs might be arranged to face each other for conversation, in which case the focal point is actually a space.

In a painting, the focal point is the point to which the viewer's eye tends to be drawn most strongly. This is usually the main subject of the work – for example, the face in a portrait, or the church tower in a village

THE GEOMETRY OF COMPOSITION

This information is by no means essential to composing a successful picture, but you may find it interesting. Absorb as much, or as little, of it as you like.

Euclid noted that a sequence of numbers (3, 5, 8, 13, 21, etc) gave a series of ratios which Renaissance artists called the 'divine proportion', otherwise the 'Golden Section' or 'Golden Mean'. If a line is drawn by combining any two successive numbers (say 5 and 8, making 13), and divided into the two component lengths (i.e. one of 5 and one of 8), then the ratio of the smaller part to the larger (5:8) is the same as the ratio of the larger part to the whole (8:13).

▶ **The Golden Section**
The diagram shows how a focal point within a rectangle is created by using the 'Golden' proportions. Giovacchino Toma (1838–91) used this principle for the main focal point in his painting *Luisa San Felice In Prison,* **below.**

This principle was used as the basis for many Classical buildings because the balance created by these divisions, either vertically or horizontally (or both), is very satisfying. In paintings, the points where the verticals and horizontals of the 'Golden Mean' intersect within the rectangle are often used as the focal point (or points) of the image. This is about a third of the way in and a third of the way up (or down).

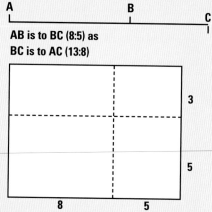

AB is to BC (8:5) as
BC is to AC (13:8)

▲ Renaissance painters used the formal geometry of vertical, horizontal and diagonal lines to form triangular compositions within the rectangle. The portrait shown here, the *Madonna of the Goldfinch* by Raphael Sanzio (1483–1520), shows the principle clearly.

Composition in practice

To understand the importance of composition, you will need to explore a little, observing how different elements relate to each other. Try these exercises.

1 Take a sheet of white paper and some coloured papers (say red and green). Cut up the colours into rectangular shapes of various sizes and practise arranging them in different ways on the white sheet, overlapping some of them if you like. Try to organise a focal point and to achieve a good balance between shapes, spaces and colours. Look at how your arrangements visually affect the rectangle. Is there a sense of space; are there 'busy' areas and 'quiet' ones; is there any sense of 'movement' or 'tension' between shapes? Try the same exercise with other colours, or with black and grey.

2 Find a reproduction of a well-known painting for this exercise. Using tracing paper, draw lines to connect up the main directions formed by the various objects, light, shadows and forms within the painting. Notice how diagonals are used to hold together different areas and create 'routes' for the eye to follow.

3 From a sheet of white paper measuring 8 x 5cm (3 x 2in), cut out a rectangle from the centre to leave a frame about 1cm (⅜in) wide all round. Hold this at arm's length and move it slowly around the room or the garden. The view you see inside the frame is your composition. Notice how a very small shift of the frame can make for a much more balanced composition.

scene. In more complex images, where no one element is more important than another, the artist has to guide the viewer's eye around the picture by the way the various elements are arranged. As in the living room, the balance of these and the 'dynamic' that is set up within the rectangle are what composition is all about.

Things to avoid

There are no firm rules, but some things are best avoided. Dividing the surface in half by placing a tall object in the centre, or positioning the horizon line exactly half-way up, makes the picture 'boring'.

Similarly, same-size objects equidistant on either side of the centre line, or a continuous row of trees running right across the middle of the picture, make for dull compositions. Remember to compose 'through' the picture as well as across the surface.

▼ The compositions of Pieter Brueghel (the Elder) (*c.* 1515–69) are full of incident and usually contain lots of different focal points with plenty of space for the eye to wander about in. Notice the position of the flying bird in his painting *Hunters in the Snow*. Is it the first thing that caught your eye?

Keeping a sketch book

Whether you use it to make preparatory drawings, try out different mediums or create a visual diary, the sketch book is an invaluable tool for the artist.

Artists have been known to make sketches on old envelopes, on shopping lists – and even on the back of the hand! It is much simpler, however, if you carry a sketch book at all times. In this way you can make on-the-spot drawings and jot down visual ideas whenever and wherever you like – and you always know where to find them when you need them.

The sketchbook habit

For most artists, carrying a sketch book is more effective than carrying a camera. True, you can take a photograph in a fraction of a second and it will give you a detailed rendition of a particular scene. Unless you are a skilled photographer, however, you cannot use the camera as creatively, as it tends to render everything in the same way.

A sketch book, on the other hand, provides a personal record. In it, you can record not only what you see, but also what you feel. You can emphasize certain elements, and leave out others entirely. If you are struck by a particular facial expression, for example, you can make a quick sketch, capturing the essence of that expression without worrying about detail, colour, texture and so on.

It is a good idea to buy a small sketch book – one which fits into your pocket or a bag that you always carry – and to use it whenever the opportunity arises. Record people and places, and sketch details of what is happening around you.

▼ **Large or small, spiral-bound or case-bound, landscape or portrait, there is a sketch book to meet the needs of every artist.**

Above all, jot down any ideas you might have for future paintings. Your sketch book – unlike your memory – won't let you down. Once you have made a drawing, it is there for ever to provide you with inspiration.

The quality of the paper in sketch books varies enormously. You can, for example, buy books of handmade paper, often bound with elaborately marbled or fabric covers. These sketch books are beautiful objects in their own right.

The right paper

However, a very expensive sketch book can be quite daunting for the amateur artist, who might be afraid to ruin it with poor sketches. Remember also that a sketch book with a delicate, ornate cover will get damaged easily if you intend to carry it around with you.

It is probably better to begin by using an inexpensive book – but avoid very cheap pads that contain thin, shiny paper. These are generally bought from stationers rather than art shops. Usually, the paper they are filled with is too hard to use with anything except a ballpoint or fountain pen.

Most art shops stock sketch books in a range of cartridge and drawing papers, from 95gsm (45lb) sketching paper to the heavier 290gsm (140lb). Also available are pads of assorted coloured and tinted papers, ideal for pastel and coloured pencil work. However, these are not usually made in pocket sizes, A5 generally being the smallest.

Choosing a sketch book

To a large extent your choice of sketch book will depend on what drawing materials you use. Cartridge paper is a good all-rounder, suitable for most drawing tools. However, bear in mind that pen and ink and technical pens are best used on very smooth papers, while chunky mediums such as soft pencil, pastel and charcoal are served well by coarse surfaces.

Sketch books come in various shapes and sizes. Some are rectangular and upright ('portrait' format); others are rectangular and horizontal ('landscape' format). The portrait format is perhaps the most versatile choice because you can always work across two pages, taking your drawing over the spine for a landscape subject.

Spiral- or case-bound?

The spine of a sketch book can be either case-bound (that is, stitched or gummed)

or spiral-bound. The spiral-bound ones don't allow you to sketch across two pages, but they do let you remove pages without ruining the book. This means you can discard substandard sketches and mount and frame exceptional ones.

What's more, the spiral-bound books can easily accommodate mounted materials. To make your book really attractive, feel free to include visually interesting items such as pressed flowers and leaves, postcards, tickets, invitations and even scraps of fabric – anything, in fact, that may prove useful as a reference, inspiration or memory jogger. Your sketchbook is, in effect, a visual diary.

You can also use your sketchbook for painting outdoors. Most heavier sketch-book papers of around 290gsm (140lb) are fine for light water-colour washes. However, for very wet colour, you should always use a watercolour pad.

▲ Carefully worked watercolours that run right up to the edge of the page can look stunning in your sketchbook.

◄ In upright sketchbooks, you can attain landscape-format drawings simply by working over the spine.

12

Watercolour pads

Like sketchbooks, watercolour pads come in a range of sizes starting from around 180 x 130mm (7 x 5in). They are made with proper watercolour paper and have a strong backing board for rigidity and stability. The papers range from very rough to smooth hot-pressed. They are available either spiral-bound or as a block which is gummed on all four edges to reduce the need for stretching.

For sketching with acrylic paints, you can buy pads of canvas-textured paper. Oil paints are not really a suitable sketching medium because they take so long to dry.

Colour notes

Painting out-of-doors can be a delight, but you often find yourself running out of time or stopped in your tracks by a change in the weather. It is difficult to finish the painting at home because you cannot remember the colours.

The answer is to make colour notes in your sketch book before you start work on the painting. Make a very rough line drawing of the subject in your sketch book. Then you can write the names of the colours on the sketch or, even better, paint an actual blob of colour in the relevant area. These approximate colour guides will provide the reference you need to complete the painting at home.

One sketch book, many styles

Use your sketch book to experiment with different drawing styles and mediums. The sketches below – which are all by the same artist – give some indication of the styles you might like to include in your book. The top picture is a line drawing in pencil, but has blocks of tone dotted across the composition to add variety. The middle picture is also in pencil – but colour has been added with washes of coffee.

The bottom sketch was done in watercolours. Paints might not seem the ideal sketching medium – but you can easily carry around a small watercolour set that contains all you need.

Enlarging your work

Producing a larger-scale version of the subject you are trying to paint or draw can be easier than you think – just follow the simple step-by-step techniques described here.

▼ Many works by Stanley Spencer (1891–1959), such as this study for his painting *The Visitation* (*c.*1912), have a visible pencil grid.

The following scenario is a familiar one to many artists. You are about to start work on a painting. You know what you want to paint and you have some reference – perhaps a drawing, photograph or small colour sketch of the subject. However, the reference is much smaller than the picture you want to paint. The problem is this: how do you transfer the small image on to a large paper or canvas without altering the shapes or losing the composition?

A freehand copy is one possibility. Draw directly on to the large support, referring to the sketch as you progress. For the experienced artist, with confidence and drawing skills to match the challenge, this is fine. However, for the beginner, freehand copying is not always as simple as it seems and can turn the very first stage of a painting into a frustrating stumbling block. For example, an over-cautious approach often leads to the enlarged drawing being too small, resulting in a lot of empty space around the subject. An easier and more accurate way of transferring and enlarging the image is to use a grid.

PROPORTIONATE RECTANGLES

The grid method of enlarging only works if both the small and large rectangles have the same proportions. To construct a proportionate large rectangle (B in the diagram) from a smaller one (A in the diagram), draw a diagonal from the bottom left-hand corner and through the top right-hand corner of rectangle A. Extend the bottom and left-hand sides of the small rectangle to form rectangle B, making sure that the top right-hand corner of rectangle B falls on the diagonal line and that each corner of the rectangle is drawn at a right angle.

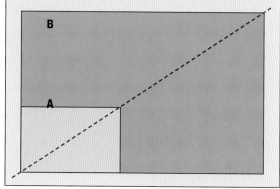

Enlarging a watercolour sketch

A small watercolour landscape is enlarged here using the grid method to provide an outline drawing for a larger watercolour. No detail is necessary, simply enough information to act as a guide for the paint. The grid is divided into twelve sections – use tracing paper to avoid drawing grid lines directly on to the colour sketch.

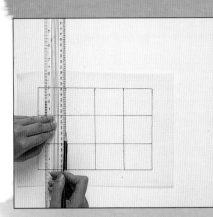

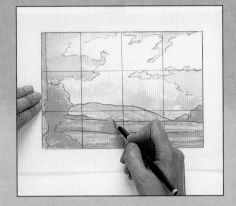

1 ▲ **Rule up a grid** Take a sheet of tracing paper and draw a rectangle the same size as the watercolour sketch. Divide the rectangle into 12 equal sections.

2 ▲ **Trace the main outlines** Use a soft pencil to trace the outlines of the landscape – the hills, trees and clouds – keeping the lines light and unfussy.

3 ▲ **Enlarge the grid** On watercolour paper, draw a large rectangle of the same proportions as the small sketch. Rule up a proportionately larger grid inside the large rectangle.

4 ▶ **Copy the image** Using the small tracing as your reference, copy the picture on to the watercolour paper section by section. Each section will be accurately reproduced on the larger-scale grid, creating an enlarged image in the correct proportions.

5 ◀ **Paint the finished picture** Erase the grid lines before you begin to paint. You can now use the enlarged outlines as a guide while you work on the various stages of the painting.

Enlarging with a grid

The grid should divide the reference sketch or photograph into a number of equal rectangles or squares. Either draw these directly on to the reference or, if you would prefer not to mark the photo or sketch, draw a grid on a piece of tracing paper and trace the reference picture on to it (see above).

The next stage is to draw a bigger grid on the large piece of paper or canvas, using the same number of squares or rectangles. It is important that the grid on the large support has exactly the same proportions as the smaller one, otherwise you will end up with a distorted image. You can now copy the smaller image section by section on to the larger support.

Confident strokes

For the enlarged drawing, try to keep your lines free and flowing. Indicate only the main shapes rather than attempting to include every detail. Avoid a cramped-looking image by drawing from the elbow rather than the wrist and by holding your drawing tool as far from the drawing tip as possible.

It helps to work with a chunky medium such as carbon pencil or graphite stick when reproducing the larger image. These tools produce thick lines which will encourage you to draw boldly, creating a drawing with a fresh, spontaneous appearance.

Photocopier method

Using a photocopier is another way of creating a larger image, enabling you to increase the size of a small sketch or photograph up to an A3 format. If you want anything bigger, you may have to enlarge your reference picture in sections, in two or more stages. However, the photocopied image still needs to be transferred by tracing, and for this you will need a lightbox.

Brushes

It's worth building up a collection of different brushes as they will help you achieve a wide range of exciting paint effects.

Artists' brushes are available in an enormous range of shapes and sizes, corresponding to the various purposes they are intended for. They may be made from several different kinds of natural bristles or from synthetic fibre, and the difference in price between the different types of bristle can be considerable. The choice is wide, but in the end the decision as to which to buy and use is a personal one, often depending on trial and error. Initially, it is a good idea to experiment with one or two brushes at a time to see how you get on.

WHAT TO LOOK FOR

FERRULE The ferrule holds the handle and the bristles of the brush securely together. The best ferrules are moulded in a single piece from a stainless, non-corrosive metal.

BRISTLES A good brush has a firm, compact and well-shaped bristle head.

HANDLE This should be lacquered or varnished to resist water and for ease of cleaning.

Small and large

Most artists' brushes come in a range of sizes, usually numbered. For example, a standard watercolour brush range can start with a tiny No. 0000, used only for the very finest work, going up to No. 20 and even larger. However, it is worth remembering that each brush manufacturer has a slightly different system. Hence a No. 2 brush made by one manufacturer is not necessarily exactly the same size as a No. 2 brush produced by another. The size of some flat brushes may be expressed in terms of total bristle width instead of numbers – 25mm (1in), 51mm (2in) and so on.

Types of brush

Each type of brush is designed to make a specific kind of mark. Choosing a brush depends very much on the effect you want to achieve, but if you have one or two of the following basic brush types they will be all you need to begin with.
Round This is a brush with a rounded ferrule, and it is a popular, general-purpose brush with a full bristle head that holds a lot of paint. Large rounds are useful for laying washes and wide expanses of colour. The point can be used for painting lines and detail.
Flat or chisel-headed This type of brush has a flattened ferrule with a square-cut

▲ **Brushes are available in many sizes. These sable rounds range in size from the finest No. 0000 to the much larger No. 20.**

bristle head. The wide bristles are good for applying paint in short dabs and for laying flat areas of colour, while the narrow edge of the bristles is useful for making thinner lines. A flat with very short bristles is sometimes referred to as a 'bright'.
Filbert Somewhere between a flat and a round, a filbert has a flattened ferrule but with tapered bristles. It is a popular and versatile brush, combining the functions of other brush types.
Fan The attractively shaped fan brush, or blender, as it is also sometimes known, has widely splayed bristles and is used primarily for blending colours together smoothly.

Watercolour brushes

Watercolour brushes are usually softer than those used with oil and acrylics.

Fan

Round

Filbert

Flat

The very best- quality watercolour brushes to be found are sable brushes. These are made from only the tail-end hairs of the sable, a small, fur-bearing animal that is found in certain regions in Siberia. This is why pure sable brushes are so expensive. To reduce cost, manufacturers sometimes mix sable with other natural hair. This is usually ox or squirrel hair, but occasionally goat, camel or even mongoose hair is used.

Why are sable brushes so good to work with? For a start, they combine strength with suppleness, and this allows you to paint in a lively yet controlled way. They also wear well, and will keep their shape. If properly cared for, a sable brush can last a lifetime.

However, manufactured bristles have improved in quality in recent years. They fall into two main categories. Soft brushes are made especially for water-colour paints and have a texture and pliancy which aim to match the qualities of natural hair. Stiffer, general-purpose nylon brushes are made mainly for use with oil and acrylics, but are occasionally used by watercolourists to give a textured surface.

Caring for watercolour brushes

Each time you use a brush, rinse it in water. Either hold your brushes in your free hand while you work, or lay them down on a flat surface. Never leave them standing head down in water because this will bend the bristles. Once this has happened, it can be difficult to restore a brush to its proper state.

At the end of a painting session, wash each brush thoroughly in warm soapy water, then rinse well under running water. Gently shake the bristle head back into its natural shape. If necessary, reshape the bristles with your thumb and index finger. Store brushes upright with the handle end downwards.

Special brushes

You may come across various eye-catching and exotic-looking brushes in the art shop. Though they may appear unusual and have intriguing names – rigger, oriental, mop and spotter – these brushes are very practical and invaluable for creating specific effects.

Rigger So-called because it was originally used to paint fine ship's rigging in marine paintings, the rigger has long, tapering bristles. Today it is used more generally for all linear work, but especially for lettering, poster writing and also calligraphy.

Oriental brushes Recognizable by their cane or bamboo handles, these brushes produce the characteristic, flowing lines which give Japanese and Chinese paintings their distinctive quality. The bristles taper to a fine point, and the brushes can be used for painting fine lines, as well as for creating broad strokes and laying washes.

Spotter Miniature paintings and all fine detail can be executed with a retouching brush, or spotter. The spotter is a small round brush with short bristles, good for all precise work.

Wash brushes There are several large brushes designed specifically for laying flat washes. Most artists use a soft, flat brush; others prefer a large round, or a mop. The mop brush has a large, rounded head and is especially good for laying textured washes such as sea and sky.

Rigger

Sable rounds

Synthetic brushes

Mop

WATERCOLOUR BRUSH MARKS

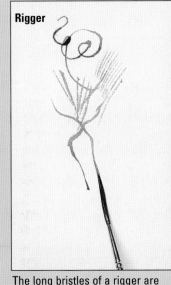

Rigger

The long bristles of a rigger are designed for linear work.

Flat or chisel-headed

A flat brush can give broad or narrow lines of paint.

Round

Use the whole brush for painting large areas, and the tip for details.

Stretching paper

Nothing is more frustrating than getting a watercolour painting just right, only for the paper to wrinkle up. Avoid disappointment with a little preparation.

Wrinkles appear in watercolour paper because it stretches when it is wet and shrinks as it dries. But it rarely dries evenly, creating wrinkles and cockles.

The degree of cockling depends on a paper's weight and quality. Paper weight is expressed in terms of grammes per square metre for metric measurements and weight per ream (500 A4 sheets) for imperial measures. With heavier papers,

those of 300gsm (140lb) and over, the paper should be sturdy enough to stand all but the heaviest soaking. Light papers will almost certainly cockle.

With light- and medium-weight papers, and those meant to take heavy washes, the answer is to soak the paper with water and dry it flat before starting work.

Stretching paper may seem a chore, but it saves time and disappointment in

the long run. You can stretch a few sheets at a time so that you have a ready supply and do not have to repeat the performance every time you want to paint.

Stretching on a board

The most usual method of paper stretching is to stick the wet sheet on to a board with gummed tape. Use a drawing board, blockboard, sturdy ply or

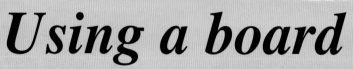

Using a board

1 ▼ Wet the paper Cut the paper so that it fits on the drawing board, leaving at least 1cm (½in) all round. Soak the sponge in water and thoroughly wet the paper all over.

2 ▼ Remove excess water When the paper has absorbed the water, squeeze the sponge dry and use it to soak up any excess moisture with long, firm strokes.

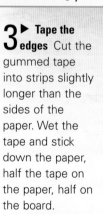

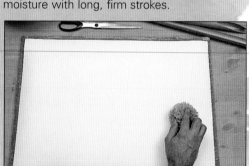

3 ▶ Tape the edges Cut the gummed tape into strips slightly longer than the sides of the paper. Wet the tape and stick down the paper, half the tape on the paper, half on the board.

4 ▶ Reinforce with drawing pins Put a drawing pin at each corner of the paper to prevent the paper from tearing or pulling off the tape. Leave the paper to dry naturally away from direct heat.

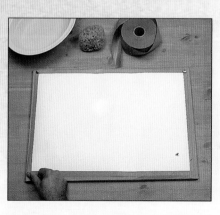

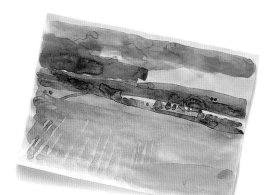

■ **Avoid the disappointment of wrinkled paper by stretching it first.**

fibreboard. Hardboard is unsuitable because it will bend as the paper dries. Nor should you use a plastic or laminated board because the tape will not stick properly. Make sure there are no bumps or flaws on the board's surface, because these will show on the stretched paper. Also, any ink or paint marks may dissolve and stain the paper.

Most papers contain size to create a receptive painting surface. Lightly sized paper takes only a minute or two to absorb water. Heavily sized paper takes longer and should be thoroughly wet. Over-soaking will eventually weaken paper and it may tear. Too little water, and the paper will not expand properly.

Use gummed brown paper tape to stick the dampened paper to the board. As the paper dries, it will often contract with a surprising force and may pull away the tape. For extra strength, cut the paper almost to the size of the board so the tape goes over the edges of the board. Always allow the paper to dry completely.

Using a stapler

A speedy method of paper-stretching is to staple the sheet to the board instead of using gummed paper. The same method can be used with a wooden canvas stretcher, in which case the stretched paper stays on the frame when you paint.

Short cuts

To avoid having to stretch paper, try using a watercolour block. This is made up of sheets of watercolour paper gummed together at the edges and mounted on cardboard to form a rigid block. Each painting is removed as it is completed. Alternatively, try watercolour boards – individual sheets of watercolour paper mounted on rigid card. These are slightly more expensive but can save a lot of time.

Using a stretcher

YOU WILL NEED

Paper

Scissors

Wooden canvas stretcher the size you require for your painting (remember the paper will be left on the frame)

Stapler and staples

Sponge

1 ▲ **Staple one side** Cut the paper to fit the stretcher, leaving about 4cm (2in) all round. Centre the stretcher on the paper and staple the paper to the edge of the stretcher at the centre of the longest side.

2 ▲ **Staple the second side** Staple the paper to the edge of the stretcher at the centre of the opposite side. The paper should not be slack, but do not try to stretch it too much at this stage otherwise it may tear.

3 ▲ **Cut the corners** Cut a slot at each corner of the paper, from the corner of the stretcher and at a right angle to the edge of the paper. Staple the paper at the centre of the two remaining shorter sides.

4 ▲ **Wet the paper** Finish stapling the paper to the stretcher. Wet the paper thoroughly and evenly with a sponge and allow to soak until the paper has absorbed the moisture.

5 ▲ **Remove excess moisture** Wipe any remaining water from the surface of the paper using the squeezed-out sponge in long, even strokes, and allow the paper to dry naturally.

Washing onto watercolour paper

Laying a flat wash onto paper is the first step that most artists take when working with watercolours. Here's how to do it.

Laying a wash onto paper is the starting point for most watercolour paintings. The wash can be flat or graduated (fading in colour towards the top or bottom of the picture) and then serves as the base colour onto which other colours can be applied.

Test the wash first

The wash technique is often used in landscape painting or for large areas of plain sky. Two good tips are to make sure that you mix enough paint to complete the wash, and to test its strength on a piece of scrap paper before you start painting. This is because watercolour dries lighter than it appears when initially applied.

The type of watercolour paper used is important as most lightweight papers require stretching to avoid cockling. The stronger and heavier papers, however, will withstand the wettest of washes and still remain fairly flat. The texture of the paper will also affect the quality of the wash. So the best option for practising laying washes is to use a sheet of cold pressed (or Not) paper heavier than 140lb. (See the section overleaf on Types of Paper for more information on this.)

Equipment

Any painting project will only benefit from good organisation, so the starting point will always be to lay out your equipment. For this exercise, make sure that you have a flat (or chisel ended) brush, a jar of clean water with a wide enough neck to accommodate the brush,

Laying a flat wash

Sheet of 140lb+ NOT watercolour paper

Jar of water

Mixing palette or dish

Flat brush

Watercolour: Cobalt blue

1 ▲ Lightly wet the paper Dip the brush into a jar of clean water and, holding it at arm's length, wet the paper using a series of horizontal and vertical brush strokes. Ensure that all the paper is covered. This allows the paint to flow freely when applied.

2 ▶ Drag the brush across the paper Leave a minute or two for the water to be absorbed. In the meantime, pour some water into a palette or white saucer and, using a wet brush, mix in some of the cobalt blue paint.

Make sure you mix enough paint to complete the wash. Then drag the loaded brush over the top of the paper in a single, smooth, even stroke, applying even pressure all the way along.

3 ▶ Continue moving downwards At the end of the stroke, lift the brush and repeat the procedure directly underneath – reloading your brush with paint if required and making sure that

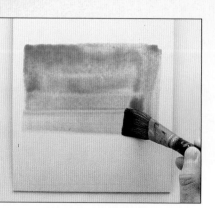

you leave no gaps between the new brushstroke and the one above. Continue moving down the paper in the same way, maintaining even pressure throughout.

4 ▶ Leave to dry Despite its initial appearance, the paint will dry to a smooth, even finish. Resist the temptation to work on the wash further.

EXPERT ADVICE
Preventing cockling

Paper lighter than 140lb should generally be 'stretched' before a wash is laid onto it. Otherwise, the wetness on the paper will cause it to contract as it dries, leaving a buckled surface. When this happens, the paper is said to be 'cockled', like the painting shown right.

Full step-by-step instructions for stretching paper will appear later in the book. Until then, use board or paper heavier than 140lb for your watercolour projects, since these are heavy enough not to need stretching, and will not cockle.

and your paint all laid out together on one side of the paper. If they are on opposite sides, you will inevitably end up reaching across the paper with a water- or paint-laden brush, which may then drip onto your work. So being prepared pays dividends.

Washing

This wash technique is best practised at arm's length to achieve fluid movement and an even result. You can also use a block to ease the flow of paint down the paper and to allow the wash to flow smoothly downward without dripping. The resulting wash will initially look rather patchy and untidy, but resist the temptation to fiddle with it, or attempt to re-work it. Just allow the paper to dry naturally and the result will be an even wash.

▲ A palette is the ideal tool for mixing washes. Clean water is placed in the round wells and colours are then mixed in the flat, slightly sloping sections below.

TYPES OF PAPER

Watercolour paper comes in three main types:

Hot-pressed or Smooth	A textureless paper which is good for pen and ink and for line work
Cold-pressed or Not	A slightly textured general purpose paper, ideal for beginners
Rough	A highly textured paper best suited to vigorous painting techniques

What next?

Having mastered the basic skills of laying a flat wash, you can try your hand at a graduated wash. This involves increasing or decreasing the intensity of colour towards the top or bottom of the wash, to give a fading effect.

This can be achieved either by adding more water to the paint mixture each time you drag the brush across the paper – or by starting off with a very watery mixture and then adding more paint with each successive application.

▼ A single streak of watercolour paint running through ten different weights and textures of paper shows clearly how the various paper types react with the paint, and how this affects its appearance.

Arches 140lb Rough

Arches 140lb Not

Arches 90lb Not

Cotman 200lb

Cotman 90lb

Bockingford 200lb

Bockingford 140lb

Bockingford 90lb

Saunders 140lb Not

Saunders 90lb Hot-pressed

Choosing the best easel

A stable easel, which holds your work rigidly in one position, will avoid the frustration of trying to work with your picture precariously propped up on a table or on your lap. You'll soon find it's a necessity rather than a luxury.

A good easel is an artist's best friend. It will last a lifetime and is one of the most important and permanent pieces of studio equipment, so take time to look around and buy a model that meets all your requirements. Your choice of easel depends on various factors – the available space in your working area, whether you like to work standing up or sitting down, and whether you tend to work mostly indoors or outdoors. It also depends on the medium you generally use and on the scale of your work. For example, watercolours are much easier to use with an easel that can be tilted to the horizontal, so your washes won't run down the paper.

Outdoor easels

Lugging a heavy easel on painting expeditions is no fun at all, so choose a compact, portable model for outdoor work. A sketching easel (see easels E–H overleaf) could be the answer, being both lightweight and foldable. These are made in wood or aluminium, are fully adjustable and can usually be positioned for both watercolour and vertical painting.

Sketching easels can accommodate surprisingly large boards and canvases, but this depends on the make and type. Check the distance between the top and bottom easel grips to make sure that the easel will take the size of support you prefer.

A box easel (see left, below and easel N overleaf) is more stable, though slightly heavier than an ordinary sketching easel. However, it is easy to fold up and carry, and also incorporates a box or drawer for holding paints, brushes and other materials.

Easels for indoor work

For large or heavy canvases, a traditional upright studio easel (easels I-L overleaf) is probably your best bet. These can be bulky – some even have castors, so that they can be moved around more easily – but they are reassuringly solid.

If your work space is limited, a radial easel (J) is a versatile alternative. This consists of an upright spine with tripod-type legs. The whole easel can be adjusted, so you can angle your work to suit the light, though not to the horizontal position necessary for watercolour painting. When it is not in use, the radial easel can be folded for easy storage.

A tilting radial easel is also known as a 'combination' easel (K) because it brings together features of both the radial and the sketching easel. It has a central joint, so

◀ **The versatile box easel is ideal for the artist who likes to work both in the studio and out-of-doors. For storage and carrying, the easel folds down to a box shape with a handle for easy carrying (right).**

that it can be adjusted to any position from upright to completely horizontal, and it is therefore an ideal choice for the artist who works in a variety of media.

If your studio space or work area is limited, a sketching easel or a box easel will be just as versatile indoors as out. Alternatively, if you work on a fairly small scale, a table-top easel in wood or aluminium (see easels A–D below) might be all you need.

Looking after your easel

Apart from the lightweight sketching easels made from aluminium, most artists' easels are robustly constructed from hardwood, traditionally beechwood. They require little regular maintenance, although the wood benefits from an occasional coat of wax polish, especially when an easel is used outside or in damp conditions. Also, the metal adjusting nuts can become stiff and should be kept lubricated with oil.

THE RIGHT EASEL FOR THE JOB

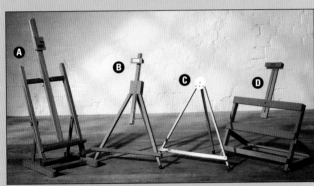

TABLE EASELS

A Sturdy wooden easel with an 'H' frame, which can be tilted to provide the ideal working angle.

B Light, portable tripod-type wooden easel with rubber-tipped non-slip feet.

C Extremely light aluminium easel with adjustable telescopic back leg and rubber-tipped feet.

D Wooden easel, which can be set at four different angles and folds flat when not in use.

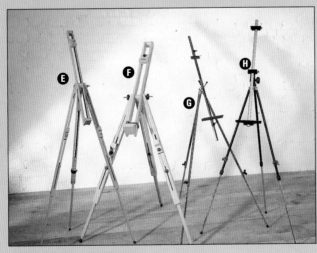

SKETCHING EASELS

E Lightweight easel with an adjustable tilting facility, making it suitable for all media, including watercolour.

F Substantial tilting, sketching easel appropriate for all media.

G Folding, tilting metal easel with telescopic legs and adjustable canvas grip.

H Fully adjustable metal easel with a camera mount fixing, so that it can be used as a photographic tripod.

STUDIO EASELS

I Sturdy studio easel with an adjustable lower shelf for the canvas or board, allowing simple adjustment of the working height.

J Rigid, adjustable radial easel, which can be tilted backwards and forwards, but not horizontally, for watercolour work.

K Combination easel, which can be secured in any position and is suitable for use with all media.

L Artist's 'donkey' or platform easel – a comfortable sitting easel which takes up very little space when folded.

M Simple, popular 'A' frame easel with a metal ratchet on the lower support for adjusting the working height.

N Box easel with a container for paints, brushes and other art materials. Ideal for studio or outdoor work.

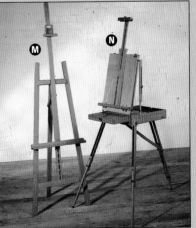

Watercolour mediums

If you would like to experiment with watercolour, try mixing it with some of the special additives that change the character of the paint.

The fluid nature of watercolour means that it is ideal for creating washes of translucent colour and delicate tones. However, this is by no means the end of the story. You can actually change the consistency of watercolour by adding one of several mediums to the paint. In this way, your colours become more versatile and you will be able to invent many different textures and surfaces. For example, watercolour mixed with the appropriate medium can be used with masking tape, painted in stiff peaks and even applied with a knife.

Gum water and gum arabic

Gum water and gum arabic are useful additives that enhance both the colour and texture of watercolour. A little of either medium mixed with the paint will give a rich gloss to the picture

WATERCOLOUR MEDIUMS

Choose a watercolour medium to make the colour thicker or thinner; to improve the flow; to slow down or speed up the drying time; to get a glossy finish; or to paint impasto textures.

Ⓐ **Thickening paste**
Ⓑ **Gum water**
Ⓒ **Gum arabic**
Ⓓ **Glycerine**
Ⓔ **Ox gall liquid**
Ⓕ **Drying medium**

USING GUM ARABIC

To achieve a glossy sheen, add a little gum arabic to the diluted watercolour with a brush, then try the following experiments.

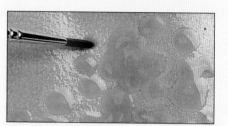

MOTTLED PATTERN
Drops of water applied with a small brush will dissolve dry, thickened colour and disperse the pigment particles to create this attractive mottled texture.

SGRAFFITO
Use a fork or other sharp tool to scratch patterns into wet, thickened colour. The white paper or underlying colour will show through the paint.

SPATTERING
Using a toothbrush, flick clean water on to dry, thickened colour. Wait for a few seconds until the water has had time to dissolve the colour, then blot the excess.

MASKING TAPE
Press strips of tape firmly down on the paper and apply the thickened colour. When the colour is dry, carefully peel back the tape to reveal the crisply painted stripes.

THICKENING PASTE

Stiffer than gum arabic, thickening paste is particularly suitable for impasto watercolour and other highly textured effects. As it is often translucent rather than transparent, too much of the paste can affect the colour of the paint and produce a cloudy effect. Once watercolour paint has been thickened with this medium, it can then be applied with a painting knife as well as with a brush.

MIXING
Blend the paste and colour together well using a stiff brush. If the mixture is too firm for your purpose, add a little water.

IMPASTO
Use the flat blade of a painting knife to apply thick layers of colour and to create wedges of overlapping paint.

SGRAFITTO
Pronounced ridges and other scratched patterns can be made using a fork, comb or other implement on the wet colour.

BRUSH MARKS
Thick colour retains the marks of a stiff brush so experiment with different types of brush stroke – dabs, swirls, and so on.

STIPPLING
Pat the wet colour with the flat blade of a painting knife to create raised peaks of colour in a coarse, stippled effect.

surface. Both mediums can be spattered or sprayed on to an area of dry colour to create a speckled or mottled texture.

Gum arabic is less fluid and more viscous (sticky) than gum water. When watercolour paint is mixed with gum arabic, it can become stiff enough to hold the shape of brush marks. The thickened colour allows you to create other surface textures such as combing or stippling. However, too much gum arabic will make the paint jelly-like and too slippery to be workable.

Thickening paste

For a heavy impasto effect, try adding thickening paste to your watercolours. The resulting mixture can be so stiff that it looks quite unlike traditional watercolour paint – in fact, many purists disapprove of the additive for this reason. However, it is always fun to experiment, and watercolour applied with a painting knife is certainly an

intriguing idea. Also, if used discerningly on selected areas of a painting, thickening paste can add textural interest and enhance the surface of the paint without detracting from its more classical qualities.

Thickening paste comes in tubes and looks similar to equivalent mediums made for oil and acrylics. Take care, when purchasing the medium, to buy a product that is made specifically for watercolour.

Flow improvers

Ox gall medium is the best known of the 'flow improvers', which are used to disperse colour evenly, particularly in washes and wet-in-wet techniques. It is a brownish-yellow liquid originally made from the gall bladders of cows and is normally added to the water rather than to the paint. Although still available, real ox gall has generally been replaced by synthetic alternatives.

In addition to ox gall, a number of other proprietary mediums are available to improve the flow of watercolour and to disperse the pigment evenly.

Drying mediums and retarders

If you have ever tried painting wet-in-wet on a very hot day, when the colour dries as soon as it touches the paper, you will appreciate the value of glycerine. A few drops of this heavy, honey-like liquid added to the watercolour will keep your painting moist and workable for considerably longer by delaying the natural drying time of the paint.

Conversely, watercolour paint dries surprisingly slowly in damp and humid conditions. This can be frustrating, especially if you are waiting to apply colour to a dry surface. Happily, you can speed up the drying time by using a proprietary drying medium. Alternatively, a few drops of alcohol added to the paint will also have the same effect.

Masking techniques

Fluffy white clouds in a blue sky, falling snowflakes or a bare tree on the horizon – all these images are easy to create using the masking technique.

► **To create the effect of falling snowflakes in this picture, dots of masking fluid were applied to the paper with a brush before any paint was put on. Once the picture was finished and the paint had dried, the masking fluid was rubbed off.**

asking is the technique used for covering specific areas of a picture so that they are protected while paint is being applied. It is a simple but very creative technique that will enable you to produce effects that might otherwise seem quite impossible.

For example, how do you fill in the background area behind a complicated flower arrangement? And how do you paint a flat blue watercolour sky whilst leaving the white clouds untouched?

You could, of course, paint around every flower and cloud in the pictures, but this would be very time-consuming. Besides which, the new colour would almost certainly be patchy and uneven because of the tight, precise brushstrokes you would be obliged to use.

The solution is masking. It is very much quicker and more effective to mask out the flowers or clouds first, so that you can simply paint over them to achieve a flat, even background or sky. When the mask is taken away, the areas underneath will be revealed untouched as well-defined shapes.

Depending on your paints and materials, masking can produce shapes that are sharp and clear, soft and subtle, or even patterned and textured. To start with, try making a simple mask from torn or cut paper. For this exercise you will need to use quite thick paper and acrylic or oil paints (watercolour is too fluid).

All kinds of lines

To paint a straight line, hold the sheet you have chosen as your mask in position on your paper, and take the colour boldly over its straight edge. Then, for a jagged effect, experiment by tearing the masking sheet into pieces and painting over the ragged torn edges.

Experimental masking

More unusual and decorative effects can be created by painting over doilies, lace, mesh and netting. It is worth experimenting to discover for yourself a few of the possibilities. For example, instead of applying paint with conventional brushstrokes, you might also try stippling the colour. Blue paint stippled over pieces of cotton wool on watercolour paper will create a realistic sky with convincing white clouds.

◄ **Masking fluid is useful for leaving white highlights or details showing on a dark background. On this leaf, every vein is clearly delineated.**

Using masking fluid

YOU WILL NEED

Small piece of watercolour paper

2B pencil

Masking fluid

Fine round brush for applying masking fluid (use an old one)

Fine round brush for applying paint

Watercolours

1 Mask out the flower Draw the outline of the fuchsia and paint inside it with masking fluid. Then add a turquoise watercolour wash over the top and leave to dry. Remove the masking fluid by rubbing gently. A distinct white image of the flower will be left showing.

2 Paint the flower To complete the fuchsia, paint the masked-out image in pink and purple. Using this masking technique, none of the paint bleeds and the edges of the flower remain clear and sharp.

Masking tape

For rigidly straight lines and geometric shapes, use masking tape – a tough, self-adhesive tape which comes in different widths and which adheres firmly to the paper or canvas. More important, it is also easy to remove. Press the tape down firmly to prevent paint from seeping underneath and use thick colour. Tapes leave hard edges, but by tearing and cutting you can introduce a softer effect.

It is safer to let the paint dry before removing the tape, but this is not always practicable, especially if you are using oils, which take a long time to dry. In this case, remove the tape carefully by lifting one end and holding the tape clear of the painting to avoid smudging.

Masking fluid

Masking fluid can be applied with a brush, a pen, a cocktail stick or even a twig, and dries to a thin, rubbery, easily-removed film. It is excellent for masking out specific areas of white for highlights and reflections, and for picking out detail. The fluid is also useful if you want to preserve selected painted areas from a surrounding wash.

Although masking fluid can achieve unexpected and attractive results, it is

wise to experiment before using it on an actual painting. First try a few brushstrokes on a piece of scrap paper. Wait till the fluid is dry, then paint over the masked marks. Allow the paint to dry completely before removing the rubbery mask using a soft rubber or a clean finger. You will normally find that the mask comes away like magic, leaving areas of pure white, although on rare occasions it can damage the surface of the paper, spoiling further applications of paint (especially watercolour).

Use an old brush

A word of caution. Masking fluid will ruin good paintbrushes. If you use a brush to apply it, make sure it is an old one. In any case, wash the brush thoroughly after use, otherwise the bristles will become like solid rubber.

Masking fluid can be used with any paints, but you should always work on a smooth paper. The fluid tends to sink into the pitted surface of a rough paper and can be tough to remove. Also, remember to take off the fluid as soon as possible after the paint has dried – if you leave it overnight or longer, this can prove difficult.

Masking fluid is excellent for certain watercolour landscape techniques. For

example, you may find it easier to depict the bare branches of trees by first masking out the shapes in masking fluid with a fine-pointed brush.

Snowflakes

Snowflakes can be dotted in with masking fluid in the early stages of a painting. For a realistic effect, mask the foreground flakes with the tip of a brush, then add smaller, distant flakes with a pen. When the masking fluid is eventually removed, the snowflakes will stand out as brilliant white flecks of paper.

Similarly, it is simple to depict water by masking out any white spray and reflections with masking fluid (the spray can be spattered on with an old toothbrush). When the fluid is removed, the white shapes stand out to create a realistic impression of moving water.

◄ **A selection of effects you can achieve with masking fluid.**

Splattering effects

Random speckled patterns are ideal for suggesting textures in painting. Effects like this are quick and easy to achieve with the spattering technique.

S pattering or flicking fluid paint on to a support allows you to create a range of dappled, speckled and mottled effects. The appeal of these effects is their spontaneity, their randomness and the fact that they do not show any brush marks.

▶ **Run your finger briskly across a toothbrush loaded with paint to create a shower of tiny droplets.**

Showing texture

Textural effects can be introduced into your paintings for a variety of reasons. You can use them to imitate rough surfaces or perhaps to represent particular elements in a landscape. Areas of spattering provide an effective shorthand for pebbles on a beach, cobblestones, foliage in the distance, stone walls, turned earth and many other 'broken' surfaces.

Textures can also be used for purely decorative effects. With various spattering techniques, you can create delicate mists of a single colour or build up complex, random patterns using a rich, varied palette of colours. Use these effects to enrich surfaces or add interest to passages of otherwise flat colour.

Suitable media

Any liquid medium, including inks, acrylics, watercolour, gouache and thinned oil paint,

▼ **A variety of tools can be used for spattering: (clockwise from far left) toothbrush, artist's soft brush, bristle brush, small stencil brush, large stencil brush, pump spray, mouth spray, nailbrush.**

can be used in spattering techniques. Spattering works best when the support is kept completely flat – if the surface is tilted, the droplets of paint might run, spoiling the effect you have created.

Methods of spattering

There are many different ways to create a spattered effect. One method is to use a stiff-bristled brush, such as a toothbrush or a stencilling brush. Mix a quantity of paint, dip the brush and shake off any surplus. Hold the brush over the support and draw your finger or something rigid, such as a metal ruler or brush handle, through the bristles. A fine spray of droplets will be deposited on the paper, creating a speckled effect. The further away you hold the brush, the larger the droplets will be.

Splashes and sprays

Another method of spattering is to load a paint brush with thinned paint and flick your wrist vigorously to deposit droplets of paint on the support. This introduces larger splashes and variation in size. Or you can load a brush with colour, hold it over the surface and then tap it across the handle of another brush. This technique allows you to cover a large area of paper and to build up dense layers of spattered colour.

A similar effect can be achieved by spraying paint, using a mouth spray or a container with a pump spray nozzle – many cosmetics and household products are supplied in such containers.

Diverse effects

A wide range of effects can be achieved with any of these spattering techniques. You can create a light stipple with a single application of colour, or build up a dense, granular surface by applying several layers of spatter, allowing the paint to dry between each application. For a subtly modulated surface, apply different tones of the same colour, or create a rich multi-coloured effect by overlaying different shades.

With soluble media, such as watercolour, you can spatter pure water on to a dry wash. The droplets of water will cause the paint to dissolve and the pigment will migrate to the outside of each splash, creating pale splodges within the wash. This effect is particularly dramatic if gum arabic is added to the base wash. To create a similar effect with oil paints, you should spatter some turpentine or methylated spirits on to the still-wet paint surface.

If you spatter watercolour paint on to a damp surface, the spatters bleed into the adjoining areas. This creates a softly diffused, mottled pattern.

Spend some time experimenting with the exciting and unpredictable effects created by spattering. You will find that you quickly build up a useful range of patterns and textures to add to your painting repertoire.

▶ **Heavy spattering fading to a lighter texture suggests pebbles on a beach stretching into the distance.**

EXPERIMENTING WITH SPATTERING TECHNIQUES

A wide range of results can be achieved using this simple technique. Explore the different effects you can create by experimenting with watercolours on scrap paper. Remember to protect the area surrounding your paper while you practise.

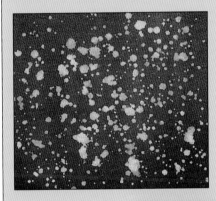

◀ **Blotting spattered water** A wash of alizarin crimson and gum arabic was applied to the support and left to dry. Water was spattered on, then blotted with kitchen paper to create irregularly shaped dapples of light tone.

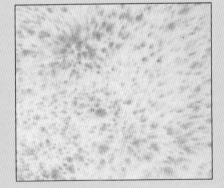

◀ **Spattering on damp paper** This softly diffused effect was created by spattering Winsor blue watercolour on to damp paper. The droplets of wash have bled across and into the paper.

▶ **Spattering water over a wash** A wash of Winsor blue mixed with gum arabic was applied to the support and allowed to dry. Water was spattered on and left to dry. This process was repeated several times, allowing the surface to dry thoroughly between each application.

▶ **Spattering in layers** This subtly variegated effect was achieved by spattering green and yellow washes on to rough watercolour paper, leaving the support to dry between applications.

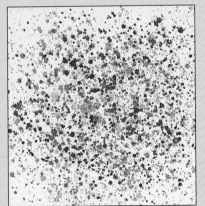

The power of colour

Colour is the painter's most versatile tool. It has the power to excite, control space, create atmosphere, express emotion and represent the illusion of reality.

I t was not until after the invention of the camera in the mid-nineteenth century that artists recognised light as the prime factor in the way we see colour. Before then, the 'local' colour was most often taken as the first consideration: sky is blue, grass is green – but is it that simple? If you look at the sky on a sunny day, it's much bluer overhead than it is on the horizon, where not only is it paler, it also has some yellow in it. Colour is dependent upon light, and we need to understand how it works.

The theory of colour

White light (sunlight), passing through a raindrop, splits into the colours of the rainbow spectrum. When these are fanned into a circle to make the colour wheel (see next page), the principles of colour mixing can be seen. Red, yellow and blue are known as the primary colours: they are pure colours and cannot be mixed from any others. The other three (orange, green and violet), are secondary colours because they are formed by an even mixture of their two immediate primary

▲ Franz Marc's (1880–1916) *The Yellow Cow*, complete with blue patches and red foreground, makes the point that colour can be used to great effect expressively, as well as realistically.

neighbours in the circle.

This can be extended to make tertiary colours by mixing any of the primaries with either of its secondary neighbours. For example, blue and green will produce a colour generally called turquoise. In fact mixed colours are

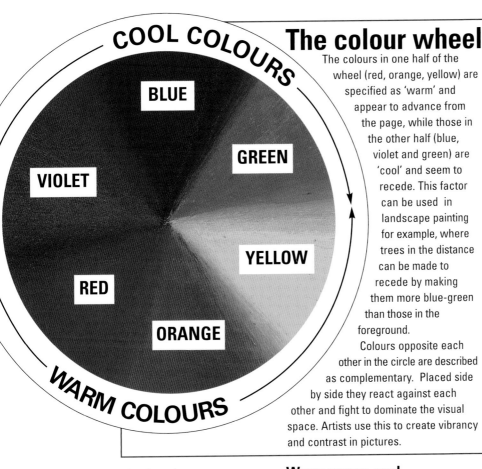

COOL COLOURS

BLUE

GREEN

VIOLET

YELLOW

RED

ORANGE

WARM COLOURS

The colour wheel

The colours in one half of the wheel (red, orange, yellow) are specified as 'warm' and appear to advance from the page, while those in the other half (blue, violet and green) are 'cool' and seem to recede. This factor can be used in landscape painting for example, where trees in the distance can be made to recede by making them more blue-green than those in the foreground.

Colours opposite each other in the circle are described as complementary. Placed side by side they react against each other and fight to dominate the visual space. Artists use this to create vibrancy and contrast in pictures.

A BASIC PALETTE

There are certain colours which, when mixed together, can form the backbone of your art. The colours listed below are all good 'mixers' in any medium. If you have viridian, two blues and two yellows, you can mix most greens you are likely to need. Practise mixing pairs of all the colours without white.

Be careful when using black on its own, since it can 'deaden' a painting if overdone. Raw umber mixed with ultramarine is a good substitute.

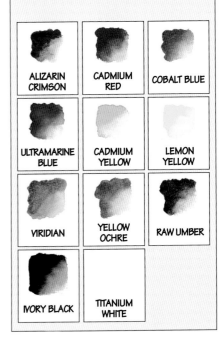

ALIZARIN CRIMSON	CADMIUM RED	COBALT BLUE
ULTRAMARINE BLUE	CADMIUM YELLOW	LEMON YELLOW
VIRIDIAN	YELLOW OCHRE	RAW UMBER
IVORY BLACK	TITANIUM WHITE	

often named after the gemstones or flowers which they resemble and these are the sort of labels you will see on tubes of paint in an art shop.

Black and white

You will notice that the circle does not contain either black or white. When light falls on an object, the object will absorb some of its wavelengths and bounce back others which make up the colour we see. Black soaks them all up and white bounces them all back, so black is the absence of any colour and white is all the colours rolled into one.

Brown

And what of brown? An object seen as brown is absorbing very few of the spectrum of light wavelengths (just those at each end of the rainbow) and bouncing all the others back. By mixing the three primaries together or the three secondaries in different proportions, a whole range of browns can be made.

Warm versus cool

Colour temperature is also part of the equation (see the colour wheel), while colour can also be said to be opaque or transparent, dark or light, translucent or impasto, flat or textured, matt or gloss, vibrant or dull.

▶ **Claude Monet (1840–1926) used colour to convey passing impressions of light and atmosphere – here waterlilies seem to dissolve into the water around them.**

Mixing orange

Mixing a secondary colour like orange is simple, right? Just mix red and yellow together. But which red and which yellow to use?

The basic rules of colour mixing are usually taught to us in primary school. There, while painstakingly scribbling one coloured pencil over another, we discover that red and yellow make orange. Easy!

As orange is a secondary colour, it can be mixed very simply by combining the two primary colours next to it on the colour wheel – that is, red and yellow. In terms of paint, the equivalents of these primaries are cadmium red and cadmium yellow.

The range of oranges

However, cadmium red and cadmium yellow alone will probably not provide you with all the oranges needed for painting a wide range of subjects. Instead, you should experiment with the many other reds and yellows that are available to the artist.

We tend to associate orange with the bright, acidic colour of the fruit – but think also of the variety of mellow tints in autumn leaves or the earthy colours of sand and brickwork. As this still-life arrangement shows, 'orange' is a very general label used to describe a wide range of colours.

Experimental mixing

Depending on the brand and type of paint, there are up to 20 yellows on a manufacturer's colour chart. Counting the earth colours, the yellows include lemon, cadmium yellow, chrome yellow, aurora, aureolin, Naples yellow and Indian yellow, as well as yellow ochre and raw sienna. The range of reds on offer is equally wide and includes cadmium red, vermilion, scarlet, rose madder, permanent rose, alizarin, Venetian red, Mars red and Indian red.

In theory, by combining every available yellow with every available red, you could have a palette of hundreds of different oranges at your fingertips. In reality, many of these mixes are so similar that you can't differentiate between them. And as no artist is likely to need such a range of oranges, confine your mixing experiments to the yellows and reds normally on your palette.

Practical mixtures

On the working palette of almost any painter you will find at least two or three reds and two or three yellows. Typically, these will be: a bright yellow, usually cadmium; an earthy yellow such as yellow ochre or raw sienna; and a cooler colour, for instance, lemon. In the painting on the left, the artist chose Naples as the cooler yellow because it is very effective at neutralizing, or 'knocking back', a strong red or orange.

The same palette will probably also contain cadmium red and a cool red such as alizarin crimson. You might also add a third red that falls somewhere between them in colour temperature – for example, cadmium scarlet. A warm earth colour, such as Venetian red, Indian red or burnt sienna, is also useful.

Note that by varying the proportions of any mixture you will get a different result. For example, cadmium red and cadmium yellow will produce a range of results from a yellowish-orange to a deep reddish-orange.

Bought colours

In addition to those colours you can mix yourself, there are also a few manufactured oranges. The most common are cadmium and chrome orange, both of which are strong and bright. The former is slightly lighter, but considered to be more permanent.

A bought orange is by no means essential, but it can provide a consistent starting point for certain standard mixtures. For example, portrait and figure painters commonly use orange mixed with white as a pale flesh tone.

Note that mixing bright yellow with bright red sometimes produces a slightly duller orange than you would expect. To avoid this, try to choose pigments with a degree of natural transparency. For example, yellow mixed with alizarin crimson will give you a brighter orange than when mixed with cadmium red, which is a more opaque pigment.

▶ The oranges in this watercolour came from cadmium yellow, yellow ochre, Naples yellow, cadmium red, cadmium scarlet and alizarin crimson, plus two bought colours – chrome orange and cadmium orange. Sepia and burnt sienna helped darken the cast shadows and top.

**Cadmium orange +
Naples yellow**

**Cadmium yellow +
alizarin crimson**

**Cadmium orange +
yellow ochre**

Chrome orange

**Sepia + cadmium yellow
+ cadmium red**

Yellow ochre + burnt sienna

Cadmium orange + cadmium red

Cadmium orange

Cadmium scarlet + cadmium orange

Mixing green

By mixing and modifying the manufacturers' greens it is possible to expand your palette well beyond the range available otherwise.

For many artists – especially those whoe are interested in the natural world – green is probably the most important colour on the palette. Rural landscapes, flowers and plants, as well as many still-life subjects, call for a variety of greens.

A common misconception

However, the great versatility of the colour green is often underestimated. Beginners sometimes believe that, because green is mixed from blue and yellow, all things green must therefore be painted from equal mixtures of these two colours.

Many first attempts at landscape painting are disappointing for this very reason – simply because the artist has failed to distinguish between the different greens in the subject.

Experiment first

One way to overcome this difficulty is to experiment with green mixtures before starting to paint. Look at the subject and pick out as many different greens as you can. Where there are highlights and shadows on a green area, take note of the light and dark tones these create.

Try your hand at mixing the greens you have detected on a separate sheet of paper. The process will initially be one of trial and error, but you will be surprised at the extraordinary range that can be achieved by mixing and modifying the colours on a very limited palette.

Mixing greens

Start by exploring the possibilities of a pair of colours, and see how many different shades of green you can get. For instance, by varying the proportions of ultramarine and cadmium lemon, you can obtain colours ranging from lime green to deep blue-green. Repeat the experiment, substituting yellow ochre for lemon yellow, and you will create an equally varied range extending from golden green to deep olive.

Modifying a green

Bought greens are also useful – in this fruit-and-vegetable still life, the artist made full use of them. However, they can be very strident – so more often than not you'll need to modify them with other colours. Again, it is useful to experiment and to extend your repertoire before painting. Choose a strong shade, such as emerald, viridian or sap green, and make some test samples. Modify the tone by adding varying amounts of a neutral colour such as raw umber or Payne's grey. This will give you a choice of rich and interesting dark greens. Avoid using black, as this can deaden the colour.

Alternatively, any green can be modified or toned down by adding a little of its complementary colour – red. Try using different reds in varying quantities to produce a range of muted greens and neutrals.

Bought greens

Five manufactured greens were used in this painting. If you have not used these pigments before, now is the opportunity to try out the new colours.

♦ **Emerald green** is more brilliant than any green you could mix yourself. It is useful for capturing man-made colours, such as the bright green band around the plate here. The clear emerald stands out beautifully from the natural greens of the fruits and vegetables.

♦ **Terre verte** is the oldest known green. Made from natural earth pigments, it works well when painting vegetation and other organic forms. Here, it is used with a little ultramarine for the blue-green broccoli. The table top and shadows are painted in a mixture of terre verte and Payne's grey to create a cool, neutral and unobtrusive background.

♦ **Olive green** varies depending on the manufacturer, but it is generally a muted natural green, good for foliage and vegetation. Here, it is used with plenty of water to put a glaze on the shadowed side of the rosy apple.

♦ **Viridian** is very powerful and needs careful handling. It can easily take over and dominate your picture. Used in small quantities and modified by other colours, it is a useful ingredient in mixtures. Otherwise, viridian is best restricted to specific areas. Here, it is mixed with varying amounts of water for the light, medium and dark tones of green on the leaves of the leek.

♦ **Sap green** is a warm, leafy green and is often used for painting grass and foliage, especially the picture is set in spring. Here, it is mixed with cadmium lemon for the green apple and with Payne's grey for the dark green pepper.

► **Although it is possible to obtain greens by mixing blues and yellows, it is often best to use bought greens and, where necessary, modify these with other colours.**

Emerald green

Payne's grey + sap green

Viridian

Ultramarine + terre verte

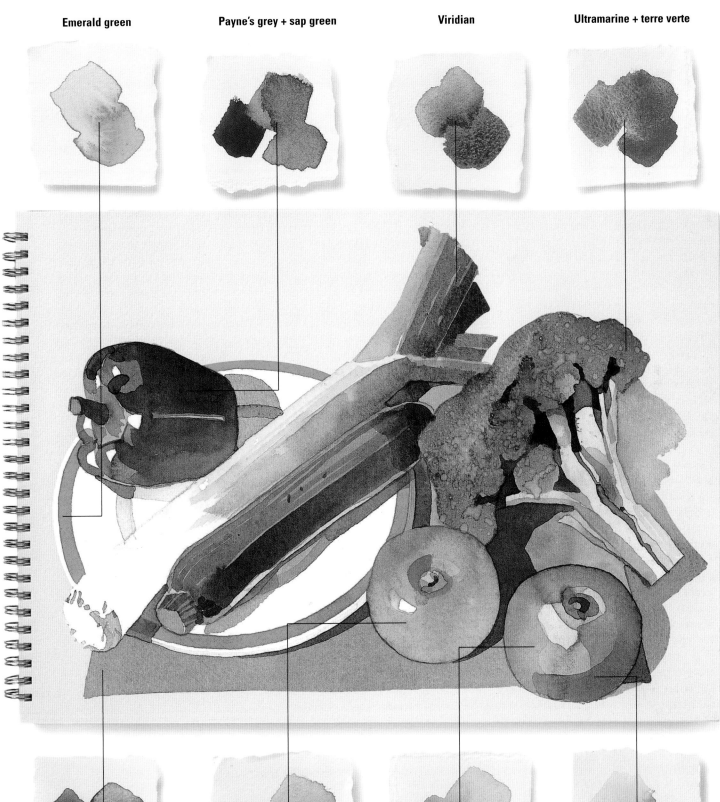

Payne's grey + terre verte

Cadmium lemon + sap green

Yellow ochre + emerald green

Olive green

Mixing purple

Discover how to create rich variations on a theme by mixing bought purples with blues, reds and neutrals.

Purple is rare in nature. The earliest purple pigment came from the shells of the 'purpura', a large whelk found on the shores of the Mediterranean. The Phoenicians are reputed to have ground several million purpura shells to make enough purple to dye their emperor's clothes. The colour they used was known as 'royal purple' and it is still produced today.

Nowadays, purple is a far more accessible colour, but even today real purple pigments are comparatively few in number. The majority of manufactured purples and violets are actually combinations of existing blues and reds.

Purple mixtures

Many artists find it unnecessary to buy ready-mixed purple. Instead, they prefer to make their own by mixing various blues and reds to get the colour they need. Fortunately, it is possible to mix a range of good purples yourself. The brightest of these are achieved by using a cool red, such as alizarin crimson, rose madder or magenta. The addition of white to these mixtures will give various shades of mauve and violet.

If you have ever tried to mix purple using cadmium red, you will know that the result is not a bright colour at all, but a muted brownish-purple. This is because cadmium red contains yellow, which gives the mixture a brown bias.

Mix your own

To discover the potential of the colours on your basic palette, try making some simple two-colour mixtures. Start with alizarin crimson and ultramarine, combining these colours in equal proportions. The result will be a strong, bright purple.

By varying the proportions of the ultramarine and alizarin crimson in the mixture, you can then go on to produce a range of purples with either a red or a blue bias.

Carry out some more tests, this time substituting cerulean blue for ultramarine. As cerulean is a cool, pale blue, the resulting purple will be less bright and slightly more opaque.

It is well worth repeating similar experiments using a number of different blues and reds. The resulting mixtures will vary enormously and not all of them will be purple. Some will be brown or muddy grey. Only by trial and error is it possible to have control over your palette and the colours it can produce.

Shadow colours

Purple is frequently used for painting shadows. If you look carefully at those that initially appear to be grey or brown, you will notice that they often contain traces of purple and violet. In this watercolour still life, the thrown shadows are mixed from the purples and violets used on the fruit and vegetables, toned down with neutral colours, such as Payne's grey or raw umber.

You can try mixing your own shadow colours by adding raw umber, Payne's grey or another neutral to any of the purples and violets below. Adding a little of their complementary colour, yellow, can also tone down purple and violet.

Bought purples

Our artist chose four manufactured purples for this still life, modifying these to acquire all the colours needed for painting the fruit and vegetables:

- **Mauve** may have a red or blue bias, depending on the manufacturer. The mauve used for the plate in this painting has a definite red tinge and stands out distinctly from the other colours. It is used here as a dilute wash.

- **Winsor violet** is a transparent colour with a powerful staining capacity. A little goes a long way, so use it sparingly. It is shown here unmixed; modified with Payne's grey and phthalo blue to obtain cool purples; and mixed with raw umber to create the neutral tone of the table top.

- **Purple madder alizarin** is a rich natural colour somewhere between brown and purple. It is popular with landscape artists for painting the warm tones of foliage and trees. Purple madder alizarin is mixed with a little Winsor violet for the dark shadow on the persimmon fruit.

- **Violet carmine** is a clear, transparent purple, used here with cadmium scarlet to depict the cool orange-violet of the persimmon fruit.

Cobalt violet is another bought purple you could try. It is not used here, but it provides an attractive warmish purple that cannot be mixed from other colours.

▶ The purples in this still life include bought colours used alone and mixed with reds, blues and neutrals (such as Payne's grey or raw umber). Don't forget to try mixing red and blue as well – such as the alizarin crimson and Prussian blue used here.

Winsor violet + phthalo blue

Winsor violet + Payne's grey

Winsor violet + raw umber

Winsor violet

Mauve

Cadmium scarlet + violet carmine

Purple madder alizarin + Winsor violet

Alizarin crimson + Prussian blue

Mixing greys

You might think that grey is simply a mixture of black and white, but you'll find that greys are actually much more subtle than that.

Making grey is not just a matter of mixing black and white. A painting with this type of grey in it would become lifeless because the grey would really be a tone, not a colour. This is valid in a monochrome work where only black and white are used, but for colour painting you will be dealing with a more exciting range of greys.

So what exactly is grey? It is important to remember that black is not a colour, but the absence of colour – in other words, the absence of light. So a grey object should be described as 'dark white' rather than 'light black', because you can't actually see black.

This concept is easier to understand if you look at some white objects placed in strong natural light or against a white window frame. Away from the light, the shadowed areas could be described as grey, and on a curved form it is immediately noticeable that there is more than one shade of grey. In addition, because the white colours are likely to be slightly different, you will see that there is also more than one *colour* of grey. This variety of grey colours might be exaggerated by colours reflected from the surroundings and the colour of the light source. Grey shadows are similarly affected. So, if you were trying to paint all these possible greys, you would struggle to be accurate using only black and white.

Mixing greys

Distinguishing subtle colour changes (hues) in greys takes practice, and a little colour theory might help here. Each of the primary colours (red, blue and yellow) is neutralised by its complementary colour (green, orange and violet). If you mix a primary colour with its complementary in varying quantities, shades of brown and grey will emerge.

Try the exercise on the right to experiment with mixing a range of greys using various combinations of warm and cool blues and reds. Once you have tried this, do the same exercise using blue and yellow pairs instead of blue and red pairs – this will provide a range of greens, the cool and warm primary mixes giving

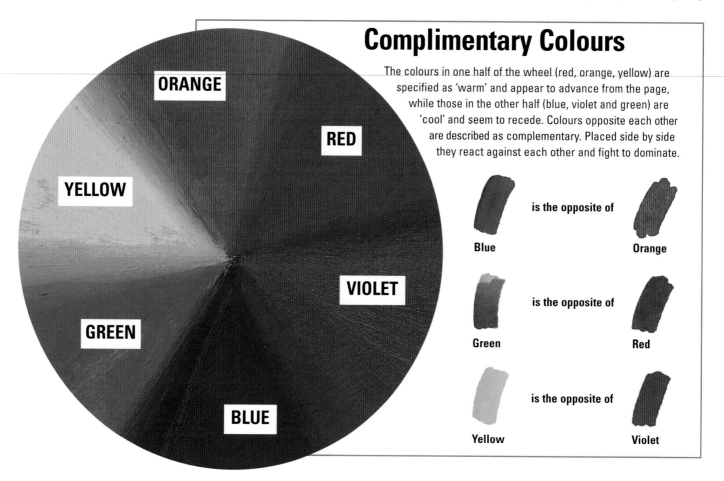

Complimentary Colours

The colours in one half of the wheel (red, orange, yellow) are specified as 'warm' and appear to advance from the page, while those in the other half (blue, violet and green) are 'cool' and seem to recede. Colours opposite each other are described as complementary. Placed side by side they react against each other and fight to dominate.

Blue   is the opposite of   Orange

Green   is the opposite of   Red

Yellow   is the opposite of   Violet

'greyer' greens. Adding a little extra of either of the two blues (warm or cold) to any of the above colour combinations will add to their 'greyness'. You should be able to make at least eight discernably different greys, from warm brownish greys through the more neutral green-greys to cool blue-violet greys.

Tones

The addition of white will, of course, give lighter shades of each of these greys. To darken them, you don't need to use black – try adding a mix of raw umber (and/or burnt umber) and ultramarine or viridian. This will affect the colour of the grey as well as the tone, but more greys will be discovered! Greys are very useful in painting landscapes, which often have more green-greys in them than actual greens. Notice, too, how often greys occur in interiors.

▼ **Being selective with detail can give pen-and-ink drawings a more lively feel: the obelisk is outlined with a fine-point brush to suggest permanency while the people are sketchily drawn to convey movement.**

Exploring a range of greys

Gather together a range of white and perhaps a few grey objects. Choose some different whites – enamel, for example, is usually bluer than china, which tends to be more creamy in colour.

1 Set up a still life Place the items on white, grey or even black paper against a white painted wall in a strong light by a window.

2 Make a painting Look hard at the objects to work out the colour bias of the different greys – are they greenish, blueish or pinkish? Start painting, using the pure colour greys you discovered in the mixing exercise opposite. Then add white or darker colours (no black) to adjust the tones.

3 Discover the greys When the painting is dry, take a strip of white paper and make half a dozen holes in it about 1cm (⅜in) across and 5cm (2in) apart. Move this around over the surface of the painting and you'll discover how many different colours of grey you have made.

YOU WILL NEED

Canvas board at least 40 x 50cm (16 x 20in)

Medium-sized round brush

Oil or acrylic paints

Seasonal palette – spring

A palette for springtime foliage should reflect the beautiful translucent greens of new leaves as well as the sunny yellows of flowering bulbs.

The green shades of spring are exceptionally fresh and vibrant. To capture them accurately in your painting, colour mixing should be kept to a minimum. Remember, the more colours you add to a mixture, the duller and more subdued the result will be. It is a good idea to limit your mixtures to no more than three colours, although, in practice, most spring greens can be mixed from simple two-colour combinations of one blue and one yellow.

Alternatively, why not introduce one of the manufactured greens into your spring landscape? Depending on the subject, there is a good selection of strong, vivid colours to choose from.

Mixing greens

The majority of greens to be found in a spring landscape contain a lot of yellow. Early flowers – including daffodils, forsythia and many crocuses – are also predominantly yellow in colour.

Later in the year, this emphasis changes. Summer flowers bloom in many different colours, and the foliage becomes darker with increased amounts of blue and other shades creeping into the leaf mixtures. For the first fresh leaves of spring, however, yellow is dominant in the garden and countryside, and as such is one of the most significant colours on the landscape artist's palette at this time of the year.

Important yellows

Cool, acid yellows are particularly useful for springtime subjects because, when mixed with blue, they create the sharp greens that are so characteristic of fresh leaves. The coolest yellows on the artist's colour wheel are those with a blue bias. A selection for your palette could include lemon yellow, cadmium yellow pale, Winsor lemon, cadmium lemon and aureolin.

Depending on the blue they are mixed with, these yellows will produce a range of the cool, vivid greens found in a typical spring landscape. The blues used in the watercolour of the verdant garden shown overleaf are ultramarine, cerulean blue and phthalo blue, but it is worth experimenting with other blues to extend your repertoire of greens.

Golden yellows – those with a red bias – produce warm or subtle greens, depending on your choice of blue. Such yellows include cadmium yellow deep, Indian yellow and yellow ochre.

For the garden scene, our artist chose cadmium lemon as a cool yellow, mixing it with one or other of the blues on the palette to make the pale greens in the foreground. For the warmer greens and yellow flowers, yellow ochre was added or used instead of cadmium lemon.

Bought greens

As a general rule, a mixed colour is more easily integrated into a composition than a single colour used directly from the tube. This is particularly so with bought greens, which can be strident and stand out jarringly from the natural colours of a rural landscape.

However, fresh spring foliage is often so bright that it really does show up against the surrounding colours. With such a subject, breaking the rules can pay off and a few splashes of a clear, brilliant green, applied unmixed, will capture this dramatic effect exactly.

Palette for new foliage

This selection of watercolours in greens, yellows and blues provides all the colours you need for the fresh new foliage and flowers in the garden picture (overleaf). The two green colours, sap green and viridian, were used neat in places. However, the main bulk of foliage was created by mixing the two yellows with the three blues to create a range of subtle, harmonious greens.

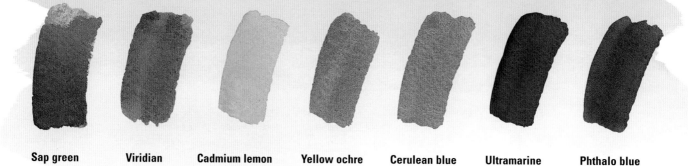

| Sap green | Viridian | Cadmium lemon | Yellow ochre | Cerulean blue | Ultramarine | Phthalo blue |

GARDEN IN FIRST LEAF

The palette shown on the preceding page was used to achieve the range of greens in this watercolour garden. Pale foliage and flowers in the foreground were painted thinly to allow the white paper to show through. Deeper greens were achieved by using stronger colour mixes with the addition of gum arabic to enhance the paint surface.

Sap green has been used on its own for the hedge in the background.

Cadmium lemon and ultramarine create a cool, fresh green for the flowerbed.

Diluted viridian has been used to add some bluish-green texture to the foreground.

Cadmium yellow and cerulean produce a bright, sharp green for the foreground foliage.

Yellow ochre and phthalo blue produce a dull green for the dark-leaved tree.

Useful bought greens include emerald, phthalo green, sap green and green-gold. Viridian is also an option, but this must be used in very small quantities only. Applied on its own, viridian can dominate the composition.

In this painting, the hedges and many of the background plants are painted in varying tones of pure sap green. Instead of adding a darker pigment for the shadows, which could dull the colour, gum arabic is mixed with undiluted sap green to create areas of deep green shadow in the hedge.

Transparent colour

Lit by the low sunlight of early spring, colours can appear particularly bright and luminous. With watercolour, you can capture this translucent effect perfectly by applying the paint in a thin layer, so that the white paper shows through the wash of colour. Avoid using white paint in a spring landscape. Adding white to watercolour tends to produce a chalky, opaque effect – particularly unwelcome when you are striving to capture the fresh, sunny colours of spring. To create white flowers and highlights, do as the artist has done in this picture and leave these as patches of unpainted white paper.

Seasonal palette – summer

In summer, the brilliance of the flowers and the diversity of foliage shades offer the artist the perfect opportunity to use a vivid and varied palette.

For the landscape painter, summer is a liberating season. The days are at their longest and, weather permitting, painting on the spot for hours on end can be a real delight. There is time to think about colours, to choose a palette, and to make colour notes and sketches if necessary.

There are no rules or restrictions on summer colours. Unlike spring, with its predominance of cool, yellow-green foliage, or autumn with its mellow earth colours, summer has no particular palette to call its own. The colours can be as bright and varied as the artist chooses or as the subject suggests.

Summer foliage

During the summer months, leaves lose the sharpness of colour that causes many spring trees and plants to look very similar. The greens begin to diversify and each one takes on its own characteristics. Leaves are often tinged with a variety of colours, including silvery grey, blue, mauve and pink. As a result, it becomes easier to spot the different greens both in the garden and in the landscape, and to pick out the local colours of the leaves.

Although greens can be mixed from the yellows and blues on the basic palette, summer is a good opportunity to try out new colours. For foliage, sap green or Hooker's green provides a good starting point. However, if you feel experimental, introduce one or two slightly more offbeat colours, such as cobalt turquoise – a strong blue-green – or green-gold – a glowing, warm shade.

Rendering flowers

For those who love to paint flowers, summer colours are often intensely brilliant and beautiful. Sometimes the colours of nature defy mixing, and only a bought colour from the manufacturer's chart can match the brightness of the subject. This is particularly so when you are painting orange or violet flowers because versions of these mixed from colours on the standard palette are rarely as bright as manufactured equivalents.

Experiment with new colours. Many summer flowers are crimson or deep vivid pinks. Again, these colours cannot be easily mixed, so try a bought version, such as carmine, permanent rose, rose madder or magenta. Not only are these cool reds beautiful in their

own right, but they are also excellent in mixtures, especially for capturing the elusive violets and oranges. For example, the orange of the Californian poppies in the picture is a mixture of permanent rose and cadmium lemon.

To capture the effect of light with paint is always a challenge. This is particular the case in summer, when sunlight often plays a dominant role. The transparent quality of watercolour is ideal for painting summer scenes, such as the on the next page, capturing both the brightness and the translucency of the petals. Even though the garden border is dense and colourful, note how the artist has still left quite a lot of white paper showing through to help capture the luminosity of summer light.

Oils and acrylics

There is no reason why a similarly colourful effect cannot be painted using oils and acrylics. The secret to success is to keep colours clean and the mixtures simple. An organized palette will help you to achieve this. Changing your turps or water frequently will also help to ensure that you retain clear, bright colours in your finished work.

Bright, summery colours

There is no single definitive palette for summer scenes – however, make sure you include some bright, hot colours. For the painting on the next page, the artist created the warm flowers from cadmium red, permanent rose and lemon yellow. For the foliage, sap green was the basis of most of the mixes, with the addition of sepia, lemon yellow and phthalo blue.

| Cadmium red | Permanent rose | Lemon yellow | Sap green | Phthalo blue | Sepia |

A GARDEN IN FULL BLOOM

A garden border in summer creates a wonderfully exciting picture – but make sure you don't get too carried away with your bright colours. As always, you should check the colour and tone of each flower carefully. In this picture, for instance, note the delicacy of the pink used for the foxgloves and the subtle changes in the mixes for the poppies in the foreground.

Dilute permanent rose made a delicate pink for the foxgloves.

Sap green and sepia created a rather neutral green for the background.

Phthalo blue with a touch of permanent rose was used for the delphiniums.

Permanent rose and cadmium lemon were used for the Californian poppies.

Permanent rose and cadmium red made a strong, hot red for these poppies.

Sap green, cadmium lemon and phthalo blue created a cool foliage colour.

Seasonal palette – autumn

Whether a riot of copper, crimson and gold, or a restrained display of browns, the colours of autumn leaves define the countryside at this time of year

Depending on the weather and prevailing climate, autumnal trees can be either brilliantly coloured or neutral and understated. New England, in the United States, is famous for its spectacular fall, where the colours of a typical autumn are crimson, orange and gold, often set off by a bright blue sky.

Sometimes, however, autumnal tints are subtler. In a damp climate, the greyness of the weather is often reflected in the colours of the leaves. An overcast day or an autumn mist can make them appear subdued and restrained. Although less dramatic than bold reds and yellows, understated colours can be equally beautiful and will often include mellow earth tones such as umbers and ochres, browns, greys and dark greens.

A quiet scene

For the painting shown on the next page, the artist deliberately chose a rather muted scene. There is no direct sunlight to bring out the colours, so the mixtures are quiet and restrained.

Subtle colours are not necessarily dull colours, however. The bronzes and coppers seen in this painting were mixed from a full palette of pigments, including cadmium red, alizarin crimson and cadmium yellow. The brightness of the palette colours is reflected in the glowing transparency of the mixtures. There are cooler colours, too, particularly in the shadows, sky and green grass.

Be experimental

As the colour swatches on the right demonstrate, autumnal hues can be mixed from the colours you are likely to have on your standard palette. However, if you feel like being adventurous, now is a good time to experiment with more unusual pigments.

For example, brown madder is a rich brownish-purple – an excellent colour for capturing mellow, autumnal tones. Earthy reds – including Venetian red,

Indian red and terra rosa – are all warm and natural, ideal for autumn leaves and trees. For shadows, try Mars violet or purple lake. Alternatively, if you have ever wanted an excuse to use the exotic-sounding caput mortuum violet or perylene maroon, these are cool purples that are excellent in autumnal mixtures.

Painting trees

The foliage on any tree is usually multi-coloured, visible as tiny flecks of colour and tone that represent the leaves. The palest flecks are the highlights – reflections caused by the bright light on the leaves; darker flecks are the shadows on the underside of the foliage. A helpful technique for capturing the effect of broken colour in foliage is that which was employed by the Pointillist painters Georges Seurat (1859–91) and Paul Signac (1863–1935).

These artists were referred to as Pointillists because of the manner in which they applied colour. For example, instead of mixing red and yellow to make orange, and thereby losing the intensity of the colours, they would dab separate dots, or points, of red and yellow onto the picture. The two colours merge in the eye of the viewer to create a vibrant orange. A similar approach was used in the autumn landscape here. Dabbing on small patches of colour gives an impression of leaves swaying in the breeze.

Hues for autumn

Although the autumnal landscape shown overleaf is characterized by subtle browns and gentle greens, the artist chose a full palette of warm and cool watercolours to create it (below). You might also try grabbing a handful of the leaves you intend to paint, matching their hues to paint colours, then adding these to your palette.

Cadmium red   Alizarin crimson   Cadmium yellow   Sepia

Payne's grey   Burnt sienna   Sap green   Phthalo blue

MIXING COLOURS FOR AN AUTUMN SCENE

Not all trees turn brilliant shades of red and gold in the autumn. Here, you can see how the brighter colours in the basic autumn palette on the previous page have been toned down to create the mainly brown shades in this peaceful scene. The brown leaves are set against a pale blue sky mixed from dilute phthalo blue with a little burnt sienna to subdue the colour.

A basic leaf colour is made from cadmium red, cadmium yellow and sepia.

Redder leaves are mixed from cadmium red, burnt sienna and cadmium yellow.

For the distant trees, a mix of burnt sienna and cadmium yellow is used.

The deep, cool shadows are created with alizarin crimson and phthalo blue.

Dark green tones are made from sap green, Payne's grey and sepia.

A muted green is achieved by neutralizing sap green with sepia.

Seasonal palette – winter

Every season demands a different palette – for a winter landscape, all you need is a small selection of subdued colours.

Even if it isn't covered with snow, the winter landscape rarely contains bright colours. Although bold red and yellow pigments may be invaluable in the other seasons, they are usually unnecessary in winter. Even bright greens may have limited use, as winter foliage tends to be dull and subdued – particularly the dark evergreen of conifers and the faded, grey-green of grass that has lost its summer freshness.

The scene opposite was painted with a palette of just five muted watercolours (see below), with the addition of a little white gouache in the final stages. The result is a moody, realistic evocation of a rather forbidding winter landscape.

Winter light

With so few local colours present in a typical winter landscape, your choice of colours will be dictated largely by the weather and the light. On a cloudy day, the landscape can almost appear monochromatic – simply a range of blacks, whites and greys with subtle tinges of green, blue and brown. In this case, the emphasis may be on the most neutral colours – Payne's grey and burnt umber.

This was certainly the case for the scene overleaf. The ultramarine used for the sky was toned down with a lot of Payne's grey. And the sap green used for the trees was neutralized by adding both Payne's grey and burnt umber.

Coloured shadows

If you're painting a winter scene in sunshine, however, the brighter colours of the palette come into their own. The sun brings out a spectrum of blues and warm golds that require the addition of ultramarine and burnt sienna. And grass and foliage that are lit by direct sunlight will demand large amounts of sap green in your mixes.

As the sun appears closer to the horizon in winter than it does in summer, it creates characteristic longer shadows. These shadows often contain a lot of colour, particularly blues and greens. Against the bright whiteness of snow, they can appear very attractive – translucent and alive with colour.

Contrasting tones

Snow creates extreme tonal contrasts. The lightest tone is the dazzling whiteness of the snow itself; the darkest tone will be created by the silhouettes of trees and other objects in what is an otherwise white landscape.

Watercolour is the perfect medium for a wintry subject because you can use the unpainted white paper to represent the snow. Inevitably, the bright whiteness of snow makes everything else in the landscape appear dark in comparison. For example, in this painting there is very little detail in the pine trees and fence posts. They are painted as dark silhouettes which stand out as sharp shapes against the white background.

Opaque white

In addition to the five watercolours on the winter palette, our artist introduced a little opaque white in the final stages of the painting. This can be seen in the spattered snowflakes, which lend a decorative and realistic touch to the scene – an effective detail, which you can add to any snowy landscape.

Simply spatter the finished painting lightly with white and grey (made up from a mixture of white and palette mud). The white will show up against the dark

Five-colour palette

A palette of five watercolours was used for the winter landscape on the right. The slightly cool Payne's grey is a good starting point for all your mixes. Use it with ultramarine for the sky and cold shadow colours; with sap green to capture foliage; and with burnt umber and burnt sienna for the warmer tones.

| Payne's grey | Ultramarine | Sap green | Burnt sienna | Burnt umber |

SNOW-COVERED HILLS

Three of the main colour mixes used by the artist for this winter landscape are shown below. Note how the strength of these mixes has been varied in the picture. For instance, the ultramarine and Payne's grey mix is quite dark below the trees, a little lighter in the sky and almost transparent in the bottom left corner. The use of the same mix across the picture helps to give it a visual unity – while varying the dilution prevents it from becoming too repetitive.

The trees and their shadows are painted in a muddy green from sap green (top), Payne's grey (left) and burnt umber (right).

The expanse of sky and the shadows reflecting it are painted with a mix of ultramarine (top) and Payne's grey (bottom).

Warmer foreground shadows are painted with a mix of ultramarine (top), Payne's grey (right) and burnt sienna (bottom).

tones; the grey stands out from the white snow. You can create a full-scale blizzard by spattering across the entire picture!

Use either white gouache or Chinese white watercolour for this finishing touch. Remember, however, that white paints contain chalk. When white is added to other pigments the resulting colours become pale and chalky, and this can destroy the natural transparency of watercolour paints. Unless you positively want a cloudy, opaque colour, don't mix white with other colours. Reserve it for special effects only.

Cold-weather warning

Painting winter landscapes is exhilarating, but it can also be very cold. You will need to protect yourself against the elements with warm clothing. A padded waistcoat or coat lining keeps your body warm, but leaves your arms free to manoeuvre the paint brush. Fingerless gloves are another good idea, keeping your hands warm, but your fingers free.

Still, the fact remains that painting on-the-spot winter landscapes is a chilly business. A practical, more comfortable alternative is to paint a view from a window. Or make rapid on-the-spot colour sketches and take photos outside, then do the painting at home.

Using coloured paper

Applying watercolour to toned paper breaks with tradition but, as these quick sketches show, the results can be both striking and instructive.

A watercolour painted on coloured paper is quite different from a classical watercolour picture on white or pale cream paper. White paper intensifies the transparent colours without changing them. On coloured paper, the underlying support shows through the paint and can alter the colours.

Underlying colour

The colour of the support will modify the painted colours in precisely the same way as if that colour had been added to the paint on the palette. Yellow paper, for instance, will push red towards orange and blue towards green.

One useful characteristic of tinted paper is the unifying effect it can have

on the finished painting. While some artists create harmony in a painting by including a little of one particular colour in every mixture on the palette, others find that they can achieve a similar effect simply by painting on coloured paper. This is because the underlying paper colour effectively mixes with each of the painted colours to create a general, unified colour theme.

Testing colours

It is helpful to make a colour test to find out how the painted colours will appear when applied to a particular paper. You can do this by cutting a small strip from the paper you intend to use for your painting. On this test strip, try out the

colours from your usual palette, as well as any of your favourite mixtures, before introducing them into the paintings.

Colour and tone

It is easier and quicker to establish light and shade on toned paper than it is when working on white paper. For example, the seated figure in the watercolour painting below is lit by an overhead window, which creates strong highlights and dark shadows. To bring out these contrasting tones, the artist chose medium-grey paper – a tone that is approximately halfway between the dark shadows and white highlights.

Having established this paper as the mid-toned colour, it was then a

WORKING ON MID-TONED PAPER

To discover the benefits of using tinted paper in a tonal study, try making a quick monochrome watercolour sketch of a figure on a sheet of medium-grey paper. Treat the paper tone as the mid tone in the picture – this stands for the limbs, the face and the clothing. Then add the background and shadows with washes of darker grey, and put in highlights with simple strokes of opaque Chinese white. Use broad brush strokes to avoid detail, relying on the tonal contrasts to build up the form.

▼ **Highlights have been picked out in Chinese white watercolour, which shines out against the grey paper.**

1 ▲ **Block in the background** Using a No.4 sable brush, wash Payne's grey over the background. Paint around the figure, and dot in one or two of the darkest shadows.

2 ▲ **Add dark tones** Change to a 25mm (1in) flat brush. Establish shadows on the chair and figure in a dilute Payne's grey that is slightly darker than the background wash.

relatively simple matter to add the shadows and a few highlights that show up clearly against the medium grey of the paper. To accentuate the tonal contrast, the artist simplified the tones, using Payne's grey for the shadows and Chinese white for the highlights.

Tinting your own paper

What happens if you cannot find paper in the colour of your choice? You can make your own tinted paper quite easily by applying a watercolour wash to a sheet of white paper or even over another colour. This will allow you to choose exactly the right tone and colour for the purpose.

The paintings opposite are both made on paper that has been tinted by the artist. An evening landscape (top) is painted over a multicoloured wash. In the second watercolour (below), a washy blue makes an attractive background for the darker blue of the painting.

▼ These strips of coloured paper, each painted with the same colours, show the considerable effect that background colour can have on the appearance of watercolour paint. Grey paper, for example, tends to mute the colours. On red paper, the yellow and orange almost disappear.

TINTING PAPER WITH A MULTICOLOURED WASH

An interesting way of tinting paper is to use more than one colour. Choose colours that will become an integral part of the painting. Here, four bands of colour are washed across the paper to represent a sky tinged with pink, and a line of foliage reflected in water. A simple landscape is added, but this method would work equally well for a more complex scene.

1 ▲ **Lay the background** Working on a slightly tilted board and using a large, flat brush, paint the background in broad overlapping stripes of dilute cadmium yellow, ultramarine, cadmium red and sap green.

2 ▲ **Add grey** Allow the background to dry. Using dilute Payne's grey and a 25mm (1in) flat brush, paint ripples on the water and dab in clouds. Suggest trees and reflections with short vertical strokes.

▲ All that is needed to finish off this simple impression of a landscape are minimal horizontal and vertical brush strokes, using Payne's grey over the sap green band.

Watercolour Landscapes

How to capture magnificent landscapes with projects ranging from holiday vistas to gritty cityscapes to your own back garden.

Portable art materials

At some stage, every artist will want the challenge of painting outdoors, but you need to make sure you take the right equipment.

Practical considerations play an important part when it comes to deciding what to take when painting away from your home or studio. You must plan in advance – taking enough materials to meet your needs, while avoiding unnecessary weight or bulk.

First and foremost, comfort is crucial. There is nothing more miserable than trying to work in extreme weather conditions without the right sort of clothing. Depending on your chosen destination, pack a wide-brimmed hat to protect against the sun, or fingerless gloves to help keep you warm.

Are you sitting comfortably?

When using oils or acrylics, working with your painting on your lap or propped up against a handy tree trunk might be okay in emergencies, but the frustration and discomfort involved will eventually make a proper easel essential.

For the travelling artist, a box easel is the ideal choice. This combines a materials container and an easel in a compact, portable case with a handle for carrying. The legs are adjustable, so you can choose to stand or sit as you paint.

Sketching easels

Alternatively, a folding sketching easel is lightweight and usually suitable for all but very large or heavy paintings. On soft ground, you can make the easel more stable by tethering the legs with string and metal skewers (just as you would stabilise a tent). If you prefer to work sitting down, a good-quality, modern folding stool or chair is a worthwhile investment.

Whatever medium you're working in, limit yourself to a few colours. This is not simply convenient, it is also a good discipline – colour mixing becomes easier and more automatic, leaving you free to observe and appreciate the subject.

Carry only as much paint as you will need. Even oils and acrylics are available in small (20ml) sizes. It is a good idea to keep the large economy tubes for the studio, and to invest in a few less bulky tubes for painting trips.

Paints of all types can be bought in handy sets – some come in lightweight carrying cases, complete with accessories such as palette, brushes, and mediums. The initial choice of colours is that of the manufacturer, but you can gradually substitute your favourite colours.

◀ Handy equipment for the travelling artist includes a backpack (A), a foldaway stool (B) and a light folding sketching easel (C). (The backpack shown here converts into a stool.)

To paint in watercolours outdoors, you need a sketch pad (D), a pencil (E) for preliminary drawings, brushes (F) and a watercolour set containing pans of paint and a palette area (G). You also need water – why not keep it in a couple of mineral water bottles? For oils and acrylics, you need a palette and paints, clip-on dippers (H) to hold thinners and mediums, perhaps a palette knife (I), and a selection of brushes (J). Canvas paper (K) is a portable, lightweight surface to paint on, and a charcoal pencil (L) can be used for an underdrawing.

Customised painting sets

Better still, why not make your own customised, portable painting set? This can be a wooden box, designed to carry your usual colours and mediums as well as your favourite palette and brushes.

Watercolourists will find that pads of paper are easier to carry than individual sheets. As the pads have a stiff card backing, there is no need for a board or other rigid surface to work on. Special blocks of paper, which are glued on three sides and do not need to be stretched, are particularly useful if you intend to work with watery washes.

For oils and acrylics, the cardboard-backed pads of canvas-textured paper are ideal for on-the-spot painting. These come with sheets of primed paper in a choice of sizes and grades – fine, medium and coarse. Alternatively, use prepared and ready-primed stretched canvases or canvas boards.

Avoid travelling with a traditional wooden drawing board, which is heavy and cumbersome to carry. If you really need a board, try a sheet of lightweight plywood or hardboard instead.

Bottles, boxes and containers

Pliable plastic food containers – the type used for freezer storage – come in a wide range of shapes and sizes and are invaluable to the artist. Use the lightweight lidded

THE COMPLETE WATERCOLOUR SET

As you need only a few lightweight materials, watercolours are particularly well suited to painting outside. You can buy compact, all-in-one sets that fit into virtually any bag and contain everything you need.

As well as a water container, palette, sketching pad and brushes, these sets have pans of colour, which are more practical than tubes because you can see and mix the colours instantly, without having to squeeze out paint and replace caps. Always carry a second bottle of water so that you have one for mixing colours and one for cleaning brushes.

For very small paintings, you can buy tiny watercolour sets – some of which will slip into your pocket.

boxes for carrying paints, crayons, pastels and other materials.

Pourers and bottles with plastic lids are excellent for holding water, turpentine and liquid mediums. You need one source of clean water or turps for diluting the colours and another for cleaning brushes. If you are travelling by air, remember that it is illegal to take flammable substances, which include turpentine and white spirit, on the plane. In some countries, real turpentine is difficult to come by, so it is worth making a few enquiries before you go.

On any painting trip, you need plenty of clean rags or kitchen paper for cleaning palettes and brushes. Also take clingfilm or plastic bags, so you can carry a dirty palette home without getting paint everywhere. Alternatively, use disposable paper palettes.

For transporting canvases with wet oils and acrylics, carry paintings face-in, as shown below. To transport drawings and watercolours, cover the surface with a sheet of clean paper, or roll them into a cardboard tube. Remember, soft pencil, pastel, chalk and charcoal smudge easily so drawings should be sprayed with fixative as soon as you have finished.

▼ The trouble with oil paints is that they take time to dry, so it is easy to smudge the colours. A convenient solution is to push panel pins through corks so that both ends of the pins protude. Then cut the blunt ends off the pins with pliers, and use these to attach two paintings, facing inwards, together. You can then carry the canvases around without touching the paint.

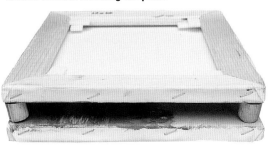

Midsummer landscape

You only need two watercolours to create this simple summer landscape. The blue and yellow are mixed together to make green.

W atercolour landscapes are one of the real joys of art. And you only need two colours to achieve this inspiring summer scene: the green is made by simply mixing the cobalt blue and cadmium yellow together.

The main thing to remember when painting a watercolour like this is that there are no rights or wrongs. You can interpret the view how you want. Because the paint will be wet on the board, where colours meet or where paint is laid directly on top of water, the colours will bleed. This lends individuality, but how much you use this technique is up to you.

Go as far as you like

How far you take the picture is also up to you. Step 11 provides a good place to stop, or you can develop the picture a bit more by following the stages shown in 'A Few Steps Further'. Take care not to keep on applying layers of paint and to overwork the picture though. Also remember to change your water often, so the colours you are mixing do not become too muddied.

Laying a graded wash

An important technique featured in this project is laying a graded wash. The block (see the 'Expert Advice' box on page 58) helps to ease the flow of the paint downward when applying the wash. This can be made by covering a piece of wood with paper – or you could just use an old book.

Finally, remember to paint onto watercolour board or paper weighing more than 140lb, since the water will cause lighter papers to wrinkle – or 'cockle' – spoiling your work.

YOU WILL NEED

Piece of watercolour board or 140lb+ watercolour paper

2B pencil

Brushes: No. 6; No. 2

Mixing palette or dish

Jar of water

'Block' to rest the board on

2 watercolours: Cadmium yellow; Cobalt blue

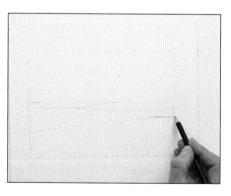

FIRST STROKES

1 ▲ **Roughly mark out the main areas of the painting** Using a 2B pencil, lightly draw a rectangle for the frame of the picture. Study the photograph, and again using light strokes, draw in the horizon. Lightly divide the foreground to mark the areas of green and yellow field.

▲ **You can achieve a lot by using just two watercolours and by mixing them in different quantities.**

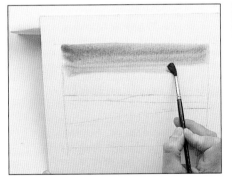

2 ▲ **Lay the wash for the sky** Lay a graduated wash over the sky area. Use the cobalt blue watercolour and a No.6 brush (rather than a flat brush, which is too large for this scale of painting). Prop the watercolour board against a block to help the paint flow smoothly down the board, and use more water in your paint mix as you move downwards to achieve the graduated effect.

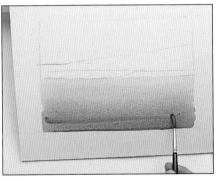

3 ▲ **Intensify the colour** Turn the board upside down and again prop it against the block. Work more of the cobalt blue mix into the top area of the sky. The angle of the board stops the paint running down into the lower sky, leaving a more intense colour at the top. Leave to dry.

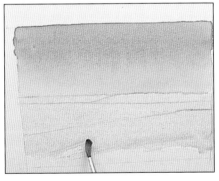

4 ▲ **Paint in the base colour for the foreground** Clean the No.6 brush, pour a little clean water into a separate palette well or saucer, and mix in some of the cadmium yellow that comes with this issue. Make sure that you mix enough paint to cover the foreground. Turn the board the right way up and work downwards, using large strokes. Leave to dry, then repeat and leave to dry again.

DEVELOPING THE PICTURE

Now you can start adding in the areas of green. First mix your colours. Pour a little clean water into a palette well or saucer, make up some cadmium yellow, then add cobalt blue, bit by bit, until you reach a shade of green you are happy with. The more blue you add, the darker the green will become.

5 ▶ Start to add in the areas of green
Remove the block and clean the No.6 brush. Then paint a thin layer of clean water around the outer edge of what will become the most distant strip of green field (shown right). Using the green mix, paint in the green strip itself, so that the paint bleeds into the adjacent area of 'wet' yellow.

▶ **The more blue that is added to the yellow, the darker the resulting green will become.**

6 ▲ Paint in the foreground Move on to the foreground area, using the same mix of green paint and working from right to left across the board. Load the brush with plenty of paint and use wide, uneven strokes, working fairly quickly.

7 ▶ Darken the background colour
Before the strip of green field on the horizon has a chance to dry thoroughly, add a touch of cobalt blue to the green mix to make it slightly darker. Then paint over the strip again to give it more depth of colour.

EXPERT ADVICE
Using a block

Watercolour board can be propped up against a block as you work, to make the paint run more easily down the page. This helps when laying washes. Once the wash has been laid from top to bottom, the board can be turned upside down. Working this time from bottom to top, the paint will again flow in a downward direction (towards the top of the painting in reality), creating greater intensity of colour.

8 ▶ Add perspective to the foreground
Using plenty of the darker green mix and working quickly so that the paint does not dry, add bold, diagonal lines to the foreground area. Move right to left and top to bottom to mimic the sloping lie of the land. This helps to emphasise the perspective.

LIFTING OFF EXCESS PAINT WITH A TISSUE

Watercolour is a flexible medium to work with, and it needn't be a problem if you make a mistake: it's easy just to blot wet paint off the paper using an absorbent material such as a tissue or kitchen towel. Even dry paint can be lifted off, with varying degrees of success, using a dampened tissue or cotton bud. The stronger the staining properties of the paint used, the more chance there is of it leaving a faint residue behind, even after lifting.

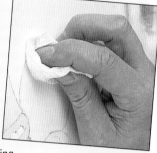

9 ▶ **Add definition to the yellow field** Paint over the yellow field again to intensify the colour, and leave to dry. Then paint a few rough 'stripes' of yellow horizontally across the field to add definition. Leave the painting to dry.

10 ▶ **Emphasise the slope of the foreground** Paint a thin layer of clean water over the entire green foreground area. Then, using the dark green mix, again paint strong, irregular diagonal lines over the foreground area, moving right to left and allowing the paint to bleed.

Master Strokes
❧

Jacob van Ruisdael (1628/9-1682)
Landscape with a Ruined Castle and a Church

A landscape specialist, Ruisdael is known for the sense of atmosphere he instilled in his paintings – largely through dramatic use of light and shade. In striking contrast to the project above, he was never known to paint a cloudless sky (we'll be tackling clouds in later projects), and in this example, a mass of towering grey cumulus threatens the serenity of the scene. Although the windmill in the centre of the painting is bathed in an almost idyllic shaft of golden light, and a sense of stillness is conveyed as in the 'Midsummer landscape', there is a suggestion that what we are actually witnessing is the calm before the storm. The shepherds to the left of the picture take a break from their work regardless.

The clouds take on a more menacing feel as they rush into the foreground, towering upwards at the same time. The shadow they cast darkens much of the foreground of the picture.

The eye is immediately drawn to this streak of pale yellow, used to depict the remaining sunlight seeping through the clouds and washing over the scene.

11 ▶ **Add the finishing touches** Load the brush with dark green mix and drag it across the bottom half of the green field on the horizon to again intensify the colour. Make sure the area of yellow field is dry, then add a touch of cobalt blue to the cadmium yellow mix to create a slightly 'dirty' yellow. Paint a few streaks of this colour across the yellow field to give an impression of shadows falling across the land. Leave the painting to dry.

A FEW STEPS FURTHER

Step 11 is a good place to stop, since you may well be entirely satisfied with the picture as it stands. However, if you want to take your work on a little further, you can add in a fence and some more foreground detail. This helps to emphasise the perspective in the scene.

12 ▶ **Paint in the fence** Make up a new mix using cobalt blue and just a dash of cadmium yellow. Then, using the fine No.2 brush and starting from the centre of the picture and working outwards, paint in the fence posts, using small, downward strokes. Space them as in the photograph, with the most distant posts appearing shorter and closer together.

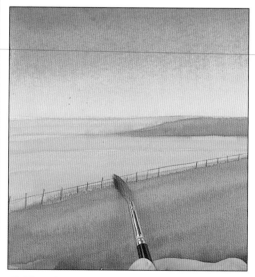

13 ▲ **Add the wire and blend in** Again using the No.2 brush and this time working left to right, add a very fine line across the upper part of the posts to depict the wire joining them together. Press the brush only lightly on the paper and try to keep your hand steady. Leave to dry, then brush a thin layer of clean water across the fencing to blend the colours and soften any harsh lines.

14 ▲ **Reinforce the perspective** Add a bit more cobalt blue to the existing green mix to darken the colour further. Then make bold, diagonal strokes across the foreground area, moving right to left with the brush. Add the most intense patch of colour in the bottom right-hand corner of the field, to reinforce the perspective of the scene. The picture is now finished and can be left to dry.

THE FINISHED PICTURE

A ──

B ──

C ──

A Area of graded wash
Using a graded, rather than flat wash, means that the blue of the sky is at its most intense at its highest point, and palest on the horizon – as it would be in a real landscape.

B Blended fencing
Brushing water over the fence softened the hard lines created by using a very fine brush. This brought the fence more into line with what is happening in the rest of the picture.

C Built up foreground
The foreground was built up by adding successive layers of green paint. The final, darkest application was allowed to bleed freely, to create a range of interesting and random effects.

Express yourself Intensified colour

In this version of the same view, the artist has intensified the colours by using more concentrated paint mixes. Complementary colours were also used – red over green and violet over yellow – to give the scene some extra zing.

Another change is the omission of the fence to give a more open view, and the use of stronger lines in the foreground to exaggerate the perspective. The time of day is also different: the pink haze on the horizon suggests early morning – a complete departure from the midday light suggested in the photograph.

Looking out over the valley

Warm and cool watercolours are used together to convey vast distances in this magnificent view from a hilltop.

We are all familiar with the great thrill that panoramic views afford and this watercolour painting certainly captures that feeling. One's emotional reaction when viewing a scene for the first time is an important element of any painting, and your aim should be to invite your viewers to share that vision. Once a scene takes your fancy, assess whether or not it will make a good painting by looking at how you can turn it into a good composition.

▼ The high viewpoint and strong curve of the path create an exciting composition in this scene. The eye tumbles into the valley then lingers over the series of thin, colourful fields in the distance.

Inviting composition

A landscape subject should have an entrance point and a destination. Try to design your composition in a way that invites the viewer to journey into the painting and roam around a little. In this painting, the rough track on the left is the directional force that carries the eye through the scene. Take note, however, that the path is not too dominant – it is interrupted by other elements such as trees and the curved line of the hill.

Colour recession

In a scene such as this, the range of tones and colours – from the nearest to the farthest – must be accurately assessed in terms of strength. If one is either too strong or too weak, the impression of a gradual recession will be destroyed. For instance, a field of oilseed rape might be a vivid yellow, but if it is in the distance it will appear to 'jump out' if you do not pay attention to how recession diminishes the intensity of the colour.

YOU WILL NEED

Piece of 400gsm (200lb) NOT watercolour paper 54 x 74cm (21 x 29in)

HB pencil

Masking fluid; colour shaper; old toothbrush

10 watercolours: rose madder; yellow ochre; cadmium yellow; burnt sienna; ultramarine; alizarin crimson; phthalo green; phthalo blue; Van Dyke brown; cerulean blue

Brushes: No. 30 squirrel mop; Nos. 10 and 2 rounds

Mixing palette or dish

Paper tissues

Craft knife

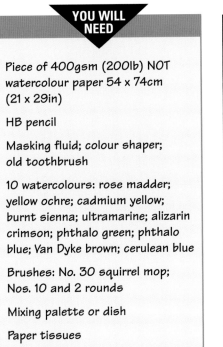

FIRST STEPS

1 ▲ Sketch the composition Using an HB pencil, sketch out the bare bones of the landscape – include the trees, path and horizon. Here, the artist drew on to a sheet of tracing paper first, then traced off the lines – this is less obtrusive than drawing directly on to the paper.

2 ◄ Work on the foreground track Draw the stones strewn across the dirt track, making them smaller in the distance. Using a colour shaper, (see Trouble Shooter on next page) mask them out with masking fluid. To represent the smallest stones, spatter some masking fluid flicked from an old toothbrush. Then apply more to the trunks and branches of the silver birch trees with the colour shaper.

TROUBLESHOOTER

BRUSH SAVER

Save wear and tear on your watercolour brushes by using a colour shaper (a type of brush with a flexible rubber tip instead of hairs) to apply the masking fluid. Even dried-on fluid is easy to remove by peeling it off the rubber tip.

3 ▲ **Apply colour to the sky** Use a No. 30 squirrel mop to wet the entire paper with clean water. Change to a No. 10 round brush and apply a narrow band of rose madder across the horizon line. Allow the colour to drift up into the sky and below the horizon. Then apply a band of yellow ochre across the top of the picture and let it merge into the pink area.

5 ▼ **Darken the sky** Rinse the No. 10 round brush in clean water and wet the sky area. Then sweep in streaks of grey-violet mixed from ultramarine warmed with a tiny drop of alizarin crimson. Add more ultramarine to the mix to make it bluer and paint a darker streak along the horizon.

4 ▲ **Underpaint the foreground** Make a fairly strong wash of cadmium yellow and work it over the foreground with broad, sweeping strokes of the No. 30 mop brush. Vary the tone with a few strokes of burnt sienna applied wet-on-wet. Allow to dry.

6 ▼ Create clouds While the sky wash is still wet, lift out cumulus clouds at the top with a small wad of tissue. Avoid rubbing, as this will spoil the surface of the paper; use a quick, press-and-lift motion. Lift out streaks of flat cloud with the 'edge' of the tissue wad.

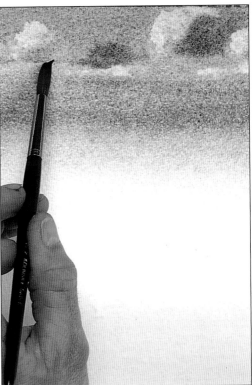

7 ▲ Develop the clouds Tilt your board downwards and soften the undersides of the clouds by 'tickling' them with a clean, damp brush. Then put in some dark clouds with small, rapid movements of the brush, using the same grey-violet mix as before, but darkened with more ultramarine.

DEVELOPING THE PICTURE

The foreground, middle ground and background are now established as simple shapes. Start to develop the landscape features and the effects of aerial perspective. As you do this, remember to keep the whole composition in mind, rather than concentrating on individual parts.

8 ▶ Start painting the foreground bushes Rinse the brush clean and shake off the excess water. Scrub the damp brush lightly over the right-hand corner of the painting, working it in different directions. Quickly dry-brush over these wet strokes with a mix of cadmium yellow and burnt sienna.

9 ▶ Establish the foreground and middle ground Use the same method as in step 8 to establish the sloping line of trees in the middle distance, behind the birch trees. Now darken the mix with a touch of ultramarine and scuff the shadows on the dirt track, again using water first so that the strokes are softened.

10 ▼ Add detail Suggest grass below the trees with a dilute mixture of cadmium yellow and phthalo green. Darken the mixture with more phthalo green and paint the grass in the foreground with quick dry-brush strokes interspersed with brown shadows mixed from burnt sienna and ultramarine. Put in shadows cast by the stones, using the No. 10 round for big ones and a No. 2 round for small ones.

11 ▼ Introduce mid tones Pick up a small amount of burnt sienna on the No. 10 brush and apply loose, scrubby strokes over the trees in the middle distance and the bushes in the foreground on the right. Mix burnt sienna and ultramarine, and suggest the cool, dark shadows between the trees with small, quick strokes of the No. 2 brush.

12 ▶ Put in distant fields Continue with the same mix for the shadows in the foreground bushes, applying the paint with upward flicks of the brush. Changing to the No. 10 round, paint the distant, bright yellow cornfield with a continuous stroke of cadmium yellow (dampen the area with clean water first). Mix in some burnt sienna and paint the field beyond the cornfield with a narrow band of colour. Add a little rose madder for the farthest fields, leaving small flashes of white paper

13 ▶ **Continue with the background** Darken the wooded area in front of the cornfield with loose, wet-on-wet strokes of burnt sienna overlaid with touches of cadmium yellow. Start to put in the distant fields with thin streaks of phthalo green. Mix ultramarine with a hint of phthalo blue (for intensity) and alizarin crimson (for warmth), and put in the line of blue hills on the horizon, using the very tip of the brush.

14 ▼ **Add more detail** Use the same blue mix to suggest lines of trees and hedgerows in the distance, working over some of the undercolours. The yellow undercolour will show through, making a green. Use bigger strokes for the trees in front of the cornfield to show that they are nearer.

15 ▶ **Paint treetops on the right** Dip the No. 10 brush in clean water, squeeze out the excess and loosely work over the middle ground on the right of the picture. Go over the area with loose strokes of Van Dyke brown and ultramarine, letting the colours run and blend on the damp paper to give an impression of treetops in hazy light. Introduce strokes of burnt sienna and cadmium yellow in the same way.

Express yourself
Nature distilled

In this version of the landscape, the elements are pared down to interlocking shapes of warm and cool colour. The paper was first wetted and broad sweeps of colour were applied with a large, soft brush, leaving flecks of white paper to offset the intense colours. Despite the lack of recognizable detail, these contrasting shapes and colours read as a landscape receding into the distance.

16 ▼ **Increase recession** Using the dampened No. 30 mop, lightly sweep over the fields to soften them. Mute the colour of the cornfield with a mix of cadmium yellow and yellow ochre. With the No. 10 brush and clean water, lift out a streak of colour from the green field, then apply cadmium yellow to suggest sunlight. Draw bands of the blue mix from step 13 across the yellow field.

17 ▶ **Paint the cast shadows** Mix a dilute wash of cerulean blue and burnt sienna and use this to suggest the rutted surface of the dirt track with quick dry-brush strokes worked in different directions. Paint more dark shadows cast by the nearby trees with an intense dark mixed from Van Dyke brown and ultramarine.

18 ▼ **Paint the twigs** Dip the tip of the No. 10 round in water, shake off the excess and paint the twigs of the birches with rapid dry-brush strokes. Then dip the brush into the dark brown wash and go over the strokes again with the brush held perpendicular. Skip it over the surface to create thick to thin calligraphic marks.

19 ◀ **Paint the birch trees** Remove the masking fluid from the birches. Mix a greenish yellow from yellow ochre, burnt sienna and a touch of phthalo green. Wet the tree trunks with clean water, then add the colour to the left edge of the trunk and let it drift across the damp paper. While this is damp, paint shadows on the trunks with Van Dyke brown and a little ultramarine. Again, touch the brush to the edge and let the colour drift.

20 ◀ **Paint the stones** Finish painting the birch trees, leaving flecks of white paper on the branches to suggest light reflecting off the silvery bark. Remove the masking fluid from the stones in the foreground. Lightly touch each stone with water, then apply a mix of cerulean blue and yellow ochre, leaving tiny flecks of white paper here and there. Just before they dry, touch in some shadows and cracks on the nearest stones with the dark brown mix.

A FEW STEPS FURTHER

There is plenty for the eye to explore in the open spaces of this atmospheric landscape. A hint of scratching out will add a final touch of subtle texture.

21 ▶ Use sgraffito With the tip of a sharp craft knife blade, scratch out a few fine, broken lines that suggest light catching the branches of young saplings in the middle distance.

22 ▲ Add shadows Paint the shadow sides of the saplings with the dark brown mix from step 17, using the very tip of the No. 10 round to produce fine lines.

THE FINISHED PICTURE

A Depth and distance
Cool, recessive blues and greens in the distance contrast with warm golds in the foreground, a device that emphasizes the effects of aerial perspective.

B Breaking the boundaries
The birch trees break the frame at the top, bringing them forward in the picture plane and pushing the landscape back into the distance by contrast.

C Counterbalance
The bushes at bottom right counterbalance the birch trees at top left, giving the composition equilibrium and forming a 'frame' for the landscape beyond.

Placing the horizon

Think carefully about where you place the horizon in your landscape painting – it has an enormous effect on the atmosphere of your composition.

The location of the horizon defines the proportion of sky to land, and has a crucial effect on the mood and sense of space within a landscape picture. Without really thinking about it, we know that the horizon line is probably the most important element in a landscape painting. In fact, if a single horizontal line is drawn anywhere on a rectangular support, most people will 'read' it as the horizon.

A low horizon

Flat, open landscapes such as plains and fenland have a broad, spacious feeling. The horizon is far away and wide, and the sky is large and important. Seascapes have a similarly open feeling. In these regions you can see weather fronts approaching and watch the shadows of clouds crossing the landscape. To recreate these conditions in a picture, place the horizon line low.

The shape of the canvas also affects the mood of the composition. A wide landscape format allows the eye to travel slowly from side to side, so it is ideal for broad, open panoramas. For his painting *Deauville, 1893*, Eugène Boudin chose a landscape format and placed the horizon low in the picture area. There is a large sky, and the clouds and the people on the beach diminish in scale towards the horizon, creating an airy, spacious feel.

Contrast this with *Poplars on the Banks of the Epte* (right) by Claude Monet (1840–1926). Here the artist has combined a very low horizon with an upright format. The tall, slender columns of the poplars and the sinuous zig-zag line of their canopy draw the eyes upwards. The viewpoint (that is, the viewer's eye-level) is an important aspect of landscape composition. If you are high up – standing on a wall, for example – you can see further than if you are sitting down, and the horizon will appear to be

▲ *Poplars on the Banks of the Epte* (1891) was painted by Claude Monet in the autumn, so the warm colours of the turning leaves emphasise the sinuous curve created as the trees follow the river bank, and increase the illusion of depth in the picture.

further away. This work was painted from a boat, and the low viewpoint means it is dominated by the sky and the towering, silhouetted trees. Although the trees get smaller as they recede into the distance, they and their reflections break the edges of the picture, drawing attention to the picture plane.

A high horizon

By contrast, a high horizon leaves little room for the sky and produces a contained and rather intimate landscape. In nature you can experience this effect in mountain valleys; towering crags crowd in upon you, casting deep shadows and limiting your view of the sky. Wooded landscapes and forests can also produce this slightly claustrophobic atmosphere.

In *Red Vineyards at Arles* (below), Vincent Van Gogh (1853–90) has taken an exaggeratedly high viewpoint, so we can see all the activity in the vineyard. A high horizon tends to flatten the picture, and the artist exploits this quality to create a graphic, almost decorative painting. Van Gogh has also created a rather ambiguous sense of space – the trees and human figures diminishing in the distance contrast with devices which emphasise the picture plane; bright colours, strong outlines and vigorous brushmarks which do not change in scale.

Experimenting with horizon lines

The horizon is just one aspect of the internal geometry (organisation) of a landscape painting. The final impact of the composition will depend on how you organise the other elements such as space, tone, colour and format. Choose a landscape and make thumbnail sketches of it, placing the horizon at different levels. You will find that each treatment demands a different internal geometry.

• If you place the horizon low in the picture area and create a thunderous sky, the painting will have a dramatic, threatening mood.

• Introduce trees on either side of the scene and the image will feel more enclosed.

• Place the horizon high within an upright format – the landscape will advance towards the viewer.

• Introduce a sweeping path or a river to lead the eye towards the horizon and you immediately create a sense of recession.

• Try placing the horizon right in the middle – you may have been told that this is 'wrong', because an even, symmetrical image can be boring, but it can work very well.

A high horizon creates an enclosed, intimate feeling and allows the artist to show greater detail in the foreground.

A central horizon can be unnaturally stable, but the right tonal balance between the areas adds dynamism.

A low horizon is ideal for showing dramatic skies to their best advantage, and to create a sense of spaciousness.

◀ Vincent Van Gogh used a high horizon in *Red Vineyards at Arles* (1888) to give him the space to show a landscape drenched in the red, orange and golden tones of a glorious sunset.

Sailing barges

A vast expanse of sky provides a luminous backdrop to traditional sailing barges with their jumble of masts, furled sails and rigging.

Harbours and estuaries are a rich source of painting material and are often more interesting when the tide is out. At low tide there are pools of water with reflections in them, boats tilted on their sides and an assortment of mooring ropes and buoys.

Rather than attempt to take in an entire scene, try to find a small area that catches your eye. Feel free to move objects around to achieve a better composition. Here, the artist felt that the jetty on the left was too obtrusive, so he pushed it back and made it smaller. He added elements on the right to balance the boats on the left.

Using a rigger brush
Rather than labouring over the barges' rigging, suggest it simply with slightly broken lines. This is where a rigger brush comes in handy. It has very long, flexible hair and the extra-fine point enables you to make hairline strokes. In fact, the name 'rigger' goes back to the days of big sailing ships, when painters of seascapes used this type of brush to render the complex rigging accurately.

▼ **In this evocative marine view, the artist combines close observation of the subject with economy of detail.**

Piece of 300gsm (140lb) NOT watercolour paper 30.5 x 40.5cm (12 x 16in)

4B pencil

8 watercolours: raw sienna; ultramarine; light red; cadmium red; lemon yellow; burnt sienna; cobalt blue; brown madder alizarin

Brushes: 25mm (1in) flat; Nos. 6, 14 and 4 rounds; No. 1 rigger

Mixing palette or dish

Jar of water

Ruler

FIRST STEPS

1 ▶ Start with a drawing Make a light pencil outline drawing of the scene. Position the horizon line low down on the page so as to give full emphasis to the boats and their tall masts. Pay attention to shapes, angles and proportions, but don't get bogged down with every last detail.

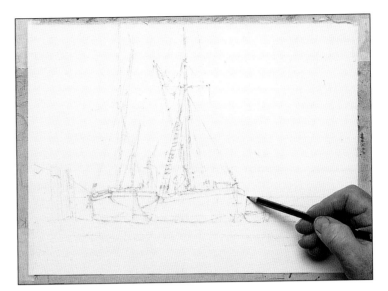

2 ◀ Apply a background wash Working with the 25mm (1in) flat brush, dampen the entire paper except for the boat hulls. Block in the sky and the foreground with a thin, transparent wash of raw sienna watercolour to give a warm tone overall.

3 ▼ Paint the clouds Just before the underwash dries, mix a dilute wash of ultramarine and make soft, diagonal strokes in the upper left of the sky with the flat brush. Put in the storm cloud at top right with a stronger wash, then sweep the brush down and across, letting the colour fade out. While the ultramarine is still damp, float a hint of light red into the lower clouds to give them a warm tint.

4 ▲ Define the horizon Make a dilute mix of ultramarine and a little cadmium red. Still using the flat brush, suggest a reddening sky by sweeping in a band of this soft mauve shade across the horizon line.

5 ▼ **Paint the water** Mix a muted green from ultramarine with a little lemon yellow and raw sienna and, using a No. 6 round brush, put in the line of trees in the far distance. Switch to a No. 14 round brush and put in the pools of water in the foreground with very dilute ultramarine.

6 ▲ **Paint the mud banks** Now put in the mud banks with sweeping strokes of raw sienna. While these are still damp, float on darker patches of mud with a brownish mix of light red and ultramarine, letting them settle softly into the underwash. Make a stronger version of the same mix and use the tip of the brush to make broken lines, suggesting ridges in the mud.

7 ◄ **Add background details** Mix varied mid tones of green and grey from ultramarine and raw sienna. Give the distant trees and mud banks a little more definition with tiny marks made with the tip of the No. 6 round brush.

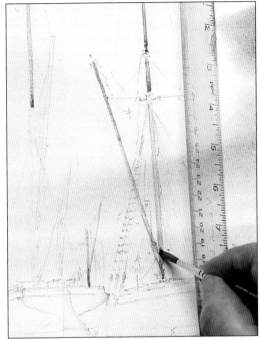

DEVELOPING THE PICTURE

Now that the sky and background are established, you can turn your attention to the boats. These are the focus of the painting, but try to integrate them naturally with the surrounding sea and sky by avoiding too many details and hard edges.

8 ▲ Paint the jetty Mix raw sienna, ultramarine and light red in varied proportions and paint the wooden jetty with vertical strokes of a No. 4 round brush. Keep these washes light and broken – the jetty is right on the edge of the picture and, if you overstate it, it will draw the eye and unbalance the composition.

9 ▲ Paint the masts Mix a warm brown from raw sienna and burnt sienna, dilute it well and begin painting the wooden masts with the No. 6 brush. To steady your hand, hold a ruler at an angle and rest the ferrule of the brush against its edge. Vary the tones of brown, and make the upper parts of the masts slightly darker where they are silhouetted against the light sky.

10 ◄ Start on the hulls Fill in the back panel of the left-hand boat with a pale wash of cobalt blue. Mix a strong blue-black from ultramarine and light red, and paint the hull of the right-hand boat, leaving slivers of white paper showing to define its form.

11 ▼ **Complete one of the hulls** Mix raw sienna and light red, and paint the base of the right-hand hull, letting this colour bleed into the darker one above. Rinse the brush, shake out the excess water and lift out some colour to show where the hull curves towards the prow and reflects more light.

12 ▲ **Complete the other hull** Paint the hull and rudder of the left-hand boat, using the same colour mixes as in steps 10 and 11, but this time making them slightly darker in tone, particularly where the back of the hull curves under. Again, leave slivers of white paper to help define the shapes.

EXPERT ADVICE
Soft focus

Although boats are solid structures, avoid using dense tones and hard edges when you paint them. In a watercolour painting, boats should harmonize with the surrounding elements of sky and water. Use a damp brush to soften the line where one colour or tone meets another, and where the bottom of the boat meets the water or the mud bank on which it is resting.

13 ▲ **Paint the sails** Use light red to put in the red trim on the little dinghy on the right. Then mix a rich brown from brown madder alizarin and raw sienna, and start painting the furled sails.

14 ▼ **Put in the rigging** Mix a dark wash of ultramarine and light red, and use the No. 1 rigger brush to put in the crosstree and ropes that make up the rigging on the right-hand boat. Use a ruler to steady your hand, but try not to make the lines too rigid. Keep the brush fairly dry, use a very light touch and vary the weight of the lines.

16 ▼ **Paint reflections** Mix a greenish-grey from ultramarine and raw sienna, and, using the No. 14 brush, paint the reflections of the boats and wooden pilings in the foreground water. Make sure each reflection sits directly beneath the object reflecting it. Add a touch more ultramarine for the darker reflections, painting them with vertical strokes while the paint is still damp so that they blend softly together.

15 ▲ **Complete the rigging** Paint the rigging on the left-hand boat in the same way. Suggest hatches and other deck details with a muted green mix of lemon yellow and ultramarine.

A FEW STEPS FURTHER

Step back from the picture and assess what is needed to complete it. Some cast shadows will strengthen the forms, and some small details on the right will give the composition better balance.

17 ▲ **Add the mooring pile** Mix a grey-brown from ultramarine and light red, and paint the mooring pile on the right with a dry No. 4 brush – its top extends above the horizon to add to the feeling of depth. Paint its reflection in the pool with broken lines in a slightly lighter tone.

Express yourself

Getting proportions right

In this rapidly executed sketch, made with a dip pen and ink, the artist focuses on capturing the 'personality' of a small fishing vessel. All boats have their own character, conveyed by the shapes of their hulls, masts and sails. However quickly and simply you draw them, it is vital to get their basic proportions right. Start by comparing the length of a boat to the height of its mast. Then check, for example, the length of the cabin against the length of the deck, and so on.

18 ▼ Add shadows Dampen the No. 14 brush and run it along the bottom of the boats to soften the line where boat and sand meet. Using darker versions of the mixes from step 8, strengthen the jetty and put in the shadows it casts on the sand. Paint the shadow on the right-hand boat with a fairly dark mix of ultramarine and light red.

19 ▲ Work on the sails Mix brown madder alizarin with a touch of ultramarine, and, with the tip of the No. 6 brush, put in the dark shadows and folds on the sails.

20 ▼ Add foreground detail With the rigger brush and a mix of ultramarine and brown madder alizarin, suggest the mooring lines tying the boats to the mooring pile and lying on the foreshore. Use a deft, light touch, letting the lines break up.

21 ▲ Add some seagulls Use the tip of the No. 6 round brush and the same dark mix to enliven the sky area with seagulls. Be sparing – scattering too many little 'V-shapes' everywhere can ruin a perfectly good painting. Include small groups as well as single birds, and vary their size, tone and wing positions.

THE FINISHED PICTURE

A Tall masts
Taking the tall masts of the barges right off the top of the picture area emphasizes their height and gives the viewer the feeling of being close to the subject.

B Lead-ins
The sweeping diagonal shape of the blue cloud leads the eye down to the centre of interest – the two sailing barges.

C Watch the birdie
Seagulls wheeling overhead on the right complement the bulk of the boats on the left, add detail to the wide expanse of sky and animate the scene.

Riverbank reflections

Various watercolour techniques are used to great effect in this painting of a cool, shady stretch of river, with the sun filtering through the trees.

There are three main elements found in this lovely river scene – water, grass and trees. Each element is treated separately and each is painted using a different technique. This jigsaw approach will enable you to complete the painting in simplified stages, and you will have the satisfaction of seeing how the pieces eventually fit together to make a realistic landscape.

Start by making the initial drawing on tracing paper. In this way you can experiment with the composition without spoiling the paper. The transferred image will always be clean and minimal – an ideal start for watercolour painting.

Grass and foliage

Spattering is the key to the fresh, grassy banks – first with clean water, then with colour, so that the paint finds its way into the wet shapes. The first spatter of colour looks like an explosion of tiny stars, but as the sequence is repeated the 'stars' eventually build up to form a perfect impression of grass and leaves.

To create perspective in the painting, make the foreground spatters larger than those in the background by spattering with the brush held closer to the paper.

Watery reflections

Paradoxically, the fluid nature of water is most effectively painted with precise brush strokes. Here, both vertical and horizontal strokes are used to create the reflections in the river. Paint the reflections wet-on-wet; when dry, they provide a soft background for more precise ripples and reflected shapes, overpainted in stronger colours.

▼ YOU WILL NEED

Piece of 400gsm (200lb) NOT watercolour paper 38 x 51cm (15 x 20in)

Tracing paper (size as above)

B pencil

Masking fluid; old toothbrush and paint brush (to apply masking fluid)

Scraps of paper to mask painting

Brushes: Nos. 6 and 4 rounds; fan blender; No. 1 rigger or fine liner

Woodcock feather (optional)

10 watercolours: cadmium lemon; phthalo green; turquoise light; indigo; burnt sienna; alizarin crimson; Naples yellow; Payne's grey; ultramarine; cerulean blue

Gum arabic; paper tissue

▲ Lively spattered texture on the foliage contrasts with the glassy surface of the river in this peaceful scene.

FIRST STEPS

1 ▼ **Trace the image** Having sketched the image on to tracing paper, draw with a B pencil over the main lines on the reverse of the paper.

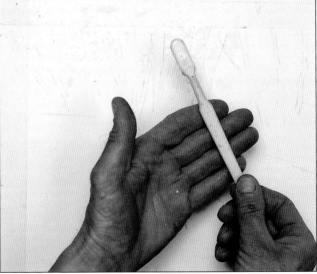

2 ▲ **Apply masking fluid** Transfer the image on to watercolour paper by turning the tracing paper the right way up and going over the lines with a sharp pencil. Use an old paint brush to dab masking fluid between the trees. Also mask distant horizontal reflections and the stumps in the foreground. Use an old toothbrush to spatter masking fluid across the background.

3 ▼ Block in the river bank Mask off the river with scrap paper. Using a No. 6 round brush, spatter water on to the grassy bank on the left. Dab on cadmium lemon, allowing the colour to run into the blobs of water. At the top, blend the yellow with more water to create a wash of solid colour.

4 ▲ Continue blocking in Wet the right-hand bank and flood the area with cadmium lemon, leaving a broad band of white along the top of the picture.

Express yourself

Down the road

Here is another watercolour, painted with many of the same techniques as the step-by-step. Here, however, the river is replaced by a road. Note how the blues and purples of the wet tarmac surface contrast with the yellows and greens of the verge. The long, linear tree shadows across the road also make a pleasing contrast with the spattered detail on the verge.

5 ▼ **Suggest the grass** Mask out all the areas around the right-hand bank. Mix phthalo green and cadmium lemon, and flick the mixture on to the wet cadmium lemon paint.

6 ▲ **Suggest the background** To suggest the distant trees on the right, lightly apply water to the paper, then spatter and dab the wet area with varying mixtures of cadmium lemon, turquoise light, indigo, burnt sienna and alizarin crimson. Allow the colours to run together on the wet paper.

7 ▼ **Continue the background** Paint the tree-trunks and branches in cadmium lemon. Moving to the left, lightly wet the paper, spatter on turquoise light and phthalo green paint, then blend the colours in the shady areas around the base of the trees.

DEVELOPING THE PICTURE

The main areas of grass and foliage have been initially blocked in with yellow and green, and it is time to start work on the trees. There is a handy technique for painting them quickly and effectively.

8 ▶ **Paint the trees** Change to a No. 4 round and paint green bands across one of the tree trunks in a dilute mix of indigo, turquoise light and Naples yellow. Define the trunk by dragging Payne's grey quickly down through the wet bands. The paint will run horizontally to suggest branches.

EXPERT ADVICE
Fine lines with a feather

In the nineteenth century, marine artists and architects often used a tail feather of a woodcock to paint fine, even lines. The feather, which is very springy and holds a surprising amount of colour, is used here taped to a brush handle to paint the long, thin branches of the trees. If you do not have a woodcock feather to hand, a No. 1 rigger or fine liner brush does a similar job.

9 ▲ **Develop the grass** With the No. 6 brush, develop the far bank, alternately spattering it with water and then with a mixture of phthalo green and indigo to create the light and dark greens. Use the tip of the brush to take the colour up to the edge of the water.

10 ▼ **Complete the trees** Use the No. 4 brush and burnt sienna to paint the bank of trees on the right-hand side. But don't overdo it – work from the wrist to achieve natural curves on trunks and branches.

11 ▼ **Build up the grass tones** Moving to the left bank, spatter the grass with drops of water, then with dilute phthalo green. Repeat to build up textured colour, adding indigo for the darker foreground tones.

12 ▼ **Paint the water** Using the No. 6 brush, block in the river in broad, horizontal strokes of ultramarine. Use deep colour in the foreground, diluting it as you move towards the distance. While the colour is wet, smooth out brush marks with water and a fan blender.

13 ▼ **Suggest reflections** Start to paint the foreground reflections into the wet blue paint, applying mixes of burnt sienna and indigo with vertical and horizontal strokes.

14 ▲ **Add distant reflections** Wet the far part of the river with water mixed with gum arabic. Using the No.4 round, work over this with vertical strokes of Naples yellow. Add darker bands with mixes of cadmium lemon, Payne's grey and burnt sienna.

15 ▲ **Remove masking fluid** Paint strokes of indigo mixed with burnt sienna between the bands of masking fluid on the water. Leave the painting to dry; rub off the masking fluid from the background and water. Paint a dilute mix of indigo, burnt sienna and phthalo green among the trees; add reflections in a mix of phthalo green, indigo and burnt sienna.

A FEW STEPS FURTHER

The picture is almost complete, but more can be made of the ripples and reflections on the river. So far, these are suggested with soft, wet-on-wet brush strokes. Now allow the painting to dry completely, so that you can add some crisper reflections to the surface of the water.

16 ▶ **Paint moving water** With the No. 6 brush, paint the reflections of the trees in the foreground in a dark mixture of indigo, burnt sienna and phthalo green, adding touches of lemon yellow for the paler tones. Use squiggly, tapering lines to capture the movement of the water.

17 ▲ **Define the bank** Continue building up reflections, diluting the mix to make lighter tones. Use the No. 4 brush for finer lines. Apply water along the edge of the river bank and flood with mixes of cerulean blue, turquoise light and cadmium yellow.

18 ▼ **Add branches** Paint the reflections of the fine branches in mixes of indigo, burnt sienna and phthalo green. Our artist used a woodcock feather for the tapering lines, but a No. 1 rigger or fine liner brush works well, too. Apply water across the far ripples, then dab off some of the colour with a paper tissue.

19 ▲ **Paint the posts** Remove the masking fluid from the wooden posts and paint the tops in a mix of burnt sienna and cadmium lemon with the No. 4 brush. Add the shadow in indigo mixed with burnt sienna.

THE FINISHED PICTURE

A Background sunlight
White sunlight filtering through the trees is established in the early stages of the painting with masking fluid.

B Grass and foliage
The river bank is built up by spattering the paper with water and paint alternately to achieve a mottled, leafy texture.

C Wavy lines
The moving surface of the water is created by using horizontal lines with squiggly and zigzag marks.

Creating foliage in watercolours

Trees, with their enormous variations in shape, colour and patterns of growth, are an important source of colour and texture in landscape paintings.

The flutter of leaves in a passing breeze is one of the most important elements in a convincing landscape painting. Using a few simple watercolour techniques, you'll soon be creating truly naturalistic effects.

When trees are in the foreground, you can make out the pattern made by the foliage and the shapes of some individual leaves. But you won't see every part of a scene with pinpoint accuracy, so don't paint every leaf. Instead, find a mark that describes the distinctive character of the foliage.

Study the subject carefully through half-closed eyes and put down the areas of tone. Gradually, a leaf-like pattern will begin to emerge. If you paint just a few leaves in detail, the viewer's brain will understand that the rest of the foliage follows the same pattern and will 'fill in the blanks'.

When a tree is further away, you can see only generalised leaf forms and the leaf masses around the boughs. And when trees are seen from even further away, only a broad silhouette of the leaves and trunk is discernible.

▲ **The grey-green foliage of this gnarled olive tree is shown in enough detail to suggest the leaves without being too precise. The trees in the distance are treated as silhouettes.**

FIRST STROKES

1 ▼ Draw the outlines Using a 2B pencil, establish the broad areas of the landscape. The branches and leaves of trees look complicated, so ignore the detail and concentrate on the underlying forms. Think about the composition – whether you are working directly from the subject or from references, adjust the drawing to create a pleasing arrangement.

YOU WILL NEED

Large piece of 300gsm (140lb) Not watercolour paper

2B pencil

Brushes: Nos.10, 6, 3 soft rounds

7 watercolours: Cobalt blue; Sap green; Sepia; Yellow ochre; Payne's grey; Cerulean blue; Black

Mixing palette or dish

Natural sponge

A mix of sepia, sap green and yellow ochre makes a good foliage colour.

2 ▶ Block in the sky Using a No.10 brush, mix a wash of cobalt blue and lay it in for the sky. Remember that, in watercolour, the paper is the lightest colour available, so leave patches of paper unpainted as clouds. Leave to dry.

4 ▲ Soften the sponged effects The stippling created by sponging can be too unsubtle, so apply more colour and roll the No.10 brush through the wash to create a variety of edges to modify the sponged effects.

3 ▲ Apply background greens Make a wash of sap green and, using a natural sponge, apply this broadly and loosely in the grassy foreground area. Use sweeping, diagonal marks that suggest swaying grasses. Mix sap green and sepia to create a lighter green for the trees in the distance, and dab it on with a sponge.

5 ▲ Add texture to the foreground Mix sap green, sepia and yellow ochre to give a vivid grass green colour. Using a No.6 brush and making vigorous diagonal strokes, add more colour to the grassy area in the foreground. Leave the painting to dry.

6 ▼ **Paint the trunks and branches** Make a wash of sepia and Payne's grey for the tree trunks. Using the No.6 brush, apply flat colour, thinking about the way a tree grows: the boughs come out of the main trunk, and the branches and twigs grow out of each other in a logical pattern, becoming gradually thinner towards the edge of the tree. Allow to dry.

DEVELOPING THE PICTURE

The background and the main silhouette of the tree are established, so it is now time to create the foliage. The patches of leaves are built up gradually in three stages by layering a light, middle and dark tone of the same basic colour. This technique creates a sense of movement, suggesting light catching fluttering leaves.

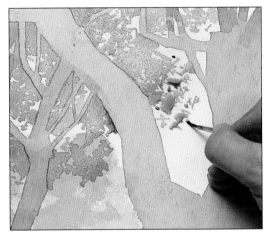

7 ▲ **Start to apply foliage to the olive trees** Mix Payne's grey, sap green and cerulean blue to make a pale blue-green for the first foliage tone. Use a small No.3 brush to apply this wash, pushing and pulling the colour with the tip of the bristles to create random clusters of leaves. Try not to space the marks too evenly, and vary the tone of the wash by adding differing amounts of water.

EXPERT ADVICE
Adding gum arabic

Gum arabic is the medium that carries the pigment in watercolour paint. Adding extra medium intensifies the colour and gives a slight sheen, as in the darkest foliage colour shown below. You can buy gum arabic in bottles from most art supply shops.

8 ▲ **Add shadows on the tree trunk** Using a more concentrated wash of the sepia/Payne's grey mix and the No.3 brush, lay in the shadows on the trunk and branches of the main olive tree. These shadows give form and solidity to the tree, and also help to describe its gnarled surface.

9 ▶ **Finish adding the first tone** Using the Payne's grey, sap green and cerulean blue wash and the No.3 brush, complete the first application of tone to the foliage. Take care to keep the marks a similar size as you work across the painting. Leave the paint to dry thoroughly.

10 ▲ **Add a second tone to the foliage** Mix a darker tone of the foliage colour and use the No.3 brush to apply another layer of leaves. Screw up your eyes to isolate the main masses of foliage. Notice that the tops of each mass, especially those on the side from which the light is coming, are lighter than the undersides. Work as before, creating patches of wash and then painting detailed leaf shapes around the edges. Leave to dry.

11 ▲ **Paint shadows on the trunk** Mix a darker tone of the sepia/Payne's grey wash and apply dark shadows to the left side of the trunk and the branches that are turned away from the light. Use the same wash to 'draw' some thin branches and twigs amongst the foliage. Allow to dry thoroughly.

Master Strokes

Gustav Klimt (1862–1918)
Roses under the Trees

The Austrian painter Gustav Klimt developed a highly decorative style. In his treatment of these trees in an orchard, the foliage is painstakingly built up dab by dab using a pointillist technique, until the surface glows with hundreds of different shades.

The painting is dominated by the vibrant foliage of the tree which fills the picture area, creating a decorative, almost abstract effect.

The ridged texture of the tree trunks is described in detail, using broken, curved lines. Patches of green lichen enliven the grey surface.

12 ▶ **Give texture to the bark** Prepare a third, dark tone of the basic foliage wash used in step 7. Add gum arabic to intensify the colour. Apply a final layer of this colour, painting clusters of leaves as before. Mix a wash of black and, using the No.3 brush, apply dark tone on the darkest side of the trunk. Use the same wash to describe fissures and textures in the bark of the tree.

13 ▲ **Apply texture and shadows** Using a wash of sap green and the No.3 brush, apply wide brush marks to the grassy area in the foreground. Allow this to dry thoroughly and then use sepia with a little sap green to paint the shadows cast by both olive trees. These attached shadows help to 'fix' the trees to the horizontal surface of the ground.

Express yourself

Band of gold

The same olive tree has been given an arresting treatment here with the addition of bright orange and green bands dividing the composition in two. These are applied as a collage of coloured paper and represent the nets used to catch the harvested olives, which have been rolled up and tied. This unusual device not only adds a splash of almost fluorescent colour to the neutral grey-green background, but also acts as a counterbalance to the vertical trunks and branches that predominate in the painting.

A FEW STEPS FURTHER

Applying the foliage as layers of washes gives the tree canopy depth and form. This area of the painting can be considered complete – it is convincing and has textural interest. You could, however, add more texture to the foreground – this will add eye-catching detail and increase the sense of recession. Consider adding to the background by painting in a line of simple silhouetted trees.

14 ▲ **Add texture to the grass** Mix sap green with sepia and paint vigorous diagonal marks with the No.3 brush to create grassy textures in the foreground. Spatter the wash over the area for varied textures.

▼ **Use increasingly concentrated mixes of sepia and Payne's grey for the bark.**

15 ▲ **Develop the textures in the bark** Mix black and sepia and, using the No.3 brush, work across the trunk adding a variety of textures. The bark of this ancient olive tree is twisted and gnarled, so you can use a range of brush marks to describe its surface.

16 ▲ **Add trees in the background** Mix Payne's grey and sap green to create a dark green. Use the No.3 brush to paint a row of trees in the middle distance. These trees add interest to the composition and create a sense of recession. However, at this distance you cannot see details of the foliage, so reduce the trees to simple silhouetted shapes.

THE FINISHED PICTURE

A Textured bark
The rough texture and fissured surface of the tree trunk is one of the interesting features of this subject. The textures were applied gradually, working light to dark.

B Foreground textures
Vigorous brush marks in the foreground capture the appearance of wild grasses. The foreground texture also helps to create a sense of space and recession.

C Simple leaf shapes
Simplified, shorthand marks capture the character of the foliage. These have been applied in layers to build up the volume and depth of the tree's canopy.

Rocks and masonry

Capture the massive solidity of a craggy cliff and the textures of aged, flaking plaster and weathered masonry in two watercolour projects.

M ost landscape subjects include some hard surfaces in the form of outcrops of rock or man-made features such as buildings or bridges. To create landscape paintings that are accurate, varied and interesting, it is important to describe these features as effectively as more fluid forms such as trees, bushes and grass.

In this project, two different 'hard' subjects are painted in watercolour. The first (above) shows a spectacular view of buildings perched on top of a sheer cliff of stratified rock. The subject of the second one is an old weathered barn with broken rendering exposing the stonework. Various watercolour techniques have been used to bring out the characteristics of the hard surfaces.

Looking and sketching

In order to paint rock features or buildings in the landscape effectively, spend time observing and sketching them. Make studies of natural and man-made structures, either outdoors or from reference photographs. In rugged landscapes, look at how the rock is

▲ The stratified formation of this towering cliff is captured very simply, using layered washes and horizontal brush strokes.

formed. Compare the appearance of bands of rock with that of hard granite outcrops or chalk cliffs. Become familiar, too, with the character of building materials – the smoothness of a rendered wall, the crumbling character of weathered stucco, the regularity of brick.

Note how distance and the play of light affect the appearance of hard surfaces. Standing close to a brick building, for example, you can see the grainy texture and subtle tonal variations of individual bricks, and the contrasting texture of the lines of mortar. Further away you can make out a regular pattern and an overall colour, while further away still you can see only an overall shape and a generalized colour.

The quality of the light and the angle of the sun also affect what you can see. On a grey day, textures appear flattened, while, on a sunny one, contrasts of light and shadow allow you to see quite small surface details.

Rendering what you see

Close observation is only part of the story. You also need to consider which techniques are best suited to representing what you see. It isn't necessary to render every last detail. Try to find a shorthand mark that suggests the material at the distance from which it is being viewed – use it here and there, but make sure that you do not overdo it.

If you give the eye enough clues, it will fill in the details. A few areas of dashes will be enough to suggest that a wall is constructed from brick, while some horizontal lines and dry-brushed marks will tell viewers that they are looking at bands of rock.

PROJECT 1

SHEER CLIFF AND BUILDINGS

A simple approach is best for this spectacular subject. Use layered washes to capture the warm honey tones and rugged qualities of the rock. Depict the different layers with horizontal brush strokes and add the vertical cracks wet-on-dry in the final stages, using the very tip of the brush.

> **YOU WILL NEED**
>
> Piece of 300gsm (140lb) NOT watercolour paper 30 x 36cm (12 x 14in)
>
> 2B pencil
>
> Brushes: Nos. 8, 4 and 3 rounds
>
> 12 watercolours: cobalt blue; yellow ochre; Alizarin crimson; indigo; cadmium yellow; cerulean blue; burnt sienna; Naples yellow; raw umber; phthalo blue; ivory black; ultramarine
>
> Scrap paper

FIRST STEPS

1 ▶ Lay in the underpainting Map out the subject using a 2B pencil. Mix a wash of cobalt blue, yellow ochre and alizarin crimson, and, with a No. 8 round brush, apply over the scene – reserve the white paper for highlights on the cliff. Paint a wash of indigo wet-on-wet over the landscape on the left.

2 ◀ Apply colour to the rock face Flood alizarin crimson and cadmium yellow into the landscape on the left. Mix a large wash of yellow ochre and use a No. 4 round brush to work the paint over the still-wet cliff face. Allow to dry.

3▼ **Build up the background** Now apply the cobalt blue, yellow ochre and alizarin crimson wash from step 1 to the background, using the No. 8 brush. Take the wash carefully along the silhouette of the cliff to sharpen it up.

DEVELOPING THE PICTURE
You can now start to capture the unique character of the rock by using layered washes applied wet-on-dry. Allow the painting to dry between washes.

5▲ **Develop the cliff** Use the No. 4 round and a mix of Naples yellow and burnt sienna on the left of the cliff. Leave to dry; add more burnt sienna to the mix and use this towards the base of the cliff.

EXPERT ADVICE
Tone matching

To check the exact tone and hue of an area of your photo, you need to view it in isolation. Cut a small hole in a sheet of paper and place it over the area – it is much easier to assess the tone when it is surrounded by white. Lay a patch of your paint mix alongside it to check its accuracy.

4▼ **Apply tone to the buildings** Mix cerulean blue and burnt sienna, and apply this dark mix over the buildings perched on top of the cliff. Use the tip of the brush to define their silhouettes.

6▲ **Add detail and vegetation** Drag raw umber into the horizontal and vertical bands on the right of the cliff to suggest layers and cracks in the rock. Add strokes of burnt sienna and a burnt sienna/Naples yellow mix on the left. Paint bushes at the top of the cliff with a wash of cobalt and indigo, then add a mix of alizarin crimson, phthalo blue and ivory black wet-on-wet, with a No. 3 round brush.

7 ▶ Work on the buildings
Use ultramarine and burnt sienna for the roofs of the buildings and for the shadowy windows. Differentiate the arched and straight tops of the windows, but don't work too precisely – the details should be in keeping with the degree of precision in the rest of the painting.

8 ◀ Add rock strata
Make sure the painting is dry. Tear a sheet of scrap paper and use the torn edge to mask the left edge of the projecting outcrop on the right. Mix ultramarine and burnt sienna, then apply horizontal strokes with the tip of the No. 8 round to indicate the layers in the rock, taking the brush marks over the mask.

9 ▲ Paint in final details Use the tip of the No. 3 round brush and a dark mix of ultramarine, burnt sienna and ivory black to apply details such as the thin vertical fissures and cracks in the rock face.

THE FINISHED PICTURE

A Simplified detail
The architectural details were rendered very simply, so as not to distract the viewer's attention from the main subject of the painting – the cliff face.

B Sunlit edge
The white of the paper was left to stand for the light area on the edge of the cliff, where it catches the full force of the sun.

C Layered washes
Layers of transparent washes applied wet-on-wet and wet-on-dry capture the complex textures of the honey and grey tones on the rock face.

PROJECT 2

OLD BARN

Capture the flaking stucco and weathered masonry of this old barn, using a combination of wax resist, masking and layered washes of watercolour. Before you begin painting, mask off the edges of the picture area with tape – this will give a crisp outline to the finished work.

FIRST STEPS

1 ▼ **Mask the stucco** Using a 2B pencil, sketch the main elements. Apply masking fluid to the outline of the white plaster with the tip of a paint shaper. Mask the top half of the window bars.

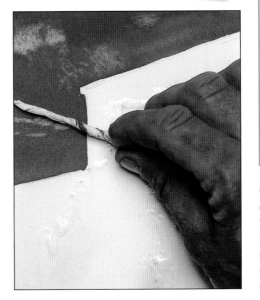

2 ◄ **Apply the sky** Apply a wash of ultramarine to the sky with a No. 8 round brush. Roll kitchen paper into a cylinder and dab it in the wet wash to create a variety of cloud

3 ▼ **Paint the masonry** Mix a wash of yellow ochre and grey it slightly with touches of alizarin crimson and ultramarine to make a buff shade. Using the No. 8 round brush, wash this colour over the masonry. Leave to dry.

DEVELOPING THE PICTURE

The main elements – the sky, the stucco and the stonework – are now broadly established. Begin to create the textures of the stonework by applying linear detail, wax resist and layers of wash.

4 ► **Add the dark tones** The shadows cast by the projecting stones allow you to see the construction of the wall. Using the tip of a No. 4 round brush and a wash of Payne's grey, draw the horizontal lines of shadows between the stones. The ragged edge of the stucco also casts a shadow, so trace this with the tip of the brush. Leave to dry.

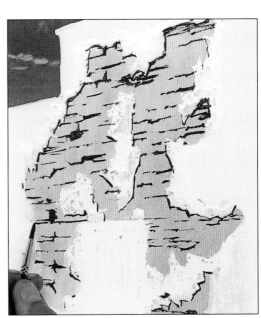

5 ▼ Apply wax resist When the painting has completely dried, rub a white candle randomly over the stonework areas.

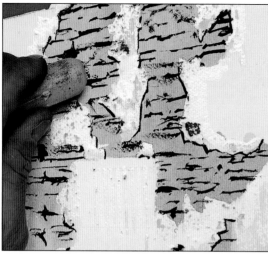

6 ▶ Apply a darker wash Paint the line of roof tiles in burnt sienna. Leave to dry. Then mix Payne's grey and burnt sienna, and, using the No. 4 round brush, apply horizontal dabs of colour over the exposed stonework. The wash separates over the waxy areas, introducing a random effect.

7 ◀ Paint the window grille With washes of Payne's grey, ivory black and a Payne's grey/burnt sienna mix, start to paint the barred window. In the top half of the window, you are painting the dark shadows cast on the wall of the interior; in the lower half you are painting the bars themselves and the shadows that they cast.

8 ◀ Apply more resist Rub the candle randomly over the stonework to create another layer of resist. Mix a darker version of the Payne's grey/ burnt sienna wash from step 7 and apply dabs of colour with the No.4 round brush. Allow to dry, then apply another layer of wax resist, and a final layer of wash, using a dry brush.

Express yourself
Surface textures

To become more familiar with painting stonework and other building materials, find locations with a variety of hard surfaces and make rapid watercolour sketches that convey their qualities as simply as possible. Here the artist has used the white of the paper and washes of pink and yellow to suggest the even surface of painted stucco on the houses by the canal. The dressed stonework of the old bridge is deftly described with freely drawn lines and dappled washes of colour. Suggest the outlines of the stone blocks, without making the marks too mechanical or overworked.

9 ▲ **Remove the masking fluid** Paint the stained edge of the roof tiles and the shadow below the tiles in Payne's grey. Leave to dry. Mix Naples yellow and cobalt blue, and paint the foliage on the left. Make sure the support is dry, then lightly rub off the masking fluid.

10 ▲ **Add tone to the plaster** Use variations of the buff mix from step 3 to apply texture to the plaster, using a dry No. 8 round brush. Mix Payne's grey and lemon yellow, and dab on this grey-green colour under the eaves.

11 ▲ **Complete the foreground** Use Payne's grey for the hanging cables and creepers, burnt sienna for the window, and the buff mix from step 3 at the base of the building. Brush in the grass with a lemon yellow/Payne's grey mix, adding more Payne's grey to paint the road.

THE FINISHED PICTURE

A Masked edges
The complicated edges of the damaged stucco were defined with masking fluid, so the exposed brickwork could be worked on freely.

B Wax resist
Alternate layers of watercolour wash and wax resist applied with a candle gave the stonework a randomly mottled appearance.

C Linear detail
A buff mix skimmed over the surface of the NOT paper with a dry brush created a patchy, weathered effect on the stuccoed wall.

Leaping salmon

The flicker of silver as salmon leap up a cascade of water provides one of nature's most thrilling wildlife spectacles – and a great subject for a loose, lively watercolour.

Water tumbling down falls and churning over a boulder-strewn riverbed simply demands to be recorded in paint. But how do you capture the lightness and brightness of the broken water without making it look too solid or laboured? Watercolour, with its potential for spontaneous effects, is the ideal medium for such a dynamic and free-flowing subject.

Spattering techniques

Spattering, for instance, is easily done with watercolour. It creates a speckled or mottled surface ideal for depicting subjects such as foam, spray and turbulent water, which are too intricate to render in any other way. Soft-fibre brushes are the best for flicking colour.

Spattering with masking fluid was also used in this painting to preserve the white of the paper for light areas such as foam and spray. To avoid damaging the bristles, you should try flicking and dribbling the fluid from the handle of your brush (or use an old brush).

Masking fluid is available in two forms: colourless or tinted (yellow or grey). The advantage of using tinted fluid, as here, is that you can see exactly where the masked areas are.

Establishing the focus

Confidence is the key to success in this painting. Rather than working from light to dark in the usual watercolour way, the artist began by establishing the dark forms of the salmon. It is important that they are introduced early on as the composition pivots around their sinuous bodies. Use bold, assertive brush strokes – you do not want to have to rework or modify them. (If necessary, practise painting on scrap paper first.)

Continue working in this confident, uninhibited way throughout the painting. Use dilute paint and gestural strokes to capture the tumbling water. Vary the colour of your washes and let them blend spontaneously – remember water picks up reflected colour from its surroundings and from the sky above. In short, try to bring something of the drama of the subject to the way you paint it.

YOU WILL NEED	
Piece of 300gsm (140lb) NOT watercolour paper 44 x 56cm (17¼ x 22in)	light red; cobalt blue; ultramarine; violet; raw umber; raw sienna; emerald green
B pencil	Brushes: 13mm (½in) flat; No. 9 round
Masking fluid	Mixing palette or dish
11 watercolours: Prussian blue; cerulean blue; neutral tint; sepia;	Jar of water
	White chalk

FIRST STEPS

1 ▲ Spatter masking fluid Use a B pencil to plot the location of the leaping fish. Dip the handle of a brush in masking fluid and flick and dribble the fluid on to the surface of the paper. Build up an area of dense spattering on the left to balance the fish on the right, then apply spattered masking fluid to the foaming water below the fish.

▲ Spattered paint, vigorous brush marks and bold contrasts of tone help to capture the drama of salmon leaping in foaming water.

2 ◀ **Block in the first fish** Mix Prussian blue and cerulean blue. Using a fairly dry 13mm (½in) flat brush, describe the back of the fish with a sweeping stroke. Drag the brush over the pitted surface of the paper so that the wash breaks up in places to create a slightly speckled effect. While the first wash is still wet, charge the same brush with a mix of neutral tint and sepia, and use this to describe the underside of the fish. Leave the stripe and eye area white, but allow the two washes to blend and fuse where they touch.

3▲ **Work on the second fish** Using the same brush, paint the second fish. Use neutral tint for the upper body and light red for the belly of the fish. Add the fins in neutral tint and light red.

4▲ **Spatter around the tail** Paint the fish's tail with the neutral tint and light red, then drag the handle of the brush through the wet paint to suggest its ribbed pattern. Load the brush with a dark mix from your palette and lightly spatter across the spray around the tail.

5▲ **Start to paint the water** Apply vigorous strokes of cobalt blue with the 13mm (½in) flat brush, then ultramarine with a touch of violet, followed by raw umber. Use gestural brush marks that trace the movement of the water. Allow the paint to flow together and puddle.

6▲ **Develop broken water** Start to apply colour over the heavily spattered area with broad strokes. Use washes of neutral tint, sepia, ultramarine, violet and Prussian blue, allowing the colours to mingle.

7 ◄ **Add more colour to the water** Still using the 13mm (½in) brush, apply a raw umber wash to the dark area in the lower left corner of the picture with vigorous brush marks. Work a pale wash of cobalt blue into the top left of the picture area.

DEVELOPING THE PICTURE

The painting is broadly established and this is a good time to stand back and see what else needs to be done. With a subject such as this, the reference photograph is a jumping-off point only – after a certain point the painting takes on a life of its own. The marks that you have made and the colours that you use will dictate your next moves.

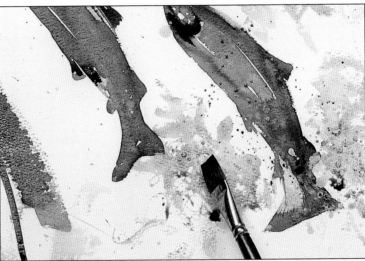

8 ▶ **Add warm colours** Mix a wash of raw sienna, adding a touch of raw umber, and scumble this colour loosely over the lower part of the painting. This will warm the area of the painting, providing a contrast with the predominantly cool palette.

▶ A range of blues and browns was used for the wet-on-wet washes and spattering to create subtly shifting tones and splashes of colour in the turbulent water. The colours include (from top to bottom): cerulean blue; cobalt blue; ultramarine; violet; sepia.

9 ▲ **Add textural marks** Mix Prussian blue and raw umber and work this into the dark area on the left. Use gestural flicking marks that suggest the splashing water. Spatter the same mix across the painting.

10 ▼ **Spatter more colours** Wash emerald green across the lower right corner and spatter over it, creating texture with the brush handle (see Expert Advice, opposite). Add raw umber and apply loosely at top left. Spatter this mix and cerulean blue over the entire painting.

11 ▲ **Remove the masking fluid** Make sure the painting is completely dry, then remove the masking fluid by rubbing it gently with your fingertips. As the mask is removed, the sparkling white paper is revealed as foam, spray and swirling water, making sense of the brushed and spattered colour.

Express yourself

Fish studies

The streamlined bodies of fish form wonderful, sinuous shapes as they flash through the water or leap up the rapids. To familiarize yourself with their movements, it is a useful exercise to make pencil sketches of fish viewed from different angles. Notice the positions of the fins and the curves of the tails as they power the fish along.

These sketches will help you when making an initial drawing for a fish painting. In the step-by-step, the bodies of the salmon are implied with just a few sweeping brush strokes, so it is important that your underlying drawing is in proportion and accurately reflects the leaping motion.

A FEW STEPS FURTHER

With the masked areas revealed, the painting assumes its final appearance. The energy of the surging water has been effectively described and the composition is nicely balanced with the dark forms of the fish silhouetted against the foaming water. At this point you could consider emphasizing the tonal contrasts by adding highlights and touches of dark tone.

12 ▲ **Suggest the scales of the fish** Drag a piece of white chalk over the surface of the fish. The powdery chalk will be deposited on the raised surface of the paper, suggesting silvery scales.

13 ▼ Contrast tones Scumble chalk across the darker areas of water. Mix a wash of neutral tint and Prussian blue and, using a No. 9 round brush, spatter on this dark tone.

EXPERT ADVICE
Drawing out paint

To create linear texture in spattered areas, draw out the wet paint into squiggly strands and tendrils of colour with the tip of the brush handle. Here, raw sienna and raw umber provide texture over an emerald green wash.

THE FINISHED PICTURE

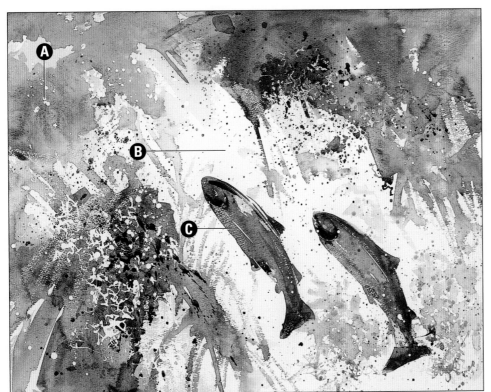

A Masked spatters
The patterns created by masking fluid spattered on to the support at the start read as foam and spray when the mask is removed.

B White paper
Extensive areas of unpainted white paper stand for the sheets of white water cascading down the waterfall.

C Scumbled chalk
Chalk scumbled over the pitted surface of the paper adds a bright, sparkling effect and lends texture to the solid washes.

Street scene

Streets can be marvellous subjects for a painting as they are full of colour, texture and detail – and usually have human interest, too.

Although it can be very rewarding to paint outdoors, one problem in town is finding somewhere to set up your easel without attracting unwanted attention from curious passers-by.

Working from photographs
This is where photographs and sketches are a boon, allowing you to gather all the information you need easily. You can use them as the basis for a painting and work on it at your leisure, at home or in your studio.

Attracted by the provincial charm of this row of small shops, the artist photographed each one separately. Back home, he laid out the photos to form a panorama of the street.

He did not slavishly copy the scene but chose to move things around in order to improve the composition. He removed the cars, for example, shuffled the figures along to make interesting groupings and moved one of the trees so that it filled the patch of sky above the single-storey shop. The artist also deliberately cut out all hints of perspective as he wanted to concentrate on the abstract elements of shape, pattern and colour.

Mood and atmosphere
The overall tonality of the scene has

▲**This simple composition of small shop fronts conveys the atmosphere of a quiet town with the residents going about their day-to-day business.**

been lightened and the grey sky has been interpreted as blue, giving the painting a fresh, spring-like mood. In addition, the loose handling of the paint and impressionistic treatment of detail lend character and energy, and there is a feeling of light moving across the buildings. What's more, there is a pleasing contrast between the solid geometric shapes of the buildings and the organic forms of the figures and trees.

► **Photographs can be used as a reference but in the painting any unwanted features, such as cars, can be left out.**

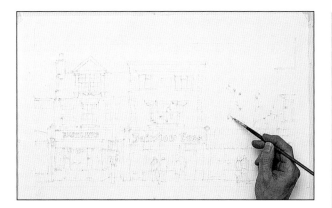

FIRST STEPS

1 ▲ **Start with an outline drawing** Using your sketches and photos as references, make a careful outline drawing of the subject, including the lettering on the shop signs, with a sharp HB pencil. Paint out the leaves on the two trees with masking fluid, applied in small flecks with an old brush. Wash the brush out immediately.

2 ▲ **Block in the sky** Dampen the sky area with clean water. Mix a strong wash of cerulean (remember it will dry lighter) and apply it loosely with the No.12 round brush. Let the paint spread and diffuse on the damp paper; this gives a more attractive effect than a flat wash.

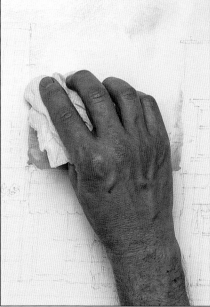

3 ▲ **Create white clouds** While the blue wash is still wet, lift out a few soft white clouds using a press-and-lift motion with a piece of crumpled paper tissue. Leave to dry (or use a hair-dryer if you're in a hurry).

YOU WILL NEED

Piece of 300gsm (140lb) Not watercolour paper 60 x 40cm (24 x 16 in)

HB pencil

10 watercolours: Cerulean; Raw sienna; Burnt sienna; Burnt umber; Ultramarine; Permanent rose; Cadmium orange; Lemon yellow; Scarlet lake; Cadmium yellow

3 brushes: Nos.12, 6 and 1 rounds

Paper tissues

Jar of water

Mixing dish or palette

Masking fluid and a small, old paintbrush

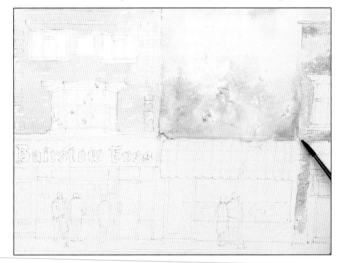

■ **Burnt and raw sienna (above) ma** **warm mix for the brickwork, whi** **a mix of cerulean, ultramarine ar** **burnt umber (right) creates the** **shadow colour.**

4 ▼ **Start painting the walls** Change to the No.6 round brush and paint in the red-brick walls of the buildings with a watery mix of raw sienna and burnt sienna. Vary the tone by adding more or less water. Apply the paint with small, broken brush strokes, leaving flecks of white paper showing.

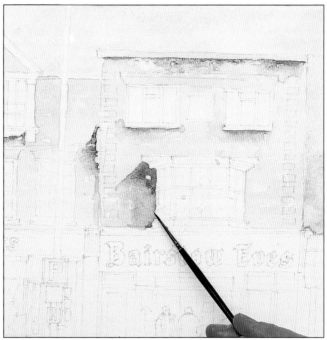

5 ▲ **Put in cast shadows** Darken the wash with some burnt umber and cerulean, plus a little ultramarine to beef it up. While the underwash is still damp, use the No.1 round brush to put in the dark shadows under the eaves and those cast on to the walls by the windows. Start at the dark, inner edge of each shadow and let the colour fade out to nothing.

DEVELOPING THE PAINTING

Now that you have established the light direction and defined the underlying structure of the buildings, you can concentrate on the architectural details and build up tone and texture.

EXPERT ADVICE
Painting windows

Windows are best suggested rather than over-defined, otherwise they can appear 'pasted on'. Here, the artist is not filling in the square panes neatly, but letting the paint hit and miss the outlines. Notice also how different tones reveal the play of light and shadow on the glass, and how flecks of white paper suggest sparkling highlights.

6 ▲ **Put in the window panes** Dilute the mixture from step 5 with more water and put in the lighter cast shadows and suggest the brickwork on the chimneys. Now change the bias of the mix. This time use ultramarine and burnt umber, with just a little cerulean, and start to fill in the dark window panes. Add water for the lighter tones, and leave tiny flecks of white paper for the reflections.

7 ▼ **Complete the windows** Continue filling in the window panes, carefully observing the light and dark tones. On the bay window in the centre, for instance, the panes are dark on the left and much lighter on the right because they face into the light; add more cerulean to your mix on the light side to suggest reflected light from the sky.

8 ▲ **Add more texture to the walls** Mix a more intense wash of raw sienna and burnt sienna than used in step 4. Using the No.1 brush, suggest the pattern and texture of the brick walls; apply the paint with tiny strokes, bringing out the negative shapes of the decorative stones and allowing the pale underwash to break through for the lighter bricks. Be selective – it is easy to overwork the detail.

EXPERT ADVICE
Painting brickwork

When painting a wall, don't try to build it brick by brick with flat strokes. A few bricks here and there, painted loosely, will give the effect in a more natural way. Put the overall tone in first, leaving chinks of white to suggest highlights. Suggest the dark bricks with darker tones of the same colour, letting the underwash show through to give the mid tone.

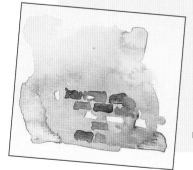

9 ▲ **Finish painting the walls** Continue building up the rough texture of the walls with small strokes. Let the paint do the work for you – the water will carry the pigment so that, as it dries, it forms hard edges that subtly suggest individual bricks. Reinforce the colour in shaded areas with touches of burnt umber.

10 ◄ **Continue working on the windows** Use permanent rose and a touch of cadmium orange, diluted to a pale tint, for the pink paintwork around the windows on the left. Paint the dark window frames on the bay window using the shadow colour mixed in step 5. In reality, the frames are black, but dark brown is a more sympathetic colour for a watercolour painting – black looks too stark.

11 ▼ **Start painting the shops** Use the No.6 round brush to suggest the baker's shop window on the extreme left with the greys and earths already on your palette. Paint the decorative green stonework next to it with a mix of lemon yellow and ultramarine, darkened with more ultramarine for the shadows. Paint the pink shop front with a wash of permanent rose and a little cadmium orange. Add some of the brick colour to this for the drainpipe.

12 ▲ **Add more detail** Fill in the lettering of the shop sign with dilute raw sienna, varying the strength of tone for a natural effect. Mix ultramarine, cerulean blue and a hint of burnt umber, dilute it well and draw the shadows on the pink shop front and in the

13 ▲ **Paint the shop window** Change to the No.1 brush and paint the glass in the shop window and door with a mix of ultramarine and cerulean blue, adding burnt umber for the dark tones. Work round the white window frame and leave chinks of white paper for the highlights. Outline the letters on the shop sign with the same colour. Suggest the plants with the lemon/ultramarine mix used earlier.

14 ▲ **Move on to the next shop front** Mix scarlet lake and a touch of cadmium orange to block in the red parts of the next shop front along. Paint the brown door and window frames with light and dark tones of raw sienna, burnt sienna and ultramarine. Use a very dark tone of this mix for the shop sign, then put in the glass windows as before, working around the outlines of the figures.

15 ▶ Paint the florist's shop

Paint the awning with cerulean and ultramarine, varying the tones to define its curved shape. When dry, use the tip of the brush to paint the red stripes with scarlet lake. Paint the flowers with lemon yellow, cadmium orange and scarlet lake. Suggest the window with loose strokes as before. Then paint the far right section with greys and reds.

Master Strokes

Anne Redpath (1895–1965)
Houses, Concarneau

This oil painting, made in 1954, shows a street scene of typical French buildings. Although it is similar in composition to the street in the step-by-step project, the side of each building is visible in perspective, giving the painting more depth. The shadowy dome in the background adds to the feeling of recession. Chiefly composed of greys, the picture has a rainy atmosphere enhanced by the heavy sky. As a result, the few patches of colour – especially the yellow shutters – really sing out.

Fine brushwork depicts decorative wrought-iron balconies.

The leafless tree is painted with great economy. Notice how each branch tapers off to a fine line.

Reflections of the buildings and trees in the pavement suggest a wet day.

A FEW STEPS FURTHER

Make sure the painting is completely dry before continuing. The row of shops is now complete and all that remains is to paint the details in the foreground, the figures in the street and the trees. Also, you need to remove the masking fluid from the trees – this will leave dots of white paper that you can then paint with a leaf colour.

16 ▲ Start painting the trees Paint the sapling in front of the florist's shop with burnt umber, adding ultramarine for the darker parts. Skip the brush tip lightly over the paper, making thin, broken lines for the branches. Leave to dry, then rub off the masking fluid. Paint the leaves with a mix of lemon yellow, cerulean and a hint of ultramarine.

Express yourself
Sketch a shop

A soft pencil was used for this sketch of just one section of the street. Thumbnail sketches are a useful adjunct to photographs when composing a panoramic view; they help you to edit out superfluous detail and simplify the subject. They also help to define the tonal values that underlie any subject.

17 ▶ Render the signpost Paint the other tree in the same way. Then mix a cool grey from ultramarine, cerulean and burnt umber for the signpost, grading the tone to make it appear rounded. Lighten the tone near the top of the post. Paint the sign with the cool grey, cadmium yellow and ultramarine.

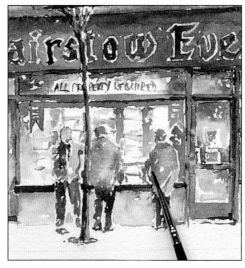

18 ◀ Paint the figures Incidental figures should be painted with the minimum of detail. Use some of the greys and earth colours already mixed on your palette to jot in the clothing, leaving tiny flecks of white paper that give movement to the figures. Mix ultramarine and scarlet lake for the woman's purple coat.

19 ▶ **Paint the pavement** To complete the painting, mix two tones of grey from burnt umber, ultramarine, cerulean blue and raw sienna, and paint the pavement with broken brush strokes.

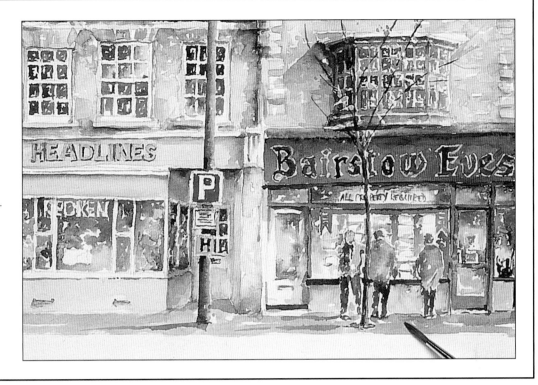

THE FINISHED PICTURE

A Spring-like atmosphere
Light tones and colours, and flecks of white paper showing through, give the feel of a crisp, spring morning with sunlight playing on the buildings.

B Minimal figures
The figures were painted with the minimum of detail so that they do not dominate the foreground. Overly precise figures tend to look like cardboard cut-outs.

C Lively detail
The details of the displays in the shop windows, such as the floral arrangements, are hinted at, but not over-defined. This allows the viewer's imagination to play a part.

Japanese bridge

A bold, uncluttered composition, a restrained palette of cool blues and greens, and a vivid splash of red produce a lyrical and memorable image.

The delicate and transparent washes of watercolour are ideal for this beautiful misty landscape. By building up layers of colour, you can capture the depth of the water and the deep, cool greens of the leafy foliage. What's more, you can use wet-on-wet techniques to create the hazy appearance of the mist-shrouded hills and wet-on-dry techniques to add crisp details, such as the structure of the bridge and the thin outer branches of the trees.

Considered composition

Before you actually begin working on any painting, make sure you consider the compositional possibilities. In this project, the eye is drawn to the area of light water in the foreground, where the sky is reflected in the lake's surface, then on to the even paler area under the bridge and hence to the bridge itself. The arcing form of the bridge frames the lower part of the painting, as do the dark blocks of foliage on the left and right. In the distance, the misty peaks allow air into the composition and prevent it from becoming claustrophobic. Note also that, as there is no foreground detail, the whole composition seems flattened just like a Japanese print.

When considering the composition, take time to look for similarities and differences. In this picture, the curved lines of the banks in the foreground are echoed by the curved tops of the mountains in the distance – and indeed by the arc of the bridge. These gentle curves are perfectly offset by the spiky edge of the tree on the left.

Complementary colours

As should always be the case, the use of colour in the picture is equally well thought out. The hot, insistent red of the bridge is set off by the cool, complementary greens of the foliage and the paler hills in the background. Note how the hills have a pinkish tinge, while the foreground is painted in much cooler blues and greens.

YOU WILL NEED

Piece of 300gsm (140lb) NOT watercolour paper 56 x 46cm (22 x 18in)

HB pencil

10 watercolours: ultramarine; Prussian blue; alizarin crimson; viridian; sap green; raw umber; cadmium red; Van Dyke brown; ivory black; yellow ochre

Brushes: 25mm (1in) hake; Nos. 12 and 4 rounds

Permanent white gouache

Mixing palette or dish

▶ Subtle changes of colour and tone create a mood of peace and tranquillity in this watercolour painting of a classic Japanese view.

FIRST STEPS

1 ▶ **Make the underdrawing** Using an HB pencil, sketch in the main outlines of the composition. Work lightly, so that the pencil lines do not dominate the final image, and make any necessary adjustments to the drawing and composition at this stage.

2 ▼ **Block in the sky** Mix a pale wash of ultramarine and Prussian blue, and, using the broad 25mm (1in) hake brush, apply the wash to the sky. Take the colour along the edge of the hills.

3 ▶ **Paint the hills** The background hills overlap like the flats in a theatre set. The interlocking shapes vary in colour and tone, depending on how far away they are, with those in the background looking paler than those nearer the foreground. Mix a watery wash of ultramarine, alizarin crimson and Prussian blue, and, using a No. 12 round brush, paint the hills in the background.

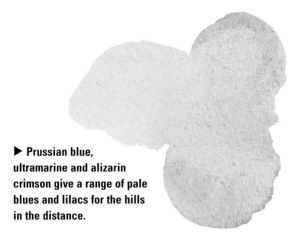

▶ **Prussian blue, ultramarine and alizarin crimson give a range of pale blues and lilacs for the hills in the distance.**

Express yourself
Pastel impression

Soft pastel is a great medium for creating misty effects. Use mauves and purples for the hills and river, applying the pastel lightly and smudging it back for distant features. Sharply drawn linear details bring the foliage forwards.

4 ▲ Intensify the hills Add more alizarin crimson to the wash and, working wet-on-wet, intensify the hills in the centre, so that they come forward in the scene. Add more ultramarine and Prussian blue to create a cooler mix for the hills on the right. Also, indicate the trees on the hills (see Expert Advice, below).

EXPERT ADVICE
Silhouetted trees

The treetops on the distant hills, seen through the mist, form hazy, spire-like silhouettes against the sky. Use the tip of the No. 12 round brush to mark these in wet-on-wet, so that they merge into the overall wash covering the hills.

5 ◀ Suggest the trees Add more Prussian blue to the cool blue mix from step 4. Still using the No. 12 round brush, stroke on this colour to represent the area of trees cladding the lower slopes of the hills on the left. Vary the texture with a stronger version of the same mix.

DEVELOPING THE PICTURE

Now move to the area below the bridge to start work on the cool blue water of the river, which relates in colour and tone to the sky and hills. Then progress to the stronger tones of the trees and foliage that frame the composition at the sides, and the painting will really start to come alive.

6 ▼ **Add more trees** Use viridian, sap green and ultramarine to create a grey-green for the trees fringing the river beyond the bridge. Use the brush tip to create the treetops. Add sap green and raw umber to the mix from step 3 and dilute with more water. Wash this pale tone over the river. Use ultramarine and Prussian blue for the darker water at the edges of the river.

▲ **Use Prussian blue, ultramarine and raw umber (above) in the water mixes. Raw umber, sap green and Prussian blue (right) produce dark foliage shades.**

7 ▼ **Develop wooded areas** Mix a dark green from sap green, Prussian blue and raw umber, and, using the No. 12 round brush and gestural marks, start to build up shadows within the clump of trees on the left.

8 ▼ **Add more foliage** Continuing with the No. 12 round, use a wash of ultramarine and sap green for the mass of bright green foliage on the left.

9 ▲ **Paint more trees** Using the same dark wash as in step 7, dab on the shadows within the trees on the right. Then return to the light green wash from step 8 and paint in the brighter foliage where the trees catch the light.

10 ▼ **Add the bridge** The bridge is the key to the whole composition. Mix cadmium red and alizarin crimson, and start to paint the bridge, using a No. 4 round brush. Work carefully, checking the reference photograph for the lattice-work pattern.

11 ▶ **Add shadows** Mix a dark brown from Van Dyke brown and ivory black. Returning to the No. 12 round brush, paint the shadows on the pillars that support the bridge. Then block in the curve of dark tone that forms the base of the bridge.

12 ◀ **Paint between the lattice** When the dark shadows are dry, use a paler version of the dark brown mix for the lighter areas of the bridge supports and for the rocks edging the water. Paint the landscape seen between the lattice-work with the No. 4 brush and a mix of sap green and ultramarine.

13 ▶ Develop the foreground water
Make a mix of Prussian blue and ultramarine, and, changing back to the No. 12 brush, apply the shadows along the water's edge and in the foreground. Use brushy horizontal marks to show the ripples on the surface of the water.

14 ▲ Add shadows to the foliage Use a mix of sap green, ultramarine and raw umber, and the tip of the No. 12 brush, to paint the shadows within the clumps of foliage on the right. These dark tones in the foliage help to describe the layering of branches and enhance the sense of depth within the tree canopy.

15 ▲ Darken the water Use a dark mix of Prussian blue, ultramarine and raw umber to add tone and depth to the edges of the water. Touch in the finials on the bridge posts and add texture to the base with a black/Van Dyke brown mix.

A FEW STEPS FURTHER

The painting is now fully resolved. All the elements are in place, and the spatial progression from front to back works well. You could add a few details, such as the fine branches on the tree and white highlights for the brass embellishments on the bridge. Be careful not to overwork the image, however, or you will lose the freshness of the watercolour.

16 ▲ **Add brass highlights** Mix yellow ochre with white gouache. Using the No. 4 round, apply this pale opaque mix to the finials and to the decorations on top of each upright.

17 ▲ **Add the branches** Mix Van Dyke brown and ultramarine, and use the tip of the No. 4 round to draw in the thin branches visible through the outer edges of the tree canopy. Work out towards the ends of the branches to achieve strokes that taper at the tip.

THE FINISHED PICTURE

A Layered greens
Layers of transparent green washes capture the depth, density and delicacy of the foliage bordering the river.

B Body colour
Opaque body colour mixed from white gouache and yellow ochre makes the metalwork sparkle.

C Paper highlights
Light catching the water is suggested by allowing the white paper to shimmer through a pale wash.

Scottish landscapes

You will need just four simple shades of watercolour to create these atmospheric studies of the beautiful Scottish countryside.

For the watercolour artist, a limited palette can be a great advantage, especially if you are painting outdoors and want to capture the scene quickly. The landscape on the following pages was painted using the same four colours: cadmium red, gamboge, ultramarine and Davy's grey. By varying the proportions of these four basic tints in each mixture, you can create an almost limitless range of colours and tones.

For example, the misty Scottish loch above contains lots of hazy blues and purples. These were mixed mainly from cadmium red, ultramarine and Davy's grey, but with a few streaks of gamboge to indicate sunlight.

The moorland landscape, by contrast, is dominated by the vast expanse of grass in the foreground. For this painting the artist worked mainly in ultramarine and gamboge, with occasional touches of grey and red.

Granulation and brushwork

Both landscapes were painted quickly, but each wash of colour was allowed to dry naturally before the next layer of colour was applied. The extra drying time allowed the pigment particles to disperse on the surface of the paper, creating the

▲ **Cool purples predominate in this painting of a Scottish loch with a background of mountains and brooding clouds.**

beautiful granular textures that can be seen in the finished paintings. (If you use a hair-dryer to speed up the process, you might diminish this effect.)

Brushwork in both landscapes is lively and bold. Decorator's brushes and a large wash brush were used to establish broad sweeps of sky, water and grassy foreground. In addition, the artist deliberately worked with an old, worn-out brush to create sharp, spiky shapes.

PROJECT 1

SCOTTISH LOCH

In the first project, the four basic watercolours are used in loose washes to convey the damp, misty atmosphere of a lake and mountains on a cloudy day. Wet-on-wet effects create beautiful blends of colour.

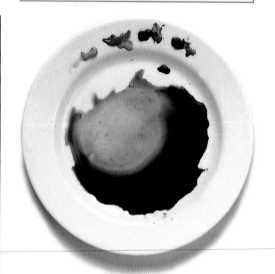

1 ▲ **Wash in the sky** Define your picture area with masking tape, then use a propelling pencil to lightly mark in the water's edge and the skyline. Mix a thin, purplish wash of ultramarine with a little cadmium red and Davy's grey, and loosely block in the sky, using a 25mm (1in) soft flat brush. Paint pure gamboge along the skyline, allowing this to run into the wet sky.

▲ Cadmium red, ultramarine and gamboge correspond to the three primary colours. From these three colours plus Davy's grey, you can mix the range of violet-based colours that predominate in this scene.

2 ◄ **Apply a wash to the water** Dip a 38mm (1½in) decorator's brush into the purple wash, then pick up a little pure gamboge on the tips of the bristles. Apply the colours horizontally along the water's edge, allowing the yellow and purple to mix on the paper. Drag the wet colours downwards, using vertical brush strokes. Allow the paint to dry.

EXPERT ADVICE
Granulation effects

Whenever you can, allow the watercolour paint to dry naturally. In this way the pigment particles disperse unevenly and create beautiful granulated effects, seen here in the sky.

3 ▲ Add the background Paint the hills with mixes of ultramarine, cadmium red and added touches of gamboge, making some of the mixes quite dilute. Use an old, misshapen brush to achieve spiky, irregular brush strokes.

Express yourself

Moody effects in the landscape

Watercolour lends itself perfectly to rendering landscapes with moody, cloud-strewn skies over hills and lakes, as no other medium captures quite so well the muted colours and indistinct shapes created by a misty atmosphere. In this variation of the Scottish loch scene, wet-on-wet effects are used for the clouds hanging over the mountaintops. Notice how the wash used for the low cloud on the right has formed a crinkled 'cauliflower' edge where the pigment has spread and dried.

4 ▼ Suggest the shore
Block in the central hill with a dilute wash of ultramarine and cadmium red. Then add Davy's grey to this mix to get a stronger colour and use the No. 6 round brush to define the shore with short, horizontal strokes.

5 ▲ Develop the water Add a splash of cadmium red at the centre of the shoreline. Then change to a 19mm (¾in) decorator's brush and, working in broad, horizontal strokes, strengthen the water with a wash of ultramarine and Davy's grey. Leave streaks of underpainting showing through between the brush strokes.

6 ▼ **Add reflections** Still using the 19mm (¾in) decorator's brush, drag the wet colour downwards in the foreground to indicate the reflections on the water.

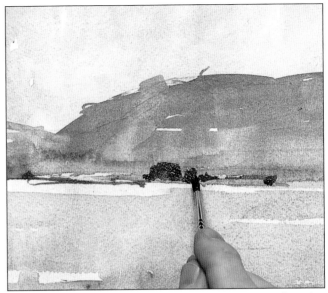

7 ▲ **Put in some tree details** Use the No. 6 round brush and ultramarine to add details of clumps of trees along the shoreline on the right-hand side. Allow the painting to dry, then remove the masking tape.

THE FINISHED PICTURE

A Directional strokes
The sky is blocked in loosely, taking the brush in different directions to create an impression of moving clouds.

B Spiky background
Some of the trees and shrubs seen in silhouette on the distant shore are painted with irregular strokes, using an old, worn brush.

C Vertical reflections
Wet colour is dragged downwards with a broad brush to suggest reflections on the surface of the water.

Choosing your palette

Painting on holiday is great fun and a good way to capture the atmosphere of the places you have visited. Make sure you take the right colours for the job.

A holiday often means the chance to pack up a few colours and brushes and take time out to do what you enjoy best – painting. If your destination is hot and sunny, you need to think in terms of bright colours and strong tonal contrasts. However, if you are visiting a cool, damp place, your colour schemes will almost certainly be more subdued and muted.

Your holiday palette

The two holiday subjects here could not be more different. One is a sunny harbour on the Greek island of Halki. The other is a windswept beach under a cloudy sky in the north of England.

However, whether you favour a sunny island or a windy coast, it is important to take the right colours for the job. For example, a palette of twelve watercolours was needed to capture the sea, sky and sunshine of Greece. The mixtures are bright with

predominantly clear, pure colours. Conversely, only eight watercolours were used to describe the wet, windy and isolated English beach and these were generally cool and more subdued.

▲ The bright Mediterranean sun helps create a colourful, sharply defined scene (top). By contrast, the cloudy, damp British climate produces a moody landscape, full of subtle colours and loose washes (above).

PROJECT 1

HALKI, A GREEK ISLAND

Don't be surprised if your paints appear to behave differently on holiday. Watercolours are affected by heat, cold and damp, so you might have to adapt your way of working to accommodate this. In strong sun, the colours slide easily from the brush on to the warm paper. Also, the paint dries quickly, making it easier to apply and control flat areas of colour, but more difficult to work wet-on-wet.

For wet-on-wet effects, you must work rapidly, painting one colour on another before the first colour has time to dry. Alternatively, add a little glycerine to your water to delay the drying time. In a damp climate, the opposite happens and watercolours can remain wet on the paper for hours. To prevent this, add a little alcohol to the colour mixtures.

The artist originally painted this scene on location (see top right). He then used it as a reference to paint the step-by-step in the studio.

YOU WILL NEED

Piece of 300gsm (140lb) Not watercolour paper 36 x 51cm (14 x 20in)

B pencil

Brushes: 19mm (³⁄₄in) flat; No.4 round; rigger

12 watercolours: Antwerp blue; Yellow ochre; Gamboge yellow; Vandyke brown; Cerulean blue; Emerald green; Payne's grey; Ultramarine; Indigo; Vermilion; Cadmium yellow; Cadmium red

1 ▶ Make a pencil drawing Draw the subject in simple lines, using a well-sharpened B pencil. Make sure all the buildings are in the correct position in relation to each other. Take special care with uprights, such as the tower. These should not be leaning!

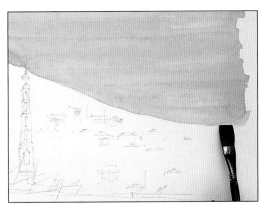

2 ◀ Paint the sky Using a 19mm (³⁄₄in) flat brush, block in the sky with Antwerp blue. Work in smooth, parallel strokes across the paper.

DEVELOPING THE PICTURE

Having established the hill and sky as solid blocks of colour, the next stage is to add the trees. These should be painted quickly as loose blobs of colour, so do not be tempted to add detail or overwork the brush strokes.

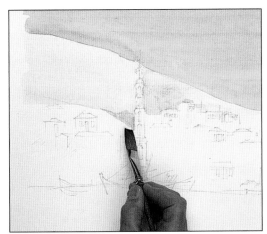

3 ▲ Add the hill Paint the hill as a flat shape using a mixture of yellow ochre and gamboge yellow. Before the paint dries, add the shadows behind the buildings using a diluted mixture of Vandyke brown and cerulean.

4 ▶ Paint trees in two tones Change to a No.4 round brush and paint the trees with a mix of emerald green, Payne's grey and ultramarine. Use diluted colour to block in the shape of the foliage, then work into the centre of each shape with a darker tone of the same colour.

TESTING THE COLOURS

Our artist describes this scrap paper as his 'mucky' sheet. He uses it to test his colours before applying them to the painting. Remember, if you make a mistake with watercolours, it is irreversible. Unlike opaque mediums such as oils and acrylics, you cannot begin afresh by simply painting over the colour.

5 ▲ Continue blocking in With the green used for the trees, paint a few of the windows, doors and steps. Add a little Payne's grey or yellow ochre to this mixture and paint more windows and doors. With a mix of indigo and emerald green, paint the steps by the tower. Block in the tower in a diluted yellow ochre, then paint the roofs in vermilion and cadmium yellow toned down with a little of the green tree mix.

6 ▶ Develop the buildings Dot in the figures under the tree with mixtures of yellow ochre, emerald and vermilion. Use indigo with a touch of emerald green for the small flight of stairs in the foreground.

7 ▲ Add detail to the tower Mix a very dark tone – almost black – from vermilion and emerald green and use this to paint the architectural detail on the tower.

8 ▲ Paint the boats and sea Paint the boats in pure cadmium red and a khaki mixed from emerald and vermilion. Using broad strokes of the 19mm (¾in) flat brush, paint the sea in an emerald green/cerulean blue mix. Add a little Vandyke brown for narrow shadows under the boats.

A FEW STEPS FURTHER

The picture is now almost complete. Allow the paint to dry before adding the final details. Watercolour appears paler as it dries, so you might also want to strengthen some of the tones and colours.

9 ▲ Add linear detail Use a rigger brush to paint the rigging and outline of the boat in a greenish-brown mixed from cadmium red and emerald. The long, tapering bristles will enable you to paint the ropes as fine, flowing lines.

10 ▲ Adjust the tones Strengthen any colours and tones that have dried too pale. For example, here, the rooftops are darkened in vermilion with a touch of emerald green.

THE FINISHED PICTURE

A Flat sky
The bright sky was painted in broad, parallel strokes. The flat colour conveys a sense of stillness, which helps create an impression of heat.

B Water effects
An intense turquoise wash over the sea suggests the translucent quality of real water. Wet-on-wet runs of colour accentuate this watery effect.

C Pure colour
To match the sunny brilliance of the scene, bright paints were used. The boats, for instance, are rendered with unmixed cadmium red.

PROJECT 2

NEAR MORECOMBE BAY, LANCASHIRE

In stark contrast to the sunny Greek island, with its bright colours and cheerful ambience, this coast has a quiet, understated beauty. Apply the paint freely wet-on-wet to capture the damp, windy weather, and limit your paint mixes to a subtle range of greys.

Do not simply mix black and white to obtain your greys. Instead, as our artist has done, just tone down blue, green or yellow with Payne's grey or by adding a little contrasting colour. This helps create 'living' greys, which appear very different when seen next to each other.

Apart from the distant buildings which are painted as dark silhouettes on the horizon, most of the tones in this painting are pale and quite similar to each other. This 'close tones' approach is usually chosen to give subtle or moody effects.

YOU WILL NEED

Piece of 300gsm (140lb) Not watercolour paper 36 x 51cm (14 x 20in)

B pencil

Brushes: 19mm (¾in) flat; Nos.4 and 5 rounds; rigger

8 watercolours: Antwerp blue; Payne's grey; Yellow ochre; Violet; Ultramarine; Emerald green; Burnt sienna; Cadmium yellow

1 ▲ Paint the sky Use a B pencil to draw the main composition, starting with the horizon, which is established as a precise single line. Using a 19mm (¾in) brush, paint the top of the sky in Antwerp blue with some Payne's grey. Add a little yellow ochre and violet towards the horizon. Make short, irregular strokes, leaving patches of white among the areas of paint.

**EXPERT ADVICE
Wet-on-wet effects**

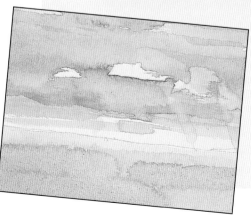

While crisp washes are ideal for simulating the effects of clear Mediterranean light, working wet-on-wet is perfect for the damp English climate. It produces unexpected and spontaneous runs of colour. If you leave these to dry naturally, you will get attractive dark edges where the pigment has collected around the runs (see left).

2 ▲ Make swirling clouds Work into the wet sky with Payne's grey mixed with touches of ultramarine and emerald green. Brush a few streaks on the white spaces, then paint some loose, swirling strokes to give a cloudy, windswept effect. Add a little more ultramarine as you paint down towards the horizon.

3 ▼ **Establish the beach** When the sky is thoroughly dry, start to paint the sand in a very diluted wash of yellow ochre. Paint darker streaks in mixtures of burnt sienna, with touches of Payne's grey and violet, allowing the wet streaks to blend together to create runs of colour.

4 ▲ **Add a few rays of light** Dip the brush in clean water and paint a few broad, diagonal strokes across the sky and sea. The water will dissolve enough colour to give the impression of pale rays of light.

5 ▲ **Dot in the buildings** Mix a cool, dark grey from Payne's grey with touches of violet and yellow ochre. Dot in the buildings around the bay with short vertical and horizontal strokes using the edge of the flat brush.

Master Strokes

Peter de Wint (1784–1849)
Mountain scene, Westmorland

This watercolour painting by British artist Peter de Wint shows a very different landscape to the one in the step-by-step, but there are some similarities in the colour palettes used to depict both scenes. At first glance the mountains may appear greyish, but look closely and you'll see ochres, greens and pinks.

Clouds hovering over the hills have been beautifully evoked by transparent washes of grey.

The dark rocks form the focal point of the painting. They also create a strong tonal contrast which helps differentiate the foreground from the pale hills beyond.

6 ▶ Paint the grass
Change to a No.4 round brush and paint the distant grass in a watery mixture of cadmium yellow with a little ultramarine. The trees in front of the grassy area are painted in a mixture of Payne's grey and cadmium yellow.

DEVELOPING THE PICTURE

At this point, the sand has been painted simply as flat washes of colour. It needs to be broken up with a few tide marks to give a sense of scale and space to the beach.

7 ▼ Add some tide marks Use the B pencil to indicate the position of the tide marks on the beach in sweeping concentric curves. Draw the curves closer together as they go off into the distance to give the scene a sense of recession and perspective.

8 ▲ Paint the tide marks With the No.4 brush dipped in a mixture of violet and yellow ochre, paint over the sweeping curves you have drawn on the beach to indicate the tide marks.

9 ▶ Add darker tones Darken the most distant houses with Payne's grey mixed with a little violet and yellow ochre. Mix a very dark green from Payne's grey with a touch of yellow ochre and add the small trees on the right with short jabs of the No.4 brush. Allow the colours to dry.

A FEW STEPS FURTHER

While you are waiting for the paint to dry, stand back and take a good look at your work. At this stage, the painting is virtually finished and needs only one or two small adjustments before it is complete. For example, the bottom edge of the composition looks rather cramped.

10 ▲ **Extend the composition** Change to a No.5 round brush and strengthen the lower edge of the painting by extending the curved tide marks on the beach, using a diluted mixture of violet and Payne's grey.

11 ▲ **Put in the distant shadows** Finally, use a stronger version of the same colour to add a few dark tones to the shadows on the far side of the beach.

THE FINISHED PICTURE

A Swirling sky
The living, moving sky was painted loosely with a large brush. Wet colours were allowed to run into each other to create amorphous shapes of muted blues and greys.

B Greyed-down colours
Local colours, such as the yellow ochre of the sand, were mixed with a little Payne's grey or a contrasting colour to create a range of cool, neutral tones.

C Suggestive brush strokes
There is no detail in the distant trees and buildings. Instead, these are suggested with tiny vertical and horizontal strokes, using the edge of a large, flat brush.

Boat on a beach

Using masking fluid with watercolour will help you to capture the wonderful array of textures in this seaside scene.

▲ **The beach is cleverly depicted by alternating spattered masking fluid with watercolour washes.**

A relatively simple subject can be lifted by paying attention to details and textures. In this project the knobbly textures of the shingle beach, together with its subtle variations of colour and tone, complement the clean, uncluttered lines of the boat.

Creating a shingle effect

The problem of rendering the complex appearance of the myriad pebbles on the beach can be solved quickly and easily by using masking fluid. When this milky liquid is applied to a support, it dries to a film that protects the

Piece of 300gsm (140lb) NOT watercolour paper 27 x 34cm (10½ x 13½in)

2B pencil

Paint shaper

Masking fluid

Toothbrush

Scrap paper

14 watercolours: cobalt blue; alizarin crimson; yellow ochre; Winsor blue; raw umber; burnt sienna; cadmium lemon; ultramarine; indigo; Payne's grey; Winsor green; light red; cadmium orange; cadmium red

Brushes: Nos. 8 and 3 rounds

Dip pen

underlying surface from subsequent paint applications. Usually used directly on white paper to create pure white areas, it can also be spattered over washes to reserve a particular colour or tone.

The shingle effect here is created by spattering masking fluid on to the previously toned support, with the small droplets creating a pebble-like pattern. A layer of wash slightly darker than the ground colour is then applied and allowed to dry. Several more layers of masking fluid are spattered over the beach area, alternated with washes of watercolour that gradually become darker in tone. When all the layers of masking fluid are finally removed, the pebble-shaped areas beneath the droplets are revealed.

Net texture

The same approach is used to render the mesh-like pattern of the heap of fishing nets in the foreground. Here the masking fluid is applied with a dip pen over a mid-toned blue in a pattern of fine crisscross lines. A darker wash is then brushed on so that the strands of the net will stand out light against dark when the mask is removed. A second application of masking fluid and wash adds depth to the heap of netting.

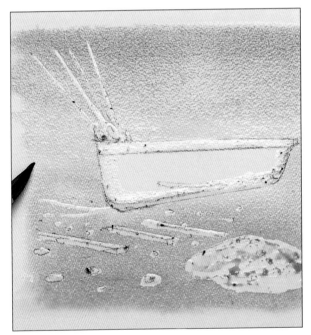

FIRST STEPS

1 ▲ Sketch the scene Use a 2B pencil to outline the boat and the heaped fishing nets, then mark in the flags and the planks that lead the eye into the scene. Now, using a paint shaper, apply masking fluid around the edge of the boat, and over the planks, flags and nets. Dot masking fluid on to the foreground of the beach, too, to reserve the shapes of the larger pebbles.

2 ▲ Lay in the sky and beach Use a No. 8 round brush to wet the paper and then flood in a mix of cobalt blue with a touch of alizarin crimson, starting at the top of the paper. Add more water to the mix as you bring the wash down the paper to the horizon line, in order to create a gradated wash. Mix a wash of yellow ochre and flood this on to the beach. Leave to dry.

3 ▶ **Darken the horizon** Wet the horizon with a No. 3 round brush. Mix a wash of Winsor blue and apply this along the horizon line so that it floods into the wet area to give a softly diffused edge. Apply a wash of raw umber below the Winsor blue and leave

4 ▼ **Spatter on masking fluid** Load an old toothbrush with masking fluid, then tap the brush against your hand to deposit droplets of masking fluid over the beach area. Leave to dry.

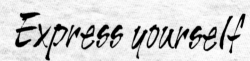

5 ▲ **Apply a wash over the beach** Mix burnt sienna and cadmium lemon, and, using the No. 8 round brush, wash this over the foreground. Leave to dry.

6 ▲ **Apply more spatter and wash** Spatter another layer of masking fluid over the beach, as in step 4. Mix a darker tone of the burnt sienna and cadmium lemon wash, and apply over the beach.

Express yourself

Into the blue

In this study, the focus is on the bright blue fishing boat rather than the beach. The artist has again opted for watercolour, but this time he has relied on a simple combination of wet-on-wet and dry-brush techniques. The boat itself is painted in strong tones of ultramarine, and with its vivid red trim it really stands out from the beach. The bold, white lettering, created by leaving the paper untouched, gives it even greater emphasis. The beach on the other hand is very loosely worked in pale tones of grey and raw umber. A little black has been flooded on to the wet beach to stand for the shadows under the boat.

7 ▲ **Apply more spattering** Once the previous wash has dried, apply another layer of spattered masking fluid to the beach. Leave to dry.

To control the size of the spattered droplets, make sure you don't overload the toothbrush with masking fluid. If the brush is too heavily loaded, the masking fluid will form droplets that are too large. Remove surplus fluid by tapping the brush over scrap paper.

8 ▲ **Apply darker washes** Mix burnt sienna with ultramarine and wash over the beach. Allow to dry, then apply another layer of spattered masking fluid, followed by a further wash of the same mix. When that is dry, apply more spattered masking fluid. Once this is dry, apply the same mix darkened with a touch of indigo. Leave to dry.

9 ▲ **Spatter paint** Mask off the areas above and below the beach with scrap paper. Load the No. 8 brush with a wash of Payne's grey and spatter dark droplets over the beach, moving the brush over the surface to get even coverage. Leave to dry.

DEVELOPING THE PICTURE

Now that the shingle – the most complex element of the picture – has been fully resolved, remove the masking fluid and move on to tackle the boat and the debris lying on the beach.

10 ▶ **Remove the masking fluid** When the support is thoroughly dry, remove the masking fluid from the beach by rubbing gently with the tips of your fingers. Notice how the layers of spattered masking fluid have reserved different layers of wash to give a wide range of pebble shades. Remove the masking fluid from the boat, the pile of nets and the planks to reveal crisp, white shapes.

11 ◄ **Work up the foreground** Mix Winsor blue, Winsor green and Payne's grey, then paint the nets with the No. 3 round. Load the brush with a mix of ultramarine and indigo and apply shadows to the underside of some of the larger stones. Apply a wash of burnt sienna and Winsor blue over the planks.

12 ▲ **Paint the boat** Apply burnt sienna with a touch of indigo along the top edge of the boat, leaving the highlight as unpainted white paper. Wet the highlit area below the brown band with clean water, then paint the hull around the wet area with cobalt blue – the colour will flow in at the edges to create a gradated tone.

13 ▲ **Add details to the boat** Apply a line of light red along the keel, then paint an indigo shadow, letting the colours blend wet-on-wet. Use the tip of the brush and a thin wash of burnt sienna to paint the flag poles. To capture movement in the flags, first paint the flag tips with clean water. Then apply indigo to the flags, allowing the colour to bleed softly into the fluttering tips.

16 ▲ **Remove the masking fluid** When the final wash is completely dry, lightly rub over the net area to remove the masking fluid and reveal a mesh of paler lines.

14 ▲ **Apply masking fluid to the pile of nets** Paint shadows on the sides of the planks with a mix of Payne's grey and raw umber. Now load a dip pen with masking fluid and draw a fine mesh of lines over the nets – the firm, pointed nib gives you considerable control. Leave to dry.

A FEW STEPS FURTHER

The painting is fully established, with the pebbles and boat convincingly rendered. Only a few details are needed to complete the image: some lines to show the timber construction of the boat and the groyne in the distance, and a couple of red flags to provide a touch of visual excitement.

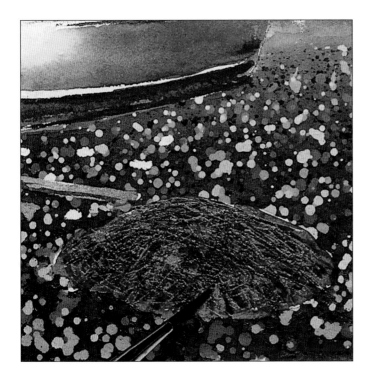

15 ▲ **Apply a wash to the nets** Mix Winsor blue with indigo and, using the No. 3 round brush, apply a wash of colour over the heap of nets. Leave to dry. Use the dip pen and masking fluid to apply a further mesh of lines over the netting. Leave to dry, then apply another layer of Winsor blue/indigo wash. Leave to dry.

17 ▲ **Add planks** Use the tip of the No. 3 round brush and Payne's grey to indicate the overlapping planks on the boat's hull. Indicate the shadows under the boat and the planks on which it is resting.

18 ▶ Add some detail around the stern

Use the burnt sienna/ indigo mix from step 12 to fill in the white strip along the side of the boat. With the tip of the No. 3 round brush and Payne's grey, add fine details and shadows around the stern of the boat. Define the top edge of the boat with a narrow line of Payne's grey to crisp up the outline.

19 ▲ Add red flags Using Payne's grey, put in patchy shadows at the base of the flag poles and flick in the groyne in the distance. Mix cadmium orange and cadmium red to paint the red flags, as described in step 13.

THE FINISHED PICTURE

A Graded stones
Lumps of white chalk (paper reserved with masking fluid) lead the eye around the foreground. They are carefully graded in size to help the illusion of recession in the scene.

B Eye-catching red
The bright, insistent colour of the two red flags contrasts with the predominant blues and browns, and provides an eye-catching focus that draws the viewer into the picture.

C Sense of scale
The simply rendered groyne gives a sense of depth, allowing the eye to read the spatial recession, from the boat and shingle in the foreground to the sea in the distance.

Colours for skies

When you've perfected the sky, your whole landscape will come together – so it's well worth practising to get it right.

Trying to capture the ever-changing moods of the sky seems rather daunting at first – where do you start? The sky changes constantly, as the sun rises and sets and as atmospheric effects such as clouds, rain and mist move across it. But if you watch the sky regularly and make notes, practise using different media and familiarise yourself with colours and techniques, you'll soon have the confidence you need to render skies skilfully and convincingly.

Sky sketches

The great landscape painter John Constable (1776–1837) sketched the sky constantly, working in oils directly from the subject – a process he called 'skying'. On 23 October 1821, Constable wrote to his friend Archdeacon Fisher, emphasising the importance of the sky in landscape painting: 'That landscape painter who does not make his skies a very material part of his composition, neglects to avail himself of one of his greatest aids.... The sky is the source of light in nature, and governs everything.'

Follow Constable's example and study the sky as often as you can. Make notes about the location, time of day, season and weather conditions. This process will help you to understand what you are seeing when on location, and will enable you to reproduce sky effects in your work.

Sky relationships

The sky is the backcloth to the landscape and should relate logically to the rest of the painting. If the sky is

▲ **This sketch in oils, *Sky Study, Clouds,* is the result of one of Constable's numerous 'skying' expeditions. He believed that skies were supremely important.**

bright blue, the landscape should be sunny. Think about where the sun is and create shadows that are appropriate: small or non-existent if the sun is overhead, long and clearly defined if the sun is lower in the sky. If the sky is overcast and leaden, the tones in the landscape will be muted and shadows absent or indistinct.

Linking sky to landscape

A toned ground laid over the entire support will subtly modify the sky and the landscape and pull the two areas

◀ A range of greys mingle with browns in this Constable study; the paint was applied loosely and the ground shows through.

together. If you add tiny dabs of sky colour to the landscape, as delicate touches or highlights, this will help to mirror the way in which light is constantly reflected from one area to another in nature.

The colour of the sky

The colour and brightness of the sky depends on factors such as the amount of cloud cover, the quantities of dust and water droplets in the air, and the position and strength of the sun. The sky is at its deepest blue between showers of rain, while on a beautiful summer's day it is often bright but not very blue because of the dust particles in the air.

To check the precise colour and tone of the sky, hold something blue or white up to it. You will find that generally the sky is brightest and whitest close to the sun, and that it often becomes paler again as it approaches the horizon.

The way you reproduce the sky will depend very much on the medium you are using and the style of your painting. In a cloudless sky, you need subtle gradations of colour and tone. You can achieve this in watercolour by laying a graduated wash, or in oil by working wet into wet to create subtle blendings. You can create skies of great depth and luminosity by applying layers of glazed and scumbled colour. You can even use a rich impasto, applying and smearing the paint with a knife – *Starry Night* by Vincent Van Gogh demonstrates the truly dramatic potential of impasto.

Special effects

Sunrise, sunset and special effects, such as rainbows, provide colourful spectacles – and each occasion is different. At sunrise and sunset, the sky is suffused with reds, oranges and yellows, which flow gradually into one another.

To describe these subtle transitions, use blending and wet-on-wet techniques. Clouds at sunset create emphatic shapes which are best painted wet-on-dry, or wet-on-damp in watercolour.

In the picture opposite, the artist Eugène Boudin (1824–98) has painted a sunny day on the beach at the seaside resort of Deauville in northern France.

KNOW YOUR SKY COLOURS

Cerulean blue
This warm blue has a slightly greenish tinge, useful near the horizon.

Prussian blue
A cold shade for rainy weather, Prussian blue also contains a hint of green.

French ultramarine
This deep shade is a warm violet-blue, perfect for sunny days.

Cobalt blue
Cobalt blue provides a good balance between warm and cold.

Payne's grey
A blue-grey, ideal for moody skies and storm clouds.

The clouds scudding across the sky give us a sense of the sea breeze.

The sky dominates the composition, occupying almost three-quarters of the canvas. The paint layer consists of thin veils of colour, which have been skimmed over the canvas so that the light itself seems trapped in a delicate web of atmospheric colours. The brushwork is soft, loose and informal, the most solid paint applications being reserved for the deep, intense blue of the sky at its highest point.

Sky moods

Despite the apparent simplicity of the subject, Boudin's painting is pervaded by a marvellous sense of space, light and airiness. If you visualise this sunny scene under a brooding, stormy sky, or gilded by the setting sun, you will see that by simply changing the sky you can create an entirely different picture.

▼ **One of Eugène Boudin's many beach paintings,** *Deauville, 1893.* **You can almost feel the blue sky and bracing air of a breezy day by the seaside.**

MIXTURES AND DILUTIONS

The colours you choose depend on the key of your painting, the effect you are trying to create and the appearance of the sky itself. So, for an intensely blue **Mix...**

A range of warm greys can be very useful when painting cloudscapes.

sky, you could use French ultramarine at the highest point, graduating through pure cobalt blue to cobalt blue muted with vermilion at the horizon.

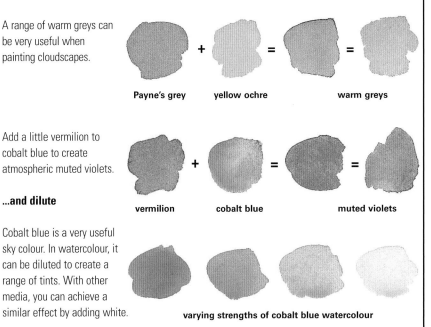

Payne's grey + **yellow ochre** = **warm greys**

Add a little vermilion to cobalt blue to create atmospheric muted violets.

vermilion + **cobalt blue** = **muted violets**

...and dilute

Cobalt blue is a very useful sky colour. In watercolour, it can be diluted to create a range of tints. With other media, you can achieve a similar effect by adding white.

varying strengths of cobalt blue watercolour

Poppies in a landscape

If your ideal landscape doesn't exist, why not create it from various sources and with a little artistic licence?

This glorious landscape with its jubilant poppies bordering a field of golden corn doesn't exist in reality. The painting is a fabrication – a work in which a still-life set-up and a landscape photograph, plus a dose of imagination, come together to create a totally plausible composition.

The photo of a luxuriant green field, a farmhouse and an ancient stone wall bordering the field (top right) formed the basis of the work, although it is considerably altered, both in content and in colour. Green fields became yellow cornfields; greyish hills became purple; stone walls vanished from view.

The poppies, which give a burst of red in the foreground, were based on a bunch of bought poppies (right). These provided an ideal visual reference.

▼ The poppies and grasses that dominate the foreground contrast in scale with the distant cottage, setting up a strong feeling of recession in the scene.

FIRST STEPS

1 ▼ **Plan the composition** Using a brown water-soluble pencil (it will wash out when you paint over it), sketch the distant hills and house. Place the poppies in the foreground, making them very large to give the sense of a receding landscape.

YOU WILL NEED

Piece of 300gsm (140lb) watercolour paper 36 x 46cm (14 x 18in)

Brown water-soluble coloured pencil

9 watercolours: cerulean blue; ultramarine; alizarin crimson; cadmium red; cadmium yellow pale; Winsor green; lemon

yellow; yellow ochre; burnt sienna

Brushes: Nos. 16 and 8 rounds; No. 2 rigger

Mixing palette or dish

Jar of water

Stiff card

Old toothbrush

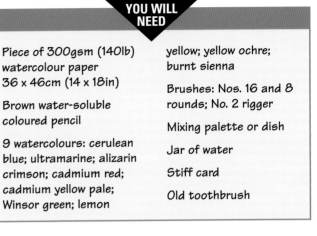

2 ▼ **Start with the sky** Using a No. 16 round brush, wet the sky area, then go over it with sweeps of cerulean blue, followed by ultramarine. Use loose, curved brush strokes rather than broad, horizontal strokes.

3 ▲ **Mix a purple** Combine alizarin crimson with ultramarine to make a purple, and use this both within the sky and on the furthest hill. Although the hill appears blue-grey in the photo, you can adapt the colours if you wish. To create some warmer accents, wash areas of cadmium red into the landscape.

▼ To prevent the red and purple mixes (left) from accidentally running into the blues and greens (below), the artist used two palettes.

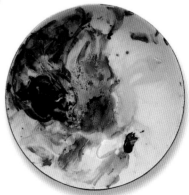

4 ◄ **Paint with water** Move forward in the scene, painting the distant fields with mixes of cerulean blue, cadmium yellow pale and Winsor green. To create a hazy effect, dip the brush in clean water and use it to slice across the sky and hills, lifting and blending the colours as you do so.

5 ▼ **Establish the cornfield** Transform the grassy field of the photograph into a cornfield by washing lemon yellow over the foreground area. Use the No. 16 round brush for this, taking care to avoid the poppies.

DEVELOPING THE PICTURE

With the broad areas of the landscape blocked in, turn your attention to the details in the scene – the house, the clumps of trees and the poppies in the foreground.

6 ▲ **Paint the farmhouse** Switch to a No. 2 rigger and cadmium red to outline the farmhouse and paint the windows. Now, with a No. 8 round brush, paint the roof and side of the house. Brush clean water on to the side wall, and draw some of the colour down from the roof to create a pale

7 ▼ Put in the trees A line of trees spans the middle distance. Paint these with mixes of Winsor green and yellow ochre, varying the proportions of the colours to create visual interest.

8 ▶ Fill in the poppies With the No. 2 rigger, define the doorway of the house, the roof and the side wall in Winsor green. Then, with the No. 8 round brush, start painting the poppies. Use varying strengths of cadmium red for the flower-heads, with occasional touches of lemon yellow.

EXPERT ADVICE
Printing techniques

Printing with the edge of a card strip is a useful way to make thin lines for stems. Don't dip the card into the paint, as it will become saturated and messy. Instead, use a brush to paint colour on to the edge of the card.

Express yourself
Change of format

Within a landscape, real or imaginary, there are often various ways of cropping into the scene to produce new and equally interesting compositions. Here, the artist has focused more closely on the farmhouse in the middle distance by cropping off the sides of the original composition, creating an unusually tall and narrow format. The verticals of the poppies and grasses in the foreground fill the paper from top to bottom, cutting across the view and bringing the viewer even closer into the scene than in the conventional landscape format. The sense of distance created by contrasting warm and cool colours is, however, just as strong.

9 ▼ **Print with card** Using the edge of a strip of stiff card, print narrow lines to stand for the dried grasses – yellow ochre on the left, burnt sienna on the right. Bend another card strip to form a V-shape and print the ears of corn, beginning at the top of each stem. Again, use yellow ochre on some of the stems and burnt sienna on others.

10 ▲ **Print the fence** Using the No. 2 rigger, strengthen the cadmium red roof of the house and add details to the windows, chimney and wall with burnt sienna and ultramarine. Then, changing to the No. 8 round, block in the foreground fence-posts with burnt sienna. Print Winsor green outlines with a card strip.

11 ▼ **Provide some dark accents** Use the No. 2 rigger and Winsor green to dot in the dark centres on the poppies. Mix ultramarine and burnt sienna to define the background hills.

12 ▲ **Build up the foreground** With the No. 2 rigger and a mix of alizarin crimson and ultramarine, define the brow of the hill in the centre by dotting dark accents along the ridge. To create visual interest in the foreground, print more hedgerow grasses, as in step 9. Use Winsor green for some and a dark mix of ultramarine and burnt sienna for others.

A FEW STEPS FURTHER

The landscape has a strong sense of recession, with the warm reds of the poppies throwing the mauves of the hills into distant relief. Complete the painting by adding a little more detail with the rigger and some spattering.

13 ▶ **Suggest some distant trees**
Return to the No. 2 rigger to add a clump of mauve-coloured trees at the top of the hill in the centre – use a dilute mix of alizarin crimson and ultramarine for this.

14 ▲ **Spatter texture** Load the bristles of an old toothbrush with burnt sienna. Draw the brush over some stiff card to spatter droplets of paint across the foreground and up into the sky.

THE FINISHED PICTURE

A Visual reference
The device of showing just the top of the fence in the foreground makes us feel that we are actually at the scene – spectators within a real landscape.

B Central landmark
The inclusion of the farmhouse in the middle distance, a recognizable landmark dwarfed by the poppies and grasses, reinforces the vast scale of the countryside.

C Sense of space
The cool hues of the hills on the horizon create a powerful sense of recession, particularly when contrasted with the warm colours in the foreground.

Picture postcards

Blank postcards made of watercolour paper are a great addition to a holiday painting kit – use them to send a unique record of your travels to your friends.

T here is a long tradition of artists sending personalized decorated correspondence. Artists such as Marcel Duchamp (1887–1968) and Kurt Schwitters (1887–1948), for example, created individual picture postcards which they sent to friends and relatives. Why not follow in their footsteps and create your own watercolour postcards to send to your friends and relatives.

Holiday postcards

A holiday away from home is a good time to try painting your own postcards, as you'll have plenty of inspiring material to work from. The challenge is to produce an image that works on a small scale – the postcards often measure about 10.5 x 15cm (4 x 6in). The secret lies in the composition – if you underpin the painting with a good, simple line drawing, you will produce an image that engages the viewer.

Working methods

To help you find a suitable composition, half-close your eyes and look at how lights and darks are distributed across the subject. See, too, if you can find interesting divisions or repeated shapes. Thumbnail sketches will help you explore the possibilities.

▲ **A combination of pencil, oil pastel and watercolour on postcard-sized watercolour paper gives impressive results quickly.**

When working on location, you'll need a portable kit. The combination of pencil, watercolour and oil pastel used for the two step-by-steps shown on the following pages is simple but effective.

The pencil is used to make fluent, calligraphic marks that contribute to the final image, rather than just plotting where the washes should go. Watercolour is a flexible medium that can be used for broad washes of transparent colour or for quite controlled detail. A small box of pan watercolours is an ideal option for the travelling artist, as it is light and the colours can be accessed directly. Tube colours are more cumbersome – using them involves deciding which colours you will need, fiddling about with lids and then squeezing out blobs of paint.

Sticks of oil pastel are portable and produce solid patches of vibrant colour as well as line. These solid areas contrast with the transparency of the watercolour. Also, because oil and watercolour are incompatible, the oil pastel is unaffected by subsequent washes.

Because of its waxy quality, white oil pastel can be used as a form of resist – you can put it down on any areas of your painting that should read as white. You can then apply watercolour washes quite freely over the top. White oil pastel is more convenient than masking fluid, so is a useful addition to your travel kit.

PROJECT 1

PLAZA MAYOR, MADRID

A café table gives you a ringside seat from which to watch the world go by and discreetly make a record of the scene. Give the image structure by simplifying the architecture and emphasizing colours and shapes in the foreground.

1 ▶ Make a drawing Using a 3B pencil, plot the key verticals and horizontals, then add the chairs and tables in the foreground to give a sense of scale and depth. Work rapidly with fluent lines that give the drawing a sense of immediacy. Indicate the shadows within the arcade around the square.

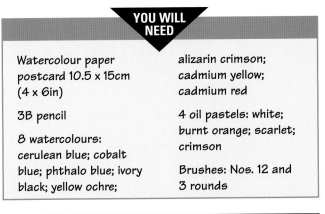

YOU WILL NEED

Watercolour paper postcard 10.5 x 15cm (4 x 6in)

3B pencil

8 watercolours: cerulean blue; cobalt blue; phthalo blue; ivory black; yellow ochre;

alizarin crimson; cadmium yellow; cadmium red

4 oil pastels: white; burnt orange; scarlet; crimson

Brushes: Nos. 12 and 3 rounds

2 ▲ Lay in the sky Mix a pale wash of cerulean blue and cobalt blue and apply to the sky with a No. 12 round brush. Use phthalo blue for the table on the left and add a little ivory black for the table on the right. Describe the curving chair backs with the tip of a No. 3 brush.

3 ▲ Paint the buildings Using the No. 12 brush, mix yellow ochre, cobalt blue and alizarin crimson for the pale grey of the roofs, pavement and arcade. By adjusting the proportions of each colour, you can create subtle shifts in tone.

4 ▶ Apply oil pastel
Use a white oil pastel as a resist for the windows on the buildings – you can then wash over the façade without any fiddly brushwork. Dab colourful touches of burnt orange, scarlet and crimson oil pastel on to the parasols and the tables.

▲ The shades of maroon and brown used for the parasols are mixed from cadmium yellow, cadmium red, alizarin crimson and phthalo blue.

5 ▼ Paint the parasols For the orange parasols, mix cadmium yellow and cadmium red watercolour; apply with the No. 3 round. For the undersides and darker parasols, make various mixes of phthalo blue, alizarin crimson, cadmium red and cadmium yellow. Use a dilute mix for the building's façade. Mix phthalo blue and black to make a grey for the shadowy arcade.

6 ▲ Add details Use the grey mix for the lamppost. Combine phthalo blue with alizarin crimson, and wash over the shadow on the façade. Use the same colour and the reddish mixes from step 5 for linear details on the chair backs and umbrella poles.

THE FINISHED PICTURE

A White pastel resist
To avoid fiddly brushwork on the façade of the building, white oil pastel was worked over the windows in order to resist the watercolour wash.

B Lively pencil lines
A lively, fluent pencil line holds the image together and complements the loose painting style.

C Bright oil pastel
Emphatic touches of brightly coloured oil pastel add emphasis to the foreground, and encourage the viewer's eyes to dance across the foreground.

PROJECT 2
CHATEAU DE CHENONCEAUX, LOIRE

The turrets of the French château of Chenonceaux looming over the surrounding waters make a romantic subject that cries out to be painted. The soaring verticals of the towers pierce the broad triangle of the sky, while the dark water below provides visual stability.

YOU WILL NEED

Watercolour paper postcard
15 x 10.5cm (6 x 4in)

3B pencil

6 oil pastels: yellow ochre;
burnt sienna; black; blue;
grey; green

6 watercolours: yellow ochre;
alizarin crimson; raw umber;
cobalt blue; phthalo blue;
cerulean blue

Brushes: Nos. 12 and
3 rounds

1 ▶ Make a drawing
Using a 3B pencil, make a drawing of the château. Start with the line of the water's edge and some other key perspective lines such as decorative bands along the façade. Where these curve around the towers, they help to describe their cylindrical forms. All these perspective lines should meet at a single vanishing point which, in this case, is beyond the picture area. Plot the verticals of the towers and check proportions and angles with your pencil at arm's length.

2 ▶ Add oil pastel Using yellow ochre, burnt sienna and black oil pastels, touch in small areas of colour on the façade of the building, echoed by reflections in the surface of the water. With blue and grey oil pastels, add the cool shadows on the slate-covered roofs.

▲ Mixes of yellow ochre, alizarin crimson, cobalt blue and raw umber provide browns and greys for the château walls and their reflections.

3 ▶ **Apply a wash** Mix a wash of yellow ochre watercolour with a touch of alizarin crimson. Using a No. 12 round brush, loosely apply this ochre wash over the façade of the building to suggest the weathered character of the masonry. The tiny touches of opaque oil pastel applied in step 2 resist the watercolour, creating areas of lively, broken colour.

Express yourself
People in the picture

Holidays are as much about people as places, so give your postcard a personal touch by including family members or new friends in the scene. This card shows a different view of the château at Chenonceaux, with a rowing boat on the lake adding foreground interest. It was quickly and loosely sketched on the spot in pen and black ink, then watercolour washes were added later – a useful method of working if you don't want to take too many art materials out with you. The boat – the focal point of the scene – has been emphasized by the pink band around it.

4 ▼ **Paint the water** Take the ochre mix from step 3 down into the water to show the reflected façade of the château, but leave parts of the paper white to suggest reflected clouds. Mix a raw umber and cobalt blue wash and paint on to the water to represent the darker reflections. Leave to dry.

5 ◄ **Paint the roof**
Use a darker tone of the warm ochre mix to define the architectural details on the façade. Apply the same wash over the furthest tower. Mix cobalt blue and a touch of alizarin crimson watercolour for the slate roofs, taking some of the colour into the window openings.

6 ► **Add the trees**
The small clump of trees on the left is an important focus, drawing the eye through the painting. Apply touches of green oil pastel followed by a wash of raw umber and phthalo blue watercolour.

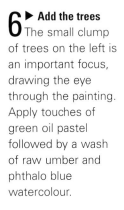

7 ▼ **Lay in the sky** Using the No. 12 brush, apply a dilute wash of cerulean blue watercolour across the sky – work loosely, leaving large patches of white for the clouds.

8 ▲ **Darken the roofs**
Use a No. 3 round brush and a mix of yellow ochre, alizarin crimson and raw umber to add more details to the building: the windows and the shadows down the sides of the towers. Using the cobalt blue/alizarin crimson mix from step 5, add darker tones on the shaded roof areas.

THE FINISHED PICTURE

A Paper clouds
In the sky area, most of the white paper was left unpainted to stand for the fluffy summer clouds.

B Economic marks
A dark wash, dabbed on with the tip of a No. 3 round brush, depicts with great economy window openings around the tower.

C Emphatic oil pastel
Streaks of black oil pastel were used to show reflections in the water. These opaque touches contrast with the transparent watercolour washes.

The artist's garden

Look for inspiration in the landscape that is closest to home – your own garden. You can return to it time and time again and never exhaust its pictorial possibilities.

The pleasure of garden paintings lies in the intrinsic beauty of the subject, as well as the enjoyment of an individual artist's treatment of it. Gardening and art have been linked for thousands of years, initially in the regions where gardening began – Egypt and China. In more recent times, Claude Monet (1840–1926) painted his gardens at Argenteuil and Vétheuil in France many times, and in the 1890s moved to Giverny and began to plant his famous and much-painted water garden.

Exploiting your garden

A garden is an ideal subject, combining nature with man-made features. But the search for a 'picturesque' landscape can lead you to overlook this very obvious view right on your doorstep. It is convenient, accessible and offers plenty of opportunities to sketch, photograph, observe and become familiar with the subject. Record your garden at different times of day, in all weather conditions and in all seasons. In art, familiarity does not breed contempt. Indeed, it can give heightened awareness, and having an understanding of the subject allows you to develop creative interpretations. Returning to it time and again has a further benefit. Because you will have solved the basic problems first time around, you will be less concerned with pure description, which can be very liberating.

Gardens in watercolour

In this project the artist worked primarily from the three photos (left), but also from her memories of a garden that she created herself, has known intimately for many years and has painted many times. The photos were particularly useful for details – leaf shapes and patterns, the fall of light, the markings on the silver birch trunks and the objects on the table.

YOU WILL NEED

Piece of 300gsm (140lb) Not watercolour paper 57 x 38cm (22½ x 15in)

2B pencil or clutch pencil

11 watercolours: Van Dyke brown; sap green; ultramarine; lemon yellow; vermilion; alizarin crimson; cadmium yellow pale; burnt sienna; Winsor violet; purple madder; Winsor blue (green shade)

Brushes: Nos. 7 and 10 rounds; old toothbrush

White gouache

▲ This fresh, light-filled painting was worked in transparent washes of watercolour. The artist painted quite slowly, building up patches of colour with a small brush.

FIRST STEPS

1 ▼ **Establish the drawing** Using a 2B pencil or clutch pencil, start on the underdrawing. The subject is fairly complex, with a still life of dishes of fruit and a jug in the foreground, a wickerwork chair by the table and a complex mosaic of leaves in the background. Use the drawing to investigate and simplify leaf shapes and patterns of foliage.

2 ◄ **Lay the preliminary washes** The three vertical columns of the silver birch trunks are key elements of the composition. Use a mix of Van Dyke brown and sap green and a No. 7 round brush to paint the foliage behind the trunks, letting the negative spaces define the positive shapes of the trees. Paint clumps of leaves with the tip of the brush, adding ultramarine to the wash to vary the tones.

3 ▼ **Continue painting the foliage** Paint the sinuous shape of the tree in the background in Van Dyke brown. Develop the foliage, looking for the character and massed shapes of the leaves. Use the Van Dyke brown/sap green wash for this, modifying it with a little ultramarine for the cooler, bluer leaves.

4 ▶ **Work on the foreground** Dilute the Van Dyke brown/ sap green/ultramarine wash and paint the glimpses of sky seen through the leaves. Paint the rest of the foliage with various mixes of these three colours, including the spiky leaves of the lily behind the wickerwork chair. Paint the lily flowers, using lemon yellow and wet-on-wet washes of vermilion/lemon yellow and alizarin crimson/cadmium yellow pale.

5 ▶ **Paint the wicker chair** Continue to work on the foliage behind the table, using variations of the Van Dyke brown/sap green/ultramarine wash. Add burnt sienna and Winsor violet for the darkest tones. Mix lemon yellow and Van Dyke brown to paint the chair – work carefully, avoiding flooding the paper with water. Paint the dark areas seen through the wickerwork in sap green and ultramarine.

6 ▶ **Add darker tones** With the tip of a No. 10 round brush, use a rich mix of Winsor violet, ultramarine and Van Dyke brown to paint the dark areas in the background and the shadows within the shrubs near the foreground. This will begin to create a sense of depth and form in the scene.

7 ▲ **Paint the jug** Switch back to the No. 7 round brush and paint the jug with separate washes of burnt sienna, Van Dyke brown and Winsor violet. Work wet-on-wet so that the colours bleed into each other, creating softly blended edges.

DEVELOPING THE PICTURE

Greens are a key component of this painting, and the range of light to dark and warm to cool greens has now been established. The next step is to work up some of the colourful features in the foreground, such as the brightly coloured cushion and the fruit.

8 ▼ Work up the chair Paint the patterned cushion on the chair, using a range of colours: vermilion, ultramarine, alizarin crimson, a mix of sap green and ultramarine, and a mix of lemon yellow and vermilion. Then paint the foliage around the chair, using your selection of green palette mixes. Fill in the holes in the wickerwork with the mix of sap green and ultramarine.

9 ▼ Describe the apple Paint the apple using the following washes applied wet-on-wet with the No. 10 round brush: lemon yellow, vermilion, sap green and a touch of Van Dyke brown. Allow the colours to blend softly.

10 ▼ Colour the cherries Paint the cherries, using alizarin crimson with a touch of lemon yellow. Add purple madder to the mix and apply to the shaded areas between the fruits – here you are using the negative spaces to define the shapes of the positive elements.

Express yourself

A different point of view

The artist has painted her garden – and the comfortable wicker chair – many times. In this study she has taken a different viewpoint, bringing the silver birch trees into the centre of the picture. She has stepped back so that a bank of white flowers fills the foreground and leads the eye into the scene. By changing your position you can create an entirely new image.

11 ▼ **Develop the 'still life'** Complete the cherries in the bowl with alizarin crimson, Winsor violet and purple madder, using Van Dyke brown for the stalks and ultramarine and Winsor blue for the bowl. Paint the second apple with lemon yellow, vermilion, sap green and a touch of Van Dyke brown. Add detail to the plate in ultramarine and Winsor blue, depicting the flower pattern and rim with a lemon yellow/vermilion mix. Finally, paint the scattered cherries with purple madder, alizarin crimson and lemon yellow.

12 ▼ **Continue with the foliage** Paint the foliage at top left with sap green and mixes of sap green with lemon yellow or ultramarine. Look for the areas of light and dark tone, the main part of the foliage and the particular leaf shapes such as those of the castor oil plant.

13 ▼ **Develop leaf shapes** Continue working down the left side of the painting, using the palest of your green washes to establish the leaf colours. Use the darker tones for the shadows that surround the leaves – these define the divided, finger-like outlines. Don't let the washes get too dry, as you need to establish the shapes but still keep the edges fairly soft.

EXPERT ADVICE
Head over heels

There are many reasons for turning your painting upside down. It helps you see the composition with fresh eyes, allowing you to focus on abstract areas of colour and tone without being distracted by the subject matter. Make any adjustments, then turn the painting back the right way up. There is also a practical reason for turning a large painting round. If you need to work on an area that is near the top edge, it is much easier to work with that edge nearest to you.

14 ◄ **Add details on the tree trunks**
Silver birches have a papery bark with dark horizontal and vertical markings. Use a sap green/Van Dyke brown mix applied with the tip of the No. 7 round brush to apply these markings.

15 ◄ **Paint the pots**
The warm tones and repeated ellipses of the terracotta pots behind the table are an important feature in this area of the painting. Paint them using burnt sienna, and a mix of burnt sienna with Van Dyke brown and touches of vermilion and lemon yellow.

16 ▶ **Paint the foliage** Apply a dilute ultramarine wash over the birch trunks to suggest their silvery tones. Using the negative/positive technique as in step 13, paint the lance-like leaves of the plant behind the jug. Begin by using sap green mixed with Winsor blue for the spaces between the leaves. Allow to dry a little, then apply a pale overall wash of sap green to colour the leaves themselves.

17 ▲ **Make some final adjustments** Apply washes of Van Dyke brown to the shaded sides of the birch trunks. Now work across the painting, making final adjustments. Use clean water to blend the colour and to soften any parts of the foliage that are too crisp and distracting.

A FEW STEPS FURTHER

You might want to carry the work further by adding some fine detail to the leaves and branches. Also, a spattering of white gouache will bring sparkling light into the painting.

18 ▲ **Apply body colour** Add white gouache to sap green watercolour and, using the No. 7 brush, add more fine, grass-like leaves in the foreground.

19 ▲ **Spatter colour** Load an old toothbrush with white gouache and spatter fine droplets of white to capture the effect of sparkling sunlight.

20 ▲ **Add cool shadows** Mix a fairly dilute wash of alizarin crimson and ultramarine, and apply purplish shadows with the No. 7 brush all over the tablecloth.

21 ▼ **Paint the branches** Mix Van Dyke brown with ultramarine and, using the tip of the brush, draw the dark tracery of branches. Work towards the tip, lifting the brush to create a line that tapers towards the end.

THE FINISHED PICTURE

A Defining negatives
Painting the dark shadows between the leaves of the castor oil plant allows the intricate indented shapes to emerge.

B Artistic licence
The artist altered the colour of the cushion on the chair so that it echoed the brighter colours of the items on the table.

C Paper whites
The white of the paper is important in watercolour – here it stands for the palest patches on the trunks of the silver birches.

Lively building site

It is not always the most picturesque scenes that provide the best subjects for the artist – urban and industrial landscapes have their own fascination.

▼ The massive machine, the mounds of mud and earth, and the active, brightly clad workers were recorded in the artist's fluent, intuitive style of painting.

The rather unusual subject matter in this project is matched by an equally unusual method of painting. Instead of working light to dark as you normally would with watercolours, start by laying in an area of dark tone to set a key for the picture. You can add the sky towards the end. Furthermore, try to approach the composition in a very direct way, applying a single layer of colour rather than building up layers of washes. Of course, this means you will have to judge and mix your colours accurately from the start, but the vibrant quality you will achieve – the white of the support glowing through a single layer of transparent colour – makes all your efforts worthwhile.

Using palette mixes

Some watercolour artists mix their colours in a very organized way, keeping each mix in a separate recess and washing their brush between each colour – an often recommended procedure. However, in keeping with your unusual approach, try working more intuitively instead, your brush dancing from one part of the palette to another.

As a result, the mixes will be gradually modified as touches of colour are blended inadvertently with those elsewhere on the palette. Inevitably they will begin to veer towards neutrals and coloured greys, the 'dirty' colours that you are sometimes warned against. In reality, these subtly modified mixes provide a range of ready-made tones that the artist can dip into. In any case, if you do not build up wash over wash, the colours retain their freshness.

With enough practice, this method can become second nature. You'll probably find that you can't tell precisely what your palette mixes consist of – just like a cook who adds a pinch of this and a bit of that to a recipe.

FIRST STROKES

1 ▶ **Make a pencil sketch** Sketch in the main elements of the composition with a B pencil. Work lightly, checking the balance of the components and the shapes they make on the paper.

YOU WILL NEED

Piece of 300gsm (140lb) NOT watercolour paper 44 x 56cm (17 x 22in)

B pencil

15 watercolours: ultramarine; cerulean blue; emerald green; cadmium yellow; Prussian blue; burnt umber; raw umber; red ochre; cadmium orange; raw sienna; yellow ochre; cobalt blue; gold ochre; madder lake; violet

Brushes: 13mm (½in) and 10mm (⅜in) flats

Mixing palette

Calligraphy pen and white chalk

Narrow stick

Round-tipped painting knife

2 ▼ **Start with the cab** Mix ultramarine, cerulean blue and emerald green. Using a 13mm (½in) flat brush, paint the back of the cab of the pile-driving rig. Load the brush with cadmium yellow and use the narrow edge of the brush to paint the warning stripes on the back. Use the flat edge to define the shape of the cab with a mix of cerulean blue, Prussian blue and burnt umber.

3 ▼ **Indicate dark tones** Block in the dark tones on the cab with a wash of raw umber, working wet-on-wet. Crisp up wet edges and draw in details with a calligraphy pen and the same wash. Sketch the head of the figure.

4 ▼ **Develop the rig** Block in the cab windows with the raw umber wash. Dip a narrow stick lengthways into the wash and apply the paint briskly to the paper to print the cables. Use the Prussian blue/cerulean mix and the 13mm (½in) brush to paint the jib (the arm of the crane) and pile-driver platform, then work into them with raw umber applied wet-on-wet.

5 ▲ **Add figures** Paint the pile-driving rod in red ochre, using the narrow edge of the 13mm (½in) brush. Hold the flat edge of the brush at an angle to the paper to mark the spiral of the auger. Block in the figures wet-on-wet. Use cadmium orange for the hats and the theodolite (a surveying instrument), cadmium yellow for the jackets, and a mix of Prussian blue and cadmium yellow for the trousers. The hat of the blue figure is emerald green, while his body is a pale version of the original blue wash from step 2.

6 ▶ **Block in the hoardings** Paint the hoardings with brush strokes of cadmium yellow, raw sienna and yellow ochre, applied wet-on-wet so that the colours run here and there. While the paint is still wet, pull a round-tipped painting knife across the wash in both directions, lifting the pigment to create highlights.

DEVELOPING THE PICTURE

Start to add details and fill in the background. Try to avoid overlaying the existing washes. The fewer layers of paint there are, the more vibrant the colours will be, so work background colours around existing shapes.

If you draw complex patterns of cables too carefully, the result won't sit comfortably with a fluid watercolour style. Instead, print lines with a tool such as a stick or card. With this quick, direct technique, you are discouraged from overworking the painting.

7 ▲ Add detail Use raw umber to print the crane and cables. Paint the rig tracks in cobalt blue, Prussian blue and raw umber. Apply foreground mixes of raw sienna, and yellow and gold ochres, using a 10mm (⅜in) brush. Mix burnt umber and Prussian blue for shadows on the auger. Put in the man on the right in emerald. Use madder lake with burnt umber for the red crane.

8 ▲ Add lettering Using raw umber and raw sienna, block in the foreground and, while the paint is still wet, scrape into it with the painting knife. Mix a wash of red ochre and use the calligraphy pen to add struts to the crane boom, and lettering to the cab of the rig.

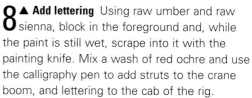

9 ◄ Define the figures Add a few defining marks to the figures with freely drawn lines made with the dip pen and red ochre mixed with burnt umber – these pull the loosely rendered figures into focus. Change back to the 13mm (½in) brush and indicate the buildings in the background with a cool grey from your palette. Add the dark figure in the foreground using burnt umber with some of your palette mixes, then use a warm, neutral palette mix to fill in the gaps between the figures.

Express yourself
Heavy machinery

This is another of the artist's vigorous watercolours, inspired by a visit to the same building site. When you have worked through this project, why not find a similar site and make some sketches on the spot? While the experience is still fresh in your mind, work up a watercolour, using the direct, single-layer approach illustrated in the step-by-step.

10 ◀ **Add the sky** Wet the upper part of the painting by flooding it with water under a tap, then dot in violet and ultramarine. Lift and tilt the paper to make the colour run and blend to create a graduated sky. The accidental softening of colours in adjacent areas, such as the pile driver and some of the figures, gives the painting a sense of fluidity and spontaneity.

11 ▲ **Add crisp details** Having softened some of the edges, pull the image into focus again by adding fine detail. Use pen and a brown palette mix to add a sketchy outline to the dark foreground figure – the crisp lines give the image a sense of movement. Use the pen to draw the rope in the foreground and the crane booms in the distance.

12 ▲ **Add texture in the foreground** Using the dark brown mix from your palette, add gestural marks to the disturbed ground in the foreground. This creates visual interest and provides a link with dark areas elsewhere in the painting.

167

A FEW STEPS FURTHER

There is now a convincing sense of noise, dust, and hustle and bustle in the painting. Decide whether you want to add more detail in the foreground – this will bring the area forward and increase the illusion of depth.

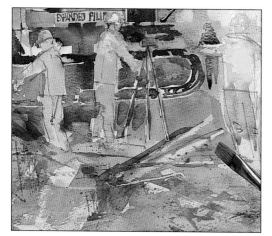

13 ▲ **Spatter the foreground** Mix a wash of cadmium orange and use this to spatter the foreground, adding lively texture here.

14 ▲ **Add highlights** Use white chalk to add a few sparkling highlights – on the edges of the auger, on the back of the dark jacket and on the ground. These highlights should be used sparingly and applied lightly, so that the stick glances over the dimpled surface of the paper to give a stippled effect.

THE FINISHED PICTURE

A One layer
Subtle areas of mixed colour, applied as a single layer, give the paint surface a sparkling, jewel-like brilliance and clarity.

B Foreground texture
Gestural marks and spattering create visually entertaining passages in the foreground. The large scale of the marks here helps to suggest recession from foreground to background.

C Lost and found
Edges that have been 'lost' by washing off, then 'found' with a pen line produce figures that have an appealing immediacy and sense of movement.

Painting with two colours

Restricting your palette has two great advantages: it makes paint mixing easier and results in paintings with wonderfully harmonious colour.

Successful watercolour painting depends to a large extent on knowing how to mix the colours you need. Experienced artists do this automatically with an ease and speed that makes the process appear almost effortless. Their secret lies in using as few colours as possible – the more limited the palette, the more harmonious and integrated the composition will appear.

The two-colour palette

As an introduction to working with a restricted palette, try painting a picture using just two colours. This sounds drastic, but you will be astonished at how much can be achieved with a pair of carefully selected colours and at how realistic the result can be.

The selection is personal and depends very much on what you are painting, but a blue combined with a warm colour provides the maximum scope for most subjects. For the watercolour seascape on the far right, our artist chose ultramarine and burnt umber which provided a varied range of browns and greys. Combinations of the two colours created the dark neutral tone of the beach behind the breakwater; the subtle warm colours of the beach and rock face; and the cool blue-greys of the sea and sky.

Alternative pairs

To continue the two-colour experiment, try painting with different pairs of colours. Apart from burnt umber and ultramarine, other effective two-colour palettes are Prussian blue, cerulean blue or indigo with any of the warm earth colours – such as Indian red, Venetian red or burnt sienna.

For flowers, still-life arrangements and other subjects that contain bright colours, try working with a pair of complementaries – two colours that fall opposite each other on the colour wheel. It is surprising how many paintings are based on the use of opposites, and how effective the colours appear as a result. Depending on the subject, choose red with green, blue with orange, or yellow with violet.

The use of opposites produces a particularly brilliant colour reaction, and artists have long made use of this visual property. By laying a colour next to its opposite, the effect is to make both appear more vibrant and bright than when viewed separately. In addition, complementary colours produce a neutral tone when mixed in equal quantities, so greys, browns and other muted colours present no problem.

Black and white

Often the addition of black to two colours gives not only an additional repertoire of dark tones, but also extends the range of greys and neutrals. However, by choosing

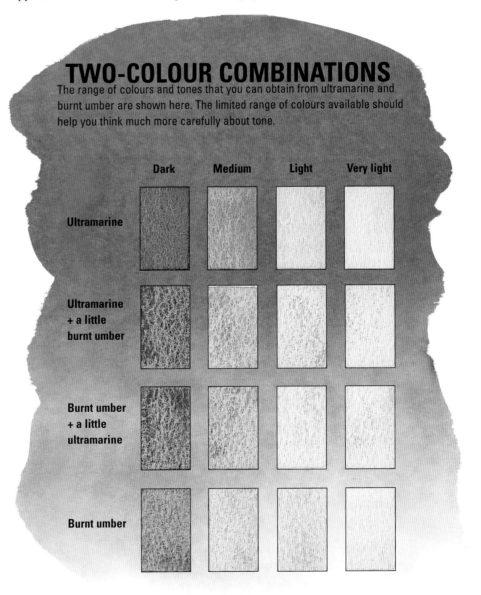

TWO-COLOUR COMBINATIONS

The range of colours and tones that you can obtain from ultramarine and burnt umber are shown here. The limited range of colours available should help you think much more carefully about tone.

	Dark	Medium	Light	Very light
Ultramarine				
Ultramarine + a little burnt umber				
Burnt umber + a little ultramarine				
Burnt umber				

A TWO-COLOUR COASTAL SCENE

This coastal landscape was completed using only burnt umber and ultramarine. A wide range of the possible mixes is shown left. Six of these mixes – together with their exact position on the painting – are shown here.

As with any landscape, think about creating an illusion of distance through aerial perspective. Objects appear cooler in colour and lighter in tone in the distance. For instance, note how a dark mix of mainly burnt umber is used for the large cliff top in the middle ground, while the small cliff top in the far distance is rendered in a very pale mix of mainly ultramarine.

A Ultramarine + a little burnt umber – dark

B Ultramarine neat – light

C Burnt umber + a little ultramarine – medium

D Burnt umber + a little ultramarine – very light

E Ultramarine + a little burnt umber – light

F Burnt umber neat – medium

colours that are dark in tone, like the burnt umber and ultramarine used here, it is not really necessary to use black at all. You can create a near-black with a strong mix of the two palette colours – look at the breakwater in the painting above. For a paler shade of any colour, simply add water to the mixture. Areas of pure white are created by leaving the paper unpainted.

Using a limited palette is, in a sense, a return to the origins of the watercolour tradition. In the eighteenth century, watercolour was considered primarily a sketching medium – useful for making studies for oil paintings. One of the main aims of these sketches was working out the tonal arrangement of the final composition. To do this, you didn't need a full range of colours. Thus a limited palette was established early as one of the traditions of watercolour painting.

Paul Sandby (1725–1809), known as the father of watercolour painting, often worked in just two or three colours. He used this palette with great success to capture the diverse effects of sunlight and atmosphere.

A little improvisation

And if Sandby ever came unstuck with his limited range of paints, he was very imaginative in his use of other materials. For example, he once mixed a 'warm' black by combining the burnt edges of his breakfast toast with gum water!

Sunny waterside scene

Bring a hot, sunny holiday afternoon alive by boldly applying vivid washes of watercolour.

The clean, bright hues that can be created with watercolour really evoke a sun-soaked, holiday mood in this picture. Large expanses of colour, such as the yellow wall, the blue water and the figures' tanned skin, all help convey the atmosphere of a hot, relaxing afternoon.

Breaking a few rules

When composing a picture, you don't have to feel tied down by conventional rules. Here, the woman basking in the sunshine is looking out of the picture, pulling our eye with it. However, together with the litter-bins on the right, she also guides the eye back into the heart of the picture. We are asked to linger on the man on the path and then move on to the house across the water. The composition moves our eye in different directions, helping create a lively, engaging picture.

Vary your technique as much as you like to add interest and texture to this casual scene. Work wet-on-wet and with overlaid washes to produce rich colour mixes, such as those on the central figure, the litter-bins on the right, and the woman's bronzed skin and vest-top.

You could also experiment with a little paint on a very dry brush. This technique is ideal for giving a stippled texture to the trees that form an attractive backdrop to the scene. For fine details, such as the ripples on the water and the slender tree branches, use well-sharpened coloured pencils.

As a reference, the artist used a sketch he made on site (above). Working in his studio on the finished picture gave him more time to think about the composition and colours. He decided to add the man in the centre of the picture as a focal point. He also painted the path and wall in the foreground in yellows and oranges. This helps give an illusion of depth – the warm colours in the foreground leap forward while the blues and greens in the background recede.

▼ **Versatility is the key to creating a picture like this. The vivid hues are rendered with intense washes of watercolour, interesting textures put in with dry brushwork and detail added with coloured pencils.**

▼

YOU WILL NEED

Piece of 400gsm (200lb) Not watercolour paper 50 x 75cm (20 x 30in)	Brushes: Nos.12 and 4 flats; Nos. 12, 4, 6, 1 rounds; No.4 fan
4B pencil	Jar of water
14 watercolours: Cerulean blue; Olive green; Cadmium yellow; Cobalt blue; Indian red; Titanium white; Yellow ochre; Winsor Blue; Permanent rose; Ivory black; Burnt umber; Winsor red; Ultramarine; Winsor green	Watercolour palette
	Kitchen paper for dabbing up watery washes
	Naples yellow gouache paint
	3 coloured pencils: Purple; Ultramarine; Mid green

1 ▲ Paint the sky Sketch the scene with a 4B pencil. Wet the sky with a No.12 flat brush and clean water. Drop in cerulean blue watercolour across the wet area and lay

2 ► Add the trees Make a watery mix of olive green, cerulean blue and cadmium yellow. Continuing with the No.12 round brush, lay this in broad areas to represent the line of trees across the back of the scene. Notice how colour variations are created where the green wash overlaps the previous blue wash. Dab off any excess or running wash with kitchen paper.

3 ▲ Lay in some strong blues Mix up a fairly bright blue with cerulean blue and cobalt blue. Use a No.4 round brush to paint in the areas of water and also the vest-top of the woman on the left of the picture. Paint wet-on-wet, adding more blue here and there to give the washes some depth and texture.

4 ◄ Wash in the wall Continuing with the blue mix, add the sunglass lenses of the woman. Put in an initial wash for the wall and path behind the woman with the No.12 round brush and a thin wash of cadmium yellow. This instantly warms up the image and helps project the woman forward.

DEVELOPING THE PICTURE

Now that the larger areas of colour are blocked in, the main shapes, such as the figures, the distant house and the litter-bins, have emerged in outline, ready to be filled in.

5 ▼ Block in the main figure Using the No.4 round, block in the woman's skin with a fairly opaque mix of Indian red, titanium white and yellow ochre. Add more Indian red to the mix to paint dark shadows on the woman's right side and under her left arm.

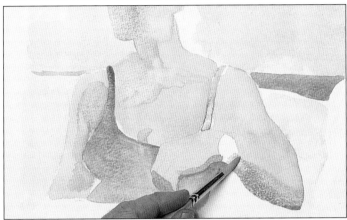

6 ▲ Establish the central area Still using the No.4 round brush, work on the central portion of the picture. Paint dense Indian red on the roof and windows of the building to bring the distance into focus – this will be the darkest colour in the painting and will help you to judge the depth of the tone across the rest of the picture. With the same brush and watery Indian red, sketch in the man in the centre, including his bag. Pick up a little yellow ochre on your brush to lift the colour on his legs.

Express yourself
A line and wash portrait

Here, the image of the woman was sketched boldly with a soft black pencil. Simple washes of black ink were then brushed on, overlapping the pencil lines in some places. Further pencil work was added on top of the thinner ink washes once they had dried.

EXPERT ADVICE
Creating light and shade

In an intensely sunny scene like this, it is important to convey a sense of light and shade throughout the picture. To create strong tonal contrast in the backdrop of trees, lay thicker paint over the top of thin colour washes with a dry, flat brush. This also builds up a sense of depth.

7 ▶ Define the foliage
Using a fairly dry No.4 flat brush, paint olive green swirls and dashes across the trees to suggest leaves and branches. Now load a very dry No.4 fan brush with the olive green paint. Dab on curved lines, creating a stippled effect by picking up tiny amounts of dense Indian red from the palette. Change the direction of the brush to vary the curves.

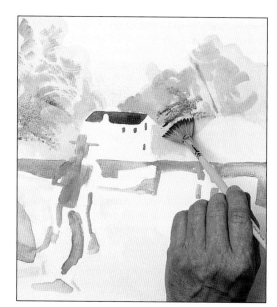

8 ▲ Paint in the litter-bins Mix Winsor blue with a little Indian red to render the rocks behind the man with the No.12 round brush. Paint the litter-bins in permanent rose – first with a light wash, then build up the shadowed sides with a stronger mix. Add touches of the same colour to the man.

9 ▲ Add shadows With the No.4 round brush, and a mix of cerulean blue, ivory black and burnt umber, wash thin shadows on to the building and thicker ones on the rocks. Paint the flag in cerulean blue. Use black with a touch of blue to paint the woman's hair, then wash cadmium yellow over the man and the bins. With watery Indian red and a cerulean blue-black, add shadows on the path. Wash burnt umber shadows on the wall.

10 ▲ Bring up some details With a No.6 round brush, add cerulean blue and black shadowing on the man's bag and left foot, and burnt umber lettering and details on the bins.

ANCHOR THE ROCKS

If you feel that the middle distance of your picture looks too flat and fades into the far distance, increase the tonal contrast here to build up form. In this painting, the dark bluish-black shadows painted on the rocks anchor this part of the picture within the whole scene.

TROUBLE SHOOTER

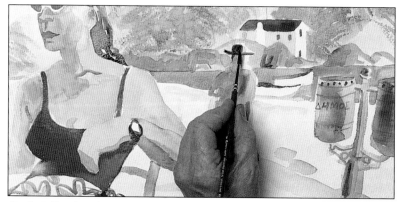

11 ▲ Develop the figures Use the Nos.1 and 6 rounds for the details. Define the woman's chair with Winsor blue. Use black for her watch-strap and hair, permanent rose for her top and a mix of permanent rose, cerulean blue and black for her sarong. Add Winsor red lips and burnt umber facial features, then put cadmium yellow on her glasses and skirt. Define the man's hat and the boats with black and burnt umber.

12 ▲ **Outline with pencils** Using a No.12 round brush, paint in some stonework on the wall with Naples yellow gouache, outlining it with a purple coloured pencil. Add linear detail across the whole picture with purple and ultramarine coloured pencils.

13 ▲ **Intensify the darks** Mix burnt umber and Winsor red to paint dark shadows across the woman's skin with the No.6 round. Add a wash of ultramarine mixed with ivory black and burnt umber to the rocks, a mix of Winsor green and ivory black to the foliage, and burnt umber and black shadow to the man's face.

Master Strokes

Paul Gauguin (1848–1903)
Tahitian Women on a Beach

This picture was painted in the year Gauguin left France to begin a new life in Tahiti. Compared to the light, airy feel of the painting in the project, it has a solidity and depth that is achieved with the emphatic application of colour. The dark bands of the sea form a decorative device behind the heads of the two women and contrast strongly with the pale yellow sand of the beach.

White foam adds a touch of realism to the sea, which is otherwise highly stylised.

Gauguin is known for flattening space, but this figure's face is subtly modelled in browns and green.

A FEW STEPS FURTHER

Step back and look at your picture to see if it could benefit from a little more depth of tone. A mix of ultramarine and ivory black is useful to deepen shadows without making them appear too harsh. Continue using coloured pencils to put in additional details and return to the fan brush to build up the tree foliage.

14 ◀ **Enrich the detail** Use the purple pencil to define details on elements, such as the litter-bins and the man's body and bag. Wash a mix of ultramarine and ivory black over the man's trousers and add burnt umber shadows along the top of the wall.

15 ▲ **Finish off the foliage** Using the No.4 fan brush, stipple more dry, olive green watercolour across the trees. Turning to the No.4 round brush and a mix of Winsor green and ultramarine, paint in some blue-green shadows at the base of the trees. Draw in fine branches with the purple pencil.

16 ▼ **Deepen the blue-blacks** Take up a mid-green coloured pencil to add the pointed cypress trees emerging from the tree-tops on the far right of the picture. Using the No.4 round brush, add more ultramarine and ivory black on the left of the painting, along the rocks and in the woman's hair.

THE FINISHED PICTURE

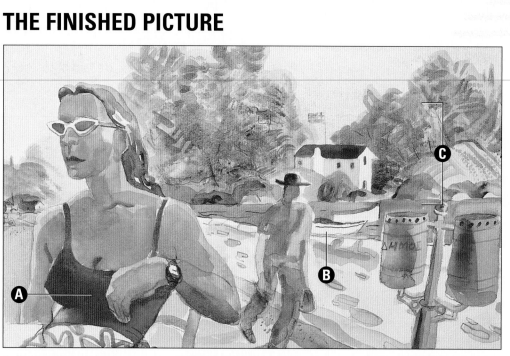

A Grainy texture
The grain of the paper shows through the thin colour washes on the woman's vest-top, and helps to suggest the texture of the fabric.

B Unpainted areas
In classic watercolour fashion, white areas such as the boats, the building and the woman's watch-face and sunglass frames were left as exposed white paper.

C Suggesting distance
The blue of the water in the mid ground and the blue-greens of the trees in the background are cool colours that help convey recession in the scene.

Tree-lined road

Transform a bleak, monochromatic winter scene into a warm, atmospheric watercolour by adding a little sunshine and touches of colourful autumn foliage.

The two stately trees outlined against the sky are a major feature of this village scene. The reference photograph was taken in the winter – a good time for artists to study trees, as, devoid of foliage, their shape, structure and proportions are easier to see. What you learn from painting winter trees will reap rewards when you come to paint trees in summer and autumn.

With his long experience of observing and painting trees, the artist felt free to add some clumps of autumn foliage to the bare winter ones in the photograph to give them colour and interest. By using warm colours throughout and adding a blue sky, the artist has created a lively interpretation of the subject.

To enliven further the colours and emphasize the contrast, the artist added sunlight to the overcast scene. In the painting, the sun is low and off to the right, throwing long shadows across the road. It also brings out the cylindrical form of the trees and the angular form of the cottage.

Using a rigger brush

The branches of the trees were painted with a rigger brush which can make very expressive marks. If you've never used one, make some practice strokes first to learn how to control the brush. Try sketching some simple trees. Hold the brush near the ferrule to make small marks, but, if you want to exploit the flexibility of the brush for creating elegant, tapering lines, hold it lightly, nearer the end of the handle. Keep your hand still and move the brush with your fingers, letting the long hairs twist and bend to make delicate strokes.

▼ **Warm, sunlit areas contrast with cooler shadows and an expanse of blue sky in this picturesque study of a tree-lined road.**

Piece of 300gsm (140lb) rough watercolour paper 30 x 42cm (11½ x 16½in)

4B pencil

7 watercolours: raw sienna; cadmium red; ultramarine; cobalt blue; light red; lemon yellow; burnt sienna

Brushes: 38mm (1½in) and 19mm (¾in) flats; Nos. 14 and 6 rounds; No. 1 rigger

Mixing palette or dish

Jar of water

Ruler

FIRST STEPS

1 ▶ Sketch the scene
Using a 4B pencil, make an outline drawing of the scene. You might find it helpful to mark the horizon line lightly and visualize the lines of the cottage roof and walls receding to the vanishing point. Feel free to omit ugly details such as the street light and road markings.

2 ◀ Lay down the initial wash
Tilt up your board slightly. Using a 38mm (1½in) flat brush, dampen the paper, except for the cottage area, with clean water. Change to a 19mm (¾in) flat and mix a pale wash of raw sienna – make the colour a little stronger than you need, as it will dilute on the damp surface of the paper. Brush the wash across the lower part of the sky and the foreground.

3 ▼ Add warmth to the sky While the paper is still just damp, sweep a band of thinly diluted cadmium red across the lower sky, just above the band of raw sienna. Allow it to melt softly into the raw sienna to give a touch of autumnal afternoon warmth.

DEVELOPING THE PICTURE

These initial blushes of colour will establish the overall warm tonality of the scene, as they will glow through the overlaid washes of colour to come.

4 ▲ Paint the upper sky Mix a wash of ultramarine and a little cobalt blue. Still using the 19mm (¾in) flat brush, sweep this across the upper sky, letting the colour drift gently down the damp paper in a graduated wash.

5 ▶ Finish the sky
Lighten the wash with more water as you work down the paper. Make flicking diagonal strokes at the edges of the picture to give some movement to the sky (as long as the paper is still damp, these will dry as soft shapes). Leave the mid-section of the sky untouched.

6 ▲ Block in the background Use some of the ultramarine sky colour to make an underwash for the line of trees glimpsed in the far distance. Make a series of short, vertical strokes with the tip of the brush.

7 ▼ Underpaint the trees Lightly place a few broad, vertical strokes of burnt sienna around the tops of the trees, keeping the brush almost dry. Pick up a little more raw sienna on the brush tip and paint the tree trunks with short, horizontal strokes.

8 ▶ **Paint the cottage roof** Add some cadmium red to the raw sienna on your palette to warm it. Change to a No. 14 round brush and paint the roofs of the cottage, leaving flecks of white paper to stand for the branches of the small tree on the right.

9 ▼ **Paint the chimneys** Darken the mix slightly with a hint of ultramarine and, using a No. 6 round brush, paint the chimneys and chimney pots. Leave slivers of bare paper for the flashing at the top and base of the chimneys.

10 ▲ **Put in the windows** Use a very dilute mix of ultramarine and cobalt blue to show the sky reflected in the window panes, varying the tone to suggest light and shadow. Leave the glazing bars white, but blur them slightly so that they are not over-defined.

11 ◀ **Paint the garden wall** Mix together cadmium red, light red and a touch of ultramarine to make a slightly cooler red than that used on the roof. Paint the garden wall with the tip of the No. 14 round brush, leaving flecks of white here and there. Paint around the posts in the foreground. Mix a green from lemon yellow and ultramarine, and use this to suggest moss and foliage growing on the wall.

12 ► **Return to the trees** Mix lemon yellow and a little raw sienna to make a light, warm yellow. With the No. 6 round brush, start to define the main clumps of foliage on the tall trees. Hold the brush almost parallel with the paper and work it with a sideways motion, letting the colour break up on the textured surface of the paper.

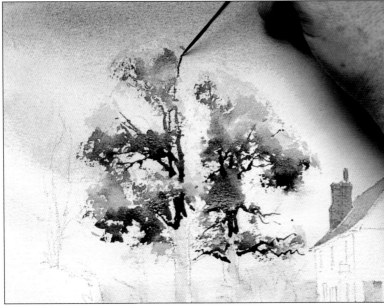

13 ▼ **Paint dark foliage** Add more raw sienna and some ultramarine to the wash. Put in the dark green clumps of foliage, again laying the brush almost flat to the paper and skipping it lightly across the surface with a sideways motion to make broken-edged marks, as before.

14 ◄ **Paint the branches** Use broken strokes of burnt sienna to suggest clumps of brown leaves, letting the colour blur into the green. Mix a near-black from ultramarine, raw sienna and light red, and paint the branches with a No. 1 rigger brush. Start at the trunk and pull the brush in the direction of growth, skipping in and out of the foliage clumps. Vary the pressure on the brush to make the lines swell and taper.

Express yourself
Pen and colour wash

This country scene has a similar composition to the one in the step-by-step. The curve of the road leads the eye into the picture and tall trees dominate the sky area. This time the scene is worked up in more detail. The initial line drawing is made with a dip pen and waterproof Indian ink and is then washed over with watercolour. The ink lines give structure to the image and sharpen up architectural features, while the freely applied washes create a fresh, lively feel. The pen has been used in a similar way to the rigger brush to suggest the tree branches.

15 ▶ **Put in distant trees** With the No. 6 round brush, model the tree trunks by painting their shadowed sides with a mix of ultramarine and light red (see Expert Advice, right). Suggest the slanting shadows cast on to the trunks by the branches. Paint the more distant trees with varied mixes of ultramarine and light red, leaving a broken glimmer of white paper along the top of the wall.

EXPERT ADVICE
Modelling the trunks

To suggest the cylindrical form of the tree trunks, first dampen them with water, then put in the shadow colour down one edge with a slightly wavering vertical stroke. The colour will fade out softly on the damp surface, creating a tonal graduation from dark to light.

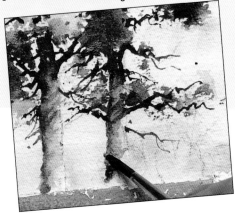

16 ◀ **Work on the foreground** Use the same colours and techniques as for the two main trees to paint the foliage and grass on the left (paint these slightly more freely – elements on the edges of the image should be understated, so as not to compete with the centre of interest). Mix lemon yellow with a touch of ultramarine and paint the grass verge on the right with loose strokes of the No. 14 brush.

17 ▲ **Model the cottage** Suggest the kerb with light red and ultramarine. Mix a dilute wash of ultramarine and a hint of light red. Using the No. 6 brush, paint shadows on the brick wall, roofs and chimneys. Clean your brush, then put in the shadows on the cottage.

18 ▲ **Add cast shadows** Indicate the kerb on the left with curved strokes of raw sienna greyed with ultramarine. Leave to dry, then use the ultramarine/light red mix to put in the shadows cast across the road by the small tree on the right. Darken the mix slightly for the broken shadow in the immediate foreground, cast by unseen trees to the right.

A FEW STEPS FURTHER

The picture is almost complete, the contrast of warm and cool colours capturing the atmosphere of a crisp, bright autumn day. All that remains is to bring in a few dark details to give the image a bit of punch.

19 ▼ **Finish painting the cottage** Paint the barge boards at the gable end of the cottage with the ultramarine/light red mix. Steady the brush by resting the ferrule on the edge of a ruler held at an angle to the paper.

20 ▲ **Paint the small tree** Use the rigger brush and mixes of raw sienna and ultramarine to put in dark reflections in the cottage windows and to paint the small tree on the right. Vary the tones to evoke the play of light and shadow on the trunk and branches. Skip the brush lightly over the paper to suggest finer branches.

THE FINISHED PICTURE

A Calligraphic strokes
The fine rigger brush makes expressive strokes that suggest the gnarled and twisted forms of the branches.

B Stable design
Both the horizon line and the tallest tree have been positioned according to the 'rule of thirds', creating a balanced composition.

C Foreground shadows
The blue-grey shadows cast by unseen trees in the foreground help to 'frame' the scene along the bottom edge.

Details and textures in watercolour

Although watercolours can be used in a free and loose manner, they can also be used to create intricate, highly finished paintings.

▼ The artist has used aerial perspective to create a sense of depth. The distant mountain is rendered in cool blues and greens, while the grassy areas are painted in warm browns. Note also that the figure in the reference photo (top right) has been omitted to create an unsullied scene.

Using a simple pocket set of watercolour paints, the artist for this step-by-step created a sweeping rendition of a Scottish landscape – full of subtle variations of colour and texture – using a simple pocket set of watercolour paints.

In the foreground, features such as the tree branches and intricate shadows are brought into sharp focus using carefully controlled lines made with a fine brush. In contrast to these lines, lively elements have been created by applying the paint in unconventional ways.

Flicking paint

Sprays of seeded grasses, for example, were added in the foreground by gently flicking paint on to the paper. And outstretched, leafy branches have been implied by blowing small pools of wet paint across the paper. These details give the impression of wind blowing across the scene, playing on the grass and foliage as it passes.

In the background, however, little detail has been added. Instead, broad strokes have been used to create the smooth surface of the mountain in a harmonious range of greens, browns and blues. To create these colours, you need constantly to mix small amounts of different colours into your main washes.

It is, therefore, vital to wash your brush often to avoid muddy colours. Dry off the brush on a wad of tissues, or flick the spare water out on to a newspaper positioned on the floor.

> **YOU WILL NEED**
>
> Piece of 300gsm (140lb) NOT watercolour paper 40 x 60cm (16 x 24 in)
>
> HB pencil
>
> Brushes: Nos. 8, 6 and 2 flats; Nos. 4 and 00 rounds
>
> Large jar of water
>
> 10 watercolours: ultramarine; cobalt blue; crimson; burnt umber; emerald green; ochre; orange; forest green; cadmium yellow; black
>
> Large flat mixing dish
>
> Paper tissues

FIRST STROKES

1 ▼ **Sketch out the scene** With an HB pencil, sketch out the main features of your scene. In the palest areas, press only lightly with the pencil, capturing the faintest impression of the ragged outlines of the foliage. In darker areas, you can block in the shadows with a firmer scribbling action. These pencil marks are an important foundation on which to build your detailed composition.

2 ▲ **Prepare the sky** Use a No. 8 flat brush and clean water to wet the sky area, making a neat edge along the line of the mountain. Do not let the area get too wet, or the paper might become wrinkled – but put on enough water to make the paper surface glisten.

3 ▶ Wash in the sky colours Put touches of ultramarine and cobalt blue into a pool of clean water on your mixing dish. Working quickly on the wet paper, boldly mark in the blue sky above the mountain. The water on the paper will make the edges of the colour blend into the white areas. Clean the brush. With tiny spots of crimson and burnt umber, colour a second pool of water and wash in the undersides of the clouds.

DEVELOPING THE PICTURE

Now that you have established the basic outlines and washed in the sky, you can begin work on the landscape itself. To achieve a range of lively textural effects, use various methods of applying the paint, from dabbing and hatching to spattering.

4 ▶ Block in the foliage With clean water, wet the paper in the main areas of foliage. Mix a wash of emerald green with touches of burnt umber and ultramarine. With a No. 4 round brush, block in the foliage, using a dabbing action. Let the patches of colour overlap and run into one another, leaving patches of plain white paper in between.

5 ◀ Establish the foreground Wash the paper in the foreground with clean water. Mix a wash of ochre and burnt umber with a touch of orange, then use the flattened tip of the No. 8 flat brush to sketch in the grass. Create strong, textural strokes to make these foreground features stand out. As you work, pull touches of other colours into your wash – emerald green, forest green, burnt umber, ochre and cadmium yellow.

6 ◄ **Work into the shadows** With a strong wash of ultramarine, forest green and a tiny touch of black, use a No. 8 flat brush to work in the deep shadows under the bushes. Visually, this makes a strong line to draw the eye across the painting. Use tight hatching marks along the edge of the grassy area to give the impression of grasses growing up across the shadows.

7 ▼ **Establish the mountain** Wait until the sky area is dry so that the edge of the mountain will remain crisp. The mountain is worked on dry paper with a wash of burnt umber, plus touches of cobalt blue and ultramarine to give it a cold, distant appearance. Use long, flat strokes of the No. 8 flat brush following the contours of the mountain. Draw a touch more ultramarine into the mix for the darker (right) side of the mountain.

8 ▲ **Develop the foliage** Using a No. 6 flat brush, dab emerald green with a little ochre and burnt umber on to the leafy areas. For a lively effect, identify pools of green paint around the edge of the tree. With your face close to the paper, blow sharply across the surface to throw spurts of paint outwards from the tree. Remove unwanted spots of paint with a tissue.

9 ▶ Mark in the twigs
Use a No. 00 round brush and burnt umber paint to mark in the trunk and main branches of the tree. Some are visible between the green patchy areas. Others stretch out sideways to support external foliage. Refer back to your subject to ensure that your marks remain characteristic of the tree. To mark out the finest twigs, see Expert Advice, opposite.

10 ▲ Work a foreground tree To create a light area, draw a wet brush along the line of the trunk. Dry the brush on a tissue, then draw it down the same line to leach out the colour. Use a mix of forest green, ultramarine and a little black for the shadows around the tree. Develop the foliage of the large tree and bushes, using the same colours as in step 8. Add ochre to help the foreground tree stand out.

TROUBLESHOOTER

REMOVING PAINT SPOTS

If paint splashes on to a plain area such as the sky, it can be removed with some quick action. While the paint is still wet, press a clean paper tissue on top of the mark. Add a drop of clean water to the mark, blot with tissue and repeat until the mark disappears.

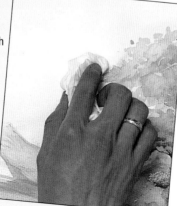

11 ▲ Enliven the foreground grass Add touches of orange and emerald green to ochre and use a No. 6 flat brush to paint in coarse, grassy marks in the foreground of the composition. For a lively texture, make some flicking marks upwards from the base of the grass stems. To do this, load the brush with paint, then hold it in one hand close to the paper and pull the bristles back with the fingers of your other hand. Release with a flick upwards to spatter paint across the picture. Remove unwanted spots of paint quickly with a tissue.

12 ▼ Develop the middle distance Using a No. 6 flat brush, mix a wash of cadmium yellow with a tiny touch of burnt umber to block in the field in the middle distance, behind the bushes. Put more burnt umber and a touch of orange into the wash, then use a stiff-bristled toothbrush to scrub the colour across the middle range of the grassy area. Mimic the textural lines of the grasses with your strokes.

**EXPERT ADVICE
Indenting fine marks**

Before you paint the finest twig lines in the tree structure, use the pointed wooden end of a paint brush to press indentations into the surface of the watercolour paper. These will make tiny 'rivulets', which will hold the dark paint neatly in delicate twig shapes.

13 ▼ Deepen the tree shadows Add a touch of black to burnt umber and, using the tip of a No. 4 round brush, work in the deepest shadows on the trunk and branches of the tree. Use the black paint very sparingly, saving it for really striking details such as these.

14 ▲ Strengthen the features Stand back from the picture and judge the tonal balance between the different areas. Using the No. 8 flat brush, strengthen the main features. Use a wash of ultramarine with touches of black and crimson to deepen the shadow areas on the mountain. Draw more ultramarine into the mix to establish the deepest shadows. Add ochre to emerald green in varying proportions to enliven the upper parts of the bushes.

15 ▼ **Add distance detail** Use the technique from step 10 to leach out colour from under one of the bushes. With a No. 00 round brush, wash in a mix of cadmium yellow with a touch of burnt umber. Once dry, paint black trunk details.

16 ▲ **Finalize the balance** Using the No. 8 flat brush and a mix of cobalt blue, ultramarine and emerald green, wash in the lower area of the mountain behind the distant trees. Add trunks and branches to the small tree on the left using the techniques from step 13. With the No. 6 flat brush and a mix of forest green and ultramarine, use a dabbing action to develop the leaf detail of both the small and large trees.

A FEW STEPS FURTHER

The composition is now complete, but you might wish to draw out some of the character of the scene with more work on fine detail, such as the grass and branches.

17 ▲ **Develop the detail** With a strong mix of burnt umber and black, and, using a No. 2 flat brush, paint in more branches and twigs on the largest tree. Strengthen existing branches to the front of the tree, but leave the ones nearer the back more washed out, to give a sense of three dimensions.

Express yourself
Focus on texture

The chosen scene is characterized by contrasting areas of smooth sky, sculpted mountain surface and detailed foliage areas. To focus on these textures rather than the colours, discard your paints and take up a piece of charcoal or, as here, a burnt umber soft pastel. Working with a loose style on NOT watercolour paper, capture the textures with a variety of strokes. Use soft, scribbling motions for the shadows, flowing marks for the contours of the mountain, and a hatching action for the grass. Use the charcoal or pastel on its side to block in larger areas of smooth shadow.

18 ▶ Add sweeps of colour
As a finishing touch, you could convey the impression of the sweeping movements of a strong wind. Make up a strong mix of burnt umber and ochre. With a No. 4 round brush, make bold, slanting marks across the foreground area to suggest the blown and tumbled grasses.

THE FINISHED PICTURE

A Sense of distance
The cool blues and greens of the distant mountain recede, helping create a sense of depth. They contrast with the warmer ochres, oranges and browns in the foreground.

B Contrasting textures
Hatched brush strokes and spattered paint created a lively texture for the scrubby grassland. This contrasts with the smooth sky and sculpted surface of the mountain.

C Strong diagonal
The line of trees and the slope in the middle distance help create dynamic diagonals that cut across the picture. They provide a pleasing echo of the sloped profile of the mountain.

Seaside studies

Explore the different effects that you can achieve by using white and tinted watercolour papers for two atmospheric seaside studies.

The colour of the support has a profound effect on the character of a watercolour painting. White paper maximises the brilliance of watercolour washes, while tinted papers create atmosphere and a sense of unity. These differences are illustrated by the two small watercolours of beach scenes on the following pages – one worked on white watercolour paper, the other on a pale blue paper.

Popular white

The most popular support for painting in watercolour is white or off-white paper.

▼ White watercolour paper left unpainted enhances the sparkle of strong sunlight on water in this lively beach scene.

A white ground gives maximum luminosity to the layers of transparent watercolour washes.

With white paper, you work from light to dark, reserving the white areas by painting around them or masking them with masking fluid or paper. The areas of unpainted white provide light local colour and bright highlights.

Moody tints

An advantage of using a tinted paper, on the other hand, is the way it instantly sets a mood. Yellow and buff tones create a warm, cheering image, while blues and greys produce more restrained studies and moody landscapes.

Tinted paper inevitably shows through here and there in a painting, pulling elements together and imposing a sense of unity. With broken-colour techniques, such as scumbling or stippling, the tinted ground can be glimpsed between the patches of overlaid colour – the paint colours combine with the colour of the support to create an optical mix. With a tinted paper, your lightest tone in a painting is the colour of the paper. If you need a lighter area or some highlights, you'll need to use semi-opaque white (Chinese white) or body colour mixed from this. In the second step-by-step project, on page 2235, Chinese white has been used to achieve the effect of white clouds against a blue sky.

If you can't find the coloured support you want or if you'd like to experiment, you can create your own tinted paper very simply by laying a flat wash, using a large wash brush or a sponge. The advantage is that you can produce any colour or tone you like – you can even introduce a scumbled or mottled texture. By using an acrylic instead of a watercolour wash, you'll reduce the chance of the background colour dissolving and mixing with subsequent layers of wash.

PROJECT 1

BEACH SCENE ON WHITE PAPER

Exploit the light-reflective qualities of white watercolour paper for this sparkling study of a sunny beach scene. The image was created quickly, using washes applied wet-on-wet to create soft blendings of colour and tone. To pull the image into focus, use wet-on-dry techniques to add a few crisp points of interest – the beach umbrellas and figures. Keep your work simple and avoid unnecessary detail. (The painting was based on the left-hand photo above, although the background bush was taken from the right image.)

1 ▲ Lay in the sky Tilt your drawing board so that it is resting at a shallow angle. Use a 3B pencil to make a very simple drawing, indicating the horizon, the shoreline and the parasols. Mix cobalt blue and phthalo blue watercolour and, using a No.12 round brush, apply a basic wash to the sky area.

2 ▶ Paint the sea Brush water over the sea, working around the parasols and the rocky outcrop. Apply cobalt blue and phthalo blue wet-on-wet, so that the colours bleed together. Leave to dry.

3 ▶ Paint the parasols
Mix Venetian red and gold ochre, then lay a pale wash of this over the sandy beach. Add touches of the same colour to the straw parasols and along the rocky outcrop.

4 ▼ Add shadows to the beach Mix phthalo blue and gold ochre and apply this colour to the distant bush. Add touches of pure colour for a variegated effect. Mix a wash of alizarin crimson and cobalt blue to create a violet for the shadows. Wet the beach area on the right and flood in this wash, allowing the paint to seep across to the left. Leave to dry.

Express yourself
A tinted background

The tinted paper used for this small sketch in acrylics provides a warm undercolour for a more intimate beach scene. The buff shade is left unpainted in places, unifying the composition and extending the palette of blues, greys and creams used for the water, rocks and sand.

EXPERT ADVICE
Creating soft edges

If you want to create a soft edge without blending two colours wet-on-wet, wait until the previous wash has dried, then wet the area where the new wash is to be applied. Flood paint into the centre of the wet area. The colour will bleed outwards from the centre, creating a softly graduated edge.

5 ▶ **Add details** Mix Venetian red and cobalt blue and paint the parasol poles. Use the same colour to indicate the figures on the beach. Strengthen the mix to add dark shadows on the parasols. For the figures' clothing, touch in dabs of alizarin crimson and a mix of alizarin and phthalo blue.

▲ **Mix colours to create subtle shades: use phthalo blue and cobalt blue for the sky; gold ochre and Venetian red for the beach; and alizarin crimson and ultramarine for the cast shadows of the figures.**

6 ◀ **Add cast shadows** Add some smaller figures in the distance – their diminishing size creates a sense of recession and space in the picture. Mix alizarin crimson and ultramarine, then add shadows under the figures. These anchor them to the beach and show the direction of the sunlight.

THE FINISHED PICTURE

A Sparkling water
The white of the paper – showing through the blue wash – suggests sunlight sparkling on the water.

B Soft shadows
A wet-on-wet technique gives soft, naturalistic edges to the shadows falling across the beach.

C Simplified figures
Simple dabs and dashes of colour come together in the eye to suggest convincing figures.

PROJECT 2

WATER SCENE ON TINTED PAPER

Use pale blue paper and a limited palette of colours to create this tranquil scene. The blue ground is allowed to stand for the distant hills and the highlights on the water. It also establishes the serene mood and provides a linking tone that holds the entire image together.

1 ▼ Lay in a wash for the sea Make a pale mix of Winsor blue watercolour. Starting at the horizon, use a No.12 round brush to apply a loose wash to the blue paper. Take the wash downwards, leaving unpainted areas where the water is lightest – the pale blue of the paper stands for the bright surface of the water.

2 ▼ Paint the clouds Mix a wash of Chinese white. Scumble this semi-opaque colour over the sky – work around the shapes of hills, which should be left as unpainted silhouettes.

3 ▲ Establish the horizon Load the No.12 brush with clean water and wet an area along and just below the horizon. Mix a wash of ultramarine and flood the colour into the wet area, creating a darker blue along the horizon.

▼ Watercolour papers are available in a range of tempting soft shades, such as green, blue, yellow and cream.

4 ▲ Paint the edge of the bay Mix gold ochre with phthalo blue. Apply this colour to the trees and vegetation that edge the bay, using the tip of the brush to describe their silhouettes. Add more blue to the mix to vary the tone on the vegetation on the right.

5 ▼ Darken the sea Wet the area of sea where the jetty will be, then flood in a pale wash of phthalo blue. While that is still wet, touch in a band of ultramarine. Notice how the paint spreads and merges subtly into adjacent wet areas.

6 ▲ Start to paint the jetty While the sea is still wet, make a mix of Winsor blue and purple lake. Using the tip of a No.3 brush, indicate the shadows on the jetty supports and under the walkway. Mix purple lake and Venetian red for the darkest shadows. Allow to dry.

Master Strokes

John Wonnacott (b. 1940)
Chalkwell Beach, Floodwater Overflow, Late Afternoon

This beach scene, painted in oils, is full of life. Figures running, playing and engaged in various other seaside activities animate the foreground. The composition is slightly unusual in that it is divided exactly in half horizontally. However, this half-and-half division is prevented from being static by the dominant diagonal of the jetty, which brings a dynamic element into the picture.

© Courtesy of Agnews & Sons

The tall verticals of the posts and masts jutting into the sky link the upper and lower halves of the picture.

Long shadows cast by the figures and the posts suggest the time of day in the painting – late afternoon.

Pools of seawater left on the beach by the receding tide add eye-catching patches of white, pale blue and grey.

197

7 ▼ Work detail on the jetty When the support is dry, mix a wash of Venetian red and use the tip of the No.3 brush to paint the jetty's walkway and the posts supporting it.

8 ▼ Add light tones Add a touch of gold ochre and Venetian red to Chinese white, and use this creamy mix for the top surface of the walkway, which is catching the light. Use the same mix for the lightest supports and for the figures on the jetty and their reflections.

9 ▶ Develop the figures Use mixes of viridian and phthalo blue to paint the clothes on the figures. Then mix a brown from viridian and Venetian red for the dark areas on the figures – the hair, the shadows on the flesh tones, and the standing figure's vest. Use the same warm colour to add definition to the structure of the jetty.

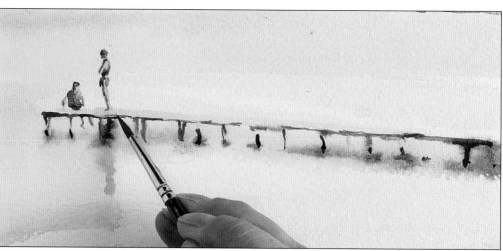

THE FINISHED PICTURE

A Hazy sky
Semi-opaque Chinese white was scumbled over the blue ground to capture the effect of a hazy blue sky.

B Blue hills
The pale blue of the support was left unpainted to stand for the hills in the distance.

C Focal point
The two figures at the end of the jetty form a point of interest in an otherwise uninterrupted landscape.

Snow scene in watercolour

Use a range of watercolour techniques to paint this tranquil landscape under a blanket of snow.

Snow transforms the landscape, softening edges and imposing a tonal harmony. In bright sunshine, its reflective quality gives the landscape a dazzling brilliance, with trees and other features standing out in contrast to the prevailing whiteness.

When painting a snow scene in watercolour, you need to work logically from light to dark, conserving the white of the paper for the snow and applying washes carefully to the surrounding areas. Use masking fluid for details such as the snow on the bridge.

Warm and cool colour contrasts are very evident in snowy landscapes. Shadows are a characteristic blue-lilac colour and were often depicted in winter scenes by Impressionist painters, who understood how they complemented the yellowish orange of the winter sunlight. In this project, the warm browns and oranges of the trees contrast with the stark white snow and the cool, blue shadows, emphasising the chilly conditions.

▼ **Dark, crisp foreground details contrast with softly blended, washed colours in this peaceful winter scene.**

YOU WILL NEED

Stretched sheet of 300gsm (140lb) Not watercolour paper

Masking tape

2B pencil

Brushes: Nos.10, 7 and 4 rounds

Watercolour palette

Masking fluid

Old brush

9 watercolours: Yellow ochre; Winsor blue; Burnt umber; Ultramarine; Cadmium orange; Cadmium red; Raw umber; Raw sienna; Sepia

FIRST STROKES

1 ▶ **Draw the landscape** To create a white border for the finished picture, stick strips of masking tape around the edge of the stretched paper. Using a 2B pencil, make a drawing of the landscape, leaving the snowy areas white. Work lightly in the background and use crisp, emphatic lines for the bridge and tree in the foreground.

2 ◀ **Lay a graduated wash** Turn the picture upside down and prop it at a shallow angle. Wet the sky area with a No.10 brush dipped in water. Lay in the area just above the horizon with a yellow ochre wash. Then lay a band of Winsor blue wash under the yellow ochre. The washes will blend to create a soft edge.

▲ Winsor blue, a cool blue, is ideal for painting a chilly, wintry sky. It was allowed to bleed into yellow ochre towards the horizon to create a delicate neutral undertone for the trees.

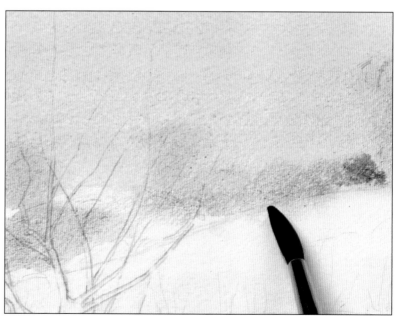

3 ▲ **Indicate the distant trees** While the sky is still wet, lay in the shapes of the distant trees, using mixes of burnt umber and ultramarine for the darker trees, and cadmium orange and cadmium red for the orange ones. The paint will bleed, creating soft edges. Leave to dry.

4 ▲ Add darker woodland Use darker versions of the same mixes to paint another layer of trees. Mix Winsor blue with burnt umber or cadmium orange for the darkest areas, working wet on wet. While the area is still wet, apply touches of Winsor blue mixed with ultramarine along the edge of the woodland. Leave to dry.

5 ▲ Spatter on masking fluid Before applying masking fluid to the vegetation on the left, protect the adjacent areas with sheets of paper. Dip an old brush in the masking fluid, then tap it with your finger to deposit droplets and streaks over the area. Leave to dry.

6 ▲ Mask the bridge Paint masking fluid over the walkway of the bridge and the tops of the plinths, then lay a band of masking fluid along each rail. Let the mask dry thoroughly.

DEVELOPING THE PICTURE

With the sky and background established and the snowy details in the foreground masked, you can get on with applying the washes and fine details that will pull the picture together. Because the white of the paper is a positive element rather than simply blank paper, the picture is actually further advanced than would be the case with any other subject.

7 ▶ Lay shadows on the snow Wet the paper where you are going to work. Using a No.7 brush, lay a very dilute wash of cadmium orange over the sunlit snow on the right. While the paper is still wet, lay a dilute wash of ultramarine over the areas of cast shadow. The edges of the orange and blue washes will bleed. Leave to dry naturally.

8 ◀ Paint the stream Mix a wash of Winsor blue for the stream and apply it using the No.7 brush. While the blue is still wet, introduce a touch of burnt umber for the reflections of the vegetation beside the stream. Add a touch of cadmium orange here and there.

EXPERT ADVICE
Painting winter trees

In order to paint trees, particularly leafless ones in a winter scene, consider their structure and growth pattern carefully. Use the flat of the brush for the main branches and the tip of the brush for the smaller ones. When you paint towards the end of a branch, the line will naturally become thinner as you complete the stroke, creating a realistic effect.

9 ▲ **Add details to the distant trees** Using a No.4 brush with raw umber and a touch of Winsor blue, apply light, delicate brush strokes to suggest the trunks and main branches of the distant trees. Use the very tip of the brush to paint in the smaller branches.

10 ◄ **Add foreground detail** Paint the fence and the hedge on the right with a mix of burnt umber and cadmium orange. Wet the paper on the left, then, with a No.10 brush, use the same wash to paint the vegetation, creating spiky stalks with the brush tip. Add Winsor blue and ultramarine, then dab touches of the raw sienna here and there. Leave to dry.

Master Strokes

Claude Monet (1840–1926)
The Magpie

Monet painted this atmospheric snow scene around 1870, when he had already become interested in working in the Impressionistic style for which he is renowned. The effects of light and shade are one of the main features of the painting.

The white of the snow is broken up by flecks of yellow, suggesting the reflections of winter sunlight glinting from the surface of the snow. The shadows are a pale grey-blue – a cool colour complementing the warmer tones of the bright snow.

The dark shape of the magpie, which stands out distinctively against the snowy landscape, forms the focal point of the painting.

Dabs of yellow and blue with a few touches of pink enliven the surface of the snow in the foreground.

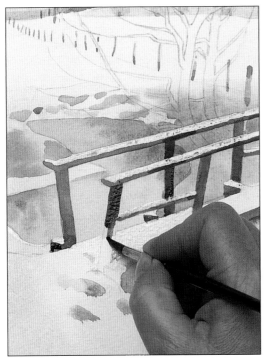

11 ▲ **Paint the bridge** Change back to the No.4 brush and paint the bridge with sepia. This man-made structure is an important focus in the picture, as its geometric shape contrasts with the soft forms elsewhere in the composition. Leave to dry thoroughly.

A FEW STEPS FURTHER

The painting is now well established. By contrasting the warm sunlight with the cool shadows on the snow, the artist has captured the sparkling light and chill of the scene. Add more texture in the foreground if you wish.

13 ◄ **Add shadows** Use the No.4 brush and an ultramarine wash to paint the shadows in the trampled snow in the foreground. With the same wash, paint the crisp shadows cast by the rails of the bridge.

12 ▲ **Paint the trees** Remove the masking fluid from the bridge and the vegetation on the left by gently rubbing the surface with your fingertips. Then use sepia and the No.4 brush to paint the trees by the bridge. Make them dark and well defined to contrast with the distant trees and create a sense of recession from foreground to background.

Express yourself
Introduce a figure

The watercolour snowscape in the step-by-step has a sense of tranquillity and solitude. By introducing a figure, the artist has created an entirely different mood. The man trudging through the snow suggests a narrative – we wonder where he is going and why. The tree on the left has changed the dynamic of the composition, providing both a counterpoint for the single human figure and another route to lead the eye into the picture.

14 ▲ **Add spattered textures** Protect adjacent areas by covering them with sheets of paper. Dip the No.4 brush in the ultramarine wash and spatter colour on the snow by tapping the brush briskly with your forefinger. Load the brush with raw sienna and repeat the process.

15 ▲ **Paint the dry grass** Mix a raw umber wash and, using the tip of the No.4 brush and a firm yet gentle flicking gesture, paint in some tufts of dry grass in the left-hand foreground area.

THE FINISHED PICTURE

A Snow white paper
The snow is represented by the white of the paper itself, washed in places with yellow ochre and in others with ultramarine.

B Cool shadows
Cool, violet-blue shadows provide a complementary contrast to the orange sunlight of winter.

C Crisp contrast
The dark, crisply painted bridge and trees create a focal point which draws the eye into the painting.

French street in watercolour

Using warm yellows, ochres and crimson, layers of watercolour are built up to create the buildings in this quiet corner of a French town.

Buildings, both old and new, can be fun and challenging to paint. France is rich with attractive buildings that make interesting paintings.

Looking at the angles

The artist has based her painting on a photograph of the small town of Soubes, near Montpellier in the south of France. The viewer is separated from the scene by the railings running right across the foreground, but the eye is drawn into the picture and down the street by the buildings that sweep in from the right and stretch away to the left.

To capture the angles of the buildings and to achieve a convincing sense of perspective, the artist took time over her preparatory drawing. She sketched in plenty of pencil guidelines running along the buildings towards their respective vanishing points on the horizon. She then used these to help her place the windows and doors correctly.

The way in which the paint is used enhances the sense of depth. The buildings and their architectural features at the end of the street are merely suggested with a light wash of colour, and this blurring helps to create the effect of the scene stretching away into the distance.

Creating a sense of place

The building on the right and the stone wall supporting the railings in the foreground have a real sense of solidity in this painting. The artist has created this impression by building up layers of colour. A light wash with a pale Naples yellow lays the foundation, then darker but still warm tones are flooded in as the painting progresses.

Selecting details

The artist has not included every detail of the original scene. Instead, she has looked for the elements that capture the sense of place: the shutters, the railings, the electric cables that snake around the buildings and hang across the street. In fact, in order to emphasise the continental feel even more, she decided to replace the flat balcony railings on the side buildings with more decorative, curved ones.

YOU WILL NEED

Piece of 300gsm (140lb) watercolour paper 44 x 38cm (17½ x 15in)

Retractable pencil

12 watercolour paints: Naples yellow; Burnt sienna; Alizarin crimson; Payne's grey; Lemon yellow; Raw sienna; Hooker's green; Cadmium yellow; Cerulean blue; Burnt umber; Cobalt blue; Cadmium orange

Brushes: Nos.10 and 5 rounds

Paper tissue

◄ Wrought-iron railings, colourful shutters and a rounded archway are distinctive architectural features in this painting.

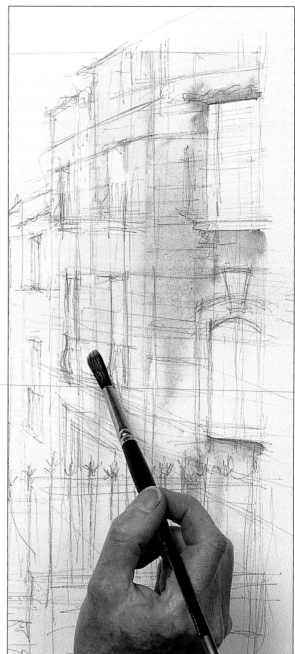

1 ▶ **Sketch the scene** Use a retractable pencil to make a fairly detailed sketch of the scene. Spend some time on getting the perspective right. The building at the front is at an angle and so has a different vanishing point from the buildings next to it. Pencil in perspective lines on the windows of these buildings, with the lines going off towards their vanishing points. You can always rub out these lines later.

2 ▲ **Wash over the buildings** Using a No.10 round brush, lay a wash of Naples yellow over the front building. Flood in a mix of burnt sienna, alizarin crimson and Payne's grey. Add lemon yellow to this mix to vary the colour.

3 ▶ Block in other areas Wash lemon yellow over the left-hand houses and into the distance. Paint the road with Payne's grey, then continue with this colour along the foreground wall. Rough in the stonework with the Payne's grey and burnt sienna. Add raw sienna to the left-hand buildings and wash it over the tree foliage.

4 ◀ Add building detail Dilute the dark mix from step 2 and use it to add some colour to the building at the front. With burnt sienna and a No.5 round brush, paint in some lines on the stonework up to the corner of the building. This will enhance the sense of perspective. Soften the lines with water if they look too stark.

6 ▲ Paint the shutters Use the No.5 brush and diluted cerulean blue to wash over the shutters on the front building. If the paint drifts, use paper tissue to pick up the excess. Using less diluted paint, add horizontal lines to the top shutter and some detail to the bottom shutters.

5 ▶ Paint the tree Mix Hooker's green with a touch of cadmium yellow. Using the No.10 brush, dilute the mix and paint the foliage of the tree, feeding in more yellow as you work from top to bottom. Add a touch of Payne's grey to the mix and dab wet-on-wet over the foliage. Use diluted Payne's grey to drift a shadow from the bottom of the tree.

7 ▲ Work on the front building Use burnt sienna, alizarin crimson and Payne's grey to work up the small roof over the top shutter. Use light and dark tones to bring out the detail. Sketch the balcony with the same mix. Build up the stonework and strengthen the shadows around the windows.

Master Strokes

Martiros Sergeevich Sar'Yan (1880–1972)
A Street, Midday, in Constantinople

In this unusual painting, worked in 1910, the effects of perspective and colour in the composition are striking. The rooftops cut into the sky, creating an abstract blue shape that is echoed by the similar orange shape of the road below. Blue and orange, being complementary colours, set up an exciting and vibrant visual effect and make the shadowy buildings on either side of the street appear even darker and more mysterious.

Sunlight catching the rooftops is shown with bands of the orange used for the road, visually linking the top and bottom of the painting.

Robed figures appear as simple dark silhouettes set against the glowing orange of the road. Like the buildings, they are worked in perspective.

8 ▶ Work on the side buildings Use the dark mix from step 7 with a touch more crimson to paint the roofs along the side buildings. Add highlights with raw sienna. Continuing with the crimson mix, mark in some of the windows along the side buildings – first use a wash, then put in detail and shadow under the balconies with heavier colour. Paint the cables using the same mix.

9 ▲ Add architectural detail Use a mix of burnt umber and Payne's grey to paint the balconies. Wash in the door at the bottom with diluted crimson, then dot crimson into the shadows under the balconies to lift the colour here and prevent it looking muddy.

10 ◀ Build up the distance Touch in the roofs of the houses on the left with crimson, adding windows with burnt umber. Strengthen the lemon yellow in the distance. Use the No.10 round brush and a diluted wash of cerulean blue to paint the sky, putting in a touch of cobalt blue where the sky meets the horizon.

11 ▶ Build up detail

Mix Hooker's green with cobalt blue and dot detail into the tree. With Payne's grey and the No.5 brush, paint the base and window of the car. Dilute the Payne's grey to add windows and balconies on the side buildings. Mix Payne's grey and burnt umber to paint the arch at bottom right, using crimson in the archway. Wash raw sienna over the first side building, then add a door and a shadow in crimson.

A FEW STEPS FURTHER

The picture is now almost complete, but there is still room for some creative detail on the metalwork of the right-hand balcony. The foreground wall and the railings above it would benefit from stronger treatment, too.

Express yourself
A pale palette

Still using watercolours, the artist worked the scene again, this time with a lighter palette. In this version, the railings in the foreground are white rather than black – this was achieved by painting them with masking fluid, which retained the white paper while the surrounding colours were applied. Being pale, these railings seem less of a barrier to the viewer than the black ones.

12 ▶ Paint the foreground

Strengthen the crimson door with burnt umber. Use Payne's grey to paint the decorative railings in the foreground. With crimson and raw umber, work on the stone wall below the railings. Add raw sienna to warm up the stones and outline some of them with Payne's grey.

TROUBLE SHOOTER

LIVELY WIRES

When painted in a dark brown shade, the cables appear to sink into the building and look like part of the stonework. Use a bright cadmium orange to help them stand out. The cables hanging across the road are worked in the darker mix.

13 ▶ **Add details**
Mix cobalt blue and Payne's grey to paint a shadow under the car. Wash in a tree at the end of the street with diluted green. Paint Naples yellow along the bottom of the railings. Then strengthen the railings with Payne's grey and the brick wall with the colours from step 12.

14 ▲ **Add the balcony pattern** Make a dry mix of burnt umber and crimson and outline the pattern on the top balcony. Finally, flood a little crimson over the wall to strengthen the colour here.

THE FINISHED PICTURE

A Aerial perspective
The buildings at the end of the street were painted very roughly and loosely to create the illusion that they are farther away.

B Build up layers
Layers of watercolour were gradually added to the buildings as the painting progressed to create a feeling of architectural solidity.

C Work creatively
The straight balcony railings were changed to curved ones to make them look more decorative. This subtle alteration enhances the continental atmosphere of the painting.

Creating the illusion of depth

Discover how to give your landscapes a real sense of depth simply by modifying the tones, colours and brush strokes you use in the background.

Ever since the Renaissance, Western painters have tried to represent three-dimensional space on a two-dimensional surface. Today, more than 500 years later, contemporary artists are still very much concerned with the same problem.

Linear perspective depends on an understanding of structure. The artist is guided by the knowledge that parallel lines on the same plane always meet at the same place – the vanishing point. If the perspective is wrong, the whole painting might look odd.

Rural landscapes

However, it can be a mistake to become too anxious about linear perspective. So long as you understand the basic principles, success will come with time and practice. In any case, when painting many subjects – such as rural landscapes – converging parallel lines might not be relevant.

Our perception of space and distance can be depicted in a number of other ways, including the use of tone and colour. This is particularly the case with landscape subjects.

INVITING THE EYE INTO THE PICTURE

Claude Lorraine (1600–82) was a master of creating the illusion of distance and enticing the eye into the painting, as shown here in his *Pastoral Landscape* (*c*.1640). Note how the warm brown-greens of the foreground turn into cool blue-greens in the distance. The actual (or local) colour of the background grass may be exactly the same as the foreground grass – but seen through the dust and damp of the atmosphere, it takes on a bluish tinge. Indicated below are other devices used to create a convincing impression of depth.

The sky is deeper in tone at the top of the image than it is in the distance – creating a sense of recession.

The foreground figure stands out clearly with his warm red skin tones and deep blue clothing.

The contrast of tones in the foreground is very bold – the dark animals are almost black, the pale ones are nearly white.

Details in the foreground are sharply defined and well-modelled.

In landscapes, the distance often seems very hazy and pale. This is caused by the blurring effect of the atmosphere. The further away an object is, the more it is dulled by the dust and moisture in the air. The effect is known as 'atmospheric' or 'aerial' perspective.

Visual clues

Distant hills may be so light that they appear to merge into the sky on the horizon. This is especially likely to happen in damp, misty conditions. In comparison, the foreground will contain greater detail and contrast and the subject matter will therefore be more clearly defined.

If a painting looks flat, you can also often improve the sense of space by adding crisp details in the foreground and blurring the objects in the distance. Look, for example, at foliage on trees. In foreground trees, you are likely to be able to see the leaves and to pick out several different shades of green within the leaves. Compare this with a similar tree in the distance on which the foliage will appear dull and faded.

A certain amount of space is created automatically in a painting simply because the subject is familiar and therefore recognisable. The subject itself provides the clues. For instance, everyone knows that a path appears to get narrower as it tapers into the distance and that faraway trees seem smaller than those in the foreground.

Even so, many paintings which should look airy and spacious often turn out disappointingly flat. Usually this is

LIGHTENED TONES

In this colour sketch, both the field of corn and the blue sky are painted in three bands of tone – dark, medium and pale. The strongest tones and colours are in the foreground – at the top and bottom of the composition – and the lightest tones represent the distance.

The eye of the viewer is led from the strong reds and browns in the foreground back towards to the horizon at the centre of the composition. The eye is then guided forward through the graded sky colours to the top front edge of the picture.

because the artist has failed to exploit the properties of the colours.

Bright, warm colours tend to jump forward, whereas cool, subdued colours appear to recede (see below). Similarly, strong colours advance from pale or diluted colours.

When these colours are used in landscapes and other figurative works, exactly the same thing happens: by using warm or strong colours in the foreground and pale or cool colours in the background, you will automatically create an illusion of space in a painting.

Large, closely packed brush marks in the foreground leap forward from the small, spaced out marks in the distance.

Back to basics

When trying to give your painting a sense of recession, keep in mind the basics of painting – in particular, your brush strokes and your palette. In the illustration on the left, brush strokes alone are used to give a sense of recession. Without varying either the tones or colours, the artist has suggested space simply by painting foreground grass and sky in larger, closer brush strokes than those used in the distance. In the illustration on the right, on the other hand, you get a feeling of recession simply from colour – the warm colours appear to come forward while the cool ones fall back.

Orange jumps forward from its cool complementary – blue – while red leaps out from its complementary – green.

For instance, if you were painting a field of poppies, you would probably need to use a warmer, strong red for the flowers in the foreground and gradually make this mix cooler and paler as you work into the distance.

Eliminate the white

To create three-dimensional space on paper or canvas, it is first necessary to destroy the flatness of the surface. For instance, any sizeable patches of white paper or primed canvas showing through between paint strokes challenge the illusion of space by reminding viewers that they are looking at a two-dimensional surface. A traditional way round the problem is to get rid of the flat white from the outset by roughly blocking in all the initial tones before starting work on specific areas and details.

However, if you work subtly, you can use a white support to lighten a tone. Look at the skies in the landscapes on this page – the artist hasn't left large areas of the support unpainted, but near the horizon he has used thin washes of blue paint so that a lot of white shows through. This helps give the sky a sense of recession.

FOREGROUND DETAIL

Here, the flowers in the foreground are painted in bold detail, immediately capturing and holding the attention of the viewer. The rest of the picture is vague and undefined in comparison. Gradually the eye moves towards the amorphous background, explores the distant landscape, and is then guided back to the more specific forms at the forefront of the image. The sense of recession is helped by the pale bluish green used for the background.

COLOUR AND ATMOSPHERE

In this landscape, the foreground fence is painted in bold green, red, black and white. The strong colours, applied undiluted and directly from the tube, stand out starkly from the lighter colours used in the rest of the picture. For example, the trees – painted in subdued green – become progressively paler as they recede into the distance.

The artist has also taken the opportunity to emphasise the three-dimensional form of the house by painting the nearest chimney in a dark tone and the farthest one in pale grey.

A second building, further away, is painted with a range of light blues and greens. This building is almost as pale as the sky and is therefore barely visible as it appears to merge with the horizon and disappear into the background.

The drama of white water

Use watercolours to capture the excitement of a river rushing over rocks.

Moving water is a compelling subject but, at first sight, you might wonder how you can possibly convey the turbulence of a rushing river or the energy and excitement of rapids or a waterfall.

The elements of swiftly flowing water that need special attention are its

▼ To capture a fast-flowing river in watercolour, the unpainted areas are as important as the painted ones.

movement, transparency and reflections, all of which can be portrayed with careful observation and the right techniques. To depict moving water effectively, you need to simplify by focusing on the main patterns and shapes being created by the flow. (Working from a photo is helpful as these patterns are frozen.)

Preserve the highlights

Working wet-on-wet with a broad wash brush is the best technique for suggesting areas of flat, undisturbed water, while wet-on-dry with broken brush strokes best describes turbulent areas of waves or spray. Avoid overlaying too many washes as the colours will become muddy.

Masking fluid is an invaluable tool as it allows you to highlight the tops of ripples, the glints of sunlight on still water or the spray thrown up by falling water. You are then free to work on the surrounding darker tones without having to worry about preserving these highlights.

In contrast to the drama of the water, the artist added a peaceful backdrop of autumnal trees. Their darker tones help guide the eye into the centre of the image.

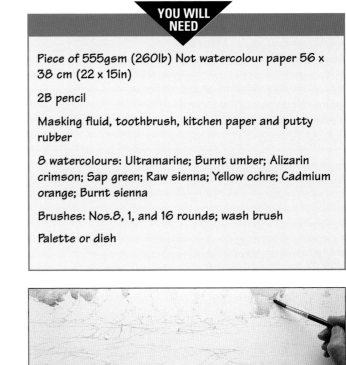

Piece of 555gsm (260lb) Not watercolour paper 56 x 38 cm (22 x 15in)

2B pencil

Masking fluid, toothbrush, kitchen paper and putty rubber

8 watercolours: Ultramarine; Burnt umber; Alizarin crimson; Sap green; Raw sienna; Yellow ochre; Cadmium orange; Burnt sienna

Brushes: Nos.8, 1, and 16 rounds; wash brush

Palette or dish

2 ▲ Paint the sky and hills Use a wash of pure ultramarine watercolour to touch in the areas of sky with a No.8 brush. Add a little burnt umber and alizarin crimson to the ultramarine, and brush on to dry paper to represent the distant hills.

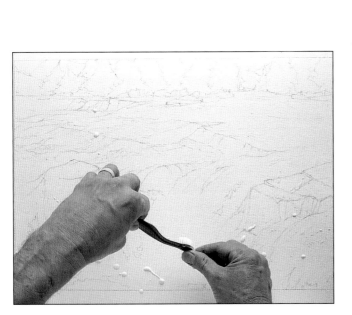

FIRST STROKES

1 ▲ Make a sketch and apply masking fluid Lightly draw the main shapes with a 2B pencil, looking at the main thrust of the water. Dip the toothbrush into the masking fluid and flick it on to the paper, starting in the centre and moving up to the left and right. Remove any unwanted blobs of fluid by blotting them with kitchen paper.

▲ The underwash for the trees was mixed from sap green, ultramarine and a touch of raw sienna.

3 ▶ Paint the trees wet-on-wet
Now dampen the paper with a No.16 brush – a damp surface rather than a wet one gives you more control over the paint. Return to the No.8 brush and mix sap green, ultramarine and a touch of raw sienna to create an underwash for the trees, laying it on more thickly towards the bottom. Create form in the trees using the same wash with less water added, then drop some yellow ochre on to the foliage to give it colour.

4 ◀ Continue to build form in the trees
Load cadmium orange on to your brush and flick it over the trees to create an autumnal effect. Repeat this technique with burnt sienna, working into the dots of paint with a clean, wet brush. Load the wash brush with water and brush it across the far water, using the chisel edge.

DEVELOPING THE PICTURE
Now begin to develop the water, using various effects to convey movement and reflections. Leave plenty of highlights of white paper showing to represent foam and spray.

EXPERT ADVICE
Painting reflections

When painting reflections, you need to create a sense of depth while retaining the horizontal plane of the water. Dilute the mix of sap green and ultramarine used to paint the trees, and make horizontal brush strokes spaced slightly apart. If objects are reflected in moving water, slight undulations in your brush strokes will help to indicate ripples.

5 ▲ Show trees reflected in water Continuing with the wash brush, use downward strokes to paint the mix of sap green, ultramarine and raw sienna (see step 3) on the water.

6 ▶ Begin to paint the rocks Add well-diluted ultramarine to this mix and begin to wash in the water. Drop in some cadmium orange to suggest more reflections. With the No.8 brush, begin to paint rocks with a light wash of ultramarine and burnt umber, adding a touch of yellow ochre.

7 ◀ Work detail into the trees Add some detail to the trees using a No.1 brush, dipping back into the green wash from step 3 and working your way across the painting from left to right. Now pull some of the foliage colours into the water, painting thin horizontal lines, and then working over them with clean water in order to diffuse the marks.

▲ Burnt umber, ultramarine and yellow ochre were mixed in varying proportions to create the colours of the rocks.

8 ▲ Develop the rocks Start to work detail on to the rocks with the same mix of ultramarine, burnt umber and yellow ochre that you used in step 6. Use broken brush strokes to allow the underwash to show through and leave flashes of paper reserved to reinforce the notion of water pouring over the rocks. Diffuse your marks with clean water.

9 ▼ Indicate turbulent water Using a wash of sap green and ultramarine, suggest the rushing movement of the water around the distant rocks with broken lines. Use a circular motion with the brush to make irregular marks that recreate the particularly turbulent water, adding a little yellow ochre in places. Again, diffuse the marks with clean water.

Express yourself
White water

This study of moving water was drawn with water-soluble pencils, and utilises the technique of reserving white paper to suggest water. By drawing rapidly, the artist was able to capture the essence of the shapes of the rocks as well as the direction of the water.

10 ▲ Move to the middle ground Work across to the middle ground in the same way. Paint more rocks with a mix of burnt umber, ultramarine and yellow ochre, using diagonal or rounded strokes and leaving some white paper showing to represent the running or foaming water. In front of these rocks, lay in a pale underwash of ultramarine and burnt umber on to dry paper, adding yellow ochre in places. Using the No.1 brush, begin to add detail with broken vertical lines.

11 ▲ Start the foreground rocks Pool your washes together to paint the water in the bottom left-hand corner. Paint the large left-hand rock, adding more ultramarine as you move towards the bottom. Leave white paper showing – broken lines suggest the direction and speed of the water, while dots and short strokes show splashes of falling water. Change to the No.1 brush to work in some detail with a stronger wash.

12 ▼ **Paint the foreground water** For the foreground water, mix washes of yellow ochre and sap green, and burnt umber and ultramarine in varying strengths. Use the No.1 brush in small, circular motions to indicate the river's turbulence, or in downward strokes to suggest falling water.

13 ▲ **Complete the rocks** Continue working across the tumbling foreground water, using the same strokes as in step 12. Then paint the right-hand rock, using the same technique as described in step 11.

Master Strokes

Frederick Edwin Church
(1826–1900)
Niagara Falls

An American landscape painter, Frederick Church specialised in paintings of spectacular natural scenery. This vista of Niagara Falls is a wonderful example of how a painter treats water at its wildest. A vast cloud of spray occupies most of the centre of the picture, echoed by a smaller cloud behind it. The rich turquoise water of the river is veined in white, conjuring up a feeling of churning movement.

Tiny figures are shown gazing at the waterfall from a viewing platform. They are used to give a sense of the awesome scale of the scene.

To convey the spray at the bottom of the waterfall, smoothed-out areas of paint have been used. Compare this to the precise strokes used for the foaming water at the top of the fall.

14 ▼ **Remove the masking fluid** Complete the water in the foreground and allow the paper to dry thoroughly. Now rub off the flecks of masking fluid with a putty rubber.

15 ▲ **Fine tune the detail** With the masking fluid removed, you will have a clearer idea of how your finished painting will look. The whiteness of the paper is revealed and the original pencil sketch is rubbed out.

A FEW STEPS FURTHER

The painting now gives a superb impression of agitated water. All that is needed is some definition in the trees and details on the surface of the water.

16 ▲ **Define the trees** Pick out shadows and define the shapes of the trees with a mix of ultramarine and sap green, using the No.1 brush. Horizontal lines of the same wash but diluted suggest reflections in the water.

TROUBLE SHOOTER

LEAVE THE PAPER TO DRY

Wait until the fibres of your paper are completely dry before you attempt to remove masking fluid with a putty rubber. Even if the paper appears to be dry to the touch, the fibres might still be damp, and rubbing masking fluid from damp paper will take off the top layer of the paper. You can use a hair-dryer to speed up the drying process.

17 ▼ **Develop the area of flowing water** Using some of the previous mixes, reinforce the notion of moving water with broken lines diffused with clean water.

18 ▲ **Strengthen the foreground** Finally, show glimpses of the rocks through the foaming water by dabbing on some of the burnt umber and ultramarine mix, using the No.1 brush.

THE FINISHED PICTURE

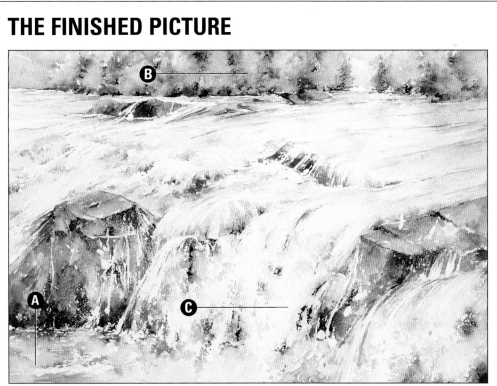

A Visual balance
Deep, strong colours in the corners provide visual balance and prevent the painting from appearing to fade away at the edges.

B Merging colours
The trees in the distance were painted wet-on-wet so that the colours merged softly, avoiding hard edges.

C Reserving paper
Moving water can appear to be largely white in colour, so allow the unpainted paper to do some of the work for you.

Watercolour landscape

By masking out areas of your watercolour painting, you can create some wonderful effects. In this image, masking fluid and tape were used to create realistic clouds and grass.

Like many landscape subjects, this striking Mediterranean view has such rich and varied surface patterns and textures that brush and paints alone might not be versatile enough to capture the full effect. The scene combines fluffy clouds, layers of earth-coloured washes and the graphic, cut-out quality of dry, spiky grasses.

Quite simply, you must look for ways to create the exact equivalents of what you see. The following are useful tips for painting two of the most common landscape features – sky and grass. Both involve masking and washes of colour which must be allowed to dry between stages. As this takes time, you can speed up the process with a hairdryer – the rivulets of colour this sometimes creates can add to the effect.

Fluffy clouds using masking fluid

The cloudy sky is painted in two straightforward stages, and the technique can be adapted to depict any type of clouds. First, paint the cloud shapes with masking fluid, then brush a wash of blue over the entire sky. Remove the masking fluid and you are left with a flat, picture-book sky complete with white, cut-out clouds.

Next, apply a second coat of fluid across the top of the cloud shapes, slightly overlapping into the sky. Paint over the sky area with a different blue, remove the fluid and you have a realistic sky with subtle veils of overlaid colour and three-dimensional clouds which reflect the sunlight.

Spiky grass using masking tape

Rather than simply painting blades of grass on top of a background colour, try masking out the grass with sticky tape before overlaying the colour. This leaves a white silhouette for each blade. Overpaint some of the blades with a streak of green while leaving others white to convey the heat and reflected sunlight of the Mediterranean landscape.

◀ **With two coats of masking fluid and two washes of paint, you can achieve beautiful, light, airy clouds.**

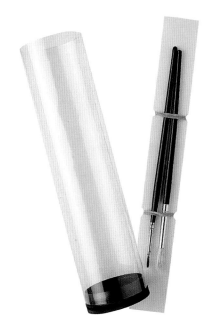

▲ **If you want to paint a scene on location, protect your brushes in a tube like the one above.**

FIRST STROKES

1 ▲ **Start with a drawing** Make a simple drawing of the subject, sketching in the outline of the clouds. To get a bold, chunky line, use a soft drawing pencil or a chisel-ended carpenter's pencil like the one used here.

2 ▶ **Mask the clouds** Using an old brush, block out the cloud area with masking fluid. Apply the fluid thickly, scrubbing it over the top half of the larger clouds. Then dab in the lower half of the larger clouds, twisting the bristles occasionally to create swirling brush marks. Pick out the distant clouds with thin slithers of fluid. Allow the masking fluid to dry.

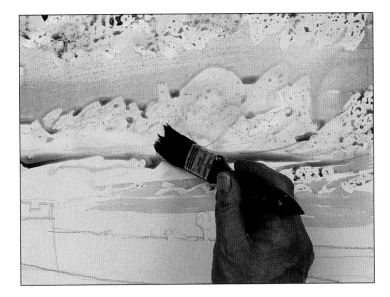

3 ◀ **Apply the first wash** Using the 38mm (1½in) brush, paint a light wash over the whole sky area in diluted cobalt blue. Load the brush generously and pull the colour in overlapping, horizontal strokes. When the wash is dry, remove the masking fluid. Rub from the centre of each shape to avoid lifting the surface of the paper.

4 ▼ **Mask out new areas** Apply a second coat of masking fluid over the sky – painting a highlight along the top side of the clouds and on selected blue areas. Let the fluid dry.

5 ▲ **Apply a second wash** Paint a dilute wash of ultramarine over the entire sky area, taking the colour over both the masked and the painted areas in broad, horizontal strokes.

DEVELOPING THE PICTURE

Allow the wash to dry, remove the masking fluid and the sky is complete. It is now time to move on to the rest of the composition, and for this you will need some masking tape and a pair of scissors.

Express yourself

Impressionistic image

A similar scene, but this time executed with no masking techniques, produces a softer, more impressionistic image. Here the emphasis is on colour and atmosphere rather than texture and shape. The paint is applied wet-in-wet, with the colours running into each other. Although no attempt has been made to render the scene realistically, the viewer can still discern sand, grass, hills and sky, as well as the fort.

▼ **Mask out the grass**

6 ▲ **Mask out the grass** Cut short, irregular strips of masking tape and stick them down to represent clumps of grass. Make the distant tufts smaller than those in the foreground.

7 ▼ **Paint the sand** Mix an earthy wash from raw sienna and plenty of water and paint this over the masking tape, using broad, criss-cross strokes.

8 ▲ **Repeat the process** Allow the wash to dry. Then, without removing the first ones, apply a few more masking tape strips in the foreground. Make the new strips larger than those further away to help create a sense of depth. Paint the wall of the fort in a mix of ivory black and alizarin crimson. Add a little Vandyke brown to the fort colour and apply this in a few broad strokes to indicate the shadows on the sand dunes.

Master Strokes

Robert Adam (1728–92)
Rocky Landscape with Castle

One of the finest architects of the eighteenth century, Robert Adam was also a skilled landscape artist. He came from the 'topographical' tradition, in which landscape was represented in an accurate, realistic way. Note how every last tree and shrub is rendered in detail in this image.

The sweeping, slanted brush strokes used for the clouds echo the strong diagonals of the path.

The eye is led up the path to the castle and on ultimately to the patch of blue sky.

▲ The coolest tones in the composition are ultramarine (left) and cobalt (top) in the sky, and the viridian (bottom) used for the grass.

▲ The warmer, landscape colours are Vandyke brown (left) and raw sienna (top). A mix of ivory black and alizarin (bottom) describes the fort and distant hills.

9 ▲ **Remove the tape** When the paint is quite dry, remove the masking tape to reveal the spiky clumps of grass. Remove stubborn bits of tape by rubbing with your finger.

10 ▶ **Paint the background** Using a No.6 round brush, paint the rest of the fort in the black and alizarin mix. Use a dark mix for the shadows and a paler wash of the same colour for the light areas. Take the same colour into the distant hills.

EXPERT ADVICE
Applying the tape

Cutting up masking tape with scissors is a sticky business. Don't worry if the strips adhere to each other and get crumpled as a result – this reflects the grass in its natural state and looks more realistic. Just press the strips down as firmly as possible, as shown here, to stop the paint from running underneath.

A FEW STEPS FURTHER

At this stage the painting is almost complete. You have established the rolling sky and the background scenery, as well as the textured scrub and grasses of the foreground. You can now go on to add a little local colour to the foreground and a few background details.

11 ▲ **Complete the background** Finish painting the distant hills in a weak wash of alizarin and black, then allow the paint to dry before moving on to the next stage.

13 ▶ **Develop the background** Finally, define the fort, using a light, broken line of ivory black and alizarin. Paint the trees in viridian mixed with a little ivory black.

12 ▲ **Add blades of green grass** Still using the No.6 round brush, paint a few blades of grass in viridian, cadmium yellow, and a mix of the two. Use short, narrow strokes for the background grass. Add more yellow to the mix and paint the foreground grass in stronger strokes.

THE FINISHED PICTURE

A Three-dimensional clouds
The undersides of the clouds are shaded by the second coat of blue – this helps the viewer to appreciate their volume.

B Two-toned fort
The whole fort is painted in a mix of black and alizarin, with a weak wash for the sunlit areas and a deep one for the shadows.

C Size matters
Small brush strokes in the background of the sky and much larger ones in the foreground give a sense of depth.

Sunlit café scene

Lively town scenes like this one needn't be difficult to paint. Learn how to focus attention on your main subject by simplifying the background.

▲ **By using a contrasting combination of bright colours and deep shadow, the artist has created a convincing outdoor scene, bathed in summer sunshine.**

Artists do not always paint exactly what is in front of them. Part of being a good painter is being able to select the features of a scene that will work well together. A lively café setting like this one might, at first glance, seem rather complicated to paint. It is possible, however, to simplify it by picking out certain shapes and colours and disregarding others.

Simplified background

There is no need, for example, to be put off by the prospect of tackling the busy area behind the main table and chairs. You don't have to make the people and buildings in the background graphically clear, as long as a few of the more obvious shapes are left in and the paint tones blend in with the rest of the picture.

The main point to remember is that the elements in the background should not overpower the clearer images of the four most important figures and their umbrella in the foreground.

Strong shadows

One of the most interesting qualities of a bright daytime setting is the role that shadows play. In the scene chosen for this exercise, the shadows are cast by the umbrellas, the café tables and chairs, and the people themselves.

Watercolour is an ideal medium for conveying both light and shade. By mixing paints together, layering one colour on top of one another and using ample water, you can create very subtle tones with traces of different colours showing through.

YOU WILL NEED

Large sheet of 140lb+ white watercolour paper

2B pencil

Round brush No.6 with a good point

Mixing palette or dish

9 watercolour paints:
Titanium white;
Cadmium orange;
Cadmium red;
Chrome yellow;
Burnt umber; Burnt sienna; Yellow ochre; Cobalt blue;
Ultramarine

FIRST STROKES

1 ▶ Make a sketch and begin adding colour Use the 2B pencil to sketch the scene. Then mix titanium white with water and add just a touch of cadmium red and chrome yellow. Test this colour on a separate sheet of paper until it makes a suitable flesh tone and paint the four main figures at the front of the scene. Clean the brush. Mix up a strong chrome yellow and paint in the large umbrella. Wipe the brush with a tissue, then use cadmium orange to paint in the T-shirt of the man on the far left. Put another patch of cadmium orange behind the man in the background on the far right.

2 ▶ Fill in the dark hair and T-shirt Clean the brush. Use burnt umber to paint the hair of three of the main figures. Vary the tone by gradually adding more water. Then mix cobalt blue with burnt sienna and paint in the blue T-shirt of the man on the right. Add more water to the mix to make the colour less intense and use this new shade of blue to define the chair on the far left, and the shadowy areas in the centre.

3 ▲ Paint the woman on the right Use yellow ochre to fill in the blonde hair and dress of the woman on the right. Clean the brush. Then mix cobalt blue with a little water and paint the legs of the chair she is sitting on. Also use cobalt blue to dab in the shady areas behind the chair on the far right.

4 ▶ Deepen the skin tones Mix up some cadmium orange and paint in the hair of the woman in the centre background. Then use a mix of burnt sienna and a little yellow ochre to paint the tanned faces and bodies of the people in the foreground.

◀ **Yellow ochre combined with a weak mix of cobalt blue gives a colour suitable for painting light shade.**

6 ▶ Add detail to the figures Now make a mix of ultramarine and burnt sienna and use it to reinforce the shadows under the left-hand chair some more. Also use this colour to paint patches and lines of shade on the faces, arms and legs of the four main figures. Add a little more detail to their facial features, too. Clean the brush.

5 ▲ Develop the main group Paint the dress of the woman on the left with a mix of cobalt blue and titanium white. Define darker shadows under the furniture using cobalt blue alone mixed with a little water. Use burnt sienna to create dark streaks on the hair and dress of the woman on the right. Add a little burnt sienna to the cobalt blue mix and use it to intensify the shadow under the left-hand chair.

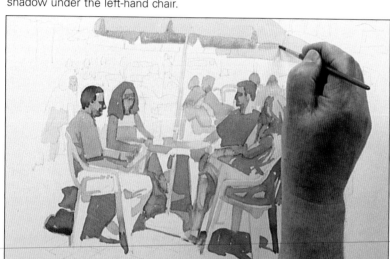

7 ▲ Continue to develop the picture Mix ultramarine with a little water and paint in the shadow under the central table. Clean the brush. Deepen the colour of the left-hand woman's blue dress using cobalt blue. Then mix burnt umber with water and paint in the faces of the people in the background. Also use this colour to reinforce the shade under the umbrella.

8 ▶ Fill in more shaded areas Make a mix of cobalt blue and a touch of burnt umber. Use it to paint in the areas of shade in the background. Add more cobalt blue to the mix and darken the T-shirt of the man at centre right. Use this colour also to fill in the shadow under the far right-hand chair and the area behind the man on the left.

EXPERT ADVICE
Creating dark colours

Watercolour painters often avoid using black paint, because it can appear too stark next to the delicate, wispy quality of other watercolours. There are many other interesting ways of arriving at dark colours using this medium. The very dark patch of shadow under the chair (below) is created with a mix of two strong colours – cobalt blue and burnt sienna. While this gives a darker tone than the others around it, the effect is not too stark. As an experiment, try to see how many different dark greys and 'blacks' you can achieve by mixing combinations of watercolours. There are many possibilities. For example, with chrome yellow, cobalt blue and cobalt green you can mix a very dark combination, almost black but with lots of interesting tones throughout.

DEVELOPING THE PICTURE

Now that you have dealt with the tables, chairs and figures in the foreground, it is time to tackle the sky and the buildings in the background. Despite their grand appearance, it is quite easy to add a few uncomplicated details to buildings such as these, as long as you have sketched the basic proportions and angles correctly.

9 ▶ Make a wash for the sky Turn the painting upside down and place it on a block. Mix ultramarine with a little water, load the brush with colour and paint in the sky area. Allow the watery paint to flow to the top of the picture. Leave to dry for a few minutes, then turn the picture the right way up again.

Master Strokes

Raoul Dufy (1877–1953)
The Terrace of the Café San Martigues

Although painted in a different medium – oils – from the café scene featured in the above watercolour exercise, this painting by Raoul Dufy has certain similarities. The emphasis is placed on the group of people set right at the front of the picture, while the rest of the outlook forms a less clearly defined backdrop to the scene. In fact, the main figures are placed so much in the foreground that the viewer feels almost part of the group around the table. As in our café scene, the detail and shading in the picture is restricted largely to the main figures. The people and the buildings in the background are painted comparatively loosely. Dufy's painting is strongly lit and shows effective contrasts between the various areas of light and shade.

The buildings are simple blocks of colour with grey rectangles for the windows. Note how the juxtaposition of the red wall and the green café front prevents the background from becoming bland.

Thick, textural brush strokes have been used to describe the figure in the foreground, creating a lively picture surface.

10 ▲ Begin painting the buildings Paint in the pale walls of the right-hand buildings with a watery mix of burnt umber and cobalt blue. Clean the brush. Mix cadmium orange with water and a little yellow ochre. Paint the roof on the right and the building on the left, leaving gaps for all the windows. Mix a strong cobalt blue with a touch of water and paint in a dark patch of colour between the buildings, just above the main umbrella.

11 ▲ Develop the left-hand building Use the same mix of cobalt blue to paint in the roof and the window tops of the building on the left. Dilute the mix with slightly more water and paint in the windows themselves.

12 ▶ **Complete the buildings** Still using the watery cobalt blue, paint the remaining wall, the windows and the roofs of the buildings on the right, as well as the shaded area below them. Add the detail behind the man on the left. Mix ultramarine with only a little water and add touches of dark blue to the dome and to the roof of the right-hand building.

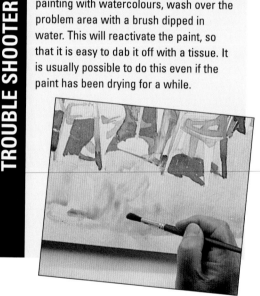

▶ **A mix of undiluted cadmium red and cobalt blue gives a deep grey colour suitable for the darkest areas of shadow in a watercolour painting.**

A FEW STEPS FURTHER

Although the main part of the painting is now complete, a further option is to work up the foreground area in front of the tables in greater detail. You can achieve this by adding some shading and a few lines to indicate the paving. With loose areas such as this, you can use plenty of water to allow colours to mingle. Don't be afraid of enjoying yourself and experimenting here. The wet areas can always be soaked up with a tissue afterwards.

13 ▶ **Add washes to the foreground** Wash over the foreground on the right-hand side using a mix made from lots of water and a touch of ultramarine and burnt sienna. Clean the brush. Use yellow ochre, again mixed with plenty of water, to wash over the foreground at centre left. Allow the two washes to seep into one another.

TROUBLE SHOOTER

THE CORRECTING POWER OF WATER

If you make a mistake while you are painting with watercolours, wash over the problem area with a brush dipped in water. This will reactivate the paint, so that it is easy to dab it off with a tissue. It is usually possible to do this even if the paint has been drying for a while.

14 ▶ **Strengthen some of the colours** While the foreground is drying, go back to the rest of the picture. Reinforce some of the existing colours if you would like to emphasise them. Here, more cadmium orange has been added to the back of the man on the far left. The hair of the people in the background could also be made a stronger shade of orange.

15 ▶ Darken the shadows and paint the paving

Darken the shadows under the table using a mix of cobalt blue and a touch of burnt sienna. Mix cadmium orange with burnt sienna and define the bottom edge of two of the yellow umbrellas with a fine line. Finally, once the paint in the foreground has dried sufficiently, use burnt umber mixed with a little water to paint in the lines of the paving stones. Paint these at an angle to convey the perspective.

Express yourself
A tonal approach

You can emphasise the effect of strong sunshine on the café scene by simplifying the colours and relying more on the tones created by light and shade. In the version of the exercise shown here, the people around the table are sketched in without adding too much detail. Once the flat orange wash has been brushed over the drawing, the light areas are taken out by brushing on more water and dabbing the paint off with a tissue. The orange tone is deepened by adding more paint in shaded areas such as the underside of the umbrella. The deep shadows on the ground are painted in a solid dark colour to offer maximum contrast, while mid-tone areas, such as the hair and clothing, are created with a dilute mix of the dark colour.

THE FINISHED PICTURE

A Strong focal point
The picture is dominated by the strong shapes and tones in the centre: the large umbrella, the four people round the table and the dark shadows.

B Simple background
The scene behind the main table was left very loose and, apart from a few patches of dark colour here and there, the paint was highly diluted with water.

C Unpainted areas
Some parts, such as the church dome and the small dome on the left, were left unpainted to allow the white paper underneath to show through.

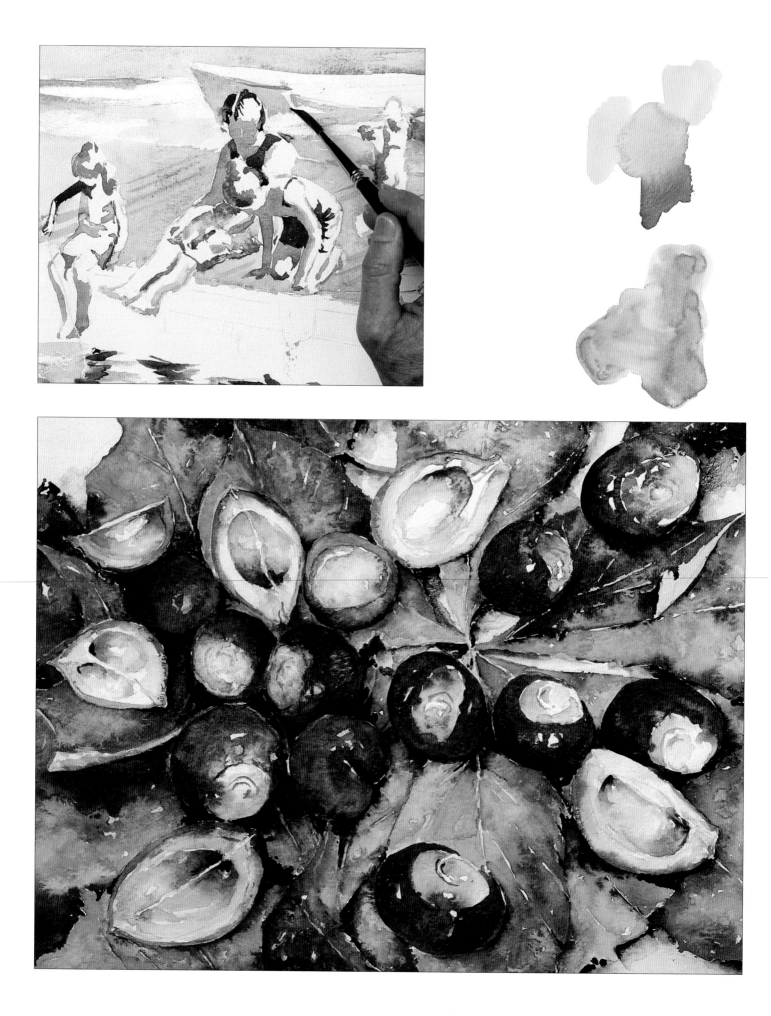

Watercolour Still Lifes and Portraits

Try out different projects from everyday scenes to painting fruit, leaves and flowers, and from group portraits to solo studies.

Still life with pumpkins

A tinted paper will give your watercolour a ready-made, even undertone and impose a pleasing sense of harmony.

◀ **The biscuit colour of the paper chosen for this still life harmonizes well with the warm tones of the apples, pumpkins, flagon and pitcher.**

YOU WILL NEED

Sheet of 300gsm (140lb) tinted NOT watercolour paper

No. 6 round brush

Watercolour palette

11 pans of watercolour: burnt sienna; burnt umber; cadmium yellow deep; scarlet; raw sienna; light red; raw umber; Payne's grey; cadmium yellow pale; viridian; permanent rose

Hair-dryer

One of the advantages of still life is the degree of control you have over the subject. You can choose objects for their shape, colour or texture, select them for their similarities or for their differences, and arrange and light them as you wish. An important aspect of the initial decision-making process is choosing the paper you want to work on, as this plays its part in creating the mood of the painting.

Pure watercolour is a translucent medium which relies on the white or off-white of the paper to provide the lightest tone. Lightly tinted papers can be very effective with watercolour, but you should choose the colour carefully.

A tinted paper has several advantages. It is less stark and therefore less daunting than starting with a pure white ground. It also serves as a key against which to judge other tones and provides a background colour to the whole painting, creating a sense of unity.

When choosing a tinted paper, find one that echoes a dominant colour in the set-up, or choose a colour to create a mood. Alternatively, you can tint your own paper by laying a flat wash over it.

'Drawing' with watercolour

For this still-life project, the artist has dispensed with an initial pencil drawing. The main forms of the two pumpkins, the basket and the pottery

items have been established with a thin wash of burnt sienna and burnt umber. If you use this direct method of working, you will find that it will give your painting a pleasingly spontaneous feel as you progress through the stages.

Don't worry if you make a few mistakes while you are outlining the objects or blocking in the tones. As long as you use a pale wash, the redrawn lines will disappear beneath the subsequent washes. Do be careful, however, to reserve the areas of lightest tone, such as the basket and the body of the flagon.

▼ **Mix permanent rose and burnt sienna for a good terra-cotta shade.**

FIRST STROKES

1 ▼ **Start blocking in the tones** Mix a dilute wash of burnt sienna and burnt umber. Using a No. 6 brush, start to block in the broad forms of the subject on tinted paper, looking for areas of dark and mid tone. If you half-close your eyes, you will be able to see the lights and darks more clearly.

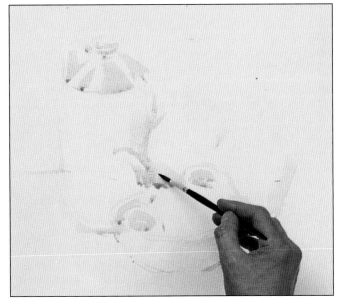

2 ▲ **Continue establishing the main tones** Add more burnt umber to the wash and lay in the shaded areas between the objects. Keep the wash very pale so that you can paint over any mistakes. Note the way the tones of the objects change as the surfaces curve away from the light source.

3 ▲ **Block in the pumpkins** Using a wash of cadmium yellow deep with a touch of scarlet, establish the broad forms of the pumpkins. Leave highlights as bare paper. Stand back and check the proportions of the objects, making any necessary adjustment by overpainting.

4 ▼ **Start to lay in the background** Mix a pale wash of raw sienna, light red and burnt umber, and use it for the body of the pitcher and the shadows on the wall. Apply the same wash as horizontal slabs of colour to suggest the pattern of the tiled surface. Allow the painting to dry thoroughly at this stage.

5 ▶ **Build up the mid and dark tones** Dark tones can be created by overlaying several thin layers of wash. Here, the convex surface of the pitcher is suggested by laying another wash over the right side and along the lower part where the body curves away from the light source. Notice the two curved lines, which suggest the ribbed surface of the pot.

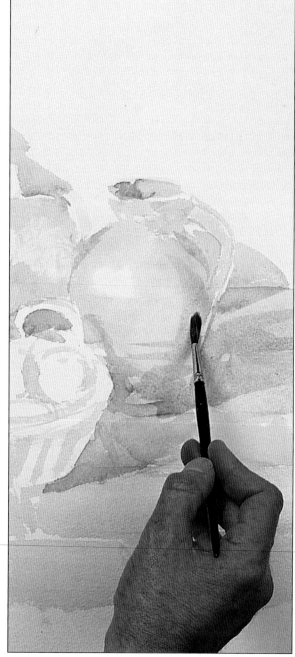

6 ◀ **Add areas of dark shadow** With a darker wash of raw umber and light red, paint the shadow behind the pumpkin at the back, defining an accurate silhouette. Now use the same mix to create the important shadow under the handle of the pitcher. Add bands of the wash around the pumpkin in the foreground to suggest its undulating surface.

7▶ Apply a light tone to the flagon The creamy paper is close to the local colour of the body of the flagon. Mix a very pale wash of Payne's grey with a touch of raw sienna and lay this over the flagon, leaving a light area on the left-hand side.

DEVELOPING THE PICTURE

You have created a monochrome study in which the shapes and broad tonal arrangements have been mapped out. You can now start to apply areas of local colour – on the apples and pumpkins, for example. From now on, the picture will progress surprisingly quickly.

REMOVING PAINT FOR HIGHLIGHTS

TROUBLESHOOTER

There are various tricks for creating lighter areas. You can lift out colour with a piece of tissue or cloth while the paint is still wet. Once the paint is dry, you can lighten it slightly by rubbing it lightly with an eraser as shown here. You can even re-wet areas with a brush, then lift out patches of colour.

8◀ Start to paint the apples Mix some cadmium yellow pale with just a touch of viridian and lay in patches of colour for the apples. Mix scarlet, permanent rose and a little raw sienna to create a warm russet tone. Apply this to the apples, following the curve of the fruit.

◀ Add burnt umber to the wash of cadmium yellow deep and scarlet to give a warm chocolate brown for the flagon.

9▶ Add local colour to the pumpkins Mix cadmium yellow deep with a touch of scarlet and apply a wash of this colour to the pumpkins. Lay the colour in bands that follow the ribbing of the vegetable, leaving some areas of paper or original wash for the highlights.

10▲ Paint the glaze on the flagon Mix burnt umber with the remains of the orange wash for the brown glaze on the flagon. Suggest the reflective surface with dabs of wash on the handle. Elsewhere, apply the wash more broadly, allowing it to build up in some areas of shadow. Leave tiny areas of bare paper for brilliant highlights.

11 ▶ **Suggest the basket weave**
Mix a dilute wash of burnt umber with a little raw sienna, and use the tip of the brush to 'draw' the dark lines of shadow between the woven strands of the basket. Don't put in every strand, otherwise the result will tend to look mechanical and unconvincing.

12 ▲ **Develop the pitcher** Wash a mix of burnt sienna and permanent rose over the pitcher. Dry the painting using a hair-dryer. Add burnt umber to the wash to paint the shadow of the basket on the pitcher and to create the dark tone within the lip. Dilute the wash for the band of dark tone down the right side of the pitcher, using the brush tip to indicate some of the ridges that run around its lower half.

13 ◀ **Add the darkest tones** Tighten up the apples with a little green and red. Mix raw umber with a little Payne's grey and, using the brush tip, add crisp details around the rim of the basket. Apply washes of dark tone between the apples to give them solidity and form. Darken the wash and paint a bold shadow on the wall behind the pumpkin.

A FEW STEPS FURTHER

The image is now fully resolved, the colours accurate and the forms solidly established. With watercolour, however, it is possible to continue tightening up the image, adding details and textures to achieve a more 'finished' result.

14 ▶ **Enhance the colour**
Mix cadmium yellow deep with a touch of scarlet and raw umber and wash colour around the left side of the left-hand pumpkin. Mix raw sienna and light red and apply this over the body of the pitcher to soften the gradations of tone.

Express yourself
A simpler composition

By removing the basket of apples from the set-up, the artist has entirely changed the mood of the composition. With fewer objects and with more space in the foreground, the arrangement is simpler and more static. The artist has developed the tones to create a dramatic *chiaroscuro* reminiscent of the carefully worked paintings of the Dutch and Spanish Masters of the seventeenth century (an example of which would be *Still Life with Brass Pot* by Floris van Schooten).

15 ▼ **Add details** Use a dilute wash of burnt umber to paint details around the stem of the pumpkin. Add light red to this wash, dilute it and lightly indicate the gaps between the tiles on the surface. Mix Payne's grey and raw sienna, and lay bands of colour to show the faceted surface of the flagon, allowing the paint to dry between each application of wash to achieve hard edges.

16 ▲ **Add highlights** When the paper is totally dry, use a sharp knife to scratch back into the paper to create an area of highlight around the rim of the pitcher.

◄ **Cadmium yellow deep is a warm yellow that makes an ideal base colour for the pumpkins. Adding a little scarlet will give a range of orange shades.**

THE FINISHED PICTURE

A Paper tone
The warm tone of the paper shows through the watercolour paint in places and becomes part of the picture in its own right.

B Layers of wash
Carefully applied layers of orange wash describe the surface appearance of the pumpkin and indicate its solid form.

C Highlights
By adding a little dark tone near the highlights on the pitcher and flagon, you can make these light touches appear brighter.

Bowl of eggs

These eggs nestling in a bed of straw create an unusual image of quiet and simple beauty. Capture their delicate colours and tones in watercolour.

Sometimes the simplest subjects make the most telling images. Inspired by the soft colours of these eggs, the artist arranged them in a bowl lined with straw, and painted them with subtle watercolour washes.

Watercolour is the ideal medium for a subject such as this. When the paint is applied in thin washes, light passes through to the white paper and reflects back through the colours, giving them a marvellous luminosity. It is important to mix the correct quantities of paint and water to obtain the right consistency.

The secret is to start off with the lightest of washes and gradually build colour, tone and form with a series of thin, transparent layers, rather like delicate sheets of tissue paper. By working in this way, you achieve tonal depth while retaining the freshness and sparkle of the colours.

▲ **The softly modelled forms and nuances of colour in this painting are achieved by laying wash over wash.**

242

FIRST STROKES

1 ▶ Draw with the brush Wet the paper with clean water and a No. 8 round brush. While it dries off a little, mix a very weak wash of raw sienna and a touch of ivory black. Use this to rough in the eggs and the shadows between them, 'drawing' with a No. 6 round brush. Next, use a cooler mix of Payne's grey and raw umber to outline the bowl.

YOU WILL NEED

Piece of 640gsm (300lb) rough watercolour paper

Watercolour brushes: Nos. 8, 6 and 2 round; No. 6 filbert

Jar of water

Mixing palette or dish

12 watercolours: raw sienna; ivory black; Payne's grey; raw umber; permanent rose; cadmium yellow; Indian yellow; Indian red; cerulean; cobalt blue; burnt umber; burnt sienna

Piece of tracing paper

Pencil

Craft knife

Stencil brush or old toothbrush

2 ◀ Define the eggs Give more definition to the eggs by painting the shadows around and between them with the Payne's grey/raw umber mix, adding a hint of permanent rose for the warmer shadows. 'Negative' painting in this way is easier than trying to draw the shapes of the eggs themselves. It also helps to integrate the objects in the composition because you are 'sculpting' them out of the page, rather than imposing them on to it.

EXPERT ADVICE
Thumbnail sketches

No matter how simple your subject, you still need to compose it well and position it effectively on the paper. Don't go for the obvious solution of placing the subject centrally. By cropping in on the bowl and placing it off-centre, you will create a more dynamic composition. Try out different ideas by observing the set-up through a viewfinder and making some small thumbnail sketches before starting to paint.

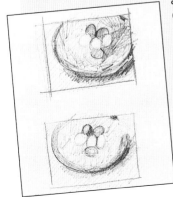

3 ▲ Make a base wash for the straw Mix a weak wash of cadmium yellow and a little permanent rose to make a warm underwash for the straw. Brush it on loosely, going over the brown eggs, too. Leave to dry.

4 ▲ **Paint the darkest brown egg** Mix a rich, warm brown from Indian yellow and Indian red, and block in the darkest of the brown eggs. While this is still damp, rinse the brush and flick it dry, then lift out the soft highlight on the egg. A white highlight would look wrong here; allow some of the surrounding colour to flow back on the damp paper, so that the highlight is just a shade lighter than the egg itself.

5 ▲ **Paint the next brown egg** Add permanent rose to the mixture and lighten it with a little more water. Paint the brown egg on the right – it is slightly cooler and paler in colour than the first one. Create a soft highlight on the top of the egg as before.

6 ▶ **Work on the blue and green eggs** Rinse the brush, then make up a weak mix of cerulean with a touch of Indian yellow to colour the blue egg. Paint the green egg with a mixture of cobalt blue and cadmium yellow, again thinly diluted. While this wash is still just damp, paint the shadow on the egg with a weak wash of ivory black and raw umber. Leave the painting to dry.

DEVELOPING THE PICTURE

Now that the basic shapes and colours of the eggs are established with pale washes, introduce deeper tones to build up form and detail.

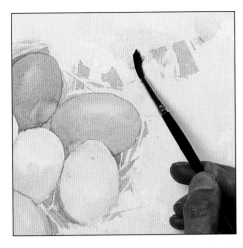

7 ◄ **Show the shadows in the straw** In this step, you will be defining the dark shadows in the centre of the straw, while leaving the thin strands unpainted. Mix a warm shadow colour from raw sienna, Indian red and a little ivory black, and touch in the shadows with the tip of the brush, cutting around the lines of the straw.

8 ▲ **Work on the straw** Make sure the shadows are completely dry before you start to paint the light tones of the straw itself. For this, you will need a pale mix of Indian yellow warmed with a touch of Indian red. Use long, sweeping strokes to suggest the tangled mass of straw, working loosely so that the pale underwash shows through.

Express yourself
Coloured pencil drawing

Here, the artist has produced the same subject using coloured pencils instead of watercolours. In fact, coloured pencils are similar to watercolours in that the coloured pigment is semi-transparent, allowing light to reflect off the paper. The artist has used the sides, rather than the points, of the pencils to drift the colours on lightly, like watercolour washes. The pigment has caught on the tooth of the cartridge paper, producing a subtle, granular finish, which adds to the delicacy of the image. Light and shadow are created by optical mixing – using a network of overlaid strokes to produce hues and tones that interact vibrantly.

9 ▲ **Deepen the shadows** Mix a strong wash of burnt umber and, using a No. 2 round brush, block in the darkest shadows around the eggs. Using the No. 6 round brush, define the bowl's rim with a mix of Payne's grey and burnt umber.

10 ▲ **Strengthen the eggs** Mix burnt sienna and burnt umber to deepen the topmost egg. Add permanent rose and more water to the wash and paint the other brown egg. Mix in Payne's grey for the shadow. Lift highlights out from the damp washes. Mix cerulean and Indian yellow for the blue egg, adding a second wash for the shadow. Wash pale cadmium yellow over the green egg, with pale raw umber and black for the shadow. Add a wash of burnt sienna, permanent rose and black to the bottom egg.

11 ▲ **Add more straw texture** Mix a base wash of Indian red and a hint of black, diluted to a mid tone. Using the No. 2 brush, suggest strands of straw with linear strokes. Define light and dark tones by adding more or less water to the wash. Where the straw is warm in colour, add cadmium yellow or permanent rose; where cool, add Payne's grey.

12 ▲ **Adjust the tones** Use the No. 2 brush to darken the shadows around the eggs with burnt umber to give a sense of the eggs 'nestling' in a well in the straw. Indicate the direction of the light by slightly darkening the tone of the straw on the left side of the bowl with further strokes of the cool colour used in step 11.

A FEW STEPS FURTHER

The picture works well at this stage, with a nice textural contrast between the smooth, round eggs and the scratchy, dry straw. All that remains is to model the eggs a little more, complete the background and add some final details.

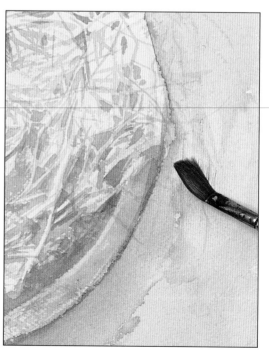

13 ▲ **Strengthen the shadows** Strengthen the shadow on the right-hand brown egg with the No. 6 brush and a mix of Indian red, burnt sienna and a little Payne's grey and Indian yellow. Use cerulean, Indian yellow and a hint of black on the blue egg, and raw umber and black on the green egg. Mix permanent rose and black for the egg next to the green one. Remember to keep all the washes thin and transparent – they are only slightly darker than the eggs themselves.

14 ▲ **Add a simple background wash** Mix a weak wash of permanent rose, Indian yellow and ivory black, and brush it loosely over the background with a No. 6 filbert brush. Darken it with more black, then add the cast shadow of the bowl while the underwash is still damp. Let it bleed out softly at the edges.

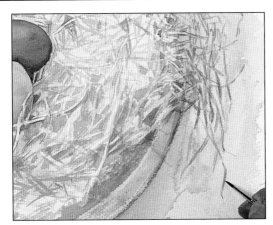

15 ▲ **Finish off the straw** Mix a base wash of Indian red, Indian yellow and ivory black, and paint the strands of straw overhanging the bowl with the No. 2 brush. Vary the tones by adding burnt umber and more ivory black for the darker strands.

16 ▶ **Add the speckles** Define the rim of the bowl with the No. 6 brush and a wash of raw umber, burnt sienna and black. Leave to dry. Dot specks of burnt umber over the rim. Place a piece of tracing paper over the picture, trace round the lower brown egg and cut it out with a craft knife. Place the tracing paper back in position. Hold it steady while you lightly spatter the brown egg with burnt umber, using a stencil brush or old toothbrush.

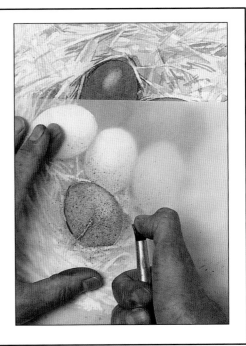

THE FINISHED PICTURE

A Transparent layers
Layers of transparent watercolour were used to build up the smooth forms of the eggs while retaining their delicacy.

B Mood
Soft tones and muted shades of blue, green and brown evoke a mood of quiet tranquillity in the composition.

C Vignetting
The simple, subdued background fades away gradually at the edges, concentrating the viewer's attention on the bowl of eggs.

Statue in watercolour

When painting statues, you can benefit from the sculptor's ability to convey interesting poses, as well as using your own figure-drawing skills.

When painting in a town or city, you don't have to record entire streets or buildings in order to create an interesting picture. Public buildings, squares and parks often have fountains, monuments and figurative sculptures in or around them, and these can make fascinating studies in their own right. If you are interested in figure painting, you will get valuable practice by drawing and painting from sculpture – with the distinct advantage that the figures never move.

In this painting, the artist has used watercolour to create a striking image of a statue of the Roman god Neptune, which stands outside the Palazzo Vecchio in Florence, Italy. Individual strokes of colour convey the strongly modelled forms of the figures, and tonal depth is built up by overlaying washes.

Accurate drawing

When painting a sculpted figure, the underlying drawing is very important. Make this as accurate as you can without recording excessive detail. Working from direct observation produces the best results, but attempting to paint in a city street or square can be difficult, so you might have to work from sketches, notes and photographs. Early morning and late afternoon are good times to paint because the sun is low in the sky and casts strong shadows that accentuate form and volume.

▶ **Sculpted figures can be as rewarding to paint as models in a life class. The muscular form of this statue has been built up with overlaid washes of watercolour.**

YOU WILL NEED

Piece of 300gsm (140lb) NOT watercolour paper 38 x 28cm (15 x 11in)

Pencil

Brushes: Nos. 4, 10 and 2 rounds

7 watercolour paints: raw umber; burnt sienna; raw sienna; crimson lake; French ultramarine; yellow ochre; Prussian blue

Jar of water

Mixing palette or dish

Craft knife or scalpel

FIRST STROKES

1 ▶ Sketch the statue Start to draw the statue in pencil, making sure the proportions of the main figure and the two smaller ones are correct. Work lightly, feeling out the forms as you go. If you make a mistake, simply re-draw on top of it. This will convey the flowing forms of the figures better than a single outline.

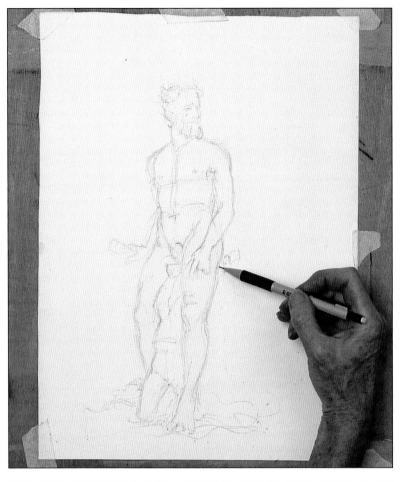

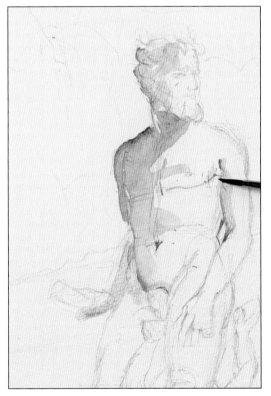

2 ▲ Start to block in the shadows Finish drawing the statue, then very lightly sketch the roof of the background building and the outlines of the clouds. Mix a cool, mid-toned wash of raw umber with a touch of burnt sienna and start to block in the shadows on the male figure with a No. 4 round brush.

3 ▲ Start to add some lights Mix a pale wash of raw sienna and start to put in the light, warm tones on the figures. Skip your brush lightly over the paper, creating flowing strokes that begin to emphasize the forms of the figures.

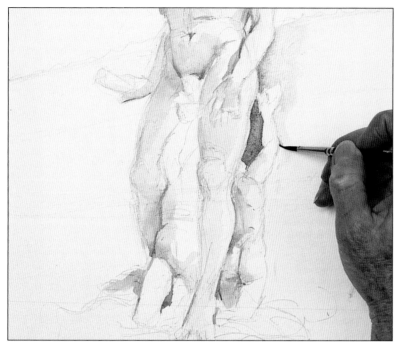

4 ▲ **Develop the light and shadow** Continue building up the forms, using the cool wash from step 2 for the shadows and the warm wash from step 3 for the lights. Strengthen the darker shadows with further washes of the raw umber/burnt sienna mix. Start to put in a light tone of the same mix around the statue to separate it from the building behind.

5 ▶ **Add more colour to the background**
Mix a dilute wash of raw umber, warmed with a touch of crimson lake. Wash this over the background building with a No. 10 round brush.

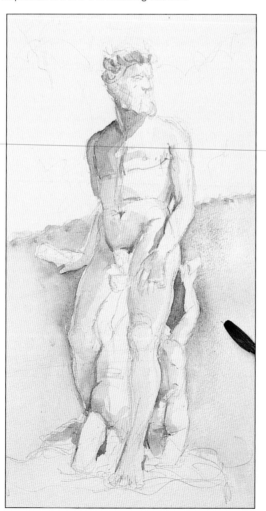

Express yourself
Working in soft pastel

Using soft pastels, you can build up layers of colour to model the forms of a figure, just as you can with watercolour. In this drawing, the dark tones on the left of the statue are achieved by applying burnt sienna and raw umber shades over the warmer golds used for the lighter side. You can achieve further modelling on the body with finely hatched lines. Create hazy, blended colours for the sky and the building by rubbing them softly with your finger or a torchon.

▶ Washes of burnt sienna, raw umber and raw sienna (clockwise from top) are used to model the figures.

DEVELOPING THE PICTURE

Now that the main elements of the composition have been blocked in, step back and review your progress so far. The next stage is to develop the detail and modelling of the statue using overlaid washes of transparent colour.

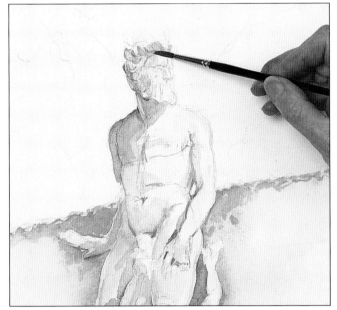

6 ▲ Add mid tones Using the No. 4 brush, emphasize the roof-line and the shadow around the statue with a darker wash of the shadow mix from step 4. Continue working over the figures and base, developing the forms with further superimposed washes. Dilute the shadow colour with more water and use this to introduce some mid tones.

7 ▲ Introduce some warmth Continue modelling the forms of the figures with overlaid washes, mixing raw sienna and a little French ultramarine for the grey shadows. Then mix a wash of crimson lake and use the No. 10 brush to apply this loosely over the background buildings, letting the underwash applied in step 5 show through the gaps.

SCRATCHING OUT

TROUBLE SHOOTER

When you are painting a small, detailed area, such as the head of the statue, it is easy to overwork with the brush, adding too much paint and losing sight of the small, white highlights that are vital in conveying the sparkle of light. To retrieve the highlights, simply allow the paint to dry, then gently scrape back to the white paper with the sharp blade of a scalpel or craft knife.

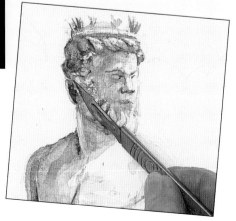

8 ▲ Develop the details of the face Mix a more concentrated wash of raw umber and burnt sienna and use this to define the details on the statue's face, hair and beard with a No. 2 brush. Keep in mind the main areas of light and shadow falling on the head, and paint the details lighter or darker accordingly.

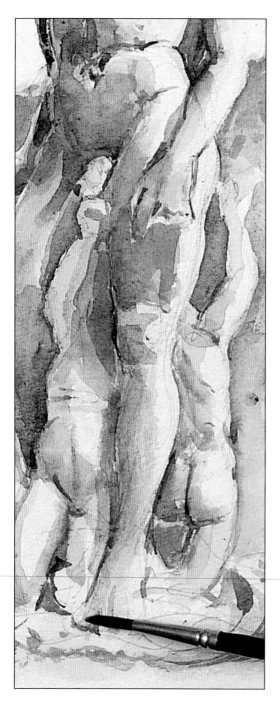

9▲ **Strengthen the forms** Using the No. 4 brush, continue to model the figures with warm and cool colours as before. Deepen the strongest shadows with transparent washes of French ultramarine and strengthen the warmest highlights with yellow ochre.

10▲ **Paint the sky** Use the No. 10 round brush to dampen the sky area, so that you can suggest storm clouds with wet-on-wet washes. Mix French ultramarine and Prussian blue for the cool grey clouds, and add touches of crimson lake for the warmer clouds. Paint some loose strokes of the blue-grey mix on to the background buildings.

A FEW STEPS FURTHER

The painting is now almost complete. All that is required are the final touches of extreme light and dark that will sharpen the image and bring it into focus.

11 ◄ **Accentuate the darks** Mix a strong dark colour from raw umber, burnt sienna and Prussian blue. Use the No. 2 brush to accentuate the figures by painting the dark shadows between them. With the same mix, define the carving on the plinth. Leave the painting to dry thoroughly.

12 ▲ **Suggest the fountains** Hint at the splashing water of the fountains around the statue by scratching into the dry paint with the tip of a sharp blade to create a few broken lines.

THE FINISHED PICTURE

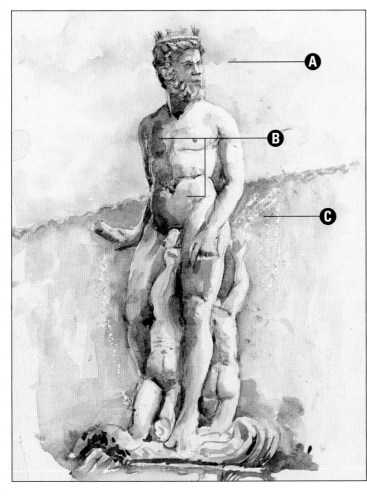

A Dramatic licence
To be in keeping with the imposing statue, the sky was deliberately made a little darker and more dramatic than in the original scene.

B Warm and cool
Overlaid strokes of warm and cool colour defined the forms of the figures.

C Simple background
The details of the background building were treated very loosely in order to focus attention on the statue.

Sunflowers and bamboo leaves

Contrasting colours and shapes give an exuberant quality to this simple but striking arrangement of flowers and leaves.

The time factor

Flowers are living things and will not stay still when placed in a vase. Blooms will open or close depending on the light, leaves may droop and petals fall – as happened during the course of this painting. The changes should not be too great, but it is important to make an accurate drawing of the group first and then leave it unchanged while the painting develops.

Watercolour has a translucency that is perfect for interpreting the delicate, filmy quality of flower petals. The secret to achieving this effect is to work from the first pale areas of wash to the final subtle details.

At first glance, this flower painting looks complex and highly finished. Closer inspection, however, shows that it is actually painted quite simply, but with careful attention to modulations of tone and colour.

Building up washes

Working with watercolour washes can be tricky. If you allow the paint to dry between each wash, the colour acquires a hard outline. Applying a wash to a still-wet area, on the other hand, can produce lovely effects, but you risk losing control and creating a mess. The best method for painting flowers is to apply a second wash while the first is still just damp; in this way the colours merge softly to produce subtle effects.

▶ **This arrangement exploits the contrast between elegant, sword-like bamboo leaves and full, rounded sunflower heads.**

FIRST STEPS

1 ▼ Make an outline drawing Using a sharp 2B pencil, draw the sunflowers and bamboo leaves in outline, but don't attempt to suggest shading or texture. Extend the image right out to the edges of the picture area.

2 ▼ Begin the first sunflower Mix a wash of cadmium yellow pale, warmed with a hint of cadmium orange. Working on dry paper, start to paint the individual flower petals with a No. 3 soft round brush. Add a touch of Winsor violet to the mix for the shaded petals.

3 ▲ Develop the petals Continue to paint the sunflower petals, looking for the subtle changes of tone and warmth or coolness created by light and shadow. When you have painted in all the palest petals, strengthen the wash with more cadmium orange, then put in the deeper tones and the shadows beneath and between the petals. Leave the painting to dry.

▶ The palette for the petals was based on cadmium orange and cadmium yellow pale, with cadmium scarlet and alizarin crimson added to darken some tones.

Cadmium orange   Cadmium yellow pale   Cadmium scarlet   Alizarin crimson

4 ▼ Paint the centre of the sunflower Make a thin, loosely mixed wash of burnt sienna, Van Dyke brown and a touch of ultramarine violet, and fill in the flower centre. Don't overwork the paint – let it puddle in places. As the individual colours are only partially mixed, you will achieve a subtly variegated effect rather than a flat wash of colour.

Express yourself
A quick impression

Speed and spontaneity are the keynotes in this very different version of the sunflowers. A rapid pencil sketch is overlaid with equally rapid brush strokes and the fluid watercolour washes are allowed to fuse while wet. The aim is to capture the exuberant 'personality' of the flowers and leaves. Elements on the left of the arrangement are half-suggested, allowing the viewer's imagination to complete the image.

5 ◀ Add darker browns When the base wash is almost dry, darken it with more ultramarine violet. Then, with the tip of the brush, make small, broken brush strokes and stippled marks to suggest the texture of the closely packed seeds.

6 ▶ Bring in some greens Mix a dilute wash of sap green, enriched with a touch of cadmium orange. Use the brush tip to paint the greenish sepals surrounding the petals. Darken the wash with a hint of ultramarine to suggest the way the sepals curl over into shadow. Use the same colours to fill in the bamboo leaf. Leave to dry.

▶ For the leaves, sap green is warmed with cadmium lemon and cadmium yellow pale, and cooled with ultramarine.

Sap green

Cadmium lemon

Cadmium yellow pale

Ultramarine

7 ▼ Paint the second sunflower Return to the yellow and green mixes used in steps 2, 3 and 6 to paint the petals and sepals of the next sunflower. Leave to dry. Add a little alizarin crimson or cadmium scarlet to the deepest yellow mix and go over some of the darker petals again.

8 ▲ Add more leaves Fill in the flower centre as in steps 4 and 5. Then paint more bamboo leaves. Use sap green as the base colour, adding a little ultramarine and cadmium lemon for the stronger, cooler greens, as on the large vertical leaf. For warmer, yellower leaves, mix cadmium yellow pale with the sap green. For the faded leaves, add a hint of Van Dyke brown. Vary the tones of the leaves by adding more or less water to the paint. Leave to dry.

EXPERT ADVICE
Sharp-edged leaves

Bamboo leaves have clean, sharp edges. To capture these, fill in the leaf with colour, then, while the paint is still wet, rinse your brush and stroke a little clean water on to the centre of the leaf. The water will carry some of the pigment to the edges of the leaf, where it will dry, leaving a dark outline.

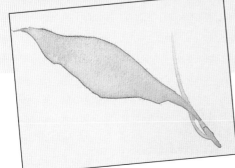

9 ▲ Complete the third flower Fill in the chinks of the blue background showing between the flowers and leaves with a wash of ultramarine. Build up the petals on the third sunflower with the mixtures used in step 7, then fill in the centre with tones of brown as before. Add cast shadows to the bamboo leaves with a mix of sap green and ultramarine.

DEVELOPING THE PICTURE

The flowers and leaves are now almost complete and it is
time to work on the other elements in the composition – the
vase and background. These should be more loosely painted,
so as not to compete with the main subject.

10 ◀ **Work on the background**
Loosely brush a
watery wash of
ultramarine over
the upper right of the
picture to give a
suggestion of
background. Make the
wash deeper near
the flowers, fading
out towards the
edges of the paper.

11 ◀ **Paint the vase**
Mix sap green,
cadmium lemon and
cadmium orange, and
paint the vase, leaving
flecks of white paper
for highlights. While
the wash is damp,
drop in a tiny bit of
ultramarine at the top
of the vase, allowing
it to bleed.

12 ▼ Paint the fallen petals Cut flowers may shed some of their petals, especially on a warm day, but you can use this to your advantage. They add interest to the bottom half of the composition, often a rather 'dead' area, and they also provide a natural colour echo of the flowers themselves. Paint the petals with different shades of yellow, just as you did for the petals on the flowers.

13 ▼ Finish the vase Complete the leaves on the left as in step 8. For the unglazed base of the vase, mix burnt sienna and chrome yellow. Dab on Van Dyke brown and alizarin crimson for the darker tones on the left, suggesting the vase's rounded form. Let these colours bleed together wet-on-wet.

14 ▼ Add more background wash With a No. 5 soft round brush, fill in the background on the left-hand side of the picture with a wash of ultramarine – make it slightly stronger than the wash on the right-hand side. Brush the colour on loosely, leaving a few tiny flecks of white paper to give it some sparkle.

15 ▲ Complete the background wash Take the blue wash down into the foreground area and into the lower right of the picture. While this is still damp, float on a few small strokes of dilute cadmium yellow pale here and there, just to the right of the flowers and also just beneath the vase.

259

A FEW STEPS FURTHER

The yellow sunflowers are almost complete and are enhanced by the blue background. Just add some final shadows and details to give the image more depth.

16 ▶ **Add a cast shadow** While the blue wash is still damp (but not wet) mix ultramarine, ultramarine violet and a hint of Van Dyke brown and put in the sliver of dark shadow underneath the vase. Let the shadow edge bleed softly into the surrounding blue wash.

17 ▲ **Create dappled light** Work over some of the leaves with very dilute ultramarine applied with crisscross strokes. This gives the effect of shadows with tiny chinks of light in between.

THE FINISHED PICTURE

18 ▲ **Complete the sunflowers** Mix cadmium yellow pale, cadmium orange and alizarin crimson. Add touches of this warm yellow to the petals and dot a few highlights on the flower centres.

A Transparent washes
Delicate washes of watercolour allow light to reflect back off the paper and suggest the translucent petals.

B Exciting shapes
The bamboo leaves were extended right to the edges of the picture to create lively positive and negative shapes.

C Blue background
A blue background wash contrasts effectively with the bright yellow flowers while harmonizing with the greens.

A lemon, a pear and an orange

How do you capture the texture of fruit? Try stippling, spattering and blotting to apply the paint – and using fine sandpaper to remove it!

Watercolour is a versatile medium and a wide range of techniques can be marshalled to build up texture. In this step-by-step, spattering, blotting and sanding down are used alongside traditional layered washes. This helps to capture the texture of three fruits and create a rich and embellished paint surface. And these interesting paint effects are combined with an understated composition to produce an unusual and striking picture.

Emphasize the abstract

Note how, as well as accurately describing the fruits, the artist has focused on the abstract qualities of the subject. Three fruits are ranged along a shelf in such a way that the picture area is divided roughly into thirds and the spaces between, below and above the lemon, pear and orange become important elements in the composition. The fruits are set in a shallow picture space against a vibrant red backdrop that emphasizes their simple shapes.

Try setting up a similar arrangement for yourself – the finished display should look contrived rather than natural. Select fruits for their shape, colour and texture, place them on a

shelf at eye level and arrange them so as to produce interesting shapes between and around them. You don't want the fruits to look as if you have just happened upon them.

Use a thick, good-quality watercolour paper and 'work' the paint surface, building up colour with layers of washes and textural effects. Add to the impact of these techniques by using gum arabic – an additive that gives the paint a more glossy finish and makes it easier to re-wet washes. (Note that it also slows the drying time.)

Tackling the subject

Work in a controlled way in the early stages, observing the subject carefully, then laying in the first simple washes on the lemon, pear and orange. Allow early first washes to dry, then apply a second layer of colour to each.

As the individual fruit images begin to emerge, you can start to introduce the textural elements and details that differentiate them – the smoothness of the pear's skin and its subtle blush of red, and the pitted surface of the orange and lemon skins. As the painting progresses, move away from pure description and add spontaneous marks, so that the forms begin to take on a life of their own.

YOU WILL NEED

Piece of 640gsm (300lb) NOT watercolour paper 38 x 56cm (15 x 22in)	permanent magenta; burnt umber; cadmium red deep; vermilion; ivory black
3B graphite stick	Brushes: Nos. 6 and 12 rounds
14 watercolours: lemon yellow; cadmium yellow; sap green; cadmium red; cadmium orange; permanent mauve; Payne's grey; yellow ochre; raw umber;	Gum arabic
	Kitchen paper
	Fine-grade sandpaper
	Ruler; stiff paper or thin card

◄ Here, the bright, flat background contrasts with the textured surfaces of the fruits.

FIRST STEPS

1 ▼ **Lay in the underdrawing** Using a 3B graphite stick, make an outline underdrawing, putting in just enough information to plot the location of your washes. Work lightly so that the lines don't show in the final painting.

2 ▲ **Wash in the lemon** Mix a wash of lemon yellow and cadmium yellow, then, using a No. 6 round brush, apply a wash of colour to the lemon. Stipple the paint on with the tip of the brush to create the highlights on the dimpled skin near the navel, where the fruit receives the light.

3 ▼ Paint the pear Add sap green to the yellow mix and use this to define the left side of the pear. While the wash is still wet, flood in a wash of cadmium red on the right. Don't be tempted to tamper with it – allow the colour to blend into the green wash in its own way.

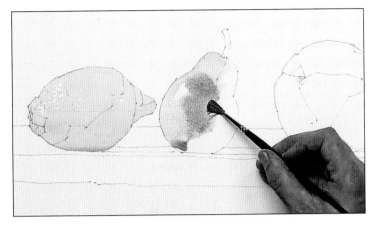

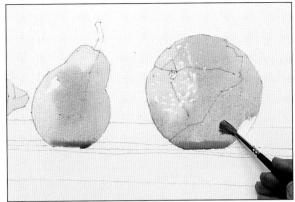

4 ▲ Paint the orange Take the green wash around the rest of the pear, allowing the red blush to flood into it. Mix a wash of cadmium orange and cadmium yellow and apply to the orange, stippling where its surface catches the light.

DEVELOPING THE PICTURE

Develop the fruits by laying a series of washes, allowing the paint to dry between applications. These overlapping transparent and semi-transparent washes give the watercolour its depth and luminosity.

5 ▼ Add texture to the lemon Check that the first wash on the lemon is thoroughly dry. Then, using a mix of cadmium yellow with a little cadmium orange, stipple colour on to the light part of the fruit. Take a flat wash over the rest of the lemon.

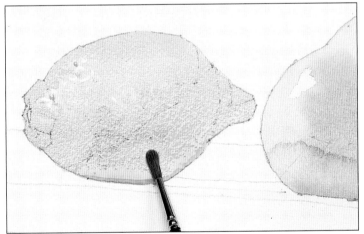

6 ▲ Develop tone on the pear Apply a sap green wash to the pear, then flood in cadmium red, allowing the colours to bleed together as in step 3. Add a touch of permanent mauve to the green wash to make a dark tone and take this around the right-hand side and base of the pear, which are turned away from the light.

7 ◄ Intensify the orange Mix a wash of cadmium orange, then use a stippling technique on the lit surface of the fruit, as in step 4. Take the rich colour over the rest of the fruit.

▼ **The warm hues of cadmium yellow (left) and cadmium orange (right) give a vibrant appearance to the orange in the still life.**

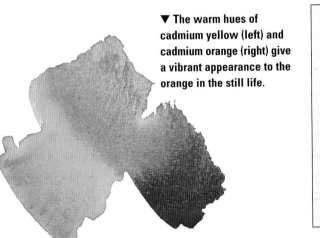

8 ▼ **Apply a third layer** Add cadmium orange to the yellow mix from step 5 and stipple over the left and centre of the lemon. Darken the mix with permanent mauve and Payne's grey, and paint the shaded part of the fruit.

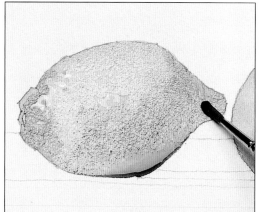

9 ▲ **Add dark tones** Mix permanent mauve and Payne's grey into the sap green wash to darken the shadow on the pear. Add cadmium red to the mix and flood into the red blush, spattering droplets for texture. Paint the stalk with dilute Payne's grey. Moving to the orange, use cadmium orange to paint furrows and stipple around the navel. Add permanent mauve, Payne's grey and gum arabic to the orange wash for the shadow.

Express yourself
Close-up pumpkin

Here, the focus is on the tough, ribbed surface of a pumpkin. Cropping in tightly removes it from its context, confusing the sense of scale and emphasizing shape, colour and texture.

10 ▲ **Spatter with water** When the orange is dry, spatter the surface with clean water. Leave the water for a few seconds to dissolve the previous wash, then gently blot the surface with kitchen paper to create random speckles of light tone that suggest the texture of the orange peel.

▼ **Washes of sap green (left) and cadmium red (right) are blended wet-on-wet to create subtly graduated colour on the pear.**

11 ▼ Develop the dark tones Use a yellow ochre and cadmium yellow mix for the ridges around the lemon's navel. Add Payne's grey and permanent mauve to the mix and darken the shadows. Develop the pear with further green and red washes, adding Payne's grey for the shadows and stalk. Using cadmium orange, add details to the top of the orange and flick droplets of colour on to the surface. Darken the mix with permanent mauve and Payne's grey, and apply these to the shaded areas.

EXPERT ADVICE
Sandpaper highlights

Once the watercolour washes are thoroughly dry, you can rub down the surface of the paint with a fine-grade sandpaper to create areas of highlight on the fruits. Tear off a piece of sandpaper, lay it on the surface of the dry wash, and rub gently until you get back to the paper, checking the effect as you work.

12 ▶ Rub down the fruits Using the technique described in Expert Advice, rub the surfaces of the fruits with fine-grade sandpaper to create highlights. On the lemon and the pear, make smooth, white patches; on the orange, rub the surface much more gently to give a stippled effect. Spatter droplets of the colour mixes from step 11 on to the three fruits.

13 ◀ Lift colour You can lift areas of colour by wetting the wash and working over the surface very gently with a brush – the effect is more subtle than that achieved with sandpaper. To do this on the orange, wet areas on the right and the bottom and work over them with the No. 6 brush to lift the colour. Rinse the brush in clean water and repeat to increase the effect.

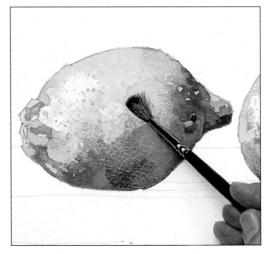

14 ▲ Soften colour on the lemon Work a moist brush over the surface of the lemon at centre right to re-wet the dry wash. Lift colour as in step 13. Varying the tone in this way helps to build up the rounded form of the fruit.

15 ◄ **Paint the shelf** Mix a wash of raw umber and cadmium orange to make a brown for the shelf. To achieve a straight edge, use a ruler as a guide – place it parallel to the shelf and lift one side away from the surface, then draw a line by resting the No. 6 brush against the raised edge and pulling it along the length of the ruler.

16 ▲ **Add shadows** Use a dark version of the same raw umber/cadmium orange mix to paint horizontal bands of colour that suggest the grain of the wood. Mix permanent magenta, burnt umber and cadmium red, and use this dark mix for the long, horizontal shadows cast by the fruits.

17 ▼ Paint the shelf edge Dilute the dark mix from step 16 and paint the shadow along the edge of the shelf. This establishes a frontal plane and creates a sense of recession.

18 ▶ Paint a bright background Mix a large quantity of cadmium red deep and vermilion. Use a No. 12 round brush to apply a flat wash of this colour over the background. Take the colour carefully around the edges of the fruits to refine their silhouettes. Work quickly, keeping the wet edge moving to avoid hard edges.

19 ▶ Add shadow under the shelf Mix ivory black, burnt umber and Payne's grey, and use this intense dark mix for the deep shadow under the shelf. Apply the wash with the No. 12 brush.

20 ▶ Complete the shadow area Take the dark mix from step 19 over the entire shadow area. Work backwards and forwards to avoid hard edges.

A FEW STEPS FURTHER

On re-evaluating the painting, you might feel that the shelf could benefit from more work to enhance the texture of the wood grain. Also, the shadow under the shelf could be darker, so as to match the depth and richness of colour in the red background.

22 ▲ **Add more texture** Use a graphite stick to draw roughly parallel lines on the surface of the shelf. This suggests more wood grain and adds linear interest.

21 ▲ **Add texture to the shelf** Cut a strip of stiff paper or thin card, and apply the dark mix from step 19 along one edge. Touch the strip on to the shelf edge to create a line of paint. Repeat the process to suggest the grain of the wood.

23 ◄ **Strengthen the shadow** Make a stronger mix of the ivory black/burnt umber/Payne's grey shadow colour. Using the No. 12 brush, apply it over the first shadow wash to make a really deep tone.

THE FINISHED PICTURE

A Dramatic background
A bold background in a flat wash of vibrant scarlet emphasizes the shallow picture space.

B Overlapping washes
A network of layered washes describes the smoothly curving surface of the pear.

C Sandpaper highlights
The surface of the orange was rubbed down with fine sandpaper to suggest the dimpled peel.

D Spatters and speckles
Spattered colour and spattered and blotted drops of water build up a rich, speckled surface.

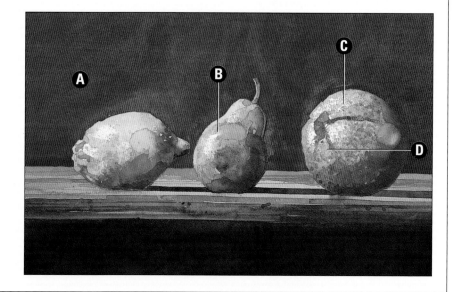

Shiny copper and glass

Combine wet-on-wet and layered washes to render the reflective surface of a copper pot and the translucency of a bottle of olive oil.

This luscious set-up with its warm colours and shiny reflective surfaces is in the great tradition of still-life painting. In the past, still lifes were usually rendered in oils, but here watercolour has been used with wonderful panache.

Arranging a still life

A major advantage of painting a still life is the degree of control you have over the subject. When selecting objects to arrange, look for features that echo each other – in this painting, the curves and colours of the brown onions repeat those of the copper cooking pot. Too many resemblances can be boring, however, so the vertical shapes of the oil and vinegar

▼ **The rich colours in this still life are reflected in the various shiny surfaces, producing a warm and harmonious picture.**

bottles and the diagonals of the ladle and the aubergine were introduced.

Looking at reflective surfaces

Reflective surfaces such as glass and metal provide all kinds of interesting effects. Clear glass takes its colour from the liquid within, as well as the colours seen through it and others reflected in it. With shiny metals such as copper, the local colour is modified by the reflections in its surface.

The trick with reflective surfaces is to paint exactly what you see. Try to envisage the subject as an abstract pattern of shapes, colours and tones.

Remember that reflections are less precise and more muted than the objects themselves. In this set-up the reflections are so distorted by the shapes of the pot and bottles that the objects reflected are barely recognizable.

YOU WILL NEED	
Piece of 300gsm (140lb) NOT watercolour paper 40 x 56cm (16 x 22in)	yellow ochre; indigo; Winsor blue
HB pencil	Brushes: Nos. 12 and 14 rounds; No. 6 Chinese
9 watercolours: alizarin crimson; Venetian red; gold ochre; cobalt blue; lemon yellow; raw umber;	Mixing palette or dish
	White candle
	White oil pastel

FIRST STEPS

1 ▲ **Sketch the set-up** Using an HB pencil, sketch the subject. Start with the sweep of the background fabric and the bigger shapes in the composition – the copper pot and the bottle of oil. Work lightly, looking for the shapes and the spaces between them. At this stage it doesn't matter if you use several tentative lines to describe a single outline – as the drawing progresses, you will decide which line is most accurate.

2 ▲ **Block in the background colour** Mix a large wash of alizarin crimson, Venetian red and gold ochre and, using a No. 12 round brush, apply this over the red cloth. Create variations of tone by alternately adding more alizarin crimson and Venetian red to the wash. Mix cobalt blue and alizarin crimson for the shadows, and touch these in while the first wash is still wet.

◄ The rich, coppery tones of the pots and bottles are mixed from varying amounts of alizarin crimson (left), gold ochre and Venetian red.

3 ▼ Add the coppery tones Mix gold ochre and alizarin crimson, and use a thin wash of this mix to underpaint the onion and the sides of the copper pot. Add more gold ochre to the mix and start to touch in the dried chillies.

4 ▼ Add candle wax Block in the red onions with wet-on-wet washes of alizarin crimson with cobalt blue, leaving white paper for highlights. Next, reserve the highlights on the shoulders and neck of the bottles by rubbing candle wax lightly over the surface of the paper.

5 ▼ Paint the oil bottle Mix a gold-coloured wash from lemon yellow, raw umber and yellow ochre. Using a No. 6 Chinese brush, apply the mix to the oil bottle. Add touches of unmixed raw umber and Venetian red wet-on-wet and allow the paint to blend to capture the gradations of colour and tone in the bottle. Leave to dry.

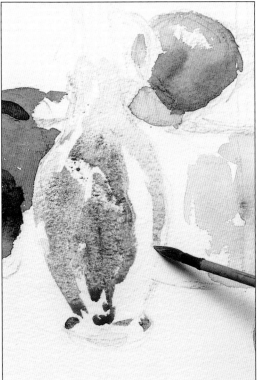

EXPERT ADVICE
Test your mixes

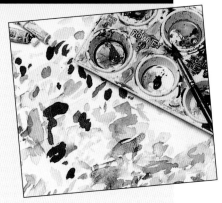

For a painting where subtle variations of colour and tone are required, work with a large palette and keep a test sheet of watercolour paper to hand so that you can check your mixes as you progress.

6 ◄ **Add darker tones**
Apply touches of a raw umber/yellow ochre mix to the surface of the copper pot where the bottle is reflected in it. Then develop the bottle itself. Use raw umber for the darkest tones, flooding in Venetian red on the right.

DEVELOPING THE PICTURE

Now begin working up the copper pot and its contents, which are the main focus of the picture. As you develop the image further, repeat colour mixes across the picture to give it harmony and visual unity.

7 ▲ **Darken the pot** Paint the top of the oil bottle in raw umber and the gold mix from step 5. Use a cobalt blue/lemon yellow mix for the aubergine stem. Apply a dilute wash of alizarin crimson and cobalt blue to the vinegar bottle. Mix indigo, alizarin crimson and raw umber for the grey inside the pot.

8 ▲ **Develop the pot** Paint the alizarin crimson and cobalt blue wash over the aubergine. Add more alizarin crimson and wash over the copper pot and the garlic. Leave to dry. Develop the surface of the pot with the grey mix from step 7 and strong and weak washes of Venetian red. Use a mix of alizarin crimson, gold ochre and cobalt blue for the warm brown reflections of the chillies.

9 ▲ **Paint the chillies** Use an indigo/alizarin crimson mix for the vinegar bottle. Leave to dry, then apply a stronger mix to establish the shadows. Paint the chillies with a mix of alizarin crimson, gold ochre and cobalt blue, leaving white highlights. Vary the colours with Venetian red and dark washes from your palette; use the dark grey mix from step 7 for the cast shadows.

10 ▲ **Add details** Paint dark tones on the aubergine in a mix of indigo and alizarin crimson. Use a dilute cobalt blue/alizarin crimson mix for the cast shadows on the table. Add a patch of gold ochre near the oil bottle. Now work over the painting, using existing mixes to develop tones and pull the

11 ▲ **Continue adding details** Paint a darker shadow on the aubergine, using a stronger version of the alizarin/indigo mix. Add deeper tones to the foreground onion, using washes based on gold ochre, Venetian red and raw umber. Define the segments of the garlic bulb with an alizarin/cobalt blue mix.

A FEW STEPS FURTHER

The painting is now fully resolved. Only a few tweaks are needed – darkening some of the shadows, adding highlights on the chillies and knocking back the stark white backdrop.

12 ▼ **Emphasize the shadows** Mix indigo with a touch of alizarin crimson and use it to darken some of the cast shadows. This helps the objects to 'sit' properly.

Express yourself

A hot background

A striking aspect of this pastel painting is the bright red paper it is worked on. Thickly applied pastel covers the red where necessary, but the hot colour is left showing through the glass bottle neck to suggest its transparency.

13 ▶ Add highlights with oil pastel

Use a white oil pastel to add extra highlights on the glossy surfaces of the dried chillies. The pastel gives you very precise marks and allows you to work light over dark. (Don't use the wax candle resist technique used in step 4 to add highlights to intricate subjects such as chillies. You can do it more accurately with a pastel or with white gouache.)

14 ▲ Tone the background
Mix Winsor blue and alizarin crimson to give a very pale blue-grey. Using a No. 14 round brush, wash this colour loosely over the background.

THE FINISHED PICTURE

A Happy accidents
Backruns, or blooms, which often occur when working with watercolour wet-on-wet, help suggest the loose folds and texture of the red fabric backdrop.

B Candle lights
Highlights made with a wax candle resist have a beautiful mottled texture. Specks of paint adhere as the wax does not completely cover the paper.

C Reflections
The sheen of the pot was suggested by showing adjacent surfaces reflected in it, such as the golden olive oil and the dark brown and red chillies.

Watercolour crab

Extend your range of watercolour techniques in responding to the challenge presented by the subtle colours and textures of a crab.

We tend to think of a still life as being a group of objects, but a single item, when painted in an interesting way, can have just as much impact as a table groaning with fruit and vegetables. The complex forms and unusual textures in this crab provide a means of challenging your watercolour skills to the full. Don't feel inhibited – the idea is not to reproduce the crab in photographic detail, but to express the essential qualities of its appearance.

Go with the flow

Watercolour is ideal for a spontaneous approach because it is so fluid and responsive. All sorts of textures and effects can be suggested, once you have found out how pigment and water behave.

Beginners are often afraid of watercolour because they think it is difficult to control. As this project shows, however, the best results are achieved by not controlling the paint too much; often you will find that it does much of the work for you! To paint the crab, wet the paper with clean water; work quickly and loosely, moving the brush in different directions to create a broken wash that is wetter in some parts than others – you don't want an even coating.

When the colours are applied they will flow with the water and dry unevenly, creating mottled patterns that mimic the crab's shell. By blotting with kitchen paper and adding further washes, you can build up complex patterns that would be difficult to achieve by more conventional means.

▼ **Look out for interesting and unusual objects for indoor painting, and be adventurous in using watercolour techniques to depict them.**

FIRST STROKES

1 ▶ Draw the outline Make a careful outline drawing of the crab using a sharp HB pencil. Don't attempt any shading, but outline the highlighted areas on the shell, some of which will be masked out.

YOU WILL NEED

Sheet of 400gsm+ (140lb+) NOT watercolour paper

HB pencil

Small, old watercolour brush for applying masking fluid

Tinted masking fluid

Brushes: Nos. 11, 6 and 2 round

Jar of water

6 watercolours: raw sienna; burnt sienna; cadmium orange; cadmium red; burnt umber; French ultramarine

Kitchen paper

Mixing palette or dish

2 ▼ Mask out the highlights Use a very small, old paint brush to apply masking fluid to the small highlights you have outlined on the shell of the crab. Leave to dry.

3 ▲ Apply the underwash Before applying any colour, load a No. 11 round brush with clean water and work it over the shape of the crab with fast, random strokes so that some areas are wetter than others. Don't worry if the water goes over the pencil lines – it will add to the unforced effect you are aiming for. Now dip the brush into some undiluted raw sienna and apply it randomly. The paint will flow with the water and create strong tones and lighter ones as it mixes with either damp or dryer areas.

TROUBLE SHOOTER

REMOVING HARD EDGES

If the underwash dries before you have a chance to apply a second wash over it, the second wash will dry with an unwanted hard edge. To avoid this, simply drop some water from the tip of the brush on to the edge where the two colours meet and gently work them together.

4 ▶ Blot with kitchen paper While the surface is still wet, blot some of the highlight areas on the main body of the crab with crumpled kitchen paper, using a press-and-lift motion. This forces the paint into the fibres of the paper, increasing the textural effects on the crab's shell.

DEVELOPING THE PICTURE

Having completed the underwash, the next stage is to develop the texture and form of the crab using wet-into-wet washes. The idea is to observe your subject carefully, then allow the paint to interpret what you see.

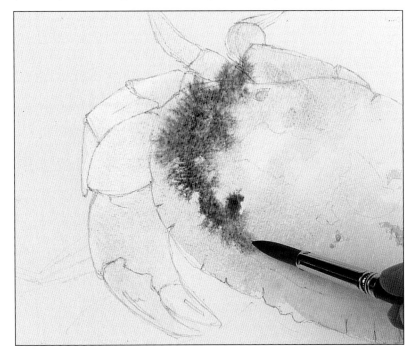

5 ▲ Apply burnt sienna Working quickly before the underwash dries, apply undiluted burnt sienna around the edge of the crab's body. Just touch the tip of the brush to the paper and let the colour flow on the damp surface.

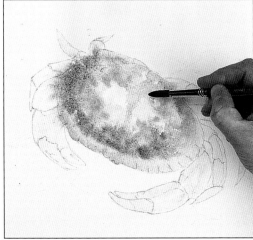

6 ▲ Start to build up form Continue darkening the body with burnt sienna, except for the top and 'pie-crust' edge of the shell, which pick up more light. Touch in some cadmium orange on the top of the shell. The rounded form of the crab is beginning to emerge: the top is pale, darkening as the shell curves away from the light.

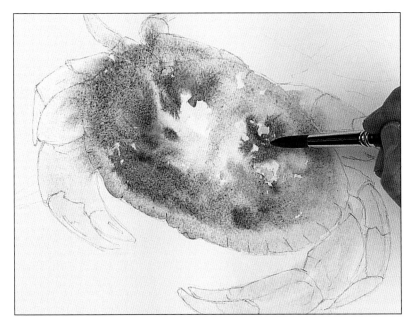

7 ▲ Add more colours Carry on building up layers of paint. To suggest the blotched patterning, drip some clean water off the brush to form small pools, then touch in a little undiluted cadmium red, then some burnt sienna. Let the colours bleed into the surrounding wash.

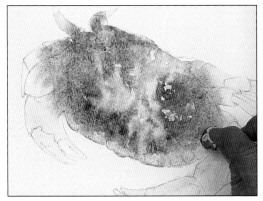

8 ▲ Work on the edge of the shell Using a wad of kitchen paper, blot the outer edge of the shell to lift out some of the paint, creating soft highlights that suggest the raised 'pie-crust' ridges. Leave the painting to dry naturally so that the water and paint settle at their own pace; using a hair-dryer will even out the marks.

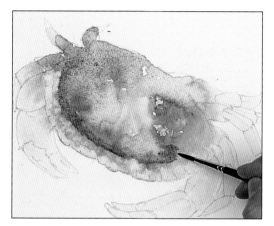

9 ◀ **Add definition**
Now drop some more water from the brush on to the shell. Use the tip of a No. 6 brush to 'draw' a line of raw sienna where the rounded body meets the flat edge of the crab, adding more definition to the shape.

EXPERT ADVICE
White highlights

Watercolour paintings have a unique freshness that owes much to the white of the paper shining through the overlaid colours. Don't forget, you can also think of the white paper as being another 'colour'. By leaving tiny slivers and flecks of paper untouched, you can create sparkling highlights that suggest shiny surfaces. These white areas also allow the painting to 'breathe', and make the whole picture dance with light.

10 ▶ **Paint the darker markings**
Mix burnt umber with a touch of raw sienna and start to paint the darker markings using a No. 2 brush. Make small, fast strokes, skipping the brush over the surface to create a mottled pattern.

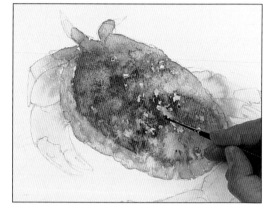

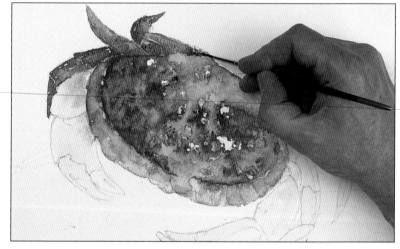

11 ◀ **Start painting the feelers** Allow the painting to dry completely, then remove the patches of masking fluid by rubbing with your finger to reveal the small, bright highlights on the shell. Now paint the first set of feelers using a slightly diluted wash of burnt sienna applied with the No. 2 brush. Don't fill in the shapes completely, but use small, broken strokes instead, allowing tiny patches of the pale underwash to show through and provide highlights. Allow to dry; because you are now working on dry paper, the paint will dry with a crisp, hard edge.

▼ **When the paint is dry you can see the interesting textural effects achieved by dropping water and wet pigment into a wet underwash, creating 'cauliflower' blooms that suggest the mottled and uneven surface of the crab's shell.**

12 ▶ **Add shadows**
Apply a dilute wash of burnt sienna over the feelers. Just before this dries, paint the shadows on the edges of the feelers and between the joints with a mixture of burnt umber and ultramarine. The edges will blend softly into the damp burnt sienna wash.

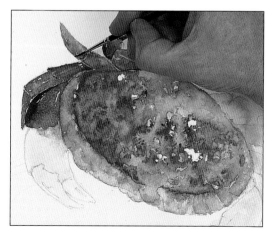

13 ◄ **Paint the claws** Repeat steps 11 and 12 to paint the first set of claws, this time making the shadows slightly stronger. Darken the mixture with more ultramarine to paint the tips of the claws. As before, use small, broken strokes and allow slivers of the underwash to provide the highlights and reflections.

14 ▼ **Complete the claws and feelers** Now paint the second set of claws and feelers, using the same method as for the first set. Leave the painting to dry.

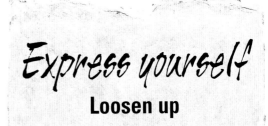

Express yourself
Loosen up

In this version of the same subject, the artist has worked even more loosely than before. He has also used more water: notice how some of the claws and feelers are partially dissolved, giving them an interesting 'lost-and-found' quality.

As well as painting a shadow under the crab, the artist has also suggested a white plate. This is understated so as not to detract attention from the crab, but serves to place it in context.

A FEW STEPS FURTHER

You might decide here that your study is complete. Sometimes adding more detail merely results in an overworked picture. But perhaps you feel your picture needs more contrast; you might also wish to add some background shadow to anchor the crab in space.

15 ► **Strengthen texture and detail** On the body of the crab, use burnt sienna and the No. 6 brush to work up the shell and emphasize form and texture. Again, use small, quick strokes to strengthen the marks already created, particularly round the edges of the shell.

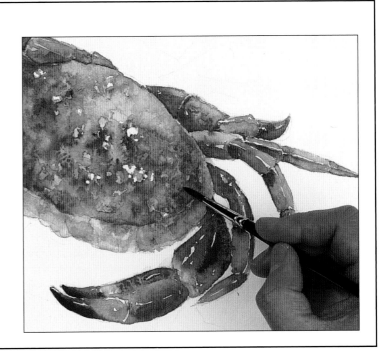

16 ▲ **Add more darks** With the No. 2 brush go over some of the shadows on the claws and feelers with a mixture of burnt sienna and ultramarine to make them stand out. Then paint a thin, broken line along the lower edge of the crab to give it more definition. Leave to dry.

17 ▲ **Paint the background shadow** Finally, add shadow beneath the crab for a three-dimensional effect. With the No. 6 brush, paint the shadow in raw sienna, overlaid with a pale mix of burnt sienna and ultramarine. Then rinse the brush and drip a little water on to the shadow area; the colour will dissolve into the water and dry with a soft edge.

THE FINISHED PICTURE

A Rounded forms
The rounded forms of the claws and feelers were suggested with overlaid washes, working from dark to light and leaving the brightest highlights unpainted.

B Mottled patterns
The blotched patterning on the crab's shell was captured perfectly by working wet-into-wet, blotting with kitchen paper and allowing the paint to flow and dry at different rates.

C Softly graded shadow
A touch of shadow helped to anchor the crab in space. The shadow is darkest directly beneath the crab, gradually fading out to nothing. This effect was achieved with a graduated wash.

Using resists

Discover the range of textures you can achieve by using watercolours with different masking materials.

W atercolour paints are unique because they are transparent. The colours contain no white or chalky pigments to make them opaque or cloudy.

For this reason, the most effective watercolour painting is done without the addition of white paint. This means you must plan ahead, leaving areas of white paper unpainted so that they represent highlights and paler tones in the picture.

Mask out the whites

Although white paper is a crucial element in most watercolour painting, you are not restricted to simply leaving certain areas unpainted. In fact, as you might have discovered, it is quite difficult to retain patches of white paper simply by painting around them. Not only do you have to remember where the white areas are, but you also have to take care not to paint over them by mistake.

The trick is to protect, or mask, the white areas before you start painting. In this way, you can work quickly, applying colour freely over the masked areas which will eventually show through the paint as patches of pure white. Any substance that temporarily blocks out the paper is called a resist.

Masking fluid

For sharply defined shapes with a hard edge, such as the crisp highlight on this shiny, ceramic plate, nothing is more effective than masking fluid. This can be applied to the paper with either a brush

▲ Masking off areas in this picture has created sparkling highlights and interesting textures.

or pen, and dries to form a thin, rubbery film. You can then paint over it and rub it off when the colours are dry to reveal the white paper underneath.

Candles and wax crayons

For a textured or linear resist, try using candles, wax crayons or oil pastels. When watercolour is painted over the oily or waxy marks, it forms droplets, which run off the resist area. However, a few drops will usually dry on top of the resist to create an attractive speckled texture. Wax crayons or oil pastels will provide a touch of colour too.

FIRST STEPS

1 ▶ Draw the still life
Start by making a simple line drawing of the bowl of fruit – a chunky carpenter's pencil will help you to keep the shapes broad and unfussy. Draw the plate as an ellipse and then establish each piece of fruit as an approximate circle. Take the spiky leaves over the edge of the plate to interrupt the elliptical shape.

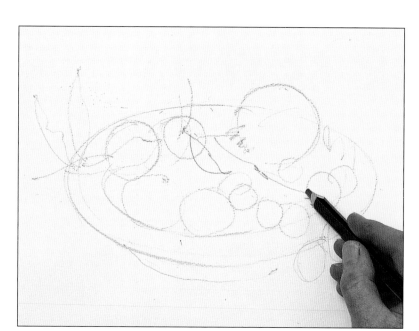

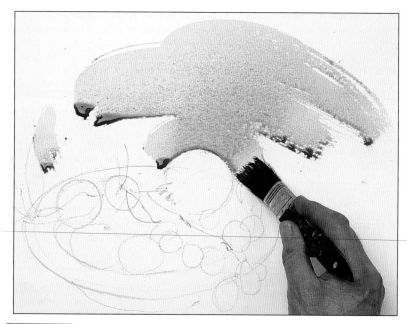

2 ◀ Apply a wash over the background
Using a 38mm (1½in) flat wash brush, paint the table top in a wash of burnt umber mixed with a little cadmium yellow. Apply the colour in broad, rapid strokes, working around the outlines of the bowl and fruit. A few drips and tidemarks will add interest to the flat table area, so don't worry if the paint looks uneven.

EXPERT ADVICE
Removing masking fluid

When removing areas of masking fluid, start rubbing from the centre of the masked shape and work outwards. In this way, the fluid should come away easily without tearing the surface of the paper.

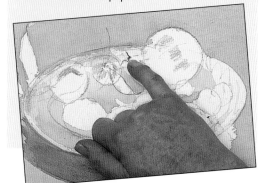

3 ▶ Mask out the highlights While the wash dries, take the opportunity to mask out some of the highlights on the fruit, using wax crayons. Make loose, sketchy strokes, but indicate the approximate rounded contours of the fruits. Choose a yellow wax crayon for the lime and an orange one for the tangerines and the pomegranate.

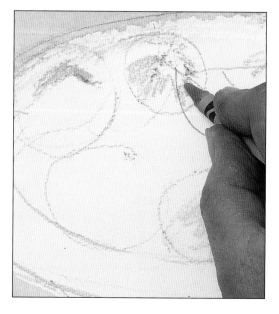

4 ▼ **Draw reflections with a candle** Continuing with the orange wax crayon, scribble over the highlight area of the pomegranate. Then use a candle to establish the white reflections on the grapes and figs. The colourless wax preserves the whiteness of the paper

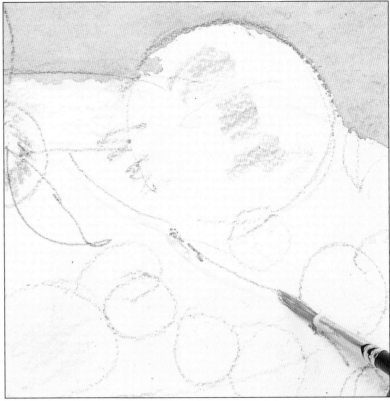

5 ▲ **Apply masking fluid** Paint the highlight around the rim of the bowl as a curved line, using masking fluid and an old round brush. Paint another line of fluid across the plate – this will be the grapes' stalk (see step 14).

DEVELOPING THE PICTURE

All the masked highlights have now been established, and it is time to start painting. Remember, the beauty of using resists is that it allows you to paint quite freely as the highlight areas are protected.

6 ▲ **Apply a wash to the plate** Using the 38mm (1½in) flat brush, paint the plate with a pale grey wash mixed from ivory black with lots of water. Follow the curved shape of the plate and use bold strokes to paint around the grapes and other fruit. Darken the tone of your wash to paint the shadow under the plate.

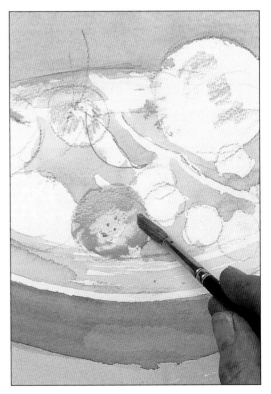

7 ▲ **Paint the lime** Change to a No.8 round brush to paint the lime in a mixture of lemon yellow and viridian, taking the brush strokes around the shape of the fruit and over the waxy crayon marks.

8 ▼ **Continue painting the fruit** Using the same technique, paint the tangerines in a mixture of cadmium red and cadmium yellow. Leave a tiny patch of white paper showing through at the centre of each fruit.

Express yourself

A sketch in wax crayons

The wax crayons used in the painting to mask out highlights on the fruit are an excellent drawing medium in their own right. They are perfect for chunky sketches in which bold line and colour are more important than a detailed rendering. This still life from the artist's sketch book was done using a basic set of 12 wax crayons. The highlights on the fruit are left as plain white paper or filled with lightly applied, smudged colour. The blue shadows on the plate echo the colour of the table.

9 ▲ **Complete the fruit** Paint the pomegranate in alizarin crimson, and the figs and grapes in a mixture of alizarin crimson and ultramarine. You will find that the candle wax resists the colour and shows up on the fruit as white reflected highlights.

10 ▲ **Paint the leaves and plate** Using viridian darkened with a little ivory black, paint each leaf as a single brush stroke of colour. Add a few darker shadows by overpainting in a darker tone of the same colour. Use the same green to paint the leaves on the ceramic plate design.

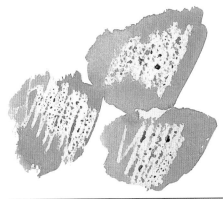

◄ The table top is burnt umber and cadmium yellow; the foliage viridian with a touch of added black; and the plate a diluted wash of ivory black. Note the rough texture created by the candle resist.

11 ▲ **Complete the bowl** Develop the leaf design on the painted ceramic plate, taking the pattern up to and around the curved shape of the pomegranate.

A FEW STEPS FURTHER

Local colours and the highlights are now in place. Shadows and dark tones need to be added – particularly on the plate, which looks a little flat at this stage.

12 ▲ **Add the bowl shadow** The shadow on the bowl is painted in a wash of ultramarine and burnt umber – the fruit shows up as lighter shapes against this dark colour. Put the paint on in broad strokes with a No.7 brush, redefining the round shapes. Flood extra colour into the darker areas.

Master Strokes

Jan van Os (1744–1808)
Fruit and Flowers

This lavish display by Jan van Os is typical of Dutch still life painting in the eighteenth century. Rather than being arranged in a formal way, the fruit and flowers spill in profusion across the table top. The light falls in a diagonal band across the centre of the picture from top right to bottom left, making this swathe of fruit stand out from the darker areas around it. In oil paintings, the highlights do not require forward planning as they do with watercolours – the bright reflected light can be added as final touches.

The highlights on the black grapes are restricted to single points of white paint; the green grapes, by contrast, are outlined in white.

Fruit of many different shapes and sizes, from tiny berries to a large melon, add variety and interest to the composition.

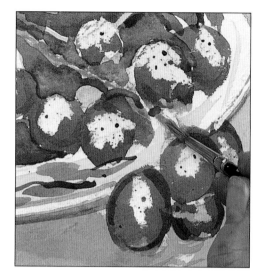

14 ▼ **Complete the grapes** Remove the masking fluid applied to the line of the grapes' stalk in step 5. Then paint the stalk with yellow ochre.

13 ▲ **Add detail to the patterned plate** Complete the rim of the plate in yellow ochre applied with the tip of a No.7 brush. Still using the tip of the brush, add dark green details to the leaves on the fruit and the plate design.

THE FINISHED PICTURE

A Textured fruit
Coloured wax crayon was used for the highlights on the citrus fruits. The slightly rough surface of the watercolour paper helped create the texture of the peel.

B Bowl highlight
The sharp linear highlight on the ceramic bowl was achieved with masking fluid, applied in a bold, unbroken line.

C White reflections
The wax from an ordinary household candle was applied in loose, sketchy strokes to create patches of reflected light on the purple grapes and the figs.

Inside the study

Watercolour is a flexible medium which can create many different effects. The 'one-stroke' wet-on-dry method gives crisp, clean images.

◄ The simple geometric shapes of the books and box are brightly lit from one side to give emphatic shadows.

The true beauty of watercolour painting is seen when it is applied layer upon layer as areas of pure colour. The building up of layers of translucent washes gives the painting a lovely, luminous brilliance.

The key to producing clear, vibrant watercolours is to keep the washes fresh and clean, and to allow each wash to dry thoroughly before you lay the next. This is called the wet-on-dry technique. Working in this way you can build up layers of fresh, jewel-like colour.

Working light to dark

When using pure watercolour, you do not have the option of adding a lighter tone over a dark tone, so the lightest tone available is the white of the paper. Plan the way you will work before you start. Look for the brightest highlights on your objects and make sure you retain these as white paper. You need to work 'light to dark' in the classic watercolour way, laying down the lightest tones of the local colours first, then gradually building up the tones by overlaying successive washes of colour.

Keep your colours fresh

Choose a large palette with many recesses, or use several saucers, so that you can keep each wash separate. Have two jars of water, one for rinsing your brushes and the other for diluting the paint for the wash, and change the water fairly frequently.

YOU WILL NEED

Sheet of 300 gsm (140lb) NOT watercolour paper

4B pencil

Kneadable rubber

Brush: round watercolour No. 6

Watercolour palette

Two jars of water

Hair-dryer

10 pan watercolours: permanent rose; Payne's grey; scarlet; burnt umber; cobalt blue; raw sienna; cadmium yellow; light red; lemon yellow; burnt sienna

287

FIRST STROKES

1 ▼ Locate the main elements Using a 4B pencil, locate the objects on the sheet, starting in the middle and working outwards. Use very light lines to provide a guide for the rest of the drawing. Refine the drawing, checking vertical and horizontal alignments, angles and 'negative shapes'. Include the outlines of the cast shadows.

2 ▶ Lay the first pale pink washes Make a pale wash of permanent rose toned down with a touch of Payne's grey. Test the wash on scrap paper and add more water if the colour is too intense. Apply to the top book with a No. 6 brush. Add scarlet to the wash to produce a warmer red for the second book. Leave to dry.

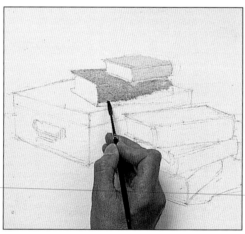

3 ◀ Establish the box and blue books Mix a wash of burnt umber with a touch of scarlet and Payne's grey. Using the No. 6 brush, apply the paint to the front and sides of the box. Add a little cobalt blue to create a cooler brown for the top. Make a dilute cobalt blue wash with a touch of Payne's grey to paint the book on the top of the pile. Using the very tip of the brush, take the wash around the golden lettering.

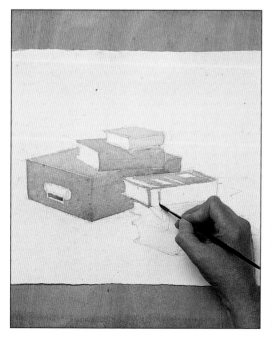

**EXPERT ADVICE
Leaving gaps between areas of wash**

To keep the image crisp, it is important to prevent colours running into each other. Do this by drying each patch of colour thoroughly before you progress to the adjoining areas. If this is too slow, you can save time by leaving a sliver of paper unpainted between adjacent areas of colour – the wash will not bleed across the dry paper.

▶ A cool red (permanent rose) and a warm red (scarlet) will give you just the right colour for the reddest books.

4 ▲ Begin to paint the surface Continue blocking in the blue books with a slightly more intense version of the colour. Leave the painting to dry. Mix a wash of raw sienna with a touch of cadmium yellow and light red. Block in the golden colour of the supporting surface, then leave it to dry.

5 ▲ **Paint the background** Mix a very pale greenish-yellow for the background. Use lemon yellow with a little cobalt blue and raw sienna. Lay this on as a single flat wash. Leave to dry.

DEVELOPING THE PICTURE

At this point all the elements of the picture have been established. Now you need to build up the darker tones with more intense versions of the initial washes. This will give the image a three-dimensional quality.

6 ▼ **Add dark tones** Mix a wash of permanent rose with a touch of burnt umber for the shaded spine of the top red book. Use the tip of the brush to lay a thin line of colour along the top edge of the cover. Add a touch of burnt umber to a wash of scarlet for the shaded parts of the second book. Notice the soft edge where the shaded area meets the light area – dip your brush in water and run it along the edge of the wash. For the shaded side of the box, use burnt sienna darkened with Payne's grey.

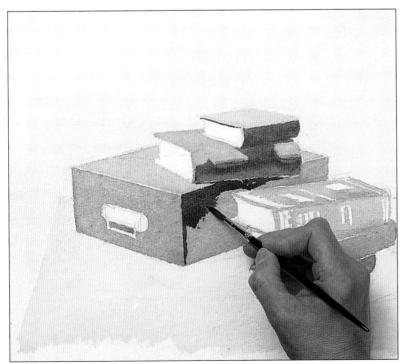

USE A HAIR-DRYER TO SPEED UP DRYING

TROUBLESHOOTER

To retain the integrity of each layer of wash, it is important that the painting is thoroughly dry before you apply successive washes. This can take time. A hair-dryer will speed things up. Don't use a dryer if there are puddles of wash, and choose a low setting – this avoids runnels of paint being blown across the support.

7 ▲ **Add more dark tones to the spines** Darken cobalt blue with Payne's grey. Using this wash, apply colour to the spine of the blue books, working carefully around the golden lettering on the spine.

◀ **Use permanent rose with a touch of Payne's grey for the cooler of the red books.**

▶ **Mix Payne's grey, burnt umber and raw sienna to create a dark but warm tone for the cast shadows.**

8 ▼ **Add the cast shadows** The shadows that fall on the supporting surface are important to establish the horizontal plane on which the objects are resting. Paint them with a wash of Payne's grey with burnt umber and raw sienna, using the No. 6 brush. Work carefully to create crisp edges. Leave to dry.

9 ▼ **Erase pencil lines** Using the previous wash, lay bands of shadow along the edge of the book covers. Leave to dry. Erase any distracting pencil lines with a kneadable rubber.

Express yourself
Editing and simplifying

The colours, shapes and textures in a subject are merely a jumping-off point for the artist. The 'picture-making' process involves manipulating, editing and emphasizing to create an image that is effective and unique. Here the subject has been simplified, which emphasizes the shapes of the objects, the pattern made by the light tone on the ends of the books, and the way this is echoed by the areas of shade and shadow. Try stripping your still-life subject down to its bare essentials and see what emerges.

10 ▲ **Add details to the box handle** Use a Payne's grey/burnt umber mix to paint the brass handle, leaving the white of the paper for the highlights. Use the tip of the brush and don't worry about precise details – a simplified version will be very convincing.

11 ▶ **Start to add the darker tones to the books** Apply a mix of permanent rose with Payne's grey to the cover of the top book, leaving a sliver of underlying colour along the edge, where light catches it. For the second book cover, apply permanent rose with scarlet.

12 ▲ **Work up details** At this point, decide which areas need to be emphasized. Warm up the side of the box that is turned to the light with a wash of burnt sienna and use the tip of the brush to add a few details to the handle. Mix cobalt blue and Payne's grey and add dark tones to the tops of the blue books, using the tip of the brush to work around the lettering.

A FEW STEPS FURTHER

The two most difficult stages in creating a picture are getting started and deciding when it is finished. The painting is complete and entirely convincing, but you might want to take it further, adding emphasis and detail.

13 ▲ **Developing the surface** The contrast between the objects and the supporting surface is a little stark. Rectify this with a flat wash of raw sienna and burnt sienna. Leave to dry. Intensifying this area pulls the entire image together. Add a wash of raw sienna with Payne's grey to the end of the bottom blue book.

14 ▲ **Adding gold lettering** The covers of the books are blocked with gold lettering. You can suggest this simply by going over the white lettered areas with raw sienna toned down with a tiny touch of Payne's grey.

15 ▲ **Warm the top of the box** Add warmth to the top of the wooden box by adding a final wash of burnt umber and burnt sienna. This final layer of colour will add both depth and warmth.

16 ▲ **Enrich the handle** Develop the brass handle further by working into it with Payne's grey warmed with burnt umber. A few touches will be surprisingly effective. Use this mix to add details and lettering on the covers of the red books.

THE FINISHED PICTURE

A Layers of crisp colour
Dry each application of watercolour before you apply the next – watercolour applied wet on dry is much easier to control.

B Small details are important
Small, generalized details, such as the scrollwork on the handle of the box, can add character and richness to a painting.

C Working light to dark
With pure watercolour you do not have a white to create light tones. The white of the paper is the lightest local colour – here, the pages of the book.

Still life with melon

Try a direct, 'no-drawing' approach to watercolour painting to achieve a bold, spontaneous effect.

For centuries, artists have used fruit and vegetables as an inspiration for still-life paintings. Works range from the lavish to the humble, from exotic fruit tumbling off silver salvers to partially peeled potatoes on scrubbed wooden tables.

Whatever your taste, you will find that fruit and vegetables make extremely versatile subjects. Fortunately, they are also easy to get hold of and a quick trip to the local market can set you up with an extraordinary range of shapes,

colours and textures with which to compose your picture.

Here, the artist chose a melon for the textural detail of its seeds, a vine of cherry tomatoes to create interesting negative shapes and a lemon and an aubergine for their strong colours and harmonious, curvaceous forms.

Fresh approach

To paint this colourful arrangement, try taking a fresh approach to a classical subject. Apply the watercolour without

a preliminary pencil drawing – a bold method that produces equally bold results. Use big brushes to keep your work immediate and lively, and avoid over-working the colours. Although a small brush was used to define the melon seeds, fine lines and details can generally be painted quickly and easily using the tip of a Chinese brush.

▲ **Bold application of watercolour brings out the strong, clear colours of the fruit and makes them stand out from the background.**

FIRST STEPS

YOU WILL NEED

Piece of 300 gsm (140lb) NOT watercolour paper 56 x 76cm (22 x 30in)

Brushes: Chinese brush; No. 3 soft round; 25mm (1in) soft flat

19 watercolours: gamboge yellow; Winsor green; lemon yellow; ivory black; cadmium orange; raw sienna; emerald green;

scarlet lake; viridian; burnt sienna; raw umber; cadmium red; Winsor violet; permanent rose; burnt umber; cobalt blue; alizarin crimson; ultramarine; sap green

Mixing dish

Rags and newspaper

Masking tape

Old toothbrush

1 ▲ Position the melon Using a Chinese brush, start by boldly blocking in the shapes of the melon flesh in dilute gamboge yellow. Make sure the proportions and positions are correct.

2 ▶ Paint the tomato stalks With the tip of the Chinese brush, paint the main tomato stalk with a mixture of gamboge yellow and Winsor green. Judge the correct position of the stalk by relating it to the painted melon, taking care to leave unpainted spaces for the tomatoes.

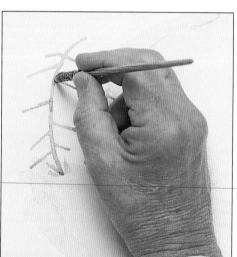

3 ▲ Add the lemon Paint the lemon in pure lemon yellow, leaving a patch of white to represent the highlight. Using the tip of the brush, dot in the dappled peel texture on the highlight. Outline the right-hand edge with a stronger lemon yellow mix.

TROUBLE SHOOTER

RESCUING HIGHLIGHTS

Leave unpainted paper for the white highlights on shiny fruit and vegetables. If you forget to do this, move quickly before the paint dries and create a highlight by soaking up the colour with a dry cotton bud.

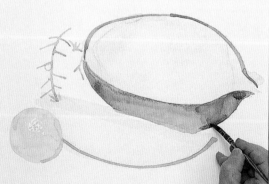

4 ▲ Develop the melon Allow the colours to dry, then outline the melon shapes with a strong mix of Winsor green with a little added ivory black and cadmium orange. Add more water and a little more orange to the mixture, and flood this into the centre of the melon half, allowing the colour to bleed into the darker tone.

5 ▼ **Add the melon seeds** Paint the shaded edge of the melon flesh in a mixture of Winsor green and lemon yellow. Add the seeds to the segment of melon in the foreground in gamboge yellow and raw sienna, leaving the pith as an unpainted white shape.

6 ▼ **Paint the tomatoes** Paint a mixture of emerald green and lemon yellow around the edge of the melon. Add three tomatoes in washes of cadmium orange and scarlet lake, leaving highlights unpainted. Paint the half-melon's seeds in mixes of raw sienna, cadmium orange and gamboge yellow.

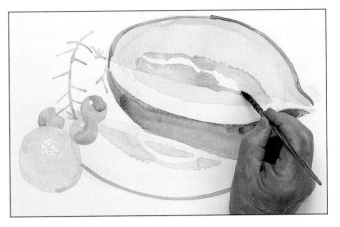

DEVELOP THE PICTURE

You will need to change to a smaller brush to put in some of the detail. It is important, however, to keep the painting generally bold and broad.

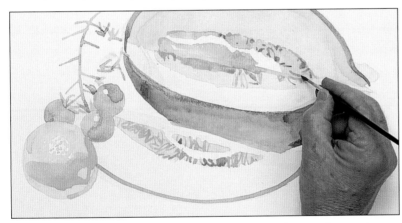

7 ▲ **Add details** Complete the tomato stalks in gamboge yellow and Winsor green. Paint the shadow on the lemon in gamboge yellow with small amounts of viridian and raw sienna. Change to a No. 3 soft round brush and define the seeds in mixtures of raw sienna, burnt sienna and raw umber.

8 ▲ **Develop the colours** With the Chinese brush, block in the remaining tomatoes in cadmium orange and cadmium red, painting around the green stalks. Add the dark stripes to the outside of the melon, painting these as broken lines of Winsor green and raw sienna.

Express yourself
Fruit substitute

You can change the emphasis of the still life by substituting one fruit or vegetable for another. In this painting of a similar subject, a watermelon dominates the colour scheme. Its bright pink centre draws the eye more than the pale green flesh of the melon used in the project. The grapes play the same role as the tomatoes in the step-by-step, creating intricate detail and interesting negative shapes. Try, too, altering the background slightly, putting in additional colours and textures.

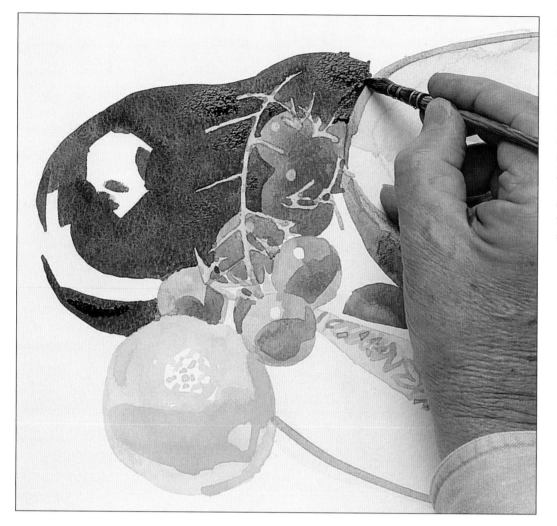

9 ◀ **Paint the aubergine** Block in the aubergine in Winsor violet with a touch of ivory black and permanent rose, painting carefully around the tomatoes and stems. Leave the jagged highlights unpainted, referring closely to the subject to find their exact shapes.

10 ▶ **Block in the shadows** Change to a 25mm (1in) soft flat brush and block in the shadows around the fruit and plate in a mixture of Winsor violet, burnt sienna and a little black. Paint the shadows on the white fabric in a diluted version of the same colour. Take the same diluted colour over the highlights on the aubergine.

11 ▼ **Paint the background** Loosely paint the glass bottle with a mixture of Winsor violet and burnt umber, leaving the lower half of the bottle unpainted to indicate the pale stone behind. Block in the background and stone with bold strokes, using dark and pale mixtures of raw sienna, ivory black and Winsor violet.

EXPERT ADVICE
Composition check

As you have not made an initial drawing, check your composition as you progress. Choose a support larger than you want the finished picture to be, then cut a card mount. By moving the mount around on the painting from time to time during the early stages, you can choose a suitable composition at any time as work progresses.

A FEW STEPS FURTHER

The watercolour is virtually finished, but you might wish to add one or two finishing touches before putting down your brushes. For example, the background and the stone are possibly rather too similar in tone and texture.

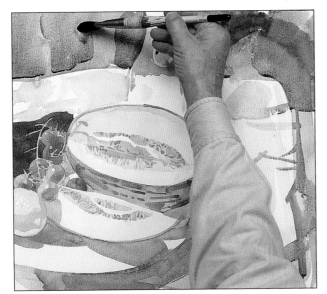

12 ▲ **Darken the background** Working in bold, broad strokes, strengthen the background with dark washes of burnt umber mixed with ivory black and a little Winsor violet. Use the same mixtures to emphasize the shadow around the right-hand side of the stone.

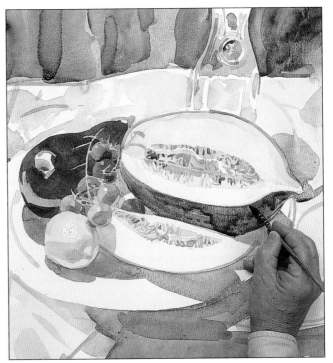

13 ▲ **Develop dark tones** With the Chinese brush, define the motif and reflections on the bottle in a mix of cobalt blue and ivory black. Paint alizarin crimson shadows on the tomatoes and add a cool shadow to the lemon in a mixture of gamboge yellow, black and ultramarine. Emphasize the melon seeds in mixtures of raw and burnt sienna, and darken the outside of the melon in sap green and black.

14 ▼ **Mask the picture** Prepare to add a spattered texture to the surface of the stone by first protecting the rest of the painting with old rags and newspaper. Stick these down with masking tape, positioning the tape carefully so that it protects the edges of the plate, cloth and bottle.

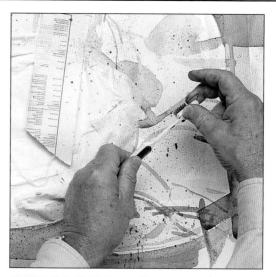

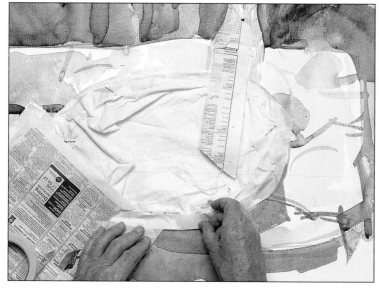

15 ▲ **Spatter the stone** To spatter, mix a wash of sap green and burnt sienna. Dip an old toothbrush into the diluted colour and hold the loaded brush a little way above the area to be spattered. Pull the bristles back and flick the colour across the paper, repeating this until the stone is covered with a speckled texture.

THE FINISHED PICTURE

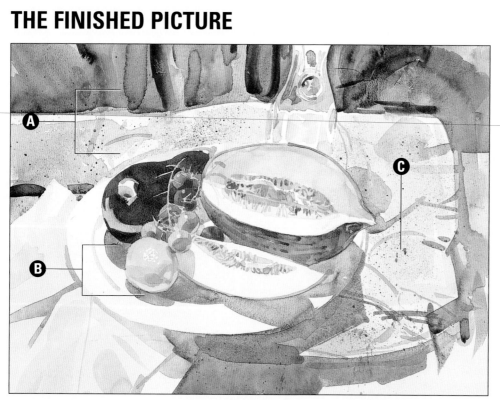

A Muted background
The background was painted in dark, neutral colours which do not compete with the central subjects: the brightly coloured fruit and shiny aubergine.

B Shadow shapes
The artist used cool violet-grey shadows on the plate to reflect curved shapes within the subject and play a positive role in the overall composition.

C Speckled stone
Spattered texture on the stone is light and minimal – just enough to differentiate it from the smooth cloth. It does not detract from the main elements in the composition.

Coffee and croissants

All the necessities for a continental breakfast are arrayed in this still life. You might find a similar scene in any French café if you want to paint on location.

▲ A spontaneous, economical style gives this watercolour painting a pleasing freshness.

Think of the painting opportunities that France has to offer and beautiful landscapes, picturesque villages and golden beaches might come to mind. But there are also paintings waiting to be made in the corner of every café. With just a few cups of coffee, a newspaper and a croissant or two, you have all the makings of an attractive and evocative still life at your disposal. Of course, you do not have to go abroad to create the ambience of the French café – you can easily do it in your own kitchen.

Arranging the composition

Take some time over the arrangement of the objects. In the painting shown here, a newspaper, a knife and a cigarette packet are positioned at an angle in the foreground to help lead the eye into the composition. The cafetière at the centre of the table provides a focal point, and the red chair helps to give depth, as well as a bold contrast to the blue of the tablecloth.

A simple approach

This type of subject matter lends itself to a simple, spontaneous approach – a rough pencil sketch, then a bold application of watercolour. In fact, the painting shouldn't take that much longer than the breakfast itself. Do not over-labour the colours by laying wash upon wash. And remember to be selective about where you apply the paint. To register the brightest highlights in the scene, simply leave the paper exposed.

As far as the watercolour paint is concerned, it is best to use the solid blocks that come in pans, rather than the semi-liquid variety in tubes. A selection of pans in a box is easier to transport if you are working on location. Watercolour paints in this form also allow you to work quickly, as each colour is on hand, ready to be mixed.

YOU WILL NEED

Sheet of 300gsm (140lb) watercolour paper

4B pencil

Brushes: Nos. 6 and 3 rounds

Mixing palette or dish

Jar of water

Paper napkin or kitchen paper

9 pan watercolours:
cobalt blue; Payne's grey; burnt umber; yellow ochre; alizarin scarlet; alizarin crimson; ultramarine; cadmium yellow; viridian

FIRST STROKES

1 ▲ **Begin the pencil sketch** With a 4B pencil, softly outline the shape of the table and chair. Then concentrate on establishing the breakfast objects. Pay particular attention to the series of ellipses formed by the cups, bowl and cafetière, and their relationship to the ellipse of the table.

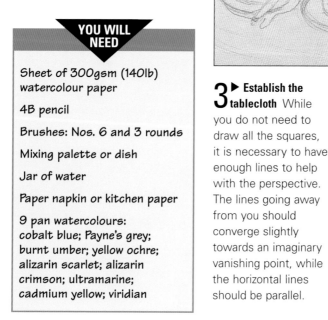

2 ◄ **Re-emphasize the outlines** Give further definition to your pencil sketch. Pay attention to the perspective, especially to that of the lettering on the newspaper. Draw two converging lines, then add the letters between them. Put a minimum of detail on the sugar cubes, as this area will be left largely as exposed paper.

3 ► **Establish the tablecloth** While you do not need to draw all the squares, it is necessary to have enough lines to help with the perspective. The lines going away from you should converge slightly towards an imaginary vanishing point, while the horizontal lines should be parallel.

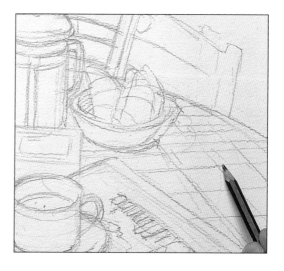

4 ▲ **Start on the background of bricks** The bricks will eventually be given only a pale wash of watercolour, so you need to put in quite a lot of detail with pencil to convey their texture. Then sit back and re-evaluate your drawing.

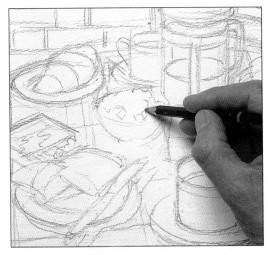

5 ▲ **Put the finishing touches on your drawing** Look over your picture and add the final details, including some definition on the edges of the sugar cubes. Remember, don't commit yourself to irreversible watercolour washes before you're totally happy with your drawing.

RESCUING DRIED PAINT

Solid blocks of watercolour dry out very easily, especially when working on a hot summer's day. To make the colours workable again, simply hold them under running water.

TROUBLE SHOOTER

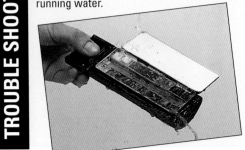

DEVELOPING THE PICTURE

Start the painting by putting initial washes of watercolour on the main objects on the table. Then move on to the table-cloth. (If the tablecloth has small checks or an intricate pattern, be prepared to spend quite a lot of time on it – or simplify it.) Finally, go back to the objects, enhancing their colour and modelling with further washes.

6 ▲ **Begin with the dark tones** Use a weak mix of cobalt blue and Payne's grey with a No. 6 brush to render the shadows cast on the cloth. Use the same wash for the lid of the cafetière and, while it is still wet, use a strong Payne's grey to show the shadow on the right of the lid and to define the handle.

7 ▲ Turn to the warmer colours Add water and burnt umber to your Payne's grey mix to render the coffee in the cafetière and cups. Add more burnt umber for the coffee on the left side of the cafetière and more Payne's grey on the shadowed side on the right. Then use a mix of burnt umber, yellow ochre and alizarin scarlet for the croissants and basket.

8 ▲ Paint the chair Clean your brush thoroughly and mix together some alizarin scarlet and alizarin crimson. Use this bright-red colour to paint the chair.

9 ▲ Fill in the tablecloth pattern Switch to a No. 3 brush and use a dark mix of Payne's grey and cobalt blue for the lettering on the newspaper and for the darker cast shadows. Dilute the mix for the mid tones on the cups. Clean the brush and, with a dilute mix of ultramarine, start defining the checks on the tablecloth. Use bold, long brush strokes. You need a steady hand and a degree of patience here.

10 ▲ Continue with the tablecloth To get the perspective right on the vertical lines of the checked pattern, follow the guidelines you established in pencil. Use a paper napkin or a piece of kitchen paper under your hand to avoid smudging any of the lines already painted.

11 ▲ **Darken the areas in shadow** Strengthen your ultramarine mix and, using the grey washes you put in earlier as a guideline, rework the areas of the tablecloth in shadow.

12 ▲ **Overlay washes** Add a lot of water and some Payne's grey to your ultramarine mix to put in the watery colours captured in the glass ashtray. Then start building up the darker tones. Use a deep burnt umber to render the areas of coffee in shadow in the cups and cafetière. Mix up alizarin scarlet, yellow ochre and cadmium yellow for the dark glaze on the croissants. Darken the tone on the cafetière lid with Payne's grey.

Express yourself
Erasing the pencil lines

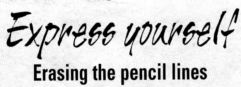

Simply by erasing the pencil marks on the painting, you will give the whole picture a fresher, more vibrant look. Much of the tone and detail of the wall was drawn in pencil. Once this is removed, the chair and table appear to leap forward towards the viewer. The bright colours seem to float and play against each other with a greater vigour. The viewer's eye is drawn across the blue tablecloth towards the areas of warmer colour.

13 ▲ **Work on the light tones** Paint in the swirling pattern on the cigarette packet using the strengthened ultramarine mix from step 11. Then add a touch of burnt umber to a mix of alizarin scarlet and alizarin crimson to put in the shaded sides of the chair. Clean your brush and use a weak mix of Payne's grey and ultramarine to paint the whitewashed wall and some of the shadows among the sugar cubes. Then add a little viridian to this mix to render the printed areas of the newspaper. Darken the mix with more Payne's grey and paint the cast shadow of the chair.

A FEW STEPS FURTHER

Squint at the set-up through half-closed eyes to check that you've got the tonal range right. Then give the picture greater punch by adding the darkest tones. Remember, as there is no going back with watercolour, don't add these tones until the end. Try not to spend too long tightening up the picture or you'll lose the freshness and spontaneity which are part of its appeal.

14 ▶ Add some detail Use a strong mix of Payne's grey for the dark tone on the knife; deepen it further for the detail on the cigarette packet. Mix burnt umber and alizarin crimson to show the red chair through the cafetière.

15 ▲ Put in the final washes Now mix up burnt umber with a touch of yellow ochre to darken the end of the left-hand croissant in the basket (where it is caught in shadow behind the cafetière). Use the same mix for the shaded side of the basket.

THE FINISHED PICTURE

A Less is more
A few dabs of grey for some shadowed sides of the sugar cubes was all that was needed to suggest their shape. The same technique was used for the cigarettes.

B Cast shadows
The artist used a considerably darker blue in the shadow areas of the tablecloth to prevent the objects from appearing to float above the table.

C Delicate touches
Changes of tone and colour were subtly applied to the ashtray to capture the reflections of the tablecloth and the cafetière in the glass.

Trout in watercolour

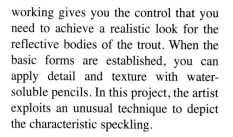

Use a combination of pure watercolour and water-soluble pencils to capture the shimmering colours of these rainbow trout.

The streamlined body shapes and iridescent colours of rainbow trout make them an absorbing subject. Arrange the pair of fish on a white plate – the austere background highlights their simple shapes and delicate hues. A more dramatic background would be distracting. If necessary, tilt the plate to provide you with a high viewpoint, as this will give a strong composition. Spray the fish with water from time to time, using a plant mister, to keep them looking fresh and glossy. Organize the lighting carefully – you should be able to see the details clearly, but strong shadows will add impact.

Combining media

This is an ideal subject for a mixed media technique. Wet-in-wet washes of watercolour are ideal for the delicate blushes of colour on the skin of the fish. Wet the paper with clean water first, then flow in very pale washes to begin with. Increase the intensity of the colour in the subsequent layers. This method of working gives you the control that you need to achieve a realistic look for the reflective bodies of the trout. When the basic forms are established, you can apply detail and texture with water-soluble pencils. In this project, the artist exploits an unusual technique to depict the characteristic speckling.

▼ You will need a delicate touch and a subtle palette of watercolours to convey the iridescent effect on the bodies of these rainbow trout.

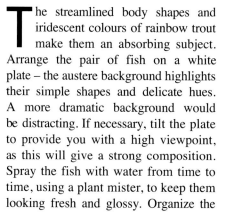

Piece of 555gsm (260lb) NOT watercolour paper

HB pencil

Masking fluid plus old brush and soap

Brushes: Nos. 10 and 7 rounds

8 watercolours: Winsor blue (if unavailable, use phthalo blue); permanent rose; viridian; ultramarine blue; burnt umber; cadmium yellow; cadmium red; permanent violet

Tissue paper

Craft knife

7 water-soluble coloured pencils: dark blue; soft green; grey; light blue; bright blue; dark brown; red

FIRST STROKES

1 ▶ Draw the subject Start by making a careful drawing of the fish and the plate, using an HB pencil. Notice how the artist has arranged the fish on a slight diagonal to produce a dynamic composition. If they had been horizontal, the image would have been quite static.

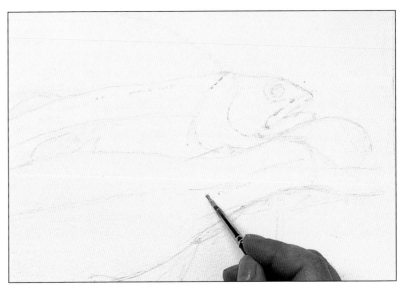

2 ▶ Mask the highlights The silvery highlights of the fish scales are represented by the white of the paper. Protect these areas with masking fluid while you lay on washes of colour. Use an old brush and rub a bit of soap into it before you dip it into the masking fluid – it will be easier to clean later. Place masking fluid over all the brightest parts of the fish. Wash the brush. Leave the mask to dry thoroughly.

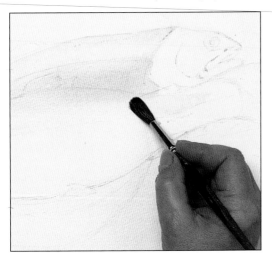

3 ▲ Apply the first washes Wet a No. 10 brush and dampen the two fish. Lay a very pale wash of Winsor blue along the back of the top fish. While this is still wet, lay a wash of permanent rose below it. Wash viridian along the back of the lower fish, overlapping the rose to make grey. Place a band of rose along the middle of the lower fish, then mix ultramarine blue and rose for the pale violet on its belly.

4 ▲ Paint the tail and fins Allow the first washes to dry completely. Mix Winsor blue and burnt umber to give an intense, warm grey for the tails and fins. Apply the colour carefully, using the tip of the No. 10 brush. Leave to dry.

5 ▼ **Paint the plate** The white, glazed surface of the plate picks up colours reflected from the adjacent surfaces, including the fish. Apply very pale washes of permanent rose, cadmium yellow and Winsor blue, allowing the washes to blend and bleed into one another to create a delicate, pearly effect. Allow these washes to dry.

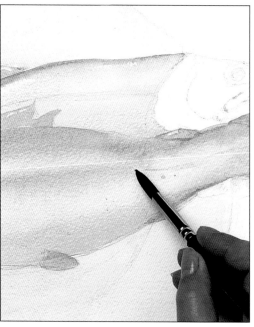

6 ▲ **Strengthen the colours** Moisten the fish with water, avoiding the overlap where you need a crisp edge. Wash a mix of Winsor blue and permanent rose along the back of the top fish, adding viridian beneath it. Flood bands of cadmium yellow on each side of the rose stripe on the lower fish. Paint a little of the pale violet mix from step 3 on the belly. Deepen the rose stripe on the side of the fish and darken its back with a mix of Winsor blue and burnt umber.

Express yourself

A new composition

Experiment with composition whenever you can. Very small adjustments can entirely change the character and impact of an image. Here, a single fish is displayed on a plain white plate. By arranging it so that it fills the picture area from corner to corner, the artist has given the image energy and has emphasized the graphic qualities of the subject.

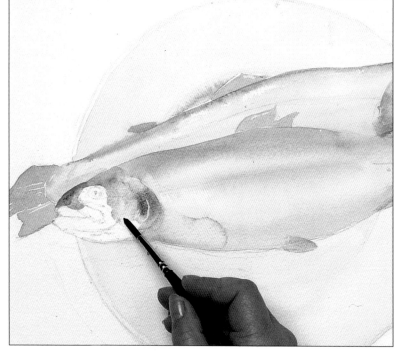

7 ▲ **Paint the heads** Add a touch of burnt umber to Winsor blue and use this for the dark areas on the right-hand fish's head. Working wet-in-wet, apply cadmium yellow and permanent rose. Develop the head on the left in the same way, using the mixed grey, permanent rose, burnt umber and a little cadmium red. Allow to dry thoroughly.

DEVELOPING THE PICTURE

The image has been established using a series of wet-in-wet washes. Now, the water-soluble pencils will come into their own. You can use them to draw details such as the eyes, to add small areas of intense colour and to develop textures using a variety of techniques.

8 ▲ **Apply texture** Re-wet the fish, then blot the surface with a tissue so that it is just damp. Using a craft knife, scrape specks of pigment from a dark blue pencil tip over the backs of both fish, dusting them with granules of colour. Repeat with soft green and grey pencils.

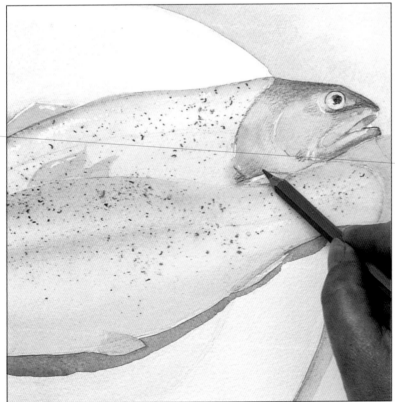

9 ▲ **Paint the shadows** Mix ultramarine and permanent rose to create a cool violet for the cast shadows. Apply this wash with the No. 10 brush, working underneath the lower fish and around the outside of the plate and crisping up the outlines at the same time. Using the same wash, add the shadows cast by the tails. Notice how the shadows give the image a three-dimensional feeling and establish the horizontal surface on which the plate is resting.

10 ▲ **Add details in water-soluble coloured pencil** Lay a very pale wash of Winsor blue over the background at the top of the image. While it is still wet, introduce touches of cadmium yellow and permanent violet to create a delicately variegated wash. Use a dark blue water-soluble pencil to create the dark pupil of the eye and the shading on the head of each fish. Go over these with grey pencil. Use this pencil to draw the details of the mouth and the eye socket. Take a light blue pencil and apply hatched shading within the mouth, along the cheek and under the head.

EXPERT ADVICE
Customize your palette

If you want to build up intense colours using water-soluble coloured pencils, make a palette on a piece of scrap paper. Hatch patches of the shades you want to use. You can dissolve the colours with a brush dipped in water, then transfer them to the image. This method allows you to control the intensity of the wash.

11 ▶ Blend the pencil colours

Using a No. 7 brush dipped in water, start to blend the water-soluble pencil colours. Work carefully, as the pigment in some water-soluble pencils is very intense and might overwhelm the subject. If the washes you create are too saturated, blot the surface gently with a tissue.

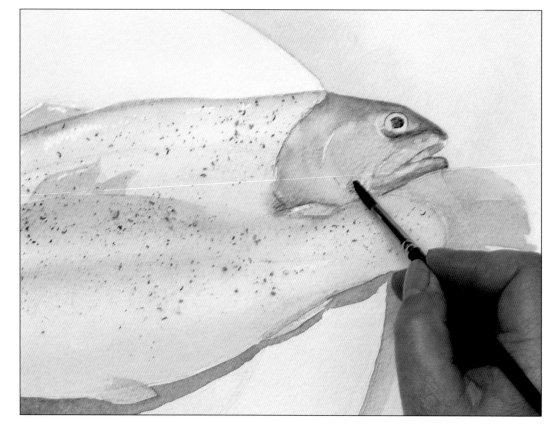

12 ▲ **Tighten up the image** Using the paper palette method, define the back of the top fish with bright blue pigment picked up on a brush, and paint the fins with dark brown. When the painting is dry, remove the film of masking fluid.

A FEW STEPS FURTHER

Deciding when your painting is finished is one of the most difficult decisions you have to make. The trick is to add a touch more detail and texture without jeopardizing the spontaneity of the image.

13 ▲ **Refine the outlines** With the dark blue water-soluble pencil, redraw the backs of the fish and the outlines of the fins. Using the blue and grey water-soluble pencils, draw spots along the back of the fish to suggest the larger dappled marks on their backs.

14 ▲ **Draw the scales** With a red pencil, draw a regular cross-hatched pattern along the side of the fish to suggest its scaly surface. If you create just a small area of detail, the eye will fill in the rest.

15 ▲ **Darken the cast shadow** Hatch in more scales in shades of blue and grey. Using the No. 7 brush and ultramarine blue with a touch of permanent rose, intensify the colour of the shadow cast by the plate.

THE FINISHED PICTURE

A Delicate wet-in-wet washes
By applying the washes to damp paper, the artist allowed the colours to flow into each other to create subtle colour blends. These perfectly captured the iridescence of the skin of the trout.

B Speckled pattern
The dots of colour on the fish were created by scraping water-soluble pencil on to damp paper, and by drawing dots on to dry paper. Combining both techniques produced visual interest and an accurate description.

C Scaly texture
Small areas of light, regular cross-hatching with the water-soluble pencils suggest the scaly bodies of the fish. If this texture had been applied more extensively, it would have looked too mechanical.

Street sign in watercolour

Watercolour is the ideal medium to re-create the faded paint and softly merging rust stains on this old and weathered Parisian street sign.

owns and cities derive much of their character from the details of their architecture. Doors, windows, balconies and decorative brick- and stonework can make lovely painting subjects in themselves, especially when they are old, faded and weathered. Even purely functional objects, such as pillar boxes and signposts, have potential due to their interesting shapes and patterns; moreover, they quite often have a characteristic design which identifies them as belonging to a certain country or era. Take the old metal street sign shown here: it is typical of the elegant Art Nouveau features that still grace many Parisian streets today.

Moving in close

It takes confidence to base an entire composition around one object placed centrally on the paper, but by cropping in close the artist can encourage the viewer to see that object with a fresh eye. It is easy, for example, to pass by a street sign like this one, but when we look at it up close we can appreciate the beauty of its design and the elegance of its lettering – and the fact that it is faded and streaked and rusting with age only adds to its appeal.

When painting architectural details in close-up, it is important to keep your brushwork and colour mixes lively and varied, otherwise there is a danger of your finished picture appearing static. Think about how your subject is lit, too; light coming from one side will create interesting shadows and emphasise form and texture, whereas front lighting tends to have a flattening effect.

▼ **Although this is a realistic interpretation of the subject, the artist has not merely copied, but also interpreted it in a personal way, capturing its character through lively brushwork.**

FIRST STROKES

1 ▼ **Draw the design** Make a careful outline drawing of the street sign and its lettering using a sharp pencil (propelling pencils are good since they give clean lines and don't need to be sharpened). Outline the two large rust patches on the main part of the sign and on the green border. Indicate the stone blocks on either side of the sign.

2 ▼ **Mask out the lettering** Use an old paint brush to fill in the lettering with masking fluid, but don't mask out the large rust marks outlined in step 1. Masking fluid tends to leave hard-edged shapes, which is fine for the lettering but not suitable for the ragged, soft-edged shapes of the rust patches. Also mask out the white edges and the highlights on the decorative roundels at the top and corners of the sign. Allow to dry thoroughly.

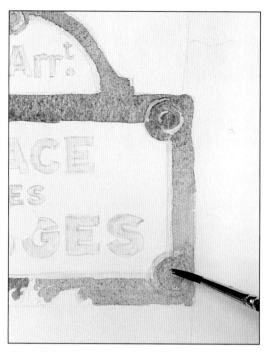

3 ▲ **Paint the green border** Mix a mid-toned green from olive green and a little Hooker's green and French ultramarine. Using a No.6 round brush, fill in the green border, again working around the outlines of the rust patches. Take care not to lean on any of the masked areas as you work, as the dried masking fluid is quite tacky and might lift off.

YOU WILL NEED

Medium-sized sheet of 240lb watercolour paper

Propelling pencil or HB pencil

Old brush for applying masking fluid

Masking fluid

Brushes: Nos.6, 2 and 11 round

6 watercolour paints: Olive green; Hooker's green; French ultramarine; Burnt sienna; Burnt umber; Raw sienna

Mixing palette or dish

Kitchen paper

4 ▲ **Start to paint the rust patches** While the previous wash is still damp, but not too wet, change to a No.2 brush and paint the rust patches on the green border with burnt sienna. Apply just a tiny drop of colour and let it bleed into the green wash so that it dries with a soft, ragged edge.

5 ▼ **Add some dark colour** When the burnt sienna base wash has dried off a little, touch in a tiny bit of burnt umber on the outer edge of each rust patch, allowing it to bleed out into the burnt sienna wash.

Express yourself
Crumbling stonework

By spraying watercolour paint on to watercolour paper using a plant mister spray, you can create a convincing stained wall surface. The artist gradually built up the rusty-looking effect shown below with layers of diluted raw sienna paint followed by layers of burnt sienna. Once these were dry, the drainpipe was painted with a brush; the textures, however, still show through.

6 ▲ **Paint the shadows and outlines** Darken the green wash prepared in step 3 by adding a little more French ultramarine to it. Use the tip of the No.2 brush to paint the dark edges of the green border and the shadowed parts of the corner roundels. This helps to give the sign a more three-dimensional appearance. Leave to dry.

7 ▲ **Fill in the blue background** Prepare a wash of French ultramarine slightly darkened with a drop of burnt umber. Fill in the blue background of the sign using a No.11 brush. To suggest the faded and distressed appearance of the old sign, vary the tone by adding more or less water, leaving some tiny slivers of white to suggest highlights. Gently blot with kitchen paper in places. You can wash over the masked-out lettering, but don't forget to leave gaps for the rust patches to go in later.

8 ▶ **Paint the large rust patches** Just before the blue wash dries, change to the No.6 brush to touch in the large rust patches with burnt sienna. Allow the colour to bleed slightly into the surrounding wash.

9 ▲ **Remove the masking fluid** Check that the previous washes are completely dry before removing the masking fluid from the lettering by rubbing with your finger. Now add more touches of burnt sienna to show where the rust has bled and run on to some of the white parts of the sign, in particular on the lettering.

DEVELOPING THE PICTURE

Now that you have completed the street sign itself, it is time to tackle the surrounding stone wall. Since the sign is the focal point of the picture, the wall should not be too strong in tone and detail, otherwise it will fight with the sign for attention. Begin by indicating the overall colour and tone of the wall, then add a suggestion of texture.

10 ▲ **Apply the underwash** Change to the No.11 brush and use it to wet the entire wall area with clean water. While this dries off a little, prepare a medium-strength wash of raw sienna. Apply this to the wall, using broad, loose strokes worked in a vertical direction. To suggest the streaked and weathered appearance of the stonework, vary the intensity of the wash by adding more pigment or water in some places and leaving other areas white.

11 ▲ **Suggest rust streaks** While the underwash is still wet, change to the No.6 brush and touch in a little burnt sienna on the wall, just beneath the main rust spots on the street sign. Encourage the colour to bleed into the underwash and run downwards to suggest streaks of rust on the wall.

12 ▼ **Start to paint the stone blocks** While the underwash is still damp, build up variations of tone and colour on the wall with random touches of raw sienna, burnt sienna, and a grey mixed from ultramarine and burnt umber. Start to paint the stone blocks to the right of the sign using raw sienna and the grey on your palette, again working wet on wet.

Master Strokes

Nick Harris (b.1948)
Blue Wall and Red Door

In this acrylic painting, the artist has made a feature of the dilapidated house wall. He has defined the cracked surface of the stucco so that it forms an intriguing pattern of hard-edged, irregular shapes – a complete contrast to the softly merging colours of the weathered wall and sign in our step-by-step. The brilliant colours and architectural lines make this a striking image.

Pink-red and green provide strong colour contrasts with the blue of the wall. The blocks of colour offset to the left are balanced by the window at top right.

Fascinated by the patterns that have been created in the cracked surface by age and weathering, the artist has made the wall the main point of interest in the painting.

13 ▲ **Continue adding tone and texture** Paint the stone blocks to the left of the sign using the same technique as before, leaving narrow strips of the pale underwash showing through for the gaps between the blocks. Suggest the weathered surface of the centre part of the wall by applying more wet-on-wet washes and streaks of colour and by blotting with crumpled kitchen paper. This gives a pleasing, granular texture to the paint.

14 ▲ **Finish off the wall** Strengthen the tone of the stone blocks with small overlaid strokes of raw sienna and grey, leaving tiny chinks of the paler underwash showing through to suggest the crumbling surface. Finally, use the same mixture to define the two long horizontal stone blocks above the street sign.

A FEW STEPS FURTHER

At this stage, when the painting is nearly complete, leave it for a while and return to it later with a fresh eye. All it will probably need to finish it off are a few crisply defined touches to bring it into focus.

15 ◀ **Add definition to the street sign** Check that the painting is dry. Mix burnt umber and French ultramarine to make a near-black, and paint a thin, broken line along the right-hand and lower edges of the street sign using the No.2 brush. This gives the sign a little more definition and makes it stand out from the wall slightly.

THE FINISHED PICTURE

16 ▲ **Strengthen the stonework** Define the shapes of the individual stone blocks by outlining some of their edges, using a slightly stronger solution of the grey mixed earlier. Finally, strengthen the colour of the lower part of the wall with a loose wash of raw sienna.

A Aged effect
The aged quality of the wall and sign were achieved by blotting wet-on-wet washes with kitchen paper.

B Asymmetric design
The space below the street sign is much larger than the space above it. This creates a more interesting composition.

C Neutral background
The wall was painted in pale, neutral tones, with just enough suggestion of texture and form to place the street sign in context.

Shades of autumn

Focus in closely on this arrangement of shiny, brown horse chestnuts and mottled autumn leaves to explore their colours and textures.

The horse chestnuts in this watercolour look real enough to pick up and put in your pocket, but beware of overworking your painting to get a realistic effect. A lifelike impression does not mean you have to make a slavish copy of what is in front of you.

For a truly naturalistic result, keep the colours and brushwork as fresh and lively as possible to match the natural freshness of what you are painting. In addition, refer constantly to the subject. In this way, you will pick up subtleties of shape and colour which will be transferred to your painting.

▼ **Bold washes on the leaves are balanced by the precise shapes of the chestnuts.**

YOU WILL NEED

Sheet of 555gsm (260lb) Not watercolour paper 46 x 41cm (18 x 16in)	Cadmium orange; Burnt umber; Ultramarine; Raw umber; Alizarin crimson
2B pencil	Brushes: Nos. 16, 6 and 1 soft rounds
10 watercolours: Raw sienna; Burnt sienna; Sap green; Cadmium yellow; Scarlet lake;	Mixing dish or palette

Wet-on-wet

Dramatic runs of colour in the red and green leaves were achieved by working wet-on-wet. Paint was dropped on to wet paper and the colours were allowed to run together and find their own way into the watery shapes.

From the very early stages, the artist encouraged the pigments in the wet colours to separate and form random textures and watermarks. The effect of this separation – or granulation, as it is sometimes called – is noticeable in the slightly dappled texture on the leaves.

The crisp outlines of the husks and horse chestnuts called for a different approach. For these hard edges, it was necessary to work wet-on-dry, which meant first allowing the surrounding colours to dry completely.

FIRST STEPS

1 ▶ Make an outline drawing Using a sharp 2B pencil, make an accurate drawing of the subject. Extend the image right out to the edges of the picture area.

2 ▼ Paint a wash Apply a very dilute wash of raw sienna with a No.16 round brush. Take the colour across the whole picture area, but paint around the white husks and the highlights on the horse chestnuts. These should be left as unpainted shapes of white paper.

3 ▼ Paint wet-on-wet leaves While the raw sienna wash is still slightly damp, change to a No.6 round brush and drop dilute burnt sienna into the reddish areas at the edges of the leaves. The colour should run slightly to form soft edges around the brush strokes.

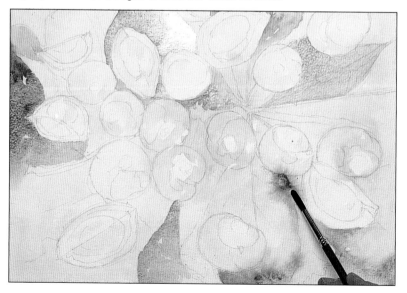

4 ▶ Add the green
Apply sap green with touches of cadmium yellow and raw sienna to the centre of the leaves. As the initial wash begins to dry, change to a No.1 round brush and define the edges of the leaves with burnt sienna.

▲ **Fresh green for the leaves is mixed from raw sienna, sap green and cadmium yellow.**

5 ▶ Strengthen the colour Pick out the brighter reds on the leaves with a dilute mixture of scarlet lake, cadmium orange and burnt sienna. Work around the veins in the leaves, leaving these as unpainted lines of paler undercolour. Paint the shadows in a more concentrated version of the same mixture.

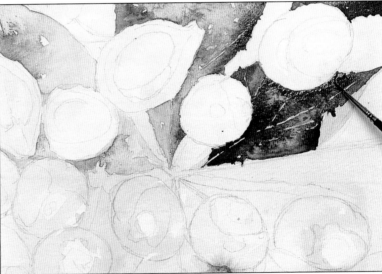

6 ▼ Add detail Returning to the green leaf colour – sap green with cadmium yellow and raw sienna – start to develop the detail in the leaves on the right-hand side of the painting. Paint the darker shadows by dropping small amounts of burnt umber into the wet green, referring constantly to the subject to make sure the colour goes in the correct places.

7 ▼ Add leaf shadows Continue building up the colours and tones on the leaves, adding a little ultramarine to the raw umber for the deepest shadows.

8 ▼ **Blend the leaf colours** Starting at the top of the painting, continue to build up the leaves in the basic green and red mixtures. It is important to keep the colours damp enough to blend the red and green areas together and avoid hard edges. If the colours become too dry, you might need to dampen the area you are working on with a little clean water to encourage the colours to merge and form soft edges.

EXPERT ADVICE
Granulation effects

To encourage granulation, drop pure water on to wet or damp colour. The water lifts the pigments, which then settle and dry to form characteristic textures and watermarks.

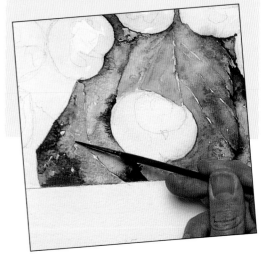

9 ▼ **Introduce texture** Continue to block in the leaves using the red and green mixtures. Try to vary the textures and tones by dropping a little clean water into areas of wet colour (see Expert Advice).

10 ▲ **Build up dark tones** Paint the deep shadows around the husks and horse chestnuts in strong mixtures of sap green, ultramarine and burnt sienna. These dark tones help to produce a three-dimensional effect, creating a sense of space in the picture.

11 ▼ **Dot in more shadows** Continue to develop the light and dark tones on the background leaves. Here, a cluster of red leaves is painted in varying strengths of burnt sienna, alizarin crimson and scarlet lake. Add a little burnt umber and ultramarine to these colours and use this to dab in the dark shadows around the husks and horse chestnuts.

◄ **Earth colours on the horse chestnuts and husks include burnt sienna, raw sienna and burnt umber.**

12 ▼ **Adjust the tones** Using the No.6 round brush, block in any remaining unpainted leaves. Take an overall look at the painting and darken any earlier shadows that might now appear pale compared with the recently painted deep tones. Allow the painting to dry.

13 ▼ **Define the white shapes** With the No.1 round brush, touch up any incomplete shadows around the husks and horse chestnuts. Take this opportunity to define the unpainted shapes prior to blocking in the local colours.

DEVELOP THE PICTURE

The background leaves are now established and it is time to block in the rest of the painting. Remember to work around the pithy areas on the husks and the reflections on the horse chestnuts – these will remain as unpainted white shapes in the finished painting.

14 ▲ **Start painting the husks** Working from the top of the composition, paint the shadows inside the husks in dilute raw sienna. Drop a little burnt sienna into the wet colour and allow this to spread. Build up the shadows and describe the concave shapes in tiny, stippled strokes of burnt sienna. Mix burnt umber, burnt sienna and a little ultramarine and use this for the darkest shadows on the inside of the husks.

15 ▼ **Build up the shadows in the husks** Moving to the husks in the foreground, paint these using an initial wash of cadmium yellow with a touch of raw umber. Build up the shading on the concave curves in small dabs of burnt umber and a little ultramarine. When you have finished painting the husks, allow the picture to dry.

16 ▲ **Paint the horse chestnuts** Start to paint the horse chestnuts, beginning with the cluster at the centre of the composition. Dampen the shapes with clean water, taking the water precisely up to the edges of the fruit, but avoiding the highlights and the pale seed scars. Drop burnt sienna on to the damp area, allowing the colour to run into the wet shape.

Master Strokes

W. S. Goodwin (*fl.*1894–1923)
Odd and Even (Pears)

The pears in this still life have a misshapen appearance that gives character to the arrangement. Their strange forms and blemishes are captured in detail – dark tones help give a sense of the deep hollows, while creamy, white paint captures the light glinting off the curves. As in the step-by-step project, colourful leaves enhance the autumnal feel of the painting. The rich, dark background throws the still life forwards, creating a sense of recession.

Specks of paint dabbed on with the tip of a fine brush build up a dappled effect on the pears.

The reds, golds and browns used for the leaves blend subtly into one another, giving realistic, graduated colour.

17 ▶ **Describe the forms** Wait until the flooded colour is almost dry. Use tiny, stippled strokes of burnt sienna to build up the darker areas of colour on the horse chestnuts. Working closely from the subject, take the shadows around the curved forms to emphasise their solidity and roundness.

A FEW STEPS FURTHER

The painting is almost complete. However, a little more work on the darker tones and shadows will give a greater sense of depth and make the subject appear even more realistic. Remember, no two shadows are the same, so it is important to work closely from the subject.

18 ▼ **Tone down the whites** Lightly wash over the pale seed scars with very dilute mixtures of burnt umber and burnt sienna. Leave tiny flecks of white around the scars to separate these areas from the surrounding darker colours.

19 ▲ **Complete the blocking in** Working across the composition, paint the remaining horse chestnuts in burnt sienna and block in any remaining unpainted areas. Allow the work to dry.

Express yourself
Experimental leaves

Before embarking on a complicated composition, why not experiment with wet-on-wet techniques on some simple leaf shapes? Start by making outline drawings of one or two interesting leaves – those beginning to turn red in the autumn have particularly exciting colours. Wet the leaf shapes, leaving the veins and highlights as dry patches. Drop paint on to the damp areas, then watch the colours as they find their own way into the wet shapes, creating a natural-looking, mottled surface.

20 ▼ **Add final shadows** In varying mixtures of sap green, raw umber, raw sienna and ultramarine, add the darkest shadows around the horse chestnuts and the husks.

21 ▲ **Complete the husks** Strengthen the shadows inside the husks in mixtures of raw umber, burnt sienna and raw sienna. Build up the graded tones in tiny dots of colour, blending these to describe the rounded, concave shapes.

THE FINISHED PICTURE

A Dark tones
Deep shadows emphasise the solid forms and create distance between the horse chestnuts and husks and the background leaves.

B Merging colours
Reddish-brown and green mixes were allowed to run into each other to give an effect of autumn leaves on the turn.

C White paper
Leaf veins, highlights on the horse chestnuts and other white areas were left as unpainted patches of paper.

Deserted beach corner

Spatter masking fluid and use a subtle combination of watercolor

paints to create areas of sand and shingle.

Any corner of a deserted beach offers a wealth of textures, from smooth pebbles scattered over the sand to the patterned grain of weathered wood and the fraying twists of old rope. With a little ingenuity, these diverse surfaces can be recreated in watercolour if you explore different ways of applying the paint.

Sand and pebbles

Spattering is a versatile technique that allows you to create droplets of colour, excellent for the grainy texture of sand with small pebbles on it. To give a sparkling texture to the sand, start by spattering masking fluid over the white paper. Paint a diluted sand-coloured wash over the dried fluid, then spatter various other colours on top of the wash for the pebbles. When the dried drops of masking fluid are removed, you will be left with tiny white highlights.

Wet-on-wet

Some of the paint on the wooden barrier and pillar is applied 'wet-on-wet'. In this technique, the colours run together spontaneously, so your colour mixing is done on the paper rather than on the palette. The exact effect can never be entirely anticipated, but the resulting accidental runs of colour usually make it well worth giving up a little control.

▼ Learn to depict rough textures in watercolour with the help of a few tricks of the trade.

FIRST STROKES

1 ▼ **Start with a light drawing** Make an outline drawing of the subject with a sharp 2B pencil, keeping the lines light and minimal. If the drawing becomes too dark, rub it over lightly with a putty eraser.

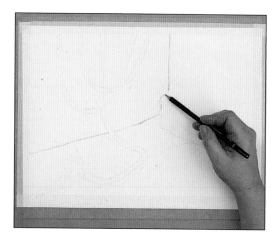

2 ▲ **Apply masking fluid to the rope** Before applying watercolour, paint out the rope with masking fluid, using an old brush. When dry, the fluid will form a protective rubbery mask, allowing you to paint over the masked area without affecting the paper underneath.

3 ▼ **Spatter the masking fluid** Cover the area of the wooden barrier and the pillar with sheets of scrap paper. Then spatter the sand areas with masking fluid by dipping the old paint brush in the masking fluid and flicking the brush at the paper. This area forms the ground of the pebble effect. Wait for the masking fluid to dry, using a hair-dryer to speed up the process if necessary.

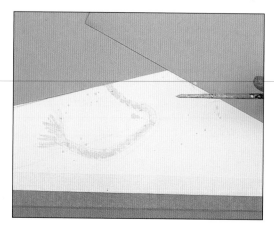

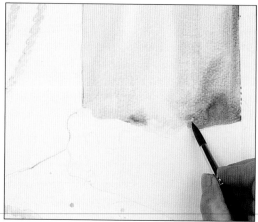

4 ▲ **Apply the first wash of colour** Using a No.10 round brush, wash a very dilute solution of raw sienna over the upright pillar. For the dark patches and the shadows, flood a mixture of French ultramarine and burnt umber into the wet wash. The small rust-coloured patch is cadmium orange applied to the wet colour.

5 ▶ **Continue to wash in the initial colours** The base of the pillar is also pale, so paint this in a very dilute wash of burnt umber. While it is still wet, add a little French ultramarine followed by a touch of raw sienna. Allow the colours to run together. When the pillar base is dry, paint the sand in a wash of equal parts cadmium orange and raw sienna, applying it loosely over the masked-out rope. Also paint a few light patches to indicate gaps in the wooden barrier.

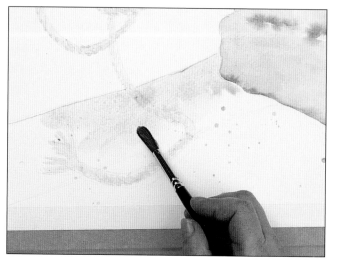

▲ **Earth colours such as the siennas and umbers are ideal to represent the tones of sand and bleached wood.**

6 ▶ Paint the barrier with graded colour
For the wooden barrier, mix a purplish-brown from approximately equal parts alizarin crimson, burnt umber and French ultramarine. Gradually add small amounts of alizarin crimson to the mixture as you progress down the shape. Note that alizarin is a strong colour, so use it sparingly.

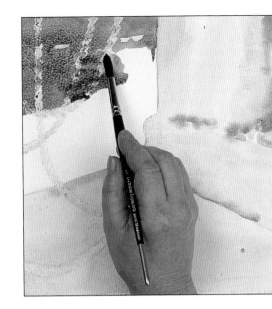

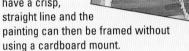

EXPERT ADVICE
Masking the edge

To give your watercolour a clean edge, stick masking tape around the border of the picture area before you start painting. Take the colour up to and over the masked edge. When the tape is removed you will have a crisp, straight line and the painting can then be framed without using a cardboard mount.

DEVELOPING THE PICTURE

The picture is now covered with washes of thin colour. It is time to work into these pale areas, strengthening the image by developing detail and adding texture.

7 ▶ Paint a shadow on to wet colour When you have reached the bottom of the barrier, introduce a little French ultramarine into the wet colour to indicate the shadow on the pillar and base. Use the same colour to paint the shadow on the sand.

8 ▲ Add more shadow Change to a No.7 round brush. Using a diluted mixture of equal parts burnt umber and raw umber, paint the wood grain on the pillar and the pebbles at its base. Then paint more shadows into the base of the pillar in burnt umber.

9 ◀ Start to spatter the sand Reposition the paper mask so that only the sand area is left uncovered. Hold the paper mask in position with something heavy if you think it might move. Using an old toothbrush, spatter the pebbles, firstly with a diluted mixture of burnt umber and French ultramarine, and then with a more concentrated version of the same colour. Work from the same place to give a strong directional feel to the spatters.

10 ▼ **Paint the grain on the barrier** Paint the dark wood grain on the barrier in a mixture of burnt umber and French ultramarine. Add a little alizarin crimson to this mixture and paint the paler grain and a few pale pebbles. Use the tip of the brush to dribble the same colour along the grain pattern to create a more natural effect.

BRUSH PROTECTION

TROUBLE SHOOTER

To avoid ruining your brush when using masking fluid, wet the bristles and rub them against an ordinary bar of soap before dipping them into the masking fluid. The rubbery fluid can then be easily washed off without destroying the brush.

11 ▼ **Develop the metal bolt heads** Paint the rusty bolt heads in cadmium orange, and the rust marks on the pillar base in burnt sienna. Use the tip of the No.7 brush to paint the wood grain on the pillar base in raw umber, applying the colour in wavy parallel lines.

Express yourself
The rope trick

In the main demonstration, the three areas of the painting – the wooden barrier, the pillar and the sandy beach – with their different textures and painting techniques, are visually united by the rope. Its loops bring the three areas into focus as a recognisable subject. You can see the effect of the rope in the version below. Without the rope bringing the three areas together, the relative shapes of the barrier, the pillar and the sand become more important. The painting loses its realism and becomes a composition of rectangular shapes. It takes on an abstract quality, an effect that is enhanced by a reduction in the amount of detail. For the painting to work as an abstract, you need to use colour – in this case, touches of alizarin crimson on all three elements – to create a sense of visual unity.

12 ▼ **Remove the masking fluid** Making sure that the paint is dry and that your finger is clean, remove the masking fluid by rubbing carefully. If it becomes difficult to remove, try using a clean eraser instead.

13 ▼ **Paint the rope** Using a No.4 brush, soften the sharp white shape of the rope by applying a pale wash of equal parts cadmium orange and French ultramarine.

14 ▼ **Define the bolt heads** Make the bolt heads stronger, darkening the tone by overpainting them with a little burnt umber.

A FEW STEPS FURTHER

At this stage, the painting is almost complete. The composition involves just four main elements – the barrier, the pillar, the sand and the rope. Yet this simple arrangement of shapes has already become a detailed and realistic painting. Now for a few finishing touches.

15 ▼ **Add shadows to the rope** Starting at the top, work down the rope, painting the shadows in burnt umber mixed with touches of French ultramarine and cadmium orange. Use the tip of the brush and keep the shadows as evenly spaced as possible.

Master Strokes

Ruskin Spear RA (1911–90)
Sea Wall, Cornwall

The individual shapes of the stones in the wall have been worked over with a smudgy layer of paint, creating a spontaneous yet weathered feel.

The lobster pots in the foreground are clearly defined, while the figures further away on the beach are much more vague and shadowy, as though melting into the distance.

Like the picture in the demonstration, Spear's painting has a spontaneous feel. He has chosen an unusual viewpoint, with the stones of the wall taking up more than half the picture space. The sombre tones of this area make the sea and clouds in the distance appear much lighter and brighter.

▲ **Cool Alizarin crimson and French ultramarine make up the picture's pinky-mauve areas, such as the wooden barrier. Raw sienna is a useful neutral tone.**

16 ▼ **Strengthen the dark tones** Still using the No.4 brush, mix burnt umber with a touch of raw umber and use this to strengthen the dark tones on the tops of the bolt heads. Change to the No.7 brush. With a fairly dark mixture of equal parts French ultramarine and raw umber, go over the dark shadows between the wooden boards in the barrier.

17 ▲ **Add more pebbles** Finally, using the left-over colour mixtures on your palette, dot in a few more pebbles with the tip of the No.7 brush.

THE FINISHED PICTURE

A Masking fluid
Instead of painting around the rope, masking fluid was used to protect this area as a crisp shape, which was then washed with light colour.

B Spattering
Spattered texture can be overdone and is most effective when used only on selected areas. Here it was confined to the small patch of sandy beach.

C Wood grain
A convincing impression of wood grain was created by using the tip of the brush to paint parallel wavy lines, spaced slightly unevenly.

Still life with oranges and a pepperpot

You learned the basics of watercolour painting in our first project. Take the skills you developed a step further and create this simple kitchen scene using cadmium red and yellow, and cobalt blue watercolour paint.

With the right paper (140lb+ to prevent cockling) and just a few colours, you can achieve some impressive results with watercolours. This project uses only three: the cobalt blue and cadmium yellow used in the first project, and cadmium red. These paints are simply mixed in varying quantities to provide all the colours you need.

Adopt a flexible approach

There's something very satisfying about mixing up watercolours, then pushing them around on the paper with your brush. You can never anticipate exactly where the paint is going to flow into thicker or thinner areas of wash. This makes watercolour an exciting medium to work with and means it's always best to retain a certain amount of flexibility in your approach.

The paint's interaction with the paper counts for a great deal because watercolours can be either opaque or translucent, depending on how much water you add. In fact the water and the paper are just as much part of an artwork as the paint itself. Irregular, grainy paper surfaces, for example, will influence the whole appearance of a picture. Paint gathers in and around the paper's peaks and troughs, mimicking the way that light plays across the surface of your subject matter.

Keep the colours thin

Remember that it's the wateriness of watercolours that gives them their delicacy, so it is important to keep colours thin and build them up stage by stage. This is one of the characteristics of watercolour painting, and part of its attraction for many people. Stick to this rule and you should be satisfied with the results you obtain.

◀ Even everyday objects are satisfying to paint. You can compose them in any number of ways to make the most of contrasts in colour and texture.

3 ▲ Paint in the mug and oranges Use the pale blue wash to paint in the mug, leaving only a trace of colour. This should be heavier along the mug's right-hand side and inside the rim. Create the base tone for the oranges with a thin layer of cadmium yellow, leaving the highlights untouched. Dab off any excess paint with kitchen towel.

4 ▲ Add some detail Once the first layer of paint has dried, you can apply stronger blue tones to the pepperpot using the No.1 brush and a less watery wash of cobalt blue. Lay the paint most heavily along the pepperpot's right-hand edge, around the bottom and under its rounded top to define the shape. Take care to work around the areas of highlight. Also make two dark lines along the side of the cup to mark the stripes, using a firm stroke.

FIRST STROKES

1 ▲ Sketch in the objects Using a 2B pencil, make a simple line drawing of the objects. If you prefer, you can use a grid – although our artist drew freehand. There's no need to worry about detail at this stage – just study how the items in the group relate to each other and draw in the outline of the shapes. Keep the pencil line quite fine and use a rubber to tidy up any lines that become too thick and rough. Also sketch in the main highlights.

2 ▲ Give shape to the pepperpot Mix up a fairly thin wash of cobalt blue in your palette and use the No.8 brush to apply this to the main area of the pepperpot. Leave the highlights blank. Then dilute the wash some more so it is translucent, and paint in the highlights so that they are a paler blue.

EXPERT ADVICE
Preventing muddy colours

When working with watercolours, you should remember to refill your jar with clean water on a regular basis. Murky water makes for dull colours and this tends to give your picture a lifeless appearance.

DEVELOPING THE PICTURE

Now that the objects are sketched in and roughly defined, it's time to add some detail. This is achieved by building up layers of colour on top of each other to create areas of light and shade and to add form. Don't be afraid to add lots of water to the page if you want to. The paper may wrinkle up as you do this, but it will become smooth again when dry.

5 ▶ **Add the pepperpot's shadows** Again using the fine brush, use a darker, more concentrated tone of cobalt blue to build up the layers and create the shadow that the cup casts against the bottom of the pepperpot. Also define its bottom right edge and add in the shadow under the rim of the pepperpot's round top.

6 ▶ **Give form to the cup** Mix the cadmium yellow, cobalt blue and cadmium red together until you achieve a violet/grey colour. Then use the fine brush to paint inside the rim of the cup. Make the application of paint heaviest around the edge, to define the shape, and fade out the wash as you move towards the cup's centre. Also use this colour to add in the cup's wide central stripe.

7 ▲ **Work on the shadows** Add more paint to the mix to create a deeper shade of violet/grey. Use this to create the shadow along the cup's right-hand and bottom edges by painting a fine line as shown. Then dab the paint with kitchen roll to spread it and remove the majority of the fluid. This creates a 'ghostly' shadow effect. Also add some colour to the cup's handle and add a strip of more dilute wash to create the vertical highlight (see Step 8).

Master Strokes

⚭

Paul Gauguin (1848–1903)
Teapot, Jug and Fruit

Gourds rather than oranges are the principal fruit in this still life by Gauguin, and this points to the fact that although a Frenchman by birth, he spent several years living in Tahiti in the South Seas.

The composition has obvious similarities to the above project in that there is the same contrast between the polished surfaces of the man-made pottery objects and the 'living' fruits. The real difference is in the media used and the way the paint is applied. Gauguin uses oils and applies the paint in flat slabs of colour – unlike the built up washes of watercolour above.

The shape of the gourd is defined by the way the fruit has been painted almost in two 'halves' – one vibrant red and the other orange.

Gauguin suggests the light source comes from the right by lightening the dull background towards the right-hand corner.

8 ▲ Give surface texture to the oranges Mix together cadmium red and cadmium yellow to produce orange. Then apply the paint to the oranges loosely and roughly, using the fine brush and allowing the lighter wash underneath to show through in places. This gives an impression of the fruits' pitted skin. Gradually increase the content of red in the paint as you move into the lower half of each orange. This helps to define their rounded shape and gives them a sense of weight.

9 ▶ Create the reflection Add the reflection of the orange in the pepperpot by dabbing a touch of the orange mix on to the highlight you created earlier. Drip a little extra water on to the orange dab to soften its edges and to blend it into the surrounding colour.

10 ▲ Sharpen up the shadows Add some more cadmium red to the mix and again build up the colour in the lower half of each orange, following the shape of each fruit round and using dabs of paint. Then mix a new colour using cadmium red with a touch of cobalt blue to produce a deep shade of blue. Load the No.1 brush with this new colour and sharpen up the edges between the pepperpot and the cup. You have now completed the work on the objects, and the painting can be left to dry.

EXPERT ADVICE
Watercolour brushes

A watercolour brush needs to come to a good point, so make sure yours does this. This will give you more control over where the paint goes on the paper. When you wash the brush after use, reshape it by pinching the bristles lightly between your fingertips. If you find any straggly hairs, these should traditionally be singed off, but a snip with a pair of scissors will do.

Express yourself
Adding a fourth colour

By adding a fourth colour, purple, the artist has heightened the sense of contrast in the scene. The effect is to create a less realistic final picture but to increase its impact. This is because the purple resonates against the blue of the pepperpot and cup (blue and violet sit next to each other on the colour wheel, so will always fight to dominate the visual space). The artist used plenty of water and allowed the purple wash to bleed extensively on the paper.

A FEW STEPS FURTHER

Add some foreground shadows then set your still life objects against a mottled background by daubing grey paint onto wet paper. Simply follow the steps.

BLOTTING OUT

Kitchen towel is a useful ally in watercolour painting. Too much water in the paint can cause it to bleed into other colours. This can quickly be remedied by using kitchen towel to soak up the excess.

TROUBLE SHOOTER

11 ▶ Add the shadows below the group Use the thicker brush and random, short strokes to daub a strong patch of violet/grey mix beneath the group. Then drop water on to it so that the colour spreads out. Dab with kitchen roll to lighten and blend.

12 ▶ Prepare the background
Paint a thin layer of clean water in a random arc shape around and above the group of objects. Take care not to drop water from the brush on to the rest of the picture, or to brush water over any areas that are by now dry.

13 ▲ Add the colour Turn the painting upside down and daub the violet/grey mix around the edges of the group with the fine brush. Encourage the paint to move into the background and to bleed into the area you painted with water. Dab the paint with kitchen towel to prevent it from running back into the central objects.

THE FINISHED PICTURE

A Surface texture
The texture of the oranges was built up by varying the intensity of paint and allowing the underlying wash to show through in places.

B Defined images
Sharp lines were allowed to bleed into shadows. These define the pepperpot and make it stand out from the cup.

C Curved shape
Light falling on the china cup was painted in as a pale blue wash and strengthened in key areas to mimic the object's curved shape.

Children fishing

*Family groups at the seaside are a favourite subject with artists.
Use watercolours to capture the atmosphere of a bright summer's
day beside the sea, with sunshine sparkling on the water.*

This seaside scene is buzzing with colour and action. In fact, most of the painting is done in just two colours – burnt sienna and cobalt blue. The impression of strong, vivid colours is created by a few well-judged splashes of bright yellow, red and green in the final stages.

The figures, too, are simplified. As a rule, the looser and more decisive you are when painting figures, the fresher and livelier the result will be.

Sketches and photographs
Instead of painting from life, try creating a scene of your own, using any available reference material together with your imagination. The scene shown here is an arrangement of figures and boats taken from photographs and sketches and put together in a colourful composition.

Painting water
Water itself has no colour and is visible only because it reflects its surroundings. Here, the sea reflects the sky, as well as the quay and figures.

It is good idea to paint the water and the children alternately. Every time you apply a new colour to the figures, add a few dabs of the same colour to the reflections. In the water, though, make sure your brushstrokes are looser to give an indication of the ripples.

▲ **The lively highlights on the figures and the water are created by using masking fluid.**

USING SKETCHES AND PHOTOS

Feel free to be selective with your reference material. For example, the figure on the right in the painting was borrowed from the black-and-white sketch of a family fishing (below right). The kneeling figure was also used in the painting, turned around to suit the composition.

A photograph of children fishing might provide you with a general starting point for your composition. From here, you could go on to alter the position of the quay and make any other changes you see fit to create an interesting composition for your painting.

Make a note of local colours on any sketches you do, as shown below left. This will help jog your memory when it comes to choosing colours for the actual painting.

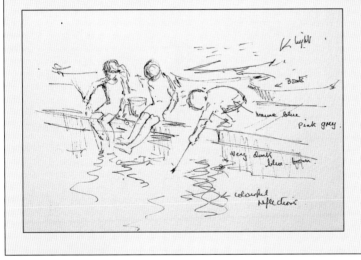

FIRST STROKES

1 ▲ Sketch in the composition Start by drawing the outlines of the figures and other main elements with a sharp HB pencil. Work from sketches and photographs, taking the best elements from each to build up your own composition. Try to draw with fluid lines to capture the movement of the figures and don't make the lines too dark, as they will show through the watercolour.

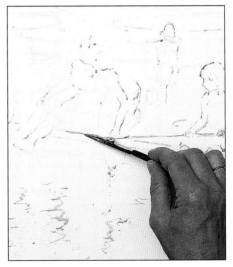

2 ▲ Mask the highlighted areas Apply masking fluid with a ruling pen on any areas that you want to remain very light in the finished picture – for example, the sunny highlights on the hair and the flickering highlights on the water.

3 ▶ Paint the water
Using a No.6 filbert brush, paint the water in a dilute mixture of cobalt blue and a little light green. Wherever the water appears slightly sandy, add a little burnt sienna to this mixture. Paint the water in long horizontal strokes, leaving slivers of white paper showing between the brush strokes to indicate the ripples.

4 ▶ Paint the flesh shadows Mix a deep tan colour from burnt sienna with a touch of raw umber and use this on the shaded side of the figures. Paint with the tip of the brush to create long, tapering shadows down the arms and legs.

EXPERT ADVICE
Choosing brushes

Your choice of brushes is a personal one and it is worth experimenting to find out which types suit your particular approach. For example, the filbert recommended for this painting was chosen specifically by the artist, who finds that the obliquely cut bristles are ideal to create both flat colour and sharp detail.

▲ Burnt sienna and cobalt blue are used extensively, forming the main colour theme in the composition.

5 ◀ Add colour to the reflections Take the flesh colour into the reflections in the sea, making irregular, wavy strokes with the filbert brush to give the impression of moving water.

DEVELOPING THE PICTURE

In this painting, the splashes of bright colour really catch the eye – namely the orange and yellow outfits, the red bucket and the emerald green fishing net. These local colours should be as bright as you can make them, so use pure colour diluted with a little clean water and applied with a clean brush.

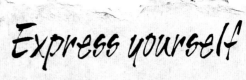

Express yourself
Trying out colours

An exploratory colour sketch enables you to work out appropriate paint mixes before starting on the main painting. In this preliminary work, note how the flesh colours, the jetty and the water are observed and painted in detail.

6 ▲ Add splashes of colour Now for some local colour. Paint the swimsuit of the right-hand figure in cobalt blue and the shorts of the kneeling figure in cobalt blue with a touch of burnt sienna. The shadow on the boy's outfit is cadmium orange, and the red swimsuit is cadmium red with a little alizarin crimson. As you use each colour on the figures, take a little of the same colour into the water to help build up the reflections.

7 ▶ Paint the hair shadows The hair shadows on all the figures are painted in a mixture of raw umber and yellow ochre. Vary the proportions of this colour mixture, using more yellow ochre for the blonde heads and more raw umber for the brunettes. Paint the woman's skirt and top in Prussian blue.

8 ▲ Block in the quay Paint the quay in a pale, dull mauve shade mixed from burnt sienna and cobalt blue. As you paint up to and around the figures, take this opportunity to redefine the contours and outlines.

9 ▲ Add the boats and wooden slats Mix a touch more cobalt blue with the basic quay colour and use this to block in the shapes of the boats and to suggest the slats of wood on the quay.

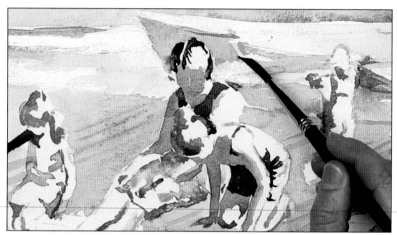

10 ▲ Develop the boats Paint the interiors of the boats in yellow ochre or emerald green, and the rims in emerald green or Prussian blue. The colours should be paler than those used on the figures and in the foreground, yet must be strong enough to show up against the white paper when you remove the masking fluid.

ADDING MORE WHITE

Forgotten to paint out some of the highlights with masking fluid? Don't worry. You can use white gouache to paint any light areas you missed. Here, a few white sparkles are added to the waves in the final stages.

11 ▲ Paint the deep shadow The shadow under the wooden quay is one of the darkest tones in the whole picture, so paint this in a strong mixture of burnt sienna and cobalt blue. Apply the colour in broad, horizontal strokes and also add a few small dabs to the reflections in the water.

12 ▶ Complete the quay Paint the edge of the quay with a mixture of Prussian blue and burnt sienna, keeping the colour slightly paler than the shadow underneath the quay. Add a splash of bright emerald green for the child's fishing net, not forgetting to add the same colour to the reflections in the water.

13 ▲ Add more bright splashes For a little more local colour, paint the bucket in cadmium red and the outfit of the standing boy in cadmium yellow. Using a dilute mixture of burnt sienna and yellow ochre, wash in any unpainted hair and skin tones on all the figures.

▼ To do justice to the colours of the buckets, fishing nets and clothes in the bright sunlight, emerald green, cadmium yellow and cadmium red were used.

Master Strokes

Cecilio Pla Y Gallardo (1860–1934)
The Beach

As in our step-by-step painting, this unusual oil painting by Spanish artist, Pla Y Gallardo captures the atmosphere of sun sparkling on water very effectively. He has used heavily textured, horizontal brush strokes for the sea, leaving the buff-coloured canvas to represent the beach. The bathers are depicted in a simple, impressionistic style with vertical brush strokes.

Several pale tints of blue and mauve are blended to provide the luminous look of the sea, which is reflecting the sky and sunlight.

The reflections of the bathers in the sea are indicated with dabs of green paint with the addition of a little flesh colour.

16 ▲ **Assess the picture** Stand back from your painting to review the overall effect. Adjust the tonal contrast if necessary, remembering that the tones in the distance should be paler. Check that you have not missed out any coloured reflections in the water.

A FEW STEPS FURTHER

14 ▲ **Remove the masking fluid** Paint the dress of the seated figure in pale cadmium red and the vest of the kneeling child in cadmium orange. Allow the paint to dry completely, then rub off the masking fluid with your finger.

15 ▲ **Soften the white shapes** Mix an extremely dilute wash of cobalt blue and burnt sienna and use this to tone down the stark white areas revealed by removing the masking fluid.

Colours are bright and the brushwork lively, evoking the warm sun and fresh air of this seaside scene. Although at this stage the picture could be considered complete, you might want to add a few more details. However, keep these to a minimum – overworking a watercolour in the final stages can reduce the natural spontaneity of the medium.

17 ▲ **Add the metal railings** Paint the railings at the far side of the quay in burnt sienna, keeping these sharp and clearly defined to contrast with the pale, hazier shapes of the boats behind.

18 ▶ Make final adjustments

Finally, you might need to soften some of the hard edges between the pale and dark flesh tones with a little clean water, dabbing off excess colour with a tissue. You could also give the woman a pair of sunglasses to protect her eyes from the strong sunlight! Using the end of your brush, simply draw the glasses with a mix of Prussian blue and cadmium red.

THE FINISHED PICTURE

A Selected elements
The figures, boats and jetty were selected from different photos and drawings. These separate elements were adapted to make the most satisfactory composition.

B Simplified colour
Flesh shadows on the figures were all painted quickly at the same time in burnt sienna mixed with a little raw umber.

C Lively reflections
Reflected colours were built up gradually as the painting progressed, with a little of each colour used elsewhere in the picture being added to the reflected patterns in the water.

Tango dancers

Watercolour is a lively medium that is well suited to an animated subject, such as this study of couples dancing the tango in a park.

When it comes to capturing quick movements, photographs really come into their own. As they freeze the motion, you have the chance to analyse what's happening and the freedom to paint at leisure what you have seen. In this painting, two shots of couples dancing the tango have been used together to make an interesting composition. The artist chose this particular dance for its precise sequence of repeated steps, which are easy to photograph.

Simplified subject

In order to focus on the movement within a scene, it is best to simplify the background. In this picture the artist has eliminated the onlookers so that all the attention is on the dancers. The figures are kept quite simple, apart from the detail in the creases of the clothes, which reflect the movement of the bodies underneath them.

Watercolour gives swift, fluid results and can be used in a loose, sketchy way. It is a spontaneous medium and, as such, is a good choice for conveying the liveliness of moving objects. In the main, it has been used here wet on

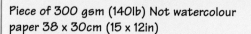

▲ Use a light, lively touch to capture the stylised steps and body stances of these tango dancers.

YOU WILL NEED

Piece of 300 gsm (140lb) Not watercolour paper 38 x 30cm (15 x 12in)

0.5 propelling pencil

Brushes: Nos.6, 4, 3 and 10 rounds

13 watercolours: Purple madder; Cadmium orange; Burnt sienna; Yellow ochre; Sepia; Antwerp blue; Payne's grey; Alizarin crimson; Ultramarine; Vandyke brown; Naples yellow; Dark emerald; Viridian

Mixing palette or dish

Jar of water

dry, with some blurred edges to enhance the sense of movement.

Purple madder and Antwerp blue are used throughout, but particularly for the two central figures. The purple madder, a strong colour, helps bring the main dancer to the front of the picture, while the blue provides a cool contrast.

SKETCHING FROM LIFE

Although working from photographs is useful, the best way to learn about the moving figure is to make a series of sketches from life. Work quickly, trying to capture the essence of the action in a series of quick sketches using a chunky medium such as charcoal or pastel.

FIRST STEPS

1 ▲ **Establish the drawing** Quickly and lightly sketch in the figures, using a 0.5 propelling pencil. Keep detail to a minimum, but mark in the folds of the clothes and lightly define the areas of shadow under the dancers' feet.

2 ▶ Paint in the main figure With a No.6 round brush and purple madder watercolour, lightly block in the woman's trousers. Change to cadmium orange and paint in her T-shirt.

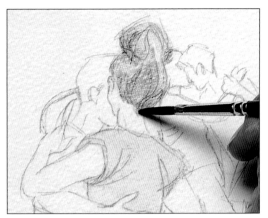

3 ▲ Add her hair Now use a No.4 round brush to mix burnt sienna and yellow ochre. Paint the woman's hair, but leave some white paper for highlights. Add sepia to the mix for shading.

DEVELOPING THE PICTURE

The main figure in your composition has now been blocked in. The light, warm tones of her clothes bring her to the front of the picture. Continue by working the other figures in relation to her.

4 ◀ Add flesh tones Use a light wash of burnt sienna to paint the woman's skin. Again, create some highlights by leaving white paper showing. Fill in the flesh tones of her partner and add shading to both with a stronger wash. Paint in the skin tones of the couple in the background. Change to Antwerp blue and paint the man's shirt.

5 ▲ Create recession With a mix of Antwerp blue and Payne's grey, paint the trousers of the dancing partner. Now use just Payne's grey to block in the man in the background. Keep your brush strokes soft and blurred, so that the figure seems to recede in the picture plane.

6 ▶ Develop the background figures Use a mix of alizarin crimson and a little ultramarine to block in the female figure's trousers, then add a little sepia to the Antwerp blue and Payne's grey mix from step 5 and paint her jumper. Using a clean brush, remove some of the colour to create highlights. Change to a No.3 round and use sepia to paint the dark hair of three dancers.

7 ▲ Focus on the small details Continuing with the careful work, use the same brush and Payne's grey to paint in the shoes of all the figures. Vary the depth of colour with stronger and weaker mixes to create highlights and shadows.

346

8 ▶ **Work wet-on-wet**
Still using the No.3
round brush, add
shading to the dark
hair with Vandyke
brown. Return to the
No.6 round brush and
use clear water to
dampen the painted
area of the blonde
woman's trousers.
Flood in some purple
madder to deepen the
tone. Now mix in a
little Payne's grey to
darken the purple and
describe the folds of
the trousers. Soften
the edges of the folds
with a clean brush.

TROUBLE SHOOTER

TAKING BACK PAINT

If you have put on too much colour,
it's simple to remedy. Take off paint with
a clean brush and clean water, blot the
area with kitchen paper and leave it to
dry. To complete the change, rework
the details in the relevant colour.

Master Strokes
John Singer Sargent (1856–1925)
El Jaleo

The impression of movement is brilliantly captured in this oil
painting of a Spanish dancer and accompanying musicians.
From the dexterous fingers of the guitarists to the dramatic poses
of the women in their fine costumes, every part of the picture

conveys lively action. Strong shadows cast on the wall echo
the shapes of the heads and arms, increasing the animated
effect. Although the palette is mainly black, white and buff, it
is enlivened by vivid splashes of scarlet, crimson and orange.

**The arcing line of the
shadow on the wall
behind the dancer
extends the backward
slant of her body.**

**Feathery brush strokes
around the dancer's shawl
convey the movement of
the swirling, fringed fabric.**

**The orange on the chair
provides a point of bright
interest in an area of light
neutral colours.**

9 ◄ **Work up shadows** Using the No.4 round and a mix of cadmium orange and purple madder, deepen the flesh tones of the foreground couple, then paint shadows on the woman's T-shirt. Change to the No.3 round and define the fabric folds with a mix of cadmium orange and Vandyke brown. Paint shadows in her hair with burnt sienna.

10 ▲ **Add shadow** Add more shadows to the flesh tones with mixes of purple madder and burnt sienna, and burnt sienna and sepia; highlight with Naples yellow. Changing to the No.6 round, define the background couple with stronger mixes of the colours used for their clothes in steps 5 and 6. Now darken the purple trousers with purple madder, the blue shirt with Antwerp blue and a dark emerald/viridian mix, and the blue trousers with a Payne's grey/Antwerp blue mix.

Express yourself

Watch your step

This version of the dancers was worked in acrylics on canvas. The artist has altered the composition significantly, working in a landscape format and adding another dynamic element – an extra dancing pair. As in the main project, the background is eliminated – but here the horizon line, too, has been removed, allowing the lively visible brush strokes to fill the canvas, further enhancing the sense of movement.

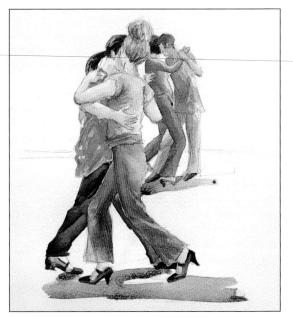

11 ▲ **Lift the details** Use the No.3 round and burnt sienna to vary the flesh tones of the male background figure. Now change to Payne's grey and work up the shadows all over the picture – on the figures, hair and shoes. Add sepia to the grey and, diluting the paint well and keeping the tone light, use the No.6 round to paint the shadows cast on the ground by the couples. Leave to dry.

A FEW STEPS FURTHER

Now that you have successfully painted in the figures, it's time to add the extra details that will tie the composition together and emphasise the picture's sense of movement.

12 ▶ Add a wash in the foreground
Using a No.10 round brush and a wash of Naples yellow, apply colour right across the foreground. Work freely, painting over the shadows cast by the figures.

13 ▲ Add refinements
Use the No.3 round brush and sepia to darken shadows on the foreground woman's T-shirt, then work over her legs with alizarin crimson and sepia. Change to a No.10 round to wash cadmium orange over the foreground. Work up the shadows on the blue shirt with Payne's grey.

THE FINISHED PICTURE

A Conveying movement
The legs and arms of the dancers create a variety of diagonals, giving them a real sense of movement.

B Softened edges
Where shadows are added to the clothing, particularly on the trousers, the edges are blurred and softened. Hard lines would give a static effect.

C Taking steps
The artist left a space between the heel of the shoe and the shadow on the ground to indicate that the foot and leg are raised in movement.

Creating highlights

To give a realistic impression of the sheen and tints of a sitter's hair in watercolours, try 'masking out' areas with an ordinary household candle.

O ne thing you learn pretty quickly when painting portraits is that a mass of hair is never one single colour. The light will always bring out unexpected tints and highlights. The model in this painting has dark brown hair, but the sun shining through the window also brought out strong glints of gold and copper in it.

Masking highlights

In watercolour, you can capture this effect by painting the hair in two or more washes of colour and masking parts of each layer with the wax of an ordinary household candle – a technique known as wax resist.

In this portrait, our artist started on the hair by masking out streaks of white paper with a wax candle to create white highlights. The waxy candle marks were then overpainted with yellow ochre, causing the masked white highlights to show through the paint. The same technique was used again to mask out a few streaks of yellow ochre before applying a wash of burnt umber. The result is pale and golden highlights in a mass of deep brown hair.

As well as the colour of the hair, pay attention to its overall shape. Try to ignore the thousands of individual hairs that spring from the skull – instead, treat the hair as a solid mass. Paint it in broad strokes exactly as you would render the face and body. In short, simplify what you see.

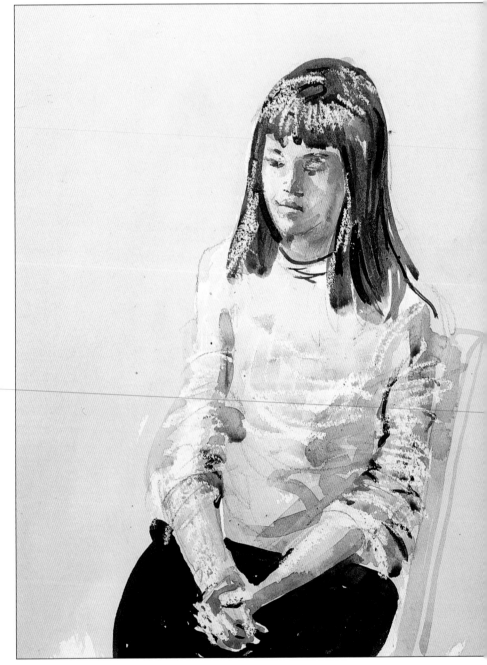

▲ Notice how the candle has been applied not only to create highlights in the hair – but also across the body and around the arms. This helps give the whole picture a lively, textural surface.

FIRST STEPS

1 ▼ Start with a basic drawing Make a simple outline drawing of your subject. Keep pencil lines to a minimum as they are only a guide to the subsequent watercolour painting. Establish the main shapes – the head, body and arms – and indicate the position of the facial features. A carpenter's pencil, available from hardware stores, has a wide, flat lead and will encourage you to concentrate on the essentials and ignore superficial details.

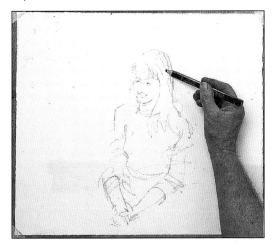

3 ▲ Block in the flesh colour Using a No.6 round brush, paint the arms and face in a mixture of yellow ochre and Indian red. The waxy candle marks will show through the watercolour, emerging as bright white highlights.

2 ▲ Mask the wax highlights Before you start painting, take a white household candle and block in any areas that you want to be white in the finished picture. These include all the light areas on the illuminated side of the face and the highlights on the face and hair.

4 ▲ Paint the sweater Changing to a 38mm (1½in) flat brush, paint the sweater in raw sienna. The candle wax will again show through the paint and help to indicate the rounded, solid form of the body.

YOU WILL NEED

Piece of 300gsm (140lb) Not watercolour paper 40 x 46cm (16in x 18in)

Carpenter's pencil

White household candle

6 watercolours:
Yellow ochre;
Indian red;
Raw sienna;
Ultramarine;
Ivory black;
Burnt umber

Brushes: Nos.6 and 5 round brushes; 38mm (1½in) flat brush

Cotton buds

DEVELOPING THE PICTURE

It is now time to work on the hair with layers of paint and more wax. Also, block in the background around the figure with a large brush, taking the opportunity to improve and redefine the outline of the figure where necessary.

5 ▼ Paint highlights in the hair Using a No.5 round brush, loosely block in the lightest hair tones in a wash of yellow ochre. There is no need to be too precise about this, because much of the yellow will eventually be covered with brown.

6 ▲ Add the background Change to the 38mm (1½in) flat brush and block in the background loosely in a mixture of ultramarine and ivory black.

EXPERT ADVICE
Removing dried paint

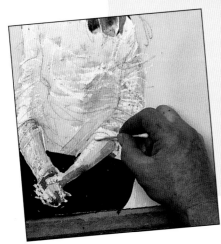

Tiny blobs of paint may collect and dry on top of the candle wax. You can remove these by lifting them carefully with a cotton bud. If the blobs have dried, try dampening the cotton bud first. Go carefully – if you press too hard you might actually rub the colour in more.

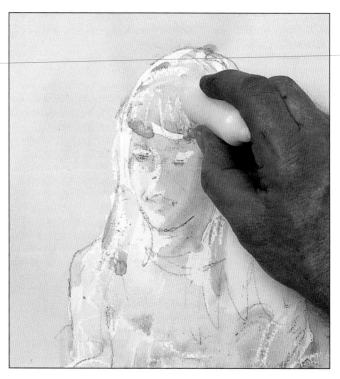

7 ▲ Use wax resist on hair highlights Make sure the yellow ochre on the hair is completely dry, then add a few strokes of candle wax to protect some yellow areas before applying the final wash of paint over the hair. Make the candle marks in the same direction as the fall of the hair.

8 ◄ Block in the brown hair Using the No.6 round brush, paint burnt umber over the entire hair area. Again, let the brush strokes follow the direction of the hair. The protected areas of yellow ochre will emerge as golden glints through the dark brown wash.

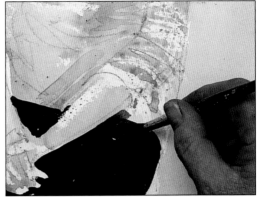

9 ▲ Paint the trousers Still using the No.6 round brush, start to block in the trousers as a flat area of ivory black with only the occasional highlight left showing.

Express yourself

A portrait sketch

This portrait sketch in black and white shows how highlights in the hair can be achieved quickly and effectively by leaving patches of the paper untouched. Shadows are blocked in as broad areas of hatched pencil tone.

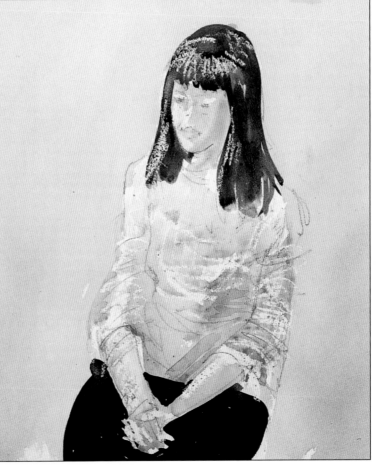

10 ▲ Define the figure Complete the trousers, taking the black up to the bottom edge of the sweater. Note that the trousers, which are painted as a flat area, do not really convey the form of the figure. It is the changes of tone in the sweater that give the impression of the three-dimensional figure beneath the clothing.

A FEW STEPS FURTHER

You have now painted all the main areas of the composition, but the figure still needs a few finishing touches. Some darker shadows, particularly on the face and hair, will help bring your portrait to life without sacrificing the freshness of the paint. However, it is important not to overdo the detail or to overwork the painting at this stage.

11 ◄ Develop the face
Still using the No.6 brush, add darker tones to the face in a mixture of Indian red and yellow ochre. The mixture must be stronger than the initial wash colour so that these darker areas show up. Leave the light patch on the far cheek unpainted. Using the No.5 round brush, define the facial features by painting grey shadows under the eyes, on the upper lip and along the eyebrows with a mixture of ultramarine and burnt umber.

Master Strokes

Valentin Serov (1865–1911)
Girl with Peaches

A renowned Russian artist, Serov is best known as a portraitist and, as his reputation grew, he painted many celebrities, particularly from the world of the arts in Russia. This beautiful, informal portrait is one of Serov's early works, painted when he was only 22 years old. It has a fresh, luminous quality that perfectly captures the dappled effect of gentle sunshine filtering into the room, highlighting the girl's hair, face and clothing.

The girl has a radiant, peachy complexion, the colours on her rosy cheeks echoing those of the fruit on the table.

The casual pose, with the arms propped up on the table, lends the portrait an air of informality.

12 ► **Paint in the shadows** With the same fleshy shadow mixture of ultramarine and burnt umber, paint broad strokes along the shaded side of the body and arms. Then paint the back of the chair in long smooth strokes of pale grey, achieved by mixing a little ivory black with plenty of water.

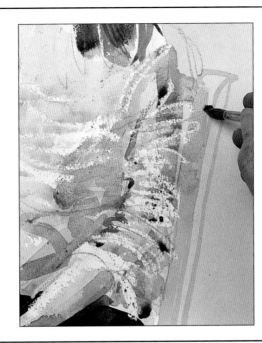

13 ▲ **Add hair shadows** Still using the No.5 brush, add a few dark streaks of shadow to the hair in ivory black. Start each streak at the crown of the head. Lift the brush to achieve a tapering effect at the end of each stroke.

THE FINISHED PICTURE

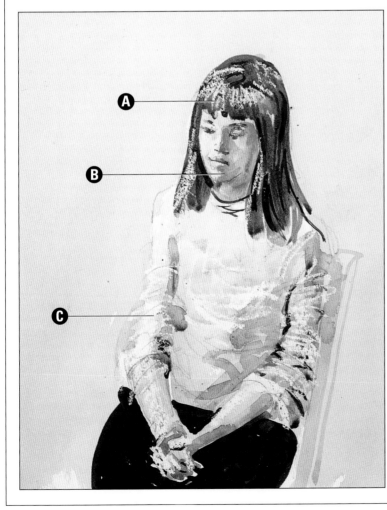

A Adding highlights to the hair
Reflections and highlights in the hair were built up gradually, using a candle wax resist. Reflected light was represented by the whiteness of the paper.

B Simplifying the flesh tones
The face was painted in a mixture of Indian red and yellow ochre. This was first applied as an overall pale wash. Shadows were then painted on top of the wash using a stronger mix of the same colours.

C Following the form
On the body, the direction of the wax highlights follows the form of the subject – helping describe the rounded arms and the torso underneath the clothing.

Relaxed study in watercolour

Cool blues, mauves, pinks and greys, enlivened with touches of brighter colour, create the right mood for this tranquil study.

This relaxed study shows off the versatility of the watercolour medium. Working with wet-in-wet washes, colours have drifted into each other to suggest the luxurious texture and the fall of the velvet throws on the sofa.

And these large expanses of colour contrast effectively with the more detailed study of the sitter. Moreover, the warmish pinks and purples of the sofa covers – together with the browns of the table and floor – also play off against the cool colours of the subject's clothes. This contrast helps to focus attention on the sitter. In terms of colour, the picture is further lifted by the lively pattern of blues and yellows on her blouse.

Looking at shape

Understanding how shapes work together is a major part of painting. The woman's pose – half lying, half sitting – creates an interesting, fluid shape. This is set off against the angularly shaped expanses of the velvet throws. The coffee table in the foreground helps lead the eye into the picture.

▲ Note how most of the detailed work in the painting has been reserved for the sitter and her clothes. The rest of the painting has been completed in relatively loose washes.

FIRST STROKES

1 ▲ **Sketch in the scene** Using a 2B pencil and light but legible strokes, sketch the model and the draped sofa, checking the angles and proportions of the figure. Don't be afraid to erase parts of the drawing with a putty rubber and start again.

▼ **YOU WILL NEED**

Piece of 300gsm (140lb) Not watercolour paper 28 x 38cm (11 x 15in)

2B pencil

Putty rubber

Brushes: Nos.10, 6 and 2 rounds

15 watercolours: Winsor violet; Naples yellow; Burnt sienna; Purple madder alizarin; Permanent rose; Payne's grey; French ultramarine; Raw sienna; Burnt umber; Sepia; Cerulean blue; Black; Emerald; Raw umber; Cadmium red

2 ▼ **Establish the back-drop** With a No.10 round brush, block in the background throw with light washes of Winsor violet. Now take up a No.6 round and work on some smaller areas. Begin on the face and hands with a very watery Naples yellow and the broad headband with burnt sienna. Throw the model's head forward by adding strong shadows in Winsor violet behind it.

3 ▲ **Fill in the scene** With the No.10 brush, paint the foreground fabric in purple madder alizarin, and deepen the background fabric with mixes of purple madder alizarin and Winsor violet, adding permanent rose highlights. With a wash of Payne's grey and a touch of French ultramarine, paint the trousers, the fringed shawl, and the shadows on the blouse and wall. Use raw sienna over burnt sienna for the sofa, raw sienna on the sitter's headband, Naples yellow for the feet and French ultramarine for the mug.

DEVELOPING THE PICTURE

The main areas of your composition are now blocked in, and the pale and brighter colour registers are established. Progress by working with a range of other colours, right across the picture, using various paint thicknesses and techniques.

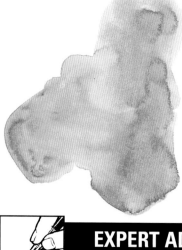

◄ Sepia (top), Winsor violet (bottom right) and purple madder alizarin (left) have been used extensively in the picture and help to set its overall colour key. They harmonise well with each other, creating an air of calm.

4 ▲ **Add upper-body detail** Changing to a No.6 round brush, use the tip to pattern the blouse with watery raw sienna. Add a little more Payne's grey on the fringed shawl. Dot in the design on the headband in burnt umber and sepia.

EXPERT ADVICE
Be complementary

By making use of complementary colours – opposites on the colour wheel – in a prominent part of the scene, you can really lift the whole. Here, placing brown-yellow and blue together in the blouse's pattern enhances the colours and brings a bright but balanced element to the picture.

5 ▲ **Brighten the blouse** Still using the pointed tip of the No.6 brush, lift the whole scene by painting in the blue parts of the blouse pattern with cerulean blue.

6 ▲ **Paint in the book** Now bring the model's book into the picture, balancing the right-hand side of the painting. Use the fine tip of the No.6 brush to sketch in an outline of the book cover in watery sepia. Put in the faintest suggestion of the pages in the same colour. Working wet-in-wet, use sepia and Payne's grey to block in the book cover. With a mix of purple madder alizarin and Payne's grey, paint the shadow of the book on the throw.

7 ▲ Work on the large areas Taking up the No.10 brush, start working up more depth and richness on the two throws. Use purple madder alizarin on both of them, laying thin washes over the dried colour to suggest the texture and sheen of velvet.

8 ▲ Define the facial features Now turn your attention to the face. With a No.2 round, start to add some fine detailing with intense sepia paint. Wash a little watery burnt sienna over the lips.

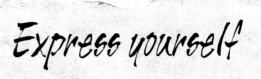

A different viewpoint

This painting, also in watercolours, creates a different mood to the step-by-step one. The high viewpoint – combined with the curled, sleeping body position – provides a highly original figure study. Note how the model's nightgown is beautifully described by controlled wet-on-wet washes. The contrast in tone here – from the white of the paper to the deep blue shadow in the middle of her curl – really brings out the form of the body. The teapot and cup and saucer in the corner pick up on blue of the nightgown and help balance the composition.

9 ▼ Intensify the darks With the No.10 and No.6 brushes, use a mix of cerulean blue and black to define the feet and legs by adding shadows on and between them. Intensify the shadows across the blouse, too. Using the No.10 brush, wash strong Naples yellow across the table as a base colour.

10 ▼ **Work on some detail** Use the same blue-black mix and the tip of the No.6 brush to define the shawl's fringe, then dot ultramarine along its border. Mix up cerulean and emerald paints and wash this across the wall behind the sofa. Notice how leaving the pencil underdrawing in has created some surface interest and definition.

11 ▲ **Adding definition** With the No.6 round, sweep lines of dry sepia, burnt umber and raw umber across the table to suggest wood grain. Using a 'palette mud' mix of black, burnt umber and ultramarine, strengthen the shadows on the legs and next to the mug. Add sepia to this mix to build up the tone of the book. Paint a little sepia and burnt sienna on the feet and hands, and a touch more detailing on the fringed border of the scarf.

Master Strokes
Paul Gauguin (1848–1903)
Fair-haired Woman on a Sofa

This painting was made in 1884, a year after Gauguin gave up paid employment to become a full-time artist. The viewpoint creates a harmonious composition of horizontals – the outstretched pose of the reclining woman is echoed by the straight lines of the *chaise longue* and the bold, wide band of brown running along the bottom of the wall.

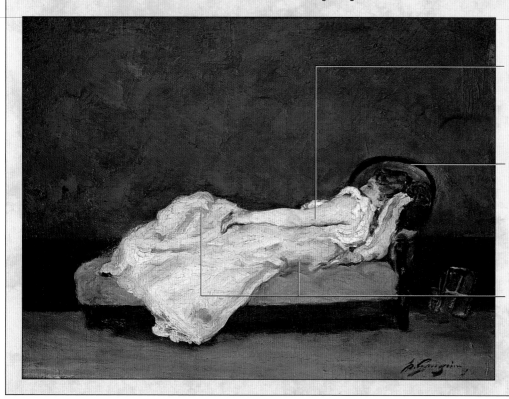

Surrounded by the dark tones of the wall, floors and *chaise longue*, the white dress and pale flesh tones really leap out.

The curved line of the *chaise longue*'s back helps frame and draw attention to the woman's head.

The greyish-browns of the walls and *chaise longue* are picked up in some of the shadow areas of the dress.

A FEW STEPS FURTHER

Now that you have worked hard on bringing up the detail on the reclining figure, even up the balance of the picture by giving a little more attention to the larger expanses of plain colour on the throws and sofa seat.

12 ▶ Finish the drapes Wash some plain water across the throws to give them more drama and depth. Using Winsor violet and the No.6 brush, strengthen the shadows on the background throw. Wash a little cadmium red lightly over the foreground throw.

13 ▲ Bring up the sofa Using the No.10 round, add the final touch by washing watery sepia across the front of the sofa seat. Now the drapes, table and model are all well-balanced, and the central figure retains its solidity, strength and interesting visual detail.

THE FINISHED PICTURE

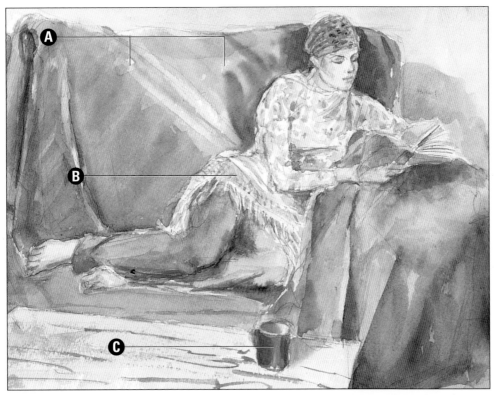

A White highlights
The tiniest flecks of unpainted white paper are sufficient to represent white highlights on the luxurious fabric.

B Central interest
Attention to detail by painting the pattern on the fringed shawl brings a point of interest to the centre of the picture.

C Drawing the viewer in
The artist has placed a strongly coloured object – the mug – in the foreground to help draw the viewer into the picture.

Watercolour Interiors

Working with watercolours to paint interiors as varied as a sunlit room in your own home, a sombre church, a boatyard or a railway station.

Conservatory in watercolour

Watercolour is the ideal medium to use for the fresh colours in this conservatory scene. The sunlight streaming in creates strong diagonal shadows that offer a contrasting tonal element.

I f you are lucky enough to own – or have access to – a conservatory, be sure to use it in a painting. Flooded with natural light, it provides a great subject – you not only have the plants and furniture inside to paint, but also the views of the world outside.

▶ **The light tones in this painting were laid down first, then the darker areas were put in, some wet-on-wet and others wet-on-dry.**

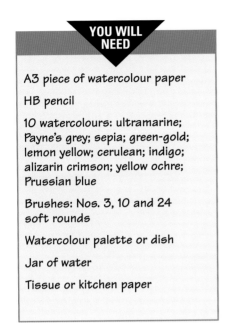

A3 piece of watercolour paper

HB pencil

10 watercolours: ultramarine; Payne's grey; sepia; green-gold; lemon yellow; cerulean; indigo; alizarin crimson; yellow ochre; Prussian blue

Brushes: Nos. 3, 10 and 24 soft rounds

Watercolour palette or dish

Jar of water

Tissue or kitchen paper

Balanced composition

The conservatory that our artist chose to paint has the added advantage of providing a simple, symmetrical composition. The bare floorboards in the foreground slant in from each side and extend into the distance, helping to create a sense of perspective and pulling the viewer's eye into the picture. The sofa balances the table in the middle of the composition, while the bushy plants on the shelf on the left are complemented by the spindly one in the hanging basket on the right-hand side.

The view outside

Beyond all this, we can see into the garden. As our artist painted in spring, the foliage is pale and golden. To capture the freshness of its colours, she found green-gold and lemon yellow particularly useful paints. These were applied unmixed for the sunlit areas of the garden, and with added touches of Payne's grey, cerulean and indigo for the shadow area.

If you are painting later, in the summer, you'll find that the greenery is darker in tone and cooler in colour. You'll need to increase the blue bias of your mixes to compensate for this.

FIRST STROKES

1 ▶ Sketch the scene
With the HB pencil, carefully draw the interior. The drawing should be relatively detailed. Correct any mistakes you make at this stage. When you move on to the watercolour, it will be too late!

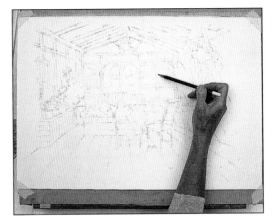

2 ◀ Establish the architecture
Using a mix of ultramarine, Payne's grey and sepia, draw the frame of the conservatory and trellis with a No. 3 round brush. To establish the right-hand shadow, let watery washes of all three colours run into each other.

DEVELOPING THE PICTURE

Having established the framework of the conservatory, move on to the garden. Don't worry about putting in too much detail here. Instead, look carefully at the variety of colours in the foliage – they range from inky blues to pale, golden yellows.

3 ▲ Move outside to the garden Switch to a No. 10 round brush to begin painting the garden. Use a mix of green-gold and lemon yellow to capture the effect of sunshine falling on the spring foliage.

4 ▲ **Add some darker tones** To put in the darker foliage, add cerulean and indigo to your mix of green-gold and lemon yellow. Keep varying the proportion of each colour in your mix to do justice to the variety of colours in the garden. Add sepia to your mix to render the woodwork outside.

5 ▲ **Continue the garden** For the wall outside, add alizarin crimson to the green-gold/lemon yellow mix. Add a little yellow ochre to a yellow mix to work the trees.

6 ▶ **Build up the pot plants** Apply a weak Payne's grey (with touches of the dark green mix) over the pot plants on the left. Create a range of greens by adding lemon yellow, green-gold and yellow ochre to indigo, cerulean and Payne's grey. Use these mixes to work up the leaves of the indoor plants with the No. 3 brush.

7 ▲ **Render the floor** Throw away your dirty water and replace it. Dip a No. 24 brush into the clean water and wet the bottom of the picture. Then add a wash of yellow ochre.

8 ▲ **Add alizarin crimson** While the floor wash is still wet, add some alizarin crimson to the immediate foreground. Then use the same colour on the No. 10 brush to paint the sofa and the plant pot on the left.

▲ Lemon yellow, Prussian blue and a touch of Payne's grey were some of the colours used to mix a range of grey-greens for the indoor plants.

9 ▲ **Lay the tablecloth** Use a wash of yellow ochre on the hanging basket in the top-right corner. Then apply a watery cerulean to the tablecloth. Surrounded by warm reds and yellows, this colour really stands out.

10 ▲ **Render the chairs** Use sepia with a little alizarin crimson to darken the underside of the hanging basket, then use the same mix to render the chairs and sofa cushions. Mix lemon yellow and yellow ochre for the pattern on the tablecloth.

11 ▲ **Darken the tone** Apply a wash of Prussian blue with touches of Payne's grey to darken the tone of the tablecloth. Also use this mix for the chair-seat covers.

Express yourself
A detailed rendering

This version of the painting is a much more detailed interpretation of the scene, both inside and outside the conservatory. The wall and fence in the garden are defined more precisely, as are the floorboards and checked pattern on the tablecloth.

Note also how the artist has used a deep-toned green for the foliage in the top-left corner. Like the wet-on-wet shadow at bottom left, this helps to direct the viewer's eye towards the garden in the centre of the composition.

12 ▼ **Add the hanging plant** Create a green with a mix of yellow ochre and cerulean to draw the plant in the hanging basket. Vary the colour and tone of the stalks as you work downwards.

13 ▲ **Finish the plant** Add a little indigo to your mix of yellow ochre and cerulean to put in more stalks of the hanging plant. For other stalks, use almost neat yellow ochre. Then, with the No. 24 brush, wet the paper at the bottom and loosely wash in Payne's grey with touches of Prussian blue for the shadows on the floor.

A FEW STEPS FURTHER

To complete the painting, intensify the shadow on the right to help draw the eye into the centre of the composition. Then simply refine a few of the details, including the chair legs and flowerpots.

14 ▶ **Strengthen the shadow** Still working with watery washes, reinforce the shadow tone on the right wall with Payne's grey and touches of alizarin crimson. Also re-establish the legs of the table and chairs if they have been altered by the wash put on the floor in the previous step.

15 ▲ **Add the finishing touches** Model the flower pots on the window ledge by adding darker tones with Payne's grey, sepia and alizarin crimson. Then put in some final details on the sofa's upholstery.

THE FINISHED PICTURE

A Muted shades
The leaves of the potted plants were rendered with a beautifully subtle range of blues, yellows and greens painted over a pale grey underwash.

B Warm colours
The glowing golden yellows of the foliage outside the conservatory help to pull the viewer's eye through the picture and into the garden.

C Wet-on-wet washes
Working wet-on-wet has created bold, dramatic shadows in the bottom-right corner. These contrast with the light, airy tones at the top of the picture.

Moody church interior

Capture the magnificent interior of this church using a combination of watercolour and gouache.

This candlelit church presents the artist with a double challenge – how to portray accurately the impressive scale and detail of the

▼ Precise pencil drawing is combined with a loose painting style and strong tonal contrasts in this atmospheric interior.

building, while at the same time conveying a sense of drama and atmosphere.

As with any architectural subject, accuracy is essential. Begin by making a precise line drawing, establishing the perspective and including as many features as possible. Once you have drawn the subject correctly in pencil, you can then apply the colour freely and with confidence.

Watercolour and gouache

The artist first blocked in the dark and mid tones, applying watercolour washes with a large brush, to create the effect of flickering candlelight and contrasting dark shadows. The washes range from deep, cool purple to warm, earthy brown and are mixed from just three basic colours: black, indigo and burnt sienna.

If you have taken the time to make an accurate drawing, you can be much looser when painting. Let spontaneous runs and splashes form and don't worry about painting over the drawn lines. However, do make sure you leave plenty of unpainted paper between each area of colour to enhance the tonal contrast.

Gouache is reserved for the later stages as it is stronger and more opaque than watercolour. It is used to accentuate the dark shadows and to add local colour and highlights.

YOU WILL NEED

Piece of 300gsm (140lb) NOT watercolour paper 35.5 x 35.5cm (14 x 14in)

Propelling pencil

7 watercolours: ivory black; indigo; burnt sienna; cadmium red; cadmium yellow; yellow ochre; ultramarine

7 gouache paints: ultramarine; orange; burnt sienna; cadmium yellow; titanium white; ivory black; indigo

Brushes: 25mm (1in) flat wash brush; Nos. 10, 4 and 2 rounds

Mixing palette or dish

Paper tissue

Ruler

Small sponge

FIRST STEPS

1 ▼ Start with a drawing Make a detailed drawing of the subject, using a propelling pencil. Take great care to be accurate with the proportions and perspective.

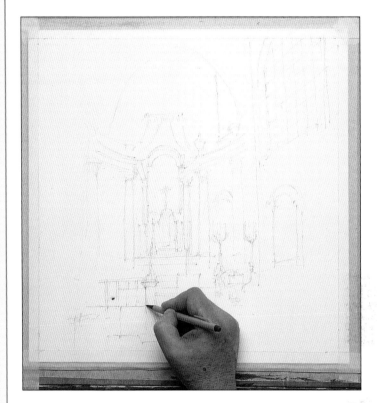

2 ▼ Block in the dark tones Mix a wash of ivory black and indigo watercolour. Prop up the top of the board slightly, then start to block in the darkest areas of the vaulted ceiling, using a 25mm (1in) flat wash brush. Add a little water to the wash to vary the tones slightly.

3 ▼ **Add warm tones** Change to a No. 10 round brush and continue blocking in the dark tones. Add burnt sienna to the wash for the warmer areas, such as inside the arch behind the altar. Use the point of the bristles for detail and to paint around the candlesticks.

◄ **Golden tones are mixed from cadmium yellow (far left), burnt sienna (top) and orange gouache.**

4 ▲ **Continue blocking in** Returning to the flat wash brush, block in the remaining cool shadows with varying mixtures of black, indigo and burnt sienna. Work with short, vertical strokes to create the rectangular architectural shapes (see Expert Advice, below).

EXPERT ADVICE
Using a flat brush

The chisel-shaped bristles of a flat brush are ideal for painting sharp angles and geometric shapes. The rectangular shadows on the right side of the picture are blocked in quickly using controlled vertical strokes. The stairs are painted by dragging the brush sideways along each step.

6 ▼ Create mid tones Dilute the warm and cool washes further and block in mid tones, such as on the columns and the religious painting. Add cadmium red and cadmium yellow for warm tones behind the altar. Use paper tissue to absorb runs of paint and lighten the tones.

7 ▲ Add local colour Add more cadmium yellow and cadmium red to the warm wash from step 6 for local colour on the columns and altar. Mix cadmium yellow and yellow ochre for the candlelit recess on the right. With the wash brush, paint the windows in dilute ultramarine – use short, vertical strokes, allowing plenty of white paper to show

5 ▶ Use fluid strokes Using the same warm and cool mixes, depict the steps, rails, columns and the area behind the altar with the tip of the No. 10 round. Paint the frieze and the arch on the right as continuous strokes of colour. Leave to dry.

DEVELOPING THE PICTURE

Put aside the watercolours and continue the painting using opaque gouache colours to accentuate the deepest shadows, including the vaulted ceiling.

8 ▼ Introduce gouache Working with the No. 10 round brush, strengthen the shadows on the left with a deep purple mixed from ultramarine and orange gouache. Use the brush tip to paint around the altar drapes and carved stonework.

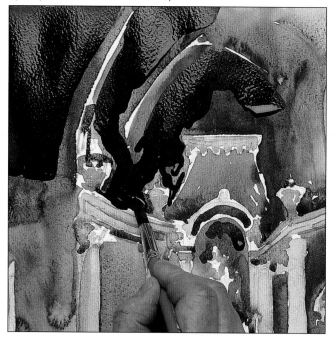

9 ▲ Develop the shadows Dilute the mixture and add a little more orange to paint the shadows in the altar drapes and on the right-hand arches.

**EXPERT ADVICE
Paint straight lines**

Ruled lines of paint give stonework in buildings a realistic appearance – but you only need a few. Too many straight lines will make the image look flat and mechanical. Use a ruler to help you pick out some of the fluting on the columns, holding the edge of the ruler above the paper surface in order to avoid smudging.

10 ▲ Add fine detail For the finer shading, change to a No. 4 round brush and use the tip to paint around the candlesticks. Depict carving on the cornice and columns, and paint the rails. Define the column on the left of the altar with a mix of burnt sienna and ultramarine (see Expert Advice, left).

11 ▼ **Paint the recess** Paint the candlelit recess with mixes of orange, cadmium yellow and burnt sienna gouache, toned down with ultramarine. Add a shadow to the right-hand pillar with a well-diluted mix of ultramarine and orange.

Express yourself

Capturing the atmosphere

Try painting the church without first making a detailed drawing. This version is done in watercolour and oil pastel and is a quarter of the size of the main painting. The small scale and chunky pastel sticks emphasize colour and atmosphere, rather than architectural details.

A FEW STEPS FURTHER

The golden ornaments and light reflections are focal points of the painting and must show up clearly against the surrounding darkness. Use pure white gouache, or white mixed with cadmium yellow and orange.

12 ▲ **Introduce white gouache** Paint the fluting at the top of the columns, using titanium white gouache and a No. 2 round brush. Mix the white with a little cadmium yellow for the candlesticks and ornaments, leaving flecks of unpainted paper to represent the reflections and highlights.

13 ▲ **Develop the columns** Model the candlesticks by adding orange to the mix. Use a ruler and the tip of the brush to pick out some of the fluted shadows in a mix of orange and ivory black. Blend the fluted lines at the base of the column to create solid shadow.

14 ▼ **Paint the window panes** With the help of a ruler, use the tip of the No. 2 brush to paint the leading on the large window in a dilute mix of black and indigo gouache.

15 ▲ **Lighten the window** Finally, use a small, damp sponge to soften the leading and give the impression of sunlight streaming through the window panes.

THE FINISHED PICTURE

A Cool lighting
The cool, blue daylight seen through the arched windows contrasts effectively with the warm glow of the interior candlelight.

B Offset composition
To avoid a symmetrical painting, the altar is deliberately offset to the left of the composition.

C Focal colour
The strongest colour in the painting is the bright orange gouache used on the easel in the centre of the composition. The eye is immediately attracted to this and the other areas of warm colour.

Going underground

Most of the time, travelling on crowded trains might seem a bit of a chore. But remember, there's a potential painting in every carriage and on every platform.

Although painting from real life has much to commend it, there are occasions when working from a photographic reference is useful, and sometimes essential. This step-by-step is a good example. The scene at a London Underground station would be almost impossible to render working from real life. Instead, the artist has photographed it and painted it later in the comfort of his home. Remember, a compact camera can fit into a pocket or handbag and – if used with an eye for the potential of everyday situations – can provide a wealth of painting material.

A painterly subject

In choosing what to photograph, the artist's eye for colour and composition led him to focus on a man sitting alone on his suitcase, oblivious to all around him. The subject is naturally framed by the wall on the left, and by the rail tracks on the top right-hand side. The colours in the photo also work well – the red of the jacket throws the subject to the fore, while the muted clothes of the other figures help them to recede.

When it came to translating the photo into a painting, the artist tweaked colours and details. The figures and objects surrounding the seated man were reduced to simple planes of colour and restricted to a palette of blues and greens in order to emphasize the solitary figure in his red jacket.

▲ Dabbing cotton wool on damp washes of paint has helped to create the wonderful array of textures, tones and edges in this picture of a traveller on the London Underground.

377

FIRST STROKES

1 ▼ Sketch the main outline Using the photo as a guide, sketch the image with a 4B pencil. The key elements to capture are the strong diagonal lines of the rail tracks in the top right-hand corner, the seated man in the foreground and the outlines of the figures behind him.

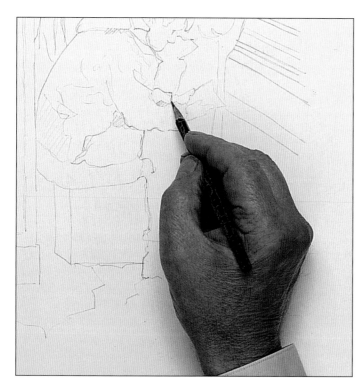

YOU WILL NEED

Piece of 300gsm (140lb) hot-pressed watercolour paper 36 x 26cm (14 x 10in)

4B pencil

10 watercolours: cadmium scarlet; ultramarine; Prussian blue; cadmium yellow pale; yellow ochre;

Payne's grey; indigo; cadmium red light; carmine; aureolin

Brushes: Nos. 6, 8, 4 and 2 soft rounds

Mixing palette or dish

Clean water

Cotton wool

Cotton bud

2 ▼ Block in the clothes Mix a dilute wash of cadmium scarlet and ultramarine; apply to the jacket, using a No. 6 brush. Mix Prussian blue and cadmium yellow pale to paint the bag next to the face of the seated figure. Using dilute yellow ochre, wash the jacketed figure at upper left. Add a little Prussian blue to the wash to make a green for the trousers of the figure on the right. Now mix Prussian blue and Payne's grey, and paint the trousers of the seated figure. Dilute the wash and apply to the figure's shoe.

EXPERT ADVICE
Special effects

To achieve areas of lighter tone just after you have applied a watercolour wash, gently rub out sections of paint with a small piece of damp cotton wool. Here, a pale patch has been lifted from the seat of the dark blue trousers, and another area is being removed from the green trousers.

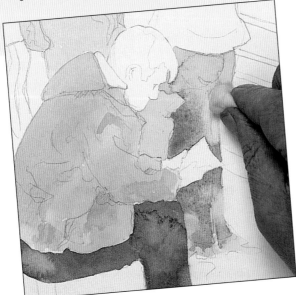

3 ▼ **Continue blocking in** Mix yellow ochre, cadmium yellow pale and a dot of Prussian blue; paint the undefined figure on the left. Mix ultramarine and Prussian blue and wash the jacket of the figure on the right. To this mix, add cadmium scarlet, yellow ochre, and a little more ultramarine to creaate a black-brown for the suitcase. Use a dilute wash of ultramarine to fill in the small area behind the seated figure.

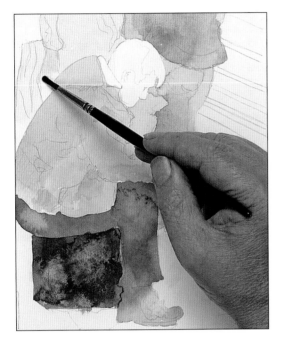

4 ▶ **Paint the platform** Mix yellow ochre and cadmium yellow to 'draw' the line on the platform. Add cadmium scarlet to make a skin tone for the face. Mix indigo, ultramarine and yellow ochre; paint the tracks, using a No. 8 brush. Wash dilute cadmium yellow pale, Prussian blue and ultramarine over the platform, and dilute ultramarine on the wall. Mix cadmium red light and Payne's grey for the background.

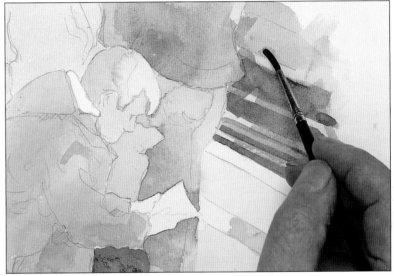

5 ▶ **Add tracks** Using a No. 4 brush, apply a yellow ochre/ultramarine wash to the back of the hair. Then paint the tracks with the blue trouser mix and allow to dry. Wash yellow ochre across the tracks. Add ultramarine and Payne's grey and define their contours.

6 ▼ **Silhouette head and hands** Define the hood with Payne's grey. Make an ultramarine/yellow ochre mix and wash over the jacket at upper left. Mix indigo and yellow ochre to darken the green trousers, adding small dabs of pure yellow ochre and indigo while the paint is still wet.

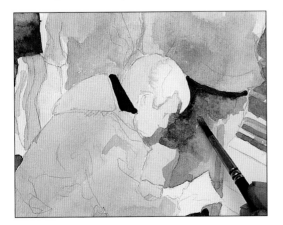

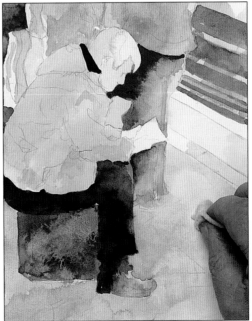

7 ◀ **Build up tone** Mix Payne's grey and ultramarine, and, using the No. 6 brush, apply this to the dark blue trousers. Leave the knee section lighter, and rub back the whole area with damp cotton wool. Mix ultramarine and cadmium yellow pale and wash over the platform with the No. 8 brush. Squeeze damp cotton wool so that a few drops of water fall on to this area and rub gently to give a mottled effect to the paint surface.

DEVELOPING THE PICTURE

The basic areas of colour are now blocked in and it is time to develop the forms with tonal shading. Continue using damp cotton wool or a cotton bud to rub back any hard edges.

9 ▲ **Build up tone** With a cadmium scarlet/yellow ochre mix, vary the tone on the red jacket. Define areas of the green trousers with indigo and cadmium yellow pale. Mix cadmium yellow, scarlet, yellow ochre and cadmium yellow pale; paint the hands. Now mix indigo, carmine, cadmium red light and yellow ochre, and apply to the suitcase. Wash an ultramarine/yellow ochre/Prussian blue mix over the blue jacket and bag.

8 ▲ **Add texture to the platform** Returning to the No. 6 brush, overlay a wash of ultramarine and Payne's grey on the platform area in the bottom left-hand corner.

10 ▶ **Add detail** Return to the jacket, mixing Payne's grey and cadmium scarlet and dotting under the arm with the No. 4 brush. Use the brush to smudge the colour from under the arm to the edge of the jacket. Draw a curve at the side of the jacket to indicate a fold line.

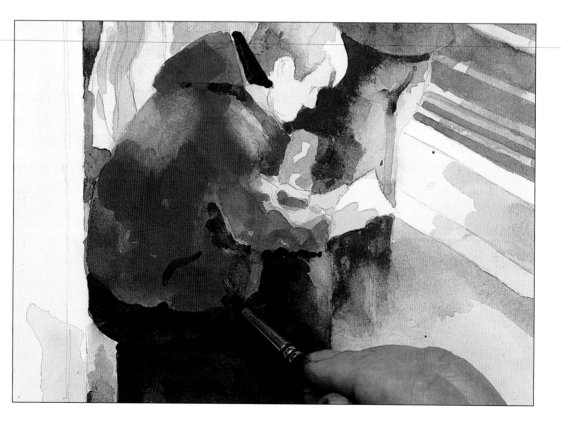

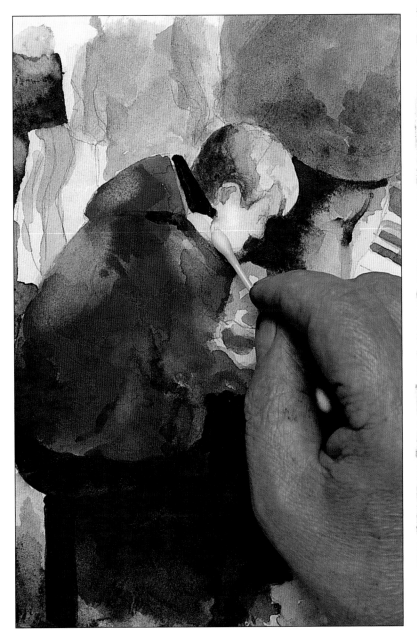

Express yourself
Single or return?

Another familiar scene at an Underground station, this composition is full of graphic linear elements, such as the ticket-office window, the noticeboard and the bands on the wall.

11 ▶ **Add features** Use cotton wool to smudge any hard red edges. Mix yellow ochre, cadmium scarlet and a little ultramarine. With a No. 2 brush, define the ear, nose, forehead and cheek. Rub back the cheek with a damp cotton bud. Apply a mix of yellow ochre and ultramarine to the hair.

▼ **Cadmium scarlet/yellow ochre (left) and cadmium scarlet/ultramarine (right) are the two basic mixes used for the red jacket.**

12 ▶ **Vary tones** Mix cadmium yellow, ultramarine and cadmium scarlet, then wash along the platform edge with the No. 8 brush. Darken the rails with a Payne's grey/ultramarine mix.

A FEW STEPS FURTHER

Finish off the picture by working some additional surface interest to give the painting character.

13 ▲ Add foreground interest Mix indigo and aureolin, and wash over the platform area. Flick a few drops of water on to the wet paint. Allow to dry, and wash roughly over the top with dilute cadmium yellow, using the No. 8 brush. Rub back with a piece of damp cotton wool.

14 ▲ Spotting and dribbling Using the No. 4 brush, apply dilute washes of cadmium yellow, cadmium red light and ultramarine to the wall. Using the No. 2 brush, draw an ultramarine border on the wall and platform. To create a lively picture surface, dribble a line of cadmium yellow pale on the left, then add dots and lines of cadmium red light.

THE FINISHED PICTURE

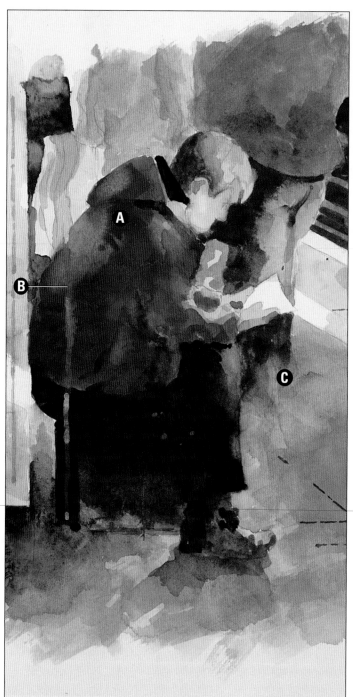

A Textured paint
The red jacket is the focus of the painting. It has been given a deep, textured appearance through the layering of colour and rubbing back of the paint with pieces of damp cotton wool.

B Distressed finish
By purposefully adding dribbles and spots of brightly coloured paint to the darker areas of the finished composition, the artist has given the painting a lift and a feeling of immediacy.

C Abstract shapes
The washes of colour around the central seated figure have been intentionally kept loose and abstract. They are represented as blocks of toned-down colour with little detail.

The summer house

This conservatory interior has the delicacy of a tinted etching, but it was drawn with ordinary ballpoint pens. The 'tinting' was done in watercolour.

Ballpoint pens might not be the obvious choice of tools when making a drawing for a watercolour painting, but they provide an unusual, detailed effect that is very successful. The pen marks do not run, so you can apply washes of watercolour over the lines without spoiling the drawing or smudging the colour.

Regular line work

Lines can be made lighter or darker by varying the pressure as you draw. What you can't do with a ballpoint pen is vary the thickness of the line itself. The pen tends to suit small- and medium-sized drawings, as the pen lines can appear overly fine and insubstantial in larger pictures. This painting of a conservatory is worked at quite a small scale, so the pen lines look firm and decisive.

You must draw 'positively' with ballpoint for your picture to be successful. Once a mark has been made it cannot easily be erased, so there is little room for error. To achieve a lively yet accurate ballpoint drawing, it is a good idea to start with a very light, preliminary pencil drawing. Once this is established to your satisfaction, the overdrawn ballpoint lines can be as bold and spontaneous as you like.

Coloured outlines

This painting was executed from inside a conservatory, taking in a view of the garden beyond. The colours indoors were predominantly warm and cheerful, while outside the light was brighter and cooler. To capture this effect in the painting, the watercolour mixtures for the garden

contained slightly more blue than those used in the conservatory. To emphasize the difference, the artist chose a black ballpoint for drawing the interior, while the garden was worked with a blue ballpoint.

In the final stages of the work, brightly coloured felt-tip pens were used to pick out some of the interior local colours and to highlight the ivy on the garden wall outside.

▲ There is plenty to engage the viewer both inside and outside. The eye moves naturally from the room to the garden.

YOU WILL NEED

Piece of stretched cartridge paper 30 x 40cm (12 x 16in)	Mixing palette or dish
HB pencil	10 watercolours: viridian; ultramarine; raw umber; cerulean; burnt umber; raw sienna; lemon yellow; yellow ochre; burnt sienna; cadmium red
2 ballpoint pens: black; blue	
Liquid paper for corrections	
No. 8 round brush	4 felt-tip pens: yellow; blue; red; grey

FIRST STROKES

1 ▼ **Draw the outline** Using an HB pencil, sketch in the position of the window, table and other main elements in the composition.

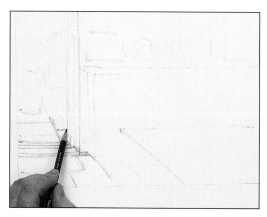

2 ◄ **Begin using ballpoint pens** Now start to work over the pencil lines with ballpoint pens, using black for the interior of the conservatory and blue for the garden visible through the door and window. Establish the main shapes with strong, clear lines.

3 ▼ **Vary the lines** Continuing with ballpoint pen, complete the drawing. Use light, broken lines in blue for the bricks and foliage seen through the window. For the ornaments and objects inside the conservatory, work in heavier, black lines.

4 ▼ **Suggest tones** Look for the darkest tones in the subject and indicate these with hatched and cross-hatched lines. These patches of tone will show through subsequent watercolour to represent pronounced areas of deep shadow.

DEVELOPING THE PICTURE

The drawing is done and it is now time to add colour. Don't worry if you feel the drawing might need a little more work. Ballpoint pen can be used over watercolour, so you can always go back and do more drawing when the paint is dry.

5 ▶ **Introduce colour** Mix a dilute watercolour wash of viridian with a touch of ultramarine. Using a No. 8 round brush, apply this loosely to the plant in the tub and the ivy on the garden wall. Allow some of the green to overlap on to the bricked area.

6 ▲ **Paint the exterior** Mix raw umber with a little cerulean and block in the shadow under the garden chair, allowing the cross-hatched ballpoint lines to show through. Apply the same mix to the brickwork on the garden wall.

Express yourself
Garden in bloom

Painting a smaller section of the same subject has allowed the artist to concentrate on the relationship between the exterior and interior. The red of the pot plant outside picks up on the cut flowers on the shelf. The cool blues of the climbing plant are repeated in the colours of the crockery. To suggest the presence of glass panes, the colours viewed through the window are pale and washy. Note, for instance, how the garden wall is described with well-defined, strong washes on the left of the picture, while pale mixes and lots of exposed white paper predominate in the middle section.

7 ▼ **Develop the garden** Block in the paved terrace in burnt umber with touches of raw sienna and cerulean. Paint the bench with a mix of viridian and ultramarine. Using a stronger mix of the same colour, dot in a few dark green shadows on the underside of the ivy leaves.

8 ▼ **Start the interior** Paint the shaded areas on the door and window frames in dilute raw umber mixed with a little lemon yellow. Use the same colour for the interior brickwork. Add a little viridian to the mixture and block in the two wicker chairs. Paint the table in yellow ochre.

▶ **Mixes used in the interior include cerulean with burnt sienna (top) for the ornaments; viridian, lemon yellow and raw umber (centre) for the chairs; burnt sienna and yellow ochre (bottom) for the tiles.**

9 ▲ **Develop the interior** Paint the tiles in a weak mix of burnt sienna and yellow ochre. Add the floor shadow, mat, floor joins, step and plant pot in varying mixes of yellow ochre and raw umber. Paint the cushion pattern in burnt sienna and cadmium red, and the plant, cushion and chair detail with a mix of viridian and ultramarine.

TROUBLESHOOTER

MAKING CORRECTIONS

Mistakes made with a ballpoint pen cannot be rubbed out, but you can correct them with a small amount of liquid paper. Note that watercolour applied over liquid paper is often paler than normal, so keep any corrections as small as possible.

A FEW STEPS FURTHER

A few details and one or two splashes of colour and the interior will be complete. In these final stages, introduce brightly coloured felt-tip pens to sharpen the colours.

10 ▲ **Define the ornaments** Paint the shadows on the wooden window sill in raw sienna and raw umber. Use the tip of the brush to define the china jug and plate in cerulean with a touch of raw sienna. Paint the bottle, plant and remaining ornaments in the same colour mixed with viridian. Add ultramarine shadows to the plant.

11 ▲ **Add more detail** Define the outlines of the ornaments in burnt sienna and ultramarine. Paint the second chair and cushion in viridian with touches of ultramarine and burnt sienna. Moving to the objects on the table, paint the crockery and newspaper in lemon and cerulean with a touch of burnt sienna. Add the cup pattern and the shadow on the newspaper in a mixture of burnt sienna and viridian. Blot excess paint from the newspaper to lighten the tones.

12 ▶ **Paint the teapot** Complete the tableware, including the teapot, which is painted in burnt umber and viridian with cadmium red decoration.

13 ▼ **Add dark tones** Using the tip of the brush, define the wickerwork on the second chair in viridian and paint the red flowers on the cushion. Depict the newspaper text and crossword in a greyish mixture of ultramarine and burnt umber. Add shadows to the table top in raw umber and yellow ochre.

14 ▲ **Introduce felt-tips** Use felt-tip pens for some final splashes of strong tone and colour. Use yellow on the outdoor foliage, blue on the garden seat, and red on the cushion pattern. With a grey felt-tip pen, outline the newspaper, chairs and cushions.

THE FINISHED PICTURE

A Ballpoint pen effects
The original lines made with ballpoint pen show through the paint to give fine detail in some areas and dark tone in others.

B Defining shadows
Fine lines of shadow applied with grey felt-tip pen define the newspaper and other objects on the table.

C Linear perspective
The converging lines of the table and floor tiles lead the viewer's eye through the open door into the garden beyond.

Boatyard

The jumble of boatyard paraphernalia and splashes of bright colour keep your eye on the move around this watercolour painting.

This study was inspired by one of the artist's favourite haunts, his local boatyard in Cornwall. What captured his imagination was the array of textures and patterns. In the densely packed yard are tools of all shapes, sizes and textures. There are the undulations of the corrugated iron walls and a jumble of ropes dangling from the ceiling. The result is a tapestry of random shapes, in

▼ Elements from two photographs were combined to develop this composition, which is packed with detail.

which even the figures of the men at work are just part of the overall design.

Working on gesso

The artist decided to work on a textured surface to heighten these effects within the painting. He covered the line board used by graphic designers – available at art shops – with acrylic gesso. Painting on a gesso ground involves a different approach to traditional watercolour techniques. The gesso seals the board, so that the paint floats on the surface rather than sinking into the support, creating interesting pools when it dries. The paint takes longer to dry and you have to work carefully when building up layers, as the original colour tends to lift off the surface. Be prepared for some happy accidents, but don't worry about mistakes – you can alter areas when they have dried.

YOU WILL NEED

Line board 34 x 46cm (13½ x 18in) primed with white acrylic gesso

4H pencil

12 watercolours: cerulean blue; ivory black; chrome yellow; phthalo blue; vermilion; magenta; Payne's grey; raw sienna; ultramarine; burnt sienna;

phthalo green; raw umber

Brushes: Small and large squirrel brushes; No. 3 sable round

Mixing palette or dish

Putty rubber

Steel ruler

FIRST STEPS

1 ▼ Scale up the scene Prime your line board with acrylic gesso and let it dry. Using a well-sharpened 4H pencil, copy the scene on to the board, including as much detail as you can. As it is an intricate drawing, it's best to copy the grid below, shown in light blue, on to your support – that is, with a ruler lightly pencil in eight equally spaced lines down the support and five equally spaced lines across it. This means you will be able to execture the drawing accurately, square by square.

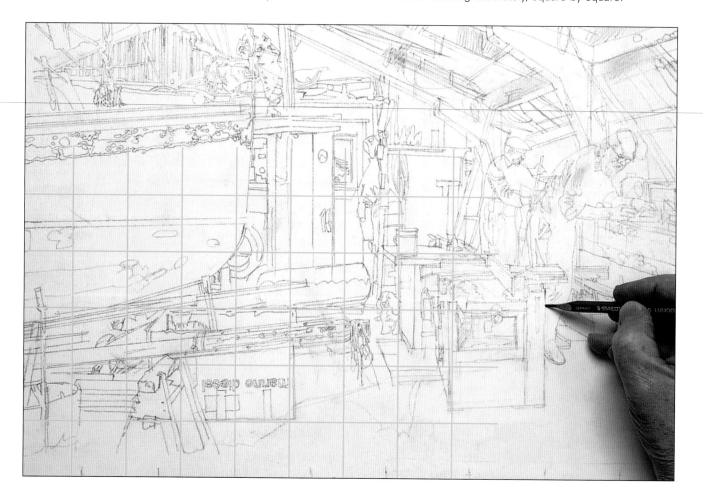

2 ▼ **Begin with a blue** Dilute some cerulean blue watercolour and, using a small squirrel brush, apply it along the rubbed-down paintwork on the boat. Then move on to other areas of blue. Add a little ivory black to the cerulean wash and make a subtle blue-grey to apply over the pale grey areas, such as details around the roof, workbench and on the window frame. When dry, feel free to use a putty rubber to soften the drawing so that it doesn't interfere with the painting.

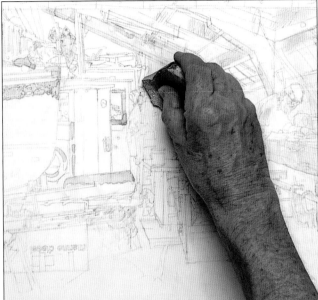

3 ▲ **Test your colours** Using the small squirrel brush and a dilute mix of chrome yellow, fill in the pale band along the hull and leave it to dry. Make a strong phthalo blue and try it out at the edge of the gesso board – testing colours is important when working on gesso, because it is difficult to modify them once they are down. Then use a large squirrel brush to apply this colour over the top half of the hull.

4 ▼ **Work wet-on-wet** Paint the base of the hull in a red mix of vermilion with a touch of magenta, working carefully around the drawn details. While the paint is still wet, drop some Payne's grey into it to suggest staining on the boat.

5 ▲ **Work around the board** Paint the overalls and oil drum in phthalo blue. Use the red mix to add bright details, modifying it with raw sienna and black where you need an orange tone, and ultramarine where you want a bluer effect. Now mix a very dilute brown from chrome yellow, phthalo blue and a hint of vermilion and wash this over the floor.

DEVELOPING THE PICTURE

Continue working up all the browns in the scene, varying their tones by making the mixes progressively stronger and darker.

6 ▶ Start on the background
Mix a mid brown from raw sienna, burnt sienna and chrome yellow. Using a No. 3 round sable brush, paint the background, taking care to avoid the various ropes and other items that cut across the area.

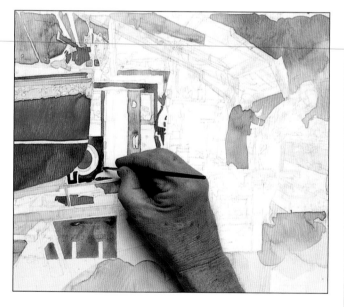

7 ▲ Add more browns Still working with the mix from step 6, paint other mid brown areas, such as the planks and door. Strengthen the tone and paint the box in the foreground. Then mix a dark brown from raw sienna, black and vermilion, and use the various brown mixes to paint lines along the top of the hull. Apply the dark brown to the door frame and behind the lifebelt.

8 ▲ Suggest weathering on the hull To represent the weather-beaten appearance of the hull, apply a watery mix of magenta and Payne's grey with the large squirrel brush. Work carefully – if you paint the new colour on too roughly, it will lift off the colour underneath.

EXPERT ADVICE
Taking colour off

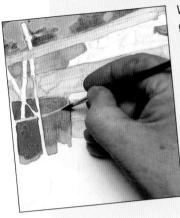

When working on gesso, it is easy to remove colour because the paint sits on the surface of the board rather than sinking into it. Here, the artist is using the tip of a brush dipped in clean water to take some blue off the top of the oil drum and suggest its metal lip.

9 ▶ Bring in some green
Using the small squirrel brush, paint the workman's jumper in ultramarine. Then mix a little black and raw sienna into phthalo green to make the muddy brown hues around the doorway. Overpaint some areas with black. Use phthalo green plus varying amounts of raw sienna and water for the small workbench in front of the figures – paint it wet-on-wet so that the colours pool together.

10 ▲ Add detail to the hull Paint a darker shade of blue over the weathered band on the boat's hull with a mix of cerulean blue and a little Payne's grey. Take care to avoid the pale patches as before.

11 ▶ Darken the man's overalls
Now give the men's clothes some texture. Using your original drawing to guide you, paint a layer of phthalo blue over the areas of the workman's overalls which are in shadow. Once the paint has dried, the texture of the board shows through, giving the appearance of tough denim fabric.

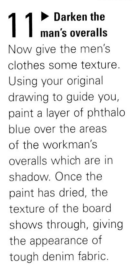

12 ▲ Paint under the boat Dilute the green mixes from step 10 and paint the trestle and other green details. Add shadows under the hull with a mix of black and varying amounts of ultramarine. It isn't necessary to know what every shape represents – just create a pleasing rhythm of patterns.

13 ▲ Add flesh tones Work up shadows on the right-hand man's clothes with mixes of phthalo blue or ultramarine and black. Paint pale skin tones on the faces with a watery mix of vermilion and raw sienna. Leave to dry, then use a stronger mix for the darker tones. Paint his beard with dilute raw umber.

14 ▼ **Fill in the background** Finish the figure in the foreground, painting his arms with the same light and dark skin tones as on his face. Now mix shades of grey from varying strengths of black plus phthalo blue and define the man's cap, glasses and watch strap. Then, with a more dilute mix of grey, add areas of shadow to the structure above his head.

15 ▼ **Paint the cocker spaniel** Define the horizontal mast with bands of dilute Payne's grey and burnt sienna. Then paint the spaniel. Use Payne's grey for the shadows on his coat, burnt sienna on his face and ears, and black for his nose, eyes and the tip of his ear. Leave the surface of the board for the white of his fur.

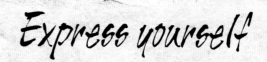

Setting up a scene

Monochrome sketches are a good way of working out the elements of a painting – the light and dark tones, the perspective and the most successful composition. In this charcoal sketch, the artist tried combining elements from his photos – putting in the two figures from one and the workbench and tea chest from the other – to see whether they held together. Without the colour, the drawing presents a more sombre view of the subject matter.

16 ▲ **Add the final details** Paint the skylights above the workbench with a mix of Payne's grey and raw umber. Mark in the tools and shadows on and around the workbenches with dilute Payne's grey, black, phthalo blue and a raw sienna/burnt sienna mix. Now, for one of the final patterns, paint the triangle of beams in the top left of the composition with the sienna mix.

A FEW STEPS FURTHER

There are a few more details that need to be brought into the painting to finish it off. For example, the lettering on the tea chest adds an authentic touch.

17 ▶ Add dark details Using the small squirrel brush and Payne's grey, work up a few dark patches of shadow in the clutter under the sloping roof. This helps to accentuate the element of pattern within the painting.

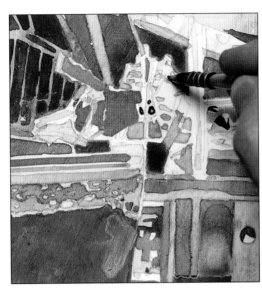

18 ▲ Add lettering Wash a cast shadow below the tea chest with a Payne's grey/burnt sienna mix, then touch in alizarin crimson on the labels. Finally, pick out the lettering with the tip of the brush.

THE FINISHED PICTURE

A Textured surface
The painted gesso ground works to heighten the sense of texture on the side of the boat and on the tea chest. Note how white ridges show through.

B Blocks of tone
The workmen, in their bold blue overalls, act as focal points in the yard's clutter. The masts in the foreground and the sloping roof help guide the eye to the men.

C Pools of colour
The tidemarks on the floor – painted wet-on-wet – add to the range and variety of textures. They work well against the geometric shapes elsewhere in the picture.

House plants in watercolour

This striking, close-up composition of three different conservatory plants shows that you do not need a grand subject or broad view to capture the beauty of nature.

Plants offer a particular challenge to the artist. The variety of forms, colours and textures require close observation and a careful choice of colours.

A painting such as this inevitably includes a lot of greens. Although green might appear to be quite a cool, fresh colour, the painting nevertheless manages to evoke the sun-drenched, humid atmosphere of the conservatory.

A range of greens

The trick is to observe the colours to be found in the light and shadowed areas. The artist has captured a wide range of greens, in both warm and

cool tones. He utilized a wet-on-wet style occasionally to let the colours run together and gain smoothly blended tones.

Visual editing

When re-creating a scene such as this, you continually need to edit the still life, simplifying the information from the original into something that can be reproduced. You are not trying to make a botanical rendering. What is important is that your painting looks believable, with an accurate representation of the shapes and light. If the composition needs a bit of help, feel free to rearrange the plants or leaves.

▲ The reds and greens that predominate in this carefully observed study of plants provide an exciting complementary colour contrast.

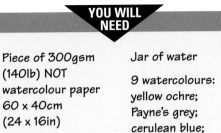

FIRST STROKES

1 ▼ **Draw in the pencil outline** Use a 2B pencil to sketch the basic picture on to the paper. Pay special attention to the shapes of the leaves and the overall forms of the plants, as they are the main focus of the composition. Close observation at this stage will pay dividends as the painting progresses.

2 ▲ **Lay a thin background wash** Leaving the highlights and the brighter parts of the composition blank, apply a very thin wash of yellow ochre and Payne's grey over the entire picture using a No. 10 round brush. Leave the wash to dry.

3 ▼ **Begin adding colour to the leaves** Look for the bluish reflections on the leaves and, using a No. 9 round brush, apply a very thin mix of cerulean blue to these areas. Use the same colour to block in the rounded plant at the front of the picture, as well as the view through the leaves and out of the window. Leave to dry.

4 ▲ **Paint the light areas** Add a little lemon yellow to your blue mix to make light green. Apply the paint from top to bottom of each leaf on the large plants. The paint will be most concentrated at the bottom of the leaves, giving the impression of light shining through the paler parts. Develop the rounded plant. The cerulean blue applied in step 3 will show through the green in places, creating a denser colour that contrasts with the translucent blue-lemon mix.

DEVELOPING THE PICTURE

Now that you have put in the palest tones of the leaves, pots and floor tiles, you can begin to build up the medium and dark tones on top. Work wet-in-wet so that the colours run into one another for a natural effect.

5 ▲ Block in the floor and pots Mix a light terra-cotta colour, adding a lot of Indian red and a little more yellow ochre to the original ochre mix used in step 2. Changing to a No. 7 round brush, block in the floor and pots. You will need to use this smaller brush in order to cut in around other areas of colour, as it is important that the terra-cotta shade does not 'bleed'. Darken the terra-cotta mix with a little more Indian red and some burnt umber. Apply to the lighter areas of the stems, using a No. 3 round brush.

6 ▲ Apply the main leaf colour Mix sap green and lemon yellow to make a more intense lime green. Using a No. 5 round brush, start to develop the detail of the lighter parts of the leaves where the sun catches them. Be very careful to render the shapes accurately.

7 ▲ Introduce the darker areas Mix lots of sap green with burnt umber and a little Payne's grey for a rich leaf colour. Add some gum arabic to intensify the colour and enable you to re-wet it once dry. Next, mix a dark stem colour with a little brown madder alizarin and lots of burnt umber. Work across the picture, painting the green mix wet-on-wet over the lime green to create the dark leaf areas. Drop brown colour on to the stems as you work across the painting.

8 ▲ Continue adding definition to the leaves Carry on adding the darker colours to all the plants. On the rounded plant, dab on the colour to show the smaller leaves. This adds density to the plants – until now, the painting has been very light and fresh. This stage takes a long time, but do not attempt to rush it, as the effect of the wet-on-wet technique is central to the whole painting. Work methodically across the picture, as you did before.

9 ▲ **Add colour to the pots** Mix burnt umber, a little yellow ochre and a little Payne's grey to make a medium brown for the soil and the insides of the pots. Apply with a No. 6 round brush. Add some Indian red to the mix to warm up the shady side of the pots, paying close attention to where the areas of light fall. The warm colours of the pots contribute to the bright, sunny atmosphere of the painting.

Express yourself

Pattern of leaves

Leaf shapes and the patterns they create are endlessly fascinating. In this pencil drawing, the artist has focused closely on the foliage of a rubber plant so that the leaves fill the paper. The pattern of leaves is more important here than the structure of the plant itself. A hint of tone and texture is achieved by the lines drawn on the foreground leaves.

10 ▲ **Define the areas of shadow** Mix sap green, Payne's grey and just a little burnt umber. Use this for the very dark green leaves and stems. As before, work methodically across the paper, introducing the dark brown colour from step 7 occasionally to add variety – use the colours together wet-on-wet.

11 ▲ **Complete the areas of shadow** Continuing with the dark brown and green mixes, work into all the shadow areas. Stand back and look at your painting. Remember that you are trying to create a believable, evocative picture, not a slavish re-creation of the original, so you can use a bit of artistic licence if necessary. If you feel the painting needs some more areas of shadow, add them, but keep it looking natural.

399

▲ Adding Payne's grey to the sap green creates a dark green for the shadow areas on the foliage.

12▲ **Embellish the background** Mix Indian red with a little brown madder alizarin. Block in the floor tiles, using the No. 9 round brush – these will make sense of the composition spatially. Add a little ultramarine, and use this mix to add detail to the pots. Make a thin mix of yellow ochre, Payne's grey and brown madder alizarin for the window frames. Paint these in as simple straight lines.

13◄ **Finish off the background** Complete the lines that form the window frames – these provide a suggestion of the setting, but do not detract from the composition's main focus. The painting is now a very believable rendering of plants in a conservatory.

A FEW STEPS FURTHER

All the main areas of light and shadow are now included, but you can improve the picture further by adding more colours to the shadows and intensifying the background.

14 ◄ **Sharpen the picture** Make a more intense mix of the dark green used on the leaves in step 10. This mix should be almost black. Using the No. 3 brush, cut in around the leaf shapes, adding more definition and sharpening up the picture. Add further accents to the pots to emphasize the light and dark areas and to strengthen the effect of bright sunlight. Make sure that you have represented all the areas of intense shadow, even the very fine ones. For close work, change to a No. 3 flat brush.

15 ▲ **Suggest the background** Mix sap green and cerulean blue. Apply using the No. 6 round brush to give a suggestion of foliage outside the conservatory. This increases the sense of depth in the picture and helps the painting to look more complete.

THE FINISHED PICTURE

A Wide tonal range
To convey the impression of strong sunlight filtering through the window and plants, a wide range of tones was used, both on the leaves and the pots.

B Simple background
In contrast to the busy subject matter in the picture's foreground, the background was kept uncluttered – the windows and floor tiles are suggested very simply.

C Dark shadows
The areas of deepest shadow on the plants were painted during the final stages. The dark colour crisply defines the lighter shapes of the leaves.

Sunlight and shadows

Watercolour is an ideal medium for capturing the subtle colours and shapes of shadows created by sunlight filtering into an interior.

What brings an interior to life? The subject matter certainly does – the room needs to have interesting objects, decoration and furniture, and these should complement each other well. The composition is also crucial – everything you choose to include should sit pleasingly within the frame. One of the most overlooked aspects of interiors, however, is the lighting.

Light and dark

In this painting, direct sunshine creates an interesting play of light and dark, with its strong shadows and bright highlights. The sunlight illuminates the right wall, yet leaves the far one in darkness. The artist has exaggerated this contrast of tone and also the contrast of colour it creates – the warmer browns of the sunlit areas beautifully offset the deeper bluish shadowed areas.

Capturing shadow areas

Key to achieving interesting, variegated shadows is layering the washes, smudging the paint while it is still wet to give a soft, uneven look that mimics the effect of shadows in real life.

As you progress with the layers of colour in the darkest area of the room – the alcove – the paint will become thicker, but you can add drops of water to dilute the wet paint already applied and thus make sections of the wall less opaque. A similar effect can be achieved with some well-judged rubbing back with damp cotton wool. Varying the tone in this way creates lively and realistic shadows. Remember, however, that you have to work quickly.

It is important to alter the colours as well as the tones in the shadow areas – for instance, halfway down the alcove, the artist added more brown to capture light reflected from the warm table.

Before building up the shadow areas, however, it pays to establish the small details you wish to retain, such as the pictures and the items on the table, in the initial stages. This then enables you to focus on the bigger picture – the overall sense of light and shadow in the room. You can return to the details in the very last stages of the painting.

FIRST STROKES

1 ▼ Sketch the room Using a 4B pencil, mark the outline of everything in the room. (Note that to attain a strong sense of recession, the artist used a slightly different viewpoint than the one in the photo on the left.) Delineate the shape of the alcove carefully, as this area is a major focus of the painting. The other key objects that should be well defined are the chair and table. Draw the items on the table carefully, too, marking in the clock face.

▲ Soft wet-on-wet washes in the shadows contrast with the crisp lines of the furniture in this atmospheric painting of an interior.

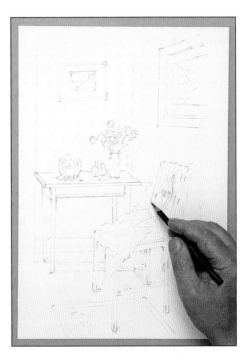

2 ◄ Paint and mask the poppies Mix carmine and cadmium scarlet to create a bright, warm red. Fill in the poppies using a No. 4 brush – don't worry about definition at this stage. Once the red paint has dried, apply masking fluid over it with an old No. 4 round brush. This will protect the flowers against being affected by the other colours you will be using around them.

3 ▶ Paint the small objects Using a No. 2 brush, mix an indigo/aureolin wash for the vase and poppy leaves. Smudge the leaves with damp cotton wool. For the bottles, mix yellow ochre with ultramarine. When dry, lighten the far bottle with aureolin. Mix cadmium scarlet, ultramarine and yellow ochre to outline the clock. Add ultramarine and Payne's grey for the picture frame.

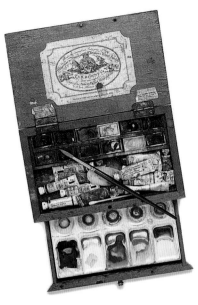

▲ The artist worked from a portable, self-contained watercolour set which is ideal if you're painting on-site.

4 ◀ Wash the right-hand wall Mix yellow ochre and cadmium yellow pale. Using a No. 8 brush, wash over the floor and right-hand wall. While the paint is still wet, rub back the light area above the chair with damp cotton wool.

5 ▶ Paint the alcove Add cadmium red light and ultramarine to the mix used in step 4 and paint the top of the right-hand wall wet-on-wet. Create an aubergine colour by adding carmine and a little more ultramarine to this mix. Work over the alcove. Add indigo, Payne's grey and more carmine to the mix and drop it on to the wash with a watery brush. Where the wall joins the alcove, smudge the paint with damp cotton wool.

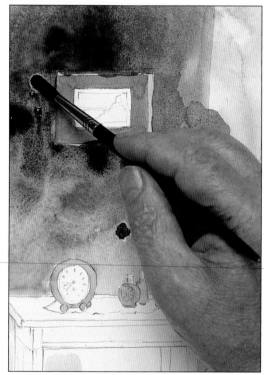

DEVELOPING THE PICTURE

Complete the main washes by lightly blocking in the table and rug. Then focus your attention on the chair and table, applying paint, then smudging it with damp cotton wool.

6 ▶ Define the chair Paint the skirting board in a pale wash of ultramarine with a little carmine. Make a dilute wash of ultramarine and yellow ochre and wash this pale shade over the table. Then mix carmine and yellow ochre and fill in the rug. Allow to dry. Mix a dark brown from indigo, cadmium red light and yellow ochre and, using the No. 2 brush, start to define the chair.

7 ▶ Smudge the paint
Use a more dilute dark brown wash for the lower part of the chair. Add cadmium scarlet and yellow ochre to the mix and apply this warmer brown to the chair-back where the light hits it. With damp cotton wool, gently smudge the paint on the chair.

Express yourself
Paint another room

This corner of a bedroom, casually strewn with clothing and jewellery, has been treated in the same way as the step-by-step picture. Diffused dark grey on the shadowed wall contrasts with pale ochre on the lit back wall, the two colours merging where the walls meet.

8 ◀ Add the chair's shadow Use the dark brown mix to paint the table top and legs. Rub back with damp cotton wool, allow to dry and reapply the paint. While still wet, gently rub back once more. Mix ultramarine and yellow ochre, and, with the good No. 4 brush, paint in the shadow of the chair. If the colour looks too dark, rub back with a piece of damp cotton wool.

9 ▼ Add detail Mix Payne's grey and cadmium scarlet, then define the far frame with the No. 2 brush. Warm the mix with cadmium red light and paint the clock rim; soften any hard lines with a damp cotton bud.

10 ▶ Build up shadows Use monestial green for the perfume bottle lid. Wash an ultramarine/yellow ochre mix over the clock face. Mix Payne's grey with cadmium scarlet and a little ultramarine. Using the No. 8 brush, wash over the top of the alcove, thinning the colour as you work downwards. Squeeze a few drops of water from a piece of cotton wool over the wet paint on the wall.

BLOW GENTLY

TROUBLESHOOTER

Using a small hair-dryer is a great way to speed up the drying process. It allows you to overlay wash on wash without fear of the colours running together. But be sure to use a low setting – if the force coming from the dryer is too strong it could accidentally blow paint across the paper.

11 ◄ **Add more detail** Apply a mix of cadmium red light, yellow ochre and Prussian blue to the top of the right-hand wall. Smudge with damp cotton wool. Wash the area around the table with a mix of yellow ochre and ultramarine, then smudge with damp cotton wool. Make various brown and beige mixes of yellow ochre, cadmium scarlet and ultramarine; using the No. 4 brush, define the main features of the two paintings.

12 ▲ **Strengthen shadows** Using a mid-beige mix from step 11, strengthen the tone on the floor. Paint the wall behind the chair, too, leaving the area above and to the left of the chair unpainted. Dip the brush in water and tap a few drops on to the painted area to add visual interest.

13 ▲ **Refine the shadows** Using the No. 2 brush, paint the shadows in the folded cloth on the chair with a weak mix of ultramarine and a touch of carmine. Mix indigo, yellow ochre and cadmium red light, and use the No. 8 brush to wash over the shadowy area under the table. With a weaker mix, paint the shadow of the chair on the floor and strengthen the wall shadow. Mix yellow ochre and ultramarine to create dark brown; using the No. 2 brush, define the edges of the table and chair.

14 ◀ **Apply greens** Mix aureolin, indigo and a little cadmium red light and paint over the vase with the No. 4 brush. Add a touch of indigo to make a darker green and apply to the foliage. Dilute this colour with water and apply around the foliage to create a halo-like shadow.

15 ▲ **Add finishing touches** Mix yellow ochre, cadmium red light and a tiny speck of Prussian blue, and apply with the No. 8 brush to the large picture frame. Leave to dry. Mix Payne's grey and cadmium red light to make a near-black, and go over the picture frame again.

16 ▶ **Enhance the details** Mix indigo, yellow ochre and carmine, and use the No. 8 brush to darken the rug. Rub away the masking fluid from the poppies with your fingertip. Mix carmine and cadmium scarlet and paint over them with the No. 4 brush, but don't cover the original colour completely. Use dilute Payne's grey and a No. 1 brush to show the markings on the chair back.

407

A FEW STEPS FURTHER

The picture now has a moody sense of shadow and light. As the painting focuses on the chair and table top, it makes sense to add a few final details to this area.

17 ▲ **Work on the fabric** Paint the clock face and hands in Payne's grey, then shade the clock face with dilute ultramarine and yellow ochre. Also add shading to the perfume bottles. Mix ultramarine and Payne's grey and, using a No. 1 brush, dot paint along the fabric edge to suggest eyelets. Using a No. 0 brush, draw tassels in white gouache.

18 ▲ **Dribble paint** Mix very dilute cadmium scarlet and cadmium yellow pale. With the No. 8 brush, tap a few drops of paint in the less detailed areas of the painting to create a lively picture surface. Tilt the paper to allow the paint to trickle down.

THE FINISHED PICTURE

A Coloured shadows
By using a palette of deep purples applied in layered washes, a very effective sense of late-afternoon shadow has been built up on the alcove wall.

B Focusing the eye
The crumpled fabric lying on the chair was left unpainted. Its dazzling whiteness creates a compelling focal point among the deep shadows that engulf the room.

C Spattered paint
The finishing touches of spattered and dripped red and yellow paint add a sense of excitement and drama to what might otherwise appear a rather sombre scene.

Chinese interior

A cool, calm interior with a view on to a sunlit exterior produces a striking pattern of lights and darks. Focus on these contrasts to create an image that lingers in the mind.

I nterior views provide the artist with a fascinating and endlessly rewarding subject. In the project on the following pages, the artist has painted the interior of the Chen Family Temple in Guangzhou in China. Two photographs provide the reference for the project. The one on the right provided the composition's broad outlines and details such as the lattice-work shutters and the play of light across the space. From the left-hand picture, the artist borrowed the details of the bright red lanterns in the courtyard beyond.

Dark against light

This study focuses on a dark interior seen against a bright exterior. The near-silhouette, or *contre jour* image, simplifies the picture into areas of light, shade and cast shadow, emphasizing the abstract qualities in the subject. And where light falls through the lattice-work, it creates interesting and intricate patterns.

The success of a *contre jour* subject depends on achieving a pleasing balance of light and dark. With watercolour, it is important to work from light to dark because you can't paint light colours over dark ones without compromising the transparency of the medium. Start by applying the sunny washes in the window openings. Work wet-on-wet with thin washes in these areas so that the paper shines through and creates a strong sense of luminosity. In the shaded areas, use wet-on-wet to give depth and vibrancy, but retain wet-on-dry for the areas where edges and decorative details are seen against the light.

YOU WILL NEED

Piece of 300gsm (140lb) NOT watercolour paper 40 x 30cm (16 x 12in)

Soft carpenter's pencil

7 watercolours: cerulean blue;
chrome yellow; indigo; yellow ochre; cadmium red; alizarin crimson; ivory black

Brushes: Nos. 12 and 10 rounds

Cotton bud

Paper tissue

◀ The fine lattice-work of the window screen and the delicately carved legs of the plant stand create dark patterns against the sunlit exterior view.

FIRST STROKES

1 ▼ **Sketch the scene** Use a soft carpenter's pencil to draw in the main outlines of the scene – the shutters framing the window openings, the angle of the floor and the low rail on the right. The flat-tipped carpenter's pencil gives a combination of thick and thin marks, so you can delineate edges and suggest areas of tone.

2 ◀ **Establish the light** Add a little cerulean blue to a chrome yellow wash to produce a pale greenish-yellow. Use a No. 12 round brush to wash in colour where the foliage is brightest. This underwash establishes the colour key for the sunlit courtyard.

3 ▶ Add more green
While the initial wash is still wet, drop touches of chrome yellow here and there. Add more of the greenish-yellow mixed in step 2 to suggest foliage outside the window. Mix indigo and yellow ochre for the darker greens and apply touches of unmixed chrome yellow. Allow the colours to bleed together. Use the brush tip to 'draw' the pot plant.

EXPERT ADVICE
Lifting wet colour

Introduce subtle textures and pale areas into the foliage by working into the still-wet wash with a cotton bud, absorbing some of the paint.

4 ◀ Introduce cool colours Mix a pale wash of indigo, cadmium red and alizarin crimson, and use this to block in the stonework of the buildings seen through the window. Use a darker wash of the same mix to depict the floor, the balcony and the shadows on the building across the courtyard.

6 ▲ Add the dark interior shadows The interior panelling is painted a deep blue-green that resonates against the sunny exterior. Mix indigo, alizarin crimson and a touch of chrome yellow. Load the No. 12 brush with the wash and drag it across the surface of the paper so that speckles of white show through here and there.

5 ◀ Dab out light areas Before the paint dries, estimate the position of the red lanterns in your composition. Then take a piece of paper tissue and begin to lift the still-wet wash in these areas.

8 ▼ Develop the foreground Block in the tables in the foreground with the indigo/alizarin crimson/chrome yellow mix. Half-close your eyes to simplify the areas of light and dark. Add ivory black and more indigo to the mix. Use the tip of a No. 10 round brush to put in the darkest shadows, which give form to the objects.

7 ▲ Block in more darks Continue painting the window screens and the pillar, using the brush to pick out details and leaving the white paper to stand for open areas and highlights. Add a little ivory black to the wash for the darkest areas.

DEVELOPING THE PICTURE

Now that the broad composition is established, you can start to add details, such as the graceful plant stands and the delicate tracery on the window screens. The trick is to provide enough information for the viewer to be able to 'read' the textures and details in the picture, without overworking or confusing the image. If every part of the painting is rendered with the same sharp detail it can be distracting, but if you add details at key points the eye will fill in the gaps.

9 ◄ Add details Load the No. 12 brush with the dark shadow mix and use the very tip of the brush to paint the delicate shapes of the plant stands. Work slowly and carefully, pulling and pushing the wash to create the solid forms of the table tops and drawing the brush very lightly down the paper for the graceful legs.

10 ▶ Add the tracery Add a touch of chrome yellow to an indigo wash and use this dark green to paint the plant on the stand. With the tip of the brush, suggest its delicate form seen against the light. Add a touch of alizarin crimson to the wash and, using the same No. 12 brush, suggest the delicate tracery on the window screens.

Express yourself
Sharp in black and white

The same balance of light and dark is retained in this pen-and-ink drawing of the Chinese interior, but the medium allows for more detail. The fine lines of the lattice-work are sharply defined, and the plant on the left is revealed as a bonsai tree.

11 ▼ Add foreground details Add black to the previous wash and use this to develop details on the furniture in the foreground. Use the tip of the brush to depict the narrow railing that divides the room.

A FEW STEPS FURTHER

The image now has a wonderful sense of light flooding into a shaded interior. While the balance of warm and cool colours is pleasing, a splash of colour contrast will enliven it and provide a focus for the eye.

12 ▲ Add the red lanterns Mix cadmium red and alizarin crimson for the lanterns. Blot with tissue, then draw the ribs on the lamp with the brush tip.

13 ▶ **Adjust the screen** Darken the shadows lying behind the lanterns with a mix of cerulean blue and indigo. Increase the brightness coming through the window screen by lightening the lower panel. Do this by dipping a cotton bud in water and lightly working it over the area to moisten it and lift some of the colour.

14 ▲ **Add details** Mix yellow ochre and indigo, and use this mossy green to paint the graceful leaves of the pot plant. Apply a pale wash of chrome yellow to add colour and detail to the foliage outside.

THE FINISHED PICTURE

A Creating recession
The details that are seen through the window are paler and less crisply defined than those found within the room, helping to create a convincing sense of depth.

B Coloured shadows
Cast shadows are rarely solid or black, but reflect colours from their surroundings. In this interior, the shadows pick up the blues from the panelling.

C Sparkling light
The dark paint used for the interior was dragged in bands across the textured paper, leaving white speckles of paper on either side to suggest sparkling light.

Sunlit interior

A soft pencil and a selection of warm colours recreate the comfortable atmosphere of this spacious, sunny sitting room.

Pencil and paint are perfect partners in this composition of a stylish interior. The artist began with a light pencil drawing to establish the composition, then painted in the main areas of colour quite loosely before drawing more tightly over the top.

Emphatic lines

The pencil used was a very dark, soft 8B, which is ideal for emphatic lines and deep, rich shading. It shows up well over the painted areas and so can be used to add details and textures once all the paintwork is complete.

Mix and match

A combination of watercolour and gouache was used to bring colour into the drawing, sunny yellow and an orange shades were used. Watercolour and gouache can be mixed together if necessary as they are both water-based paints, which is handy if

▲ Soft pencil, gouache and watercolour complement each other beautifully in this line-and-wash drawing.

you don't have all the colours you need in one or other of the mediums.

In hot weather or a warm room, gouache will dry out more quickly on the palette than watercolour, so spray the paint with water from a plant mister from time to time to keep it moist.

YOU WILL NEED

Piece of 300gsm (140lb) hot-pressed watercolour paper 46 x 61cm (16 x 24in)

8B pencil

Putty rubber (to erase mistakes and guide lines)

Craft knife (for sharpening pencil)

Brushes: No. 2 squirrel; No. 4 round

4 gouache paints: mid orange; cadmium yellow; titanium white; brilliant green

6 watercolours: brilliant purple; burnt umber; cobalt blue; gamboge; ultramarine violet; Payne's grey

Mixing palette or dish

Jar of water

SETTING THE SCENE

Before you embark on the project, make a rough, preliminary sketch to check the composition and work out the perspective of the furniture and other features in the room. The very free interpretation shown on the right is worked in the style of an interior designer's colour notes and is a great way to try out the paint mixes.

FIRST STEPS

1 ▶ Make an initial drawing Using an 8B pencil, draw the composition quite loosely. First establish the eye-level line – it runs just below the wall plaque. Make sure that the perspective lines of the sofa, rug and window frame meet at a vanishing point on this line.

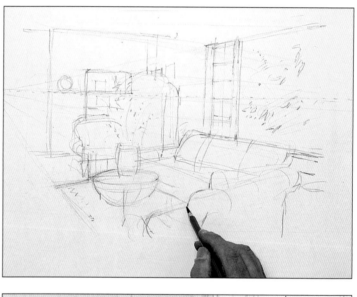

2 ▼ Colour the walls Mix mid orange and cadmium yellow gouache with titanium white to make an apricot colour. Using a No. 2 squirrel brush, wash this colour over the walls.

3 ▲ Paint the chairs and sofa Add more mid orange and water to the mix and wash over the armchairs. Now mix mid orange and a little white gouache with brilliant purple watercolour and paint the sofa and back of the foreground chair with this warm pink. Add more mid orange to the mix to make a 'burnt' orange for the far chair.

4 ▼ Mix in more colours Use the 'burnt' orange mix to block in the rug. Add brilliant green gouache to the warm pink mix from step 3 and paint the red plant. Mix in burnt umber watercolour to make a dark pinkish-brown for the shelf and floor shadows.

5 ▼ Put in the greens With the pinkish-brown mix, paint the back of the near armchair, the ceiling beam and the band around the table. Make a dilute mix of cobalt blue and gamboge watercolour for the hazy colour outside the window. For the plants, add brilliant green gouache to the apricot mix from step 2. Add extra cadmium yellow to vary the green.

DEVELOPING THE PENCIL WORK

Once you have finished washing in the colours, you can continue with the drawing. Emphasize the furniture with pencil outlines and put in pattern details on the rug and upholstery, working on top of the coloured areas.

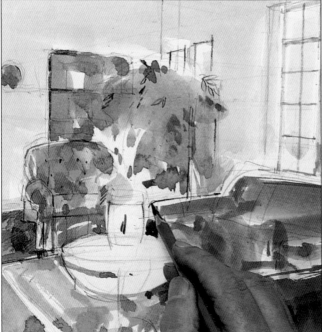

6 ▲ Draw some details Using a No. 4 round brush and a mix of ultramarine violet watercolour and white gouache, paint the window frame. Sharpen the 8B pencil and define some of the leaves on the red plant. Begin outlining the furniture and hatch shadows on the floor around the far chair.

7 ▲ Put in some more detail Add more leaf detail to the red plant and darken the shadow areas within it. Work around the sofa cushions. Firm up the outline of the table, then draw the lines on the vase and hatch in its cast shadow. Draw the pattern on the rug, emphasizing the black edge.

8 ▲ **Continue with the pencil** Describe the plant next to the sofa with outlined leaves and dark negative shapes. Hatch in the shadow on the shelves. Indicate the curved back and arms of the chair in the foreground with linear marks.

9 ▲ **Use more colour** With the No. 4 round brush, dab on spots of titanium white gouache to suggest the flowers in the vase. Paint white highlights on the armchair, sofa and plants. Mix mid orange, cadmium yellow and white and suggest the pattern on the chairs and rug with simple brush marks. Develop the pattern using the warm pink mix from step 3. Use the pink mix on the red plant, too.

A FEW STEPS FURTHER

Take a look at the picture and check whether any textures would benefit from being described in more detail. For example, the leather sofa has a mottled appearance that can be suggested with a combination of pencil and paint.

EXPERT ADVICE
Gouache highlights

As white gouache is opaque rather than translucent like watercolour, it is ideal for adding strong highlights at the end of the project. Here, titanium white is being painted over the rich pink of the sofa to create a light area.

10 ▲ **Paint dark leaves on the plants** Mix a dark green from brilliant green gouache with brilliant purple and a little Payne's grey watercolour. Use this to paint individual leaves on the large green plant. On the red plant, use the dark green to pick out a few of the leaves and also to paint dark negative shapes behind paler leaves. Finally, rub out the pencil construction lines around the drawing.

11 ▼ **Add pencil and paint details** Using the 8B pencil, add more definition to the rug pattern. Mix mid orange and cadmium yellow gouache to paint the lines on the vase. Use the pinkish-brown mix for the round table frame, then add white gouache to the mix for the pale shadows on the table.

12 ▲ **Describe the leather texture** Use pencil hatching for the dark tone behind the armchair and to add texture to the leather sofa. Bring out the paler parts of the leather with the orange/yellow vase mix plus white.

THE FINISHED PICTURE

A Hazy background
The garden, just visible through the window, was left hazy, so that it did not distract from the interior.

B Loose paint style
The paintwork was kept loose, working with the drawn elements, rather than dominating them.

C Pencil over paint
Drawing back over the paint adds weight to the linear aspect of the drawing and builds up shadow tone.

Train station

Lively pencil lines and loose washes of watercolour combine to create the distinctive appearance and atmosphere of a traditional railway terminus.

In this project, the artist has combined two photographs of a train station taken at slightly different angles. He wanted to include elements from both – the train plus the sweep of the platform on the right. The idea was to create an atmospheric rather than a realistic view: all the main elements are in place, but much of the detail, particularly the colours, is left to the imagination.

Inexperienced artists often believe that the more paints they use and the more brushes in their armoury, the better their paintings. This is rarely the case. More likely to be true is the maxim 'less is more'. This painting was, in fact, executed with just three paints – versions of the primaries red, blue and yellow – and three brushes. And rather than using costly sables, the

brushes are all inexpensive and readily available – the 13mm flat listed in the things you will need for this project is actually a pastry brush. If you don't have a similar kitchen utensil, a small household paintbrush will do.

▼ **The curved perspective lines of the platform and roof give a strong sense of depth in this painting.**

FIRST STEPS

1 ▶ **Create a frame**
Using a propelling pencil and ruler, draw a rectangle measuring 27 x 41cm (10½ x 16in) on your paper. Apply strips of masking tape to define the edges of the picture area. Now start mapping out the composition, beginning with the dramatic sweep of the platform and roof. Rough in the train and the arch at the end of the platform.

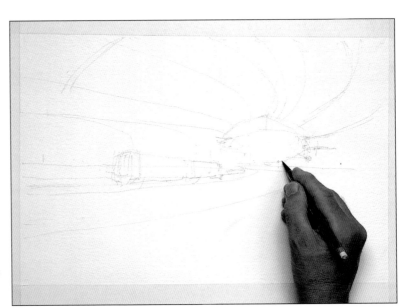

2 ▼ **Establish the perspective** Put in the main lines of the platforms and roof, making the distance between these lines progressively narrower as they recede from view. Add pockets of detail on the station building.

3 ▶ **Build up the drawing**
Continue building up the detail, paying particular attention to the arch at the end of the platform as the eye will rest here – the literal light at the end of the tunnel. Once the overall structure is correct, turn your attention to the train. Notice how this, too, appears to get smaller as it recedes from view.

4 ▲ **Firm up the detail** In this study, the pencil lines form an integral part of the composition, so continue working on the train and the main structure. Don't, however, try to follow the photographs slavishly – the eye can take in only a simplified version of the scene.

DEVELOPING THE PICTURE

With the basic drawing complete, start adding washes of watercolour. The colour in this composition relies heavily on the imagination, so allow yourself to be creative.

5 ▼ **Create atmospheric colours** Using a 25mm (1in) bristle flat brush, make a dilute red-brown mix from equal amounts of the red, blue and yellow, and wash this over the right-hand platform. Mix ultramarine and medium yellow to make a dull green wash and take this over parts of the roof and the opening at the end of the station.

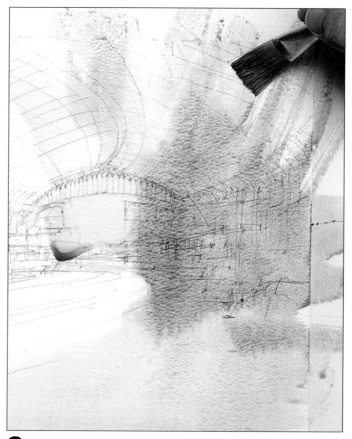

6 ▲ **Add a blue wash** Make a watery blue from the ultramarine and paint this over the right-hand side of your composition, drawing the colour out from the centre. Notice how the paint granulates as the pigment settles on the paper.

7 ▲ **Add a sweep of purple** Use a 13mm (½in) bristle flat brush to sweep a slightly darker wash of ultramarine over the far wall on the left of the painting. Add brilliant red and a touch of medium yellow to the watery ultramarine from step 6 and wash this dilute purple along the length of the tracks. Allow the paint to dry. Now that the background washes are complete, you can remove the masking tape.

TROUBLESHOOTER

REMOVING MASKING TAPE

A danger in removing masking tape is that you will lift off some of the paper at the same time and damage the surface. There is a simple way to avoid this: use a hair-dryer over the masking tape to dry out the sticky resin, then carefully peel the tape off the paper. Now you will have clean, sharp edges to your painting.

8 ▶ Start on the train With the background washes in place, turn your attention to the train. Change to a No. 3 soft round brush and varying mixes of red, blue and yellow to suggest the contours of the carriages, the dark underside wheel area and the windows on the front of the cab. Leave the front of the train white, as though light is catching it.

9 ▲ Block in the windows Using a coppery mix of brilliant red and medium yellow, paint the distinctive vertical bands on the front and back of the first carriage. Then block in the windows in a dark blue-grey mixed from ultramarine and a little brilliant red.

10 ▲ Return to the drawing The station walls – red brick and dotted with windows – support the vast expanse of roof, itself a complex structure of metal and glass. Once the paint is completely dry, return to your propelling pencil and put in some of these elements, starting with the pattern of windows along the far wall.

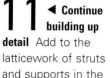

11 ◄ **Continue building up detail** Add to the latticework of struts and supports in the roof, suggest some figures waiting on the right-hand platform and draw several lines of tracks punctuating the centre of the composition and disappearing from view.

Express yourself

Bustling concourse

In this study, the artist used acrylics, starting out with a warm brown background wash, then working up to the lights. The figures are sketched very loosely with a spindly calligraphic style – this gives the impression of the bustling activity on the station concourse.

12 ▼ **Heighten contrasts** Although the intention is to have atmospheric rather than realistic colours, the lights and darks should be roughly accurate. Here, the tracks seem too light in comparison to the rest of the painting. With the 13mm (½in) flat brush, add purple mixed from ultramarine and red over the tracks to darken them. This stronger tone makes the light at the end of the station seem that much brighter.

13 ▶ **Paint figures on the far platform** With the No. 3 soft round brush and the purple mix from step 12, put in windows on the far wall. Add more ultramarine to the purple and squiggle a couple of figures on the platform.

14 ◀ **Add dark accents** Darken the right-hand side of the picture by painting a series of curved purple bands from the roof structure to the platform. Add more brilliant red and water to the mix and paint the shadows and figures along the platform. Emphasize the fact that it extends into the distance by placing dots of dark purple at the far end.

◀ Medium yellow and ultramarine were used on the carriages.

◀ Medium yellow and brilliant red were used for the details on the train.

◀ Ultramarine, brilliant red and medium yellow were used for the tracks.

A FEW STEPS FURTHER

All that's needed now is a final balancing of tones and perhaps a focal point ...

15 ▲ **Build up detail on the right** To strengthen the tonal balance, dab dark purple and a strong reddish-brown on to the shadows on the right of the composition and allow these to dry. Now use your pencil to draw more elements along this right-hand wall. Make these quite sketchy – a suggestion of architectural detail is all that you need.

16 ▲ **Draw the eye into the distance** Strengthen the appearance of the glass structure at the end of the roof by filling in a couple of the panes with purple. These dark touches serve to create a focal point, leading the eye through the station and into the distance.

THE FINISHED PICTURE

A Textural effects
Interesting variegated textural effects are created in the finished picture by the granulation of the ultramarine pigment on the paper.

B Latticework of pencil lines
An intricate pencil drawing forms the basis and body of the painting and provides plenty of detail for the eye to linger on.

C Unpainted areas
The unpainted area in the background suggests the effects of bright light beyond the covered platform and helps to pull the eye into the picture.

Inside the rustic kitchen

Break with convention by adding textural interest to your watercolours with scored and scraped lines.

Bristol board is an unusual surface for watercolour painting – it is not generally recommended because it has a smooth, slippery surface on which washes dry unevenly.

However, the technique used for this painting – textural marks are scored into the paper with a knife before washes are applied – is itself unorthodox and Bristol board is the ideal surface for this technique.

Scoring the surface

This still life features objects with a variety of textures and patterns. Such an intricate subject can be difficult to paint without overloading the picture with detail, but the artist has overcome this problem by using the scoring method to suggest detail and texture. The technique is like *sgraffito* in reverse – instead of scratching through a painted area to reveal the white paper beneath, you score

▼ **Chosen for their textural qualities, the objects in this still life make an ideal subject for the scoring technique.**

the paper to make indents in the surface, then apply colour over it.

This process reveals the more absorbent paper beneath the smooth surface coating of the board, so that the scored lines appear darker than the surrounding washes. The channels that are made by the knife, and the bumps which are created by roughing up the surface, become integral parts of the finished painting.

Choice of blade

Almost any type of sharp metal point, such as a penknife, craft knife or scalpel blade, can be used to score the lines, as long as it cuts easily through the board without slipping. A saw-tooth blade dragged across the surface is useful for making hatched and crosshatched lines, and for suggesting rough textures. Always be careful when drawing with a sharp instrument – never place your free hand in the path of your drawing hand.

FIRST STROKES

1 ◄ **Draw with a brush** Using a No. 4 soft round brush, rough in the main outlines of the still-life group with a dilute wash of ultramarine. Don't worry too much about accuracy – try to express the exuberant lines of the subject.

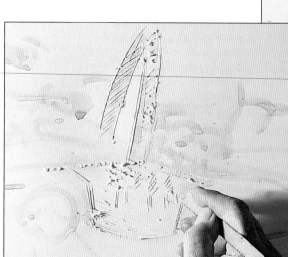

2 ▲ **Paint the basket** Draw the outline of the basket by scoring the surface of the board with the sharp point of a saw-tooth blade. Then suggest the woven pattern of the basket by scoring short, angular lines into the paper, using both the point and the teeth of the blade (see inset). Then mix a wash of yellow ochre and wash this lightly over the basket with a No. 10 wash brush. The paint darkens where it sinks into the indents made by the knife and catches on the roughened paper. Leave to dry.

DEVELOPING THE PICTURE

It can be difficult to see where the scored lines are on the white board, so the best way to proceed is section by section. Score one area of the picture and paint it before moving on to score and paint the next.

3 ▶ Score and paint Use the blade to score lines that suggest dried flowers and teasels in the basket. Work around the shapes of the white flowers. Mix a wash of burnt umber and sweep it over the dried flowers. Again, the paint darkens where it sinks into the scored marks.

4 ◀ Score the alliums With a penknife or craft knife, score fine lines at bottom left to show the allium seed-heads. Scratch tiny parallel lines for the seed capsules. Mix a pale wash from ivory black and ultramarine, and brush over the seed-heads with the wash brush to reveal the delicate stalks and seeds. Allow to dry.

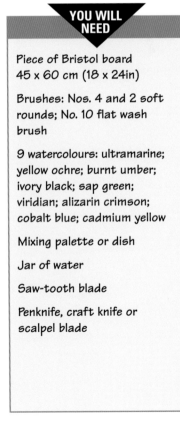

YOU WILL NEED

Piece of Bristol board 45 x 60 cm (18 x 24in)

Brushes: Nos. 4 and 2 soft rounds; No. 10 flat wash brush

9 watercolours: ultramarine; yellow ochre; burnt umber; ivory black; sap green; viridian; alizarin crimson; cobalt blue; cadmium yellow

Mixing palette or dish

Jar of water

Saw-tooth blade

Penknife, craft knife or scalpel blade

5 ▼ Work on the corn Now change to a saw-tooth blade. Use the tip and teeth to score a series of short zigzag lines into the board to suggest the heads of corn lying next to the allium seed-heads. Brush over the lines with a thin wash of yellow ochre to reveal the scored lines.

6 ▶ Add the thistle stalks Use the knife to score the long corn and thistle stalks. Suggest the texture of the thistle heads by scoring short parallel lines at varying angles. Paint a thin layer of sap green over the stalks with the wash brush. Go over the darker stalks with a wash of viridian, letting the light and dark greens mix loosely.

KNOW THE SCORE

These examples show the range of textural effects you can achieve with scored marks. Thick lines were made with a saw-tooth blade; finer ones with the tip of a penknife.

Heads of corn

Basket weave

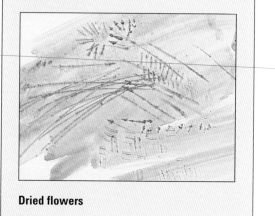

Dried flowers

Drawing with a blade

While the scoring technique is used in the step-by-step project to capture intricate detail and texture, it is equally appropriate for simpler, more minimal subject matter. Here, the artist first scored the outlines of the crockery and cutlery, the checks of the tablecloth and the vertical lines in the background. Then he added the washes of watercolour. Finally, when the blue wash was dry, he drew the blade diagonally across it to add a vigorous, lively texture to the background.

7 ▲ Add some purples Paint the red onion in the centre with a purple made from alizarin crimson and cobalt blue, loosely mixed. Let the colour settle in pools of light and dark tone that give form to the onion, and leave a white highlight near the top. Use the same mix to darken the thistle heads.

EXPERT ADVICE
Score draw

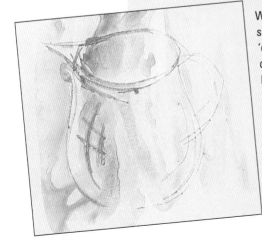

Why not try using the scoring method to 'draw' the outlines of objects? The scored lines are revealed when colour washes are added, and the contrast of soft washes and fine spidery lines is very pleasing – rather like an etching.

8 ▲ Paint the jug Lighten the mixture with more water and use the chisel edge of the wash brush to go over the outlines of the blue jug. Bring out its rounded form with overlaid washes of light and dark tone, applied wet-on-wet.

9▲ **Bring in more details** Use ivory black and cobalt blue to add dark lines to the dried flowers in the basket, and to paint the scored teasels and the shadow on the basket handle. Suggest the pink dried flowers with a sweep of alizarin crimson. Paint the cheese with cadmium yellow. Score circular lines for the texture of the broken bread and wash over it with very dilute burnt umber and ivory black.

A FEW STEPS FURTHER

The painting is now complete, but if you wish you can add just a touch more scratched and painted detail. Resist the temptation to go overboard, though, as you risk losing the spontaneity you have achieved so far.

11▶ **Scratch back** When the washes have dried fully, add texture and highlights to the crusty bread and the skin of the onion by scratching broken lines with the tip of the knife. Then scrape at the unpainted areas left in step 3 to give an impression of the fluffy texture of the white flowers.

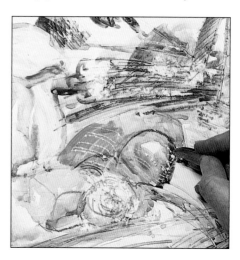

10◀ **Strengthen the image** Continue to work all over the picture, building up local colour and strengthening the dark areas. Using a mixture of alizarin crimson and burnt umber, add warm shadows to the onion and to the basket and its contents. Strengthen the jug with ultramarine, then paint the chopping board with a loose wash of burnt umber. Use viridian and sap green to add more green stalks in the foreground. Leave to dry.

12▼ **Add more highlights** In the foreground, use the knife blade to scrape out small patches of colour to suggest the highlights on the thistle heads.

13▲ **Add some seeds** Mix burnt umber and a touch of ultramarine, and dot in some seeds around the allium heads, using a No. 2 round brush. Add a few more in alizarin crimson.

THE FINISHED PICTURE

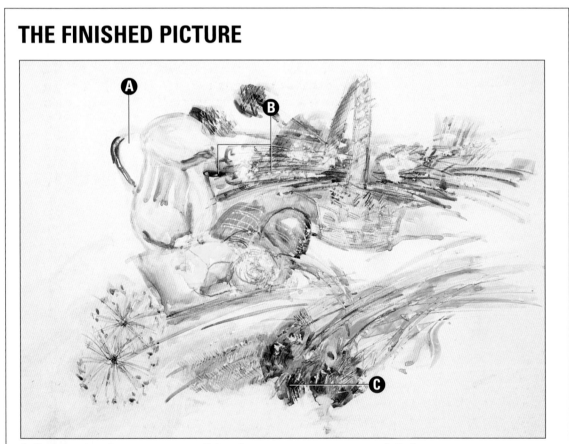

A Lively brushwork
The absence of an initial pencil sketch encouraged freedom and spontaneity in the brushwork.

B Less is more
The white flowers are not really drawn – instead their fluffy texture is registered by scuffing up the paper.

C Surface texture
Scoring and scratching the surface of the board added character to the picture, as well as suggesting more detail and texture.

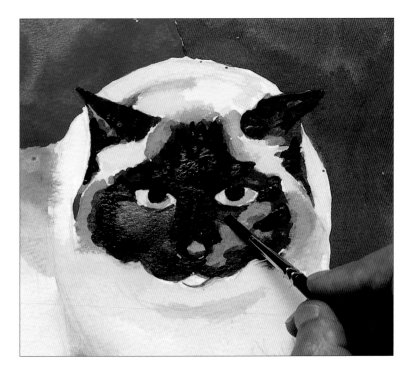

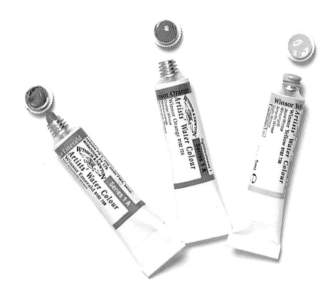

Gouache and Mixed Media

From creating landscapes, portraits, interiors and still lifes in gouache to hand-tinting photographs and using pencils, crayons and even glue.

Introducing gouache

An exciting, versatile form of watercolour, gouache can be used to create both delicate, translucent washes and bold, opaque areas of colour.

Gouache is simply an opaque form of watercolour. It is made in exactly the same way as traditional watercolour paint, except that white chalk is added to make it opaque.

Though it has never attained the popularity of watercolours or oils, gouache nevertheless has a long history. Reputedly, it was discovered in the eleventh century by an Italian monk, who added zinc white to his watercolours for illustrating manuscripts. From the sixteenth to the eighteenth centuries it was also used to paint miniatures. Some of the best-known artists to have used gouache include Joseph Turner (1775–1851), Edgar Degas (1834–1917), Pablo Picasso (1881–1973) and Henri Matisse (1869–1954).

Sometimes referred to as body colour, gouache has many of the qualities of pure watercolour, but being opaque it has a character of its own. Like watercolour, gouache flows easily, dries quickly and becomes lighter in colour as it dries. When dry, however, it has a matt, slightly chalky finish quite different from that of translucent watercolour.

Brightness of gouache

Whereas watercolour paint gains its brightness from light reflecting off the white paper beneath it, the brightness of gouache comes mainly from the reflecting power of the pigments in the paint surface itself.

As with traditional watercolours, some colours are permanent, but a few are liable to fade – so avoid using these if you intend to paint for posterity. The degree of permanence is indicated on the label. Also, try to avoid mixing too much white with a colour, as it can cause fading.

All the papers and boards recommended for pure watercolour are also suitable for gouache. Moreover, with gouache, coloured papers can be used to great effect. If the paint is applied thickly, for example, the colour of the paper is obliterated, but when it is washed on thinly, the paper colour shows through and modifies the colour applied on top. Furthermore, areas of coloured paper can be left unpainted so that the colour becomes part of the painting.

Choosing a coloured paper

With coloured paper, always choose pastel paper or mounting board, which will not fade when exposed to light.

▼ If you already work in watercolours, you have all the equipment needed for gouache, except the paints themselves. Instead of white paper, you can try a coloured support.

Lightweight papers should be stretched, as it is for watercolour painting.

Watercolour brushes are normally used for gouache, but because the paint has more body than watercolour, you can also use bristle brushes to make textural marks and strokes.

As gouache is an opaque paint, it is a more forgiving medium than watercolour. One layer of colour will conceal another, and light colours can be applied over dark. This makes it ideal for beginners, as mistakes can be corrected and tones modified with ease.

Bold, lively marks

Gouache might not have quite the radiant transparency of pure watercolour, but you can still get subtle washes of paint by diluting it with water. Alternatively, you can use it thick and undiluted to produce an effect similar to oils and acrylics, using bristle brushes to make bold, lively marks and even building up a slight impasto. Thick, near-dry paint can be scuffed and dragged across the paper to create attractive, broken-colour effects with a matt, pastel-like quality.

Flat, saturated colour

Mixed with a little water, gouache has a soft, creamy consistency. It flows smoothly and dries evenly – ideal when you want to emphasise pattern with bright areas of flat, saturated colour. It is equally good for creating fine lines and details. Illustrators are particularly fond of the medium because its bold hues, matt finish and dense covering power make it ideal for reproduction in books and magazines. When it is thinned with more water, gouache takes on a delicate, semi-transparent, milky quality, which is perfect for capturing the effects of clouds, mist and haze in landscapes.

All of these different techniques can be incorporated within a single painting. Areas of wet-in-wet dilute colour can be overlaid with areas of thick, opaque paint, and these variations help to create a lively picture surface.

Mixed media

You can obtain an even wider range of interesting textures and visual effects by mixing gouache with other media. Watercolour and gouache are often used together, the opaque colour being used to add highlights or to scumble clouds over a sky wash, for example. Gouache also combines well with acrylics, egg tempera, pastel and pen-and-ink.

THE EXPRESSIVE, VERSATILE MEDIUM

Like watercolour, gouache can be used thinned with water to attain transparent washes of paint (see the flowers, left). But it also presents you with many other options. For instance, you can also add white to your gouache paints to create opaque colour (see below). This allows you to apply light colours over dark.

The sky sketches (right) show the possibilities of this technique. In the top picture, white is used quite thickly in parts so that the blue and grey underwash is hidden and a 'silver lining' effect is achieved. In the bottom picture, near-dry paint has been 'scuffed' across the underwash to mimic wispy clouds. You can see here how gouache – like acrylics and oils – allows you to create distinct brush strokes.

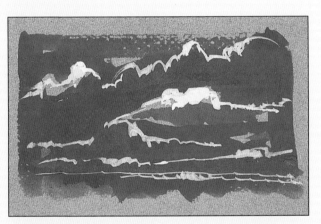

▲ After the sky and grey clouds were loosely washed in, opaque white gouache was added to create silver linings.

▲ Varying degrees of transparency, from the most transparent (top) to the least (bottom), can be attained by diluting gouache with water.

▲ Adding white to a gouache colour not only lightens it but makes it more opaque. Here the colour on the left is created by using viridian lake neat; the other two have different amounts of white added.

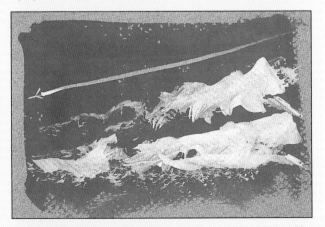

▲ Scrubbing dryish white paint over a blue wash with the side of the brush creates wispy clouds and vapour trails.

After the harvest

Panoramic landscapes offer great painting opportunities. This broad vista has been approached in an expressive, imaginative way.

▼ **Layers of scumbled gouache and pastel, together with a variety of textural marks, create a paint surface with plenty of visual interest.**

This painting was inspired by a visit the artist made to France just after the harvest had been taken in. It is not a conventionally pretty landscape, but the starkness of the rolling farm land uninterrupted by hedges and fences provides an arresting image. Big landscapes are mirrored by big skies, and the frothy white cumulus clouds are an important component of this image. The lines of stubble have a bold, graphic quality and lead the eye across the landscape and into the distance. The tawny colours and spiky textures were also an inspiration.

A sense of space and place

The artist painted this image in the studio, with the aim of capturing the sense of space and place, rather than creating a precise topographical description. He used photographs as a resource, but also relied on his memory of the scene and his experience of the landscape, the light and the mood.

Working from photographs

Indeed, the most rewarding results are achieved when you use photographs as a jumping-off point – a trigger for the imagination rather than a template to be copied exactly. Most artists treat photography as a tool alongside sketching and drawing, a valuable aid and a source of inspiration. Photos are especially useful for landscape artists because time spent on location

is often limited, not least because the weather can close in. When you find a subject that interests you, don't take just one photo, but run off a whole film. Take a series of overlapping photographs (see left) and tape the prints together to create a panorama that will give you a choice of compositions. Try different formats and crops: a broad vista will feel spacious and airy while a tight crop can produce a more dynamic image.

In this project, the artist was inspired by the trees marching along the skyline, and the colours and the beautiful sky full of light, wispy clouds. However, the field in the foreground was 'borrowed' from another series of pictures and the house was moved to the right side of the image.

Perfect partners

A combination of gouache and pastel was used for the painting. These two media, one wet and one dry, have many qualities in common. Both are strongly coloured, have a matt opaque finish and can be used as solid colour or as semi-transparent scumbles.

An underpainting in gouache establishes the division between sky and land, and sets the colour key for the image. Further colour is applied with broad strokes of the gouache or pastel, but these are knocked back by subsequent layers. Later, some layers are recovered by scratching back with a blade. Gradually the image comes into focus, but sometimes it dissolves as an area disappears under a layer of colour only to emerge in a different guise. This technique of losing and finding gives the final image a freshness and spontaneity which is often absent in more orderly and conventional methods of painting.

YOU WILL NEED

Piece of 300gsm (140lb) Not watercolour paper

Brushes: 50mm (2in) decorator's brush; Nos. 20, 10 and 4 rounds; No.16 filbert; squirrel mop

9 gouache paints: Azure blue; Madder carmine; Cadmium orange; Titanium white; Raw sienna; Burnt sienna; Alizarin crimson; Winsor green; Cobalt blue

Palette and jar of water

14 soft pastels: Cobalt blue; Indian red; Titanium white; Sage green; Sap green; Burnt umber; Cadmium yellow; Lemon yellow; Yellow ochre; Dark green; Cobalt blue; Lilac grey; Dark grey; Pale blue

Hard eraser

Kitchen paper

Blade

L-shaped card croppers

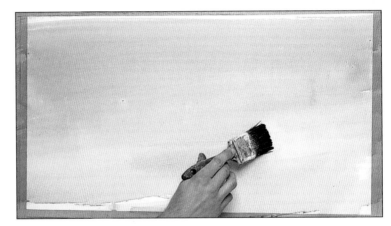

FIRST STEPS

1 ▲ Block in the underpainting Wash in the sky with a 50mm (2in) decorator's brush and a large quantity of azure blue gouache with a touch of madder carmine. Apply a broad wash of cadmium orange to the foreground to provide a warm undertone for the cornfield. Dry the painting with a hair-dryer. These areas of colour establish the broad divisions of the composition.

2 ▲ Lay in the clouds Using a No.20 round brush, scumble titanium white gouache into the sky, pushing the paint around to create cloud formations. Mix a little madder carmine with white and a touch of azure blue and drag this colour over the lower sky and horizon – this gives the lilac for the shadows on the undersides of the clouds.

3 ▶ Develop the sky Use the side of a mid-toned cobalt blue pastel to lay a band of broken colour across the orange just below the horizon. With a No.10 round brush, lay a narrow band of pure azure blue along the horizon. Use the No.20 brush to work more of the pale lilac into the upper sky, pushing the paint backwards and forwards with vigorous strokes to create descriptive marks.

4 ▶ Add foreground colour Load a No.16 filbert and lay broad, sweeping bands of a mix of cadmium orange and raw sienna across the foreground. The paint is distributed unevenly, covering thickly in some places, glancing across the surface in others to give a dry-brush effect. These bands describe the patterns of light and shadow on the field.

DEVELOPING THE PICTURE

The broad division between sky and land has been established and the orange foreground and blue/lilac sky set the colour key for the painting. Now it is time to introduce more texture in the foreground and develop the clouds on the right. The white house provides a focal point.

5 ▲ Introduce a focal point Add texture in the foreground by skimming Indian red pastel across the foreground. Now put in the white house with titanium white pastel, giving it a mid-grey roof. Located on the horizon at a key point about a third of the way up and a third of the way in from the right, the white house draws the eye and helps to tie the composition together.

6 ▲ Develop the clouds Use a hard eraser to lift out colour to create white areas of paper that stand for clouds. Apply white pastel in the cloudy areas on the right – the different qualities of the paper white and the pastel white suggest the changing nature of the clouds.

7 ▲ Darken the horizon Mix azure blue and burnt sienna gouache to give a dull green and lay a thin wash of this over the azure hills on the horizon, linking them to the foreground.

8 ▲ Knock back the foreground Add alizarin crimson to the azure blue/burnt sienna mix to produce a rich brown. Wash this colour in bold gestural marks over the foreground with the squirrel mop brush. This creates areas of solid and broken colour that describe the shadows cast over the landscape by the clouds.

9 ▶ Soften the horizon Make a pad from crumpled kitchen paper and rub this lightly over the white clouds to soften them in some areas. Then gently rub the pad over the horizon – the pastel sticking to it will soften and diffuse the colours.

TROUBLE SHOOTER

TESTING A COLOUR

If you want to make a major change to the painting, test the effect before you commit yourself. Lay a sheet of paper over the relevant area and apply the new colour to this.

10 ▲ Add linear marks Pastel is both a drawing and a painting medium. Use a sage green pastel to create lines that echo the marks in the stubble and lead the eye to the house on the horizon. These lines link the foreground to the background and create a sense of travel within the picture. Select a sap green pastel to lay in a solid block of green under the house. This provides an accent colour that draws the eye.

Express yourself
Shifting the viewpoint

This composition, also worked in gouache and pastel, shows an alternative viewpoint. The house has been moved to the left of the picture and is not such a prominent feature. The hills have been left out, so that the trees stand out more starkly against the pale clouds, linking land to sky.

11 ▼ **Add the trees** Mix azure blue, Winsor green and alizarin crimson gouache to create a dark green. Use the tip of the No.10 round brush to dot in the silhouetted tree shapes, painting the trunks with the tip of the brush.

12 ▲ **Lighten the foreground** Scumble a thin wash of titanium white gouache over the foreground – pastel picked up by the wash modifies the colour, introducing interesting random effects. While the paint is still wet, use a blade to scrape off areas of paint, revealing the underlying layers. This 'losing and finding' is part of the creative process. Stand back and review your handiwork – you might find it useful to leave it for a while so that you can come back and study it with a fresh eye.

EXPERT ADVICE
Frame the picture

It is easier to see how a picture is progressing if you contain it within a card frame. Try different crops with four strips of card or two L-shapes. Judge how the composition is working within the rectangle of the picture area and make adjustments if you wish.

13 ▶ **Develop the textures** Mix Winsor green, cobalt blue and alizarin crimson to create a dark brown and wash this over the foreground. Leave to dry. Now apply gestural marks on top with a burnt umber pastel. Use cadmium yellow, lemon yellow and yellow ochre pastels to develop the sunlit central areas.

15 ▼ **Add details to the trees** Use a dark green pastel to refine the shapes of the trees and add texture to them. The silhouettes should remain crisp, but they will look more convincing if there is a variation of tone.

14 ▲ **Add more texture** With L-shaped card croppers in place, add more texture and detail in the foreground. Use flicks and stipples of lemon yellow, yellow ochre and white pastels to suggest the texture of stubble and straw.

Master Strokes

Stanley Royle (1888–1961)
The Marshes at Sunset

Painted in oils on canvas, this richly coloured picture presents a broad vista with a wide, open sky. As in the painting in the project, trees and a house break the skyline, interrupting the horizontal aspect of the composition. The interlinked bands of colour that make up the foreground give a patterned, almost abstract quality to the flat landscape.

Brush marks in the thickly applied oil paint imply the form of the clouds. The sunlit areas are particularly heavily textured.

Lit by the setting sun, the yellow field makes a bright splash of colour among the gentler blue, green and brown hues of the marshy landscape.

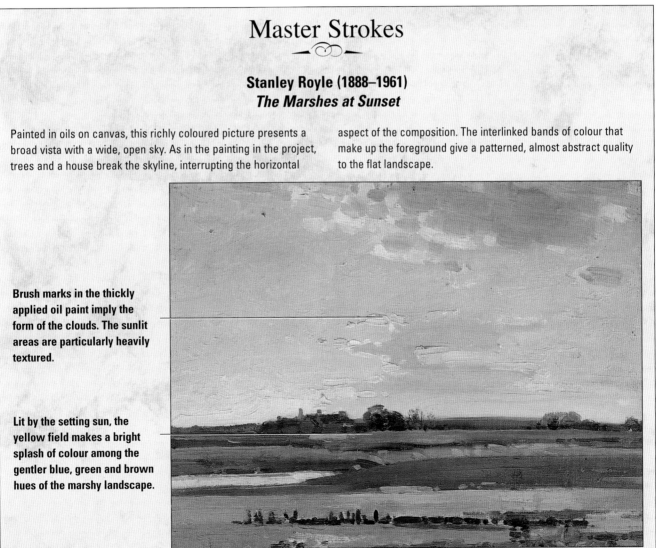

16 ▼ **Develop the sky further** It is important to achieve a sense of recession in the sky as well as on the ground. Make the sky at the top of the picture darker, with larger, more emphatic clouds forms, and leave the clouds near the horizon smaller and less defined. Scumble cobalt blue pastel over the upper sky, then add a little lilac grey.

17 ▲ **Blend the sky** Use a dark grey pastel to scumble shadow under the closest cloud formation. Then use your fingertips to soften and blend all the pastel marks across the sky.

18 ◄ **Develop the sky** Apply pale blue, lilac grey and mid grey pastel on the undersides of the clouds, using diagonal marks to give the sky a sense of movement. Blend the colour by brushing it lightly with your hand or with a piece of crumpled kitchen paper.

A FEW STEPS FURTHER

Once the painting was almost complete, the artist studied it for a while and decided that the central area needed more work. It is a good idea to leave an almost-finished painting for a while and come back to it fresh – it will often then be obvious what still needs to be done.

19 ◄ **Knock back the green field** The sap green field no longer looks quite right as a single band of colour. Begin modifying it to give it a more subtle look by applying an initial layer of cadmium yellow pastel.

20 ▶ Modify the strong yellow

Skim lemon yellow pastel over the field to lighten it. Then use a blade to scratch off some of the colour so that layers underneath are revealed.

21 ◀ Put in the birds

Add a layer of burnt umber pastel to the field and scratch back once more with the blade to create broken colour. Make a dark mix of Winsor green and alizarin crimson and use the tip of a No.4 round brush to dot in birds flying over the stubble. This final flourish provides a sense of scale and movement.

THE FINISHED PICTURE

A Luminous sky
Layers of semi-transparent gouache and scumbled and blended pastel were used to capture the shifting, ever-changing luminosity of the sky.

B Focal point
A tiny white house located at a key point on the horizon provides a solid anchor for the composition. The eye travels around the image but constantly returns to this point.

C Spiky stubble
Pastel flecked, stippled and dashed over the foreground captures the dry spikiness of the stubble. The layered approach suggests the complexity and depth of the surface.

Birman temple cat

Photographs are an invaluable reference source for painting an animal. Choose the best background and pose, then combine them for a great composition.

▼ The strong colours and shapes in the background set off the fluffy texture and pale tones of the cat's fur.

Family pets are challenging but very rewarding subjects to paint. They do, however, have a habit of getting up and strolling away just as you're about to start painting. So, unless you have an unusually obliging specimen, your best option is to use photos to help you.

A danger with painting from photos is that you can end up with a picture that looks two-dimensional. Purists often reject the practice and claim that they can tell when something has been painted from a photo because it lacks vitality. The secret is not to base your picture entirely on photographs, but to use them as a springboard for your work while also referring to your actual pet.

The Birman legend

An unusual breed of cat – the Birman temple cat – was chosen for this project.

The story goes that this breed originally had yellow eyes and white fur, and guarded the Temple of Lao-Tsun in Myanmar (formerly Burma). One day, the temple was attacked and the head priest killed. At the moment of the priest's death, his favourite cat placed its feet on him and its markings changed for ever. Its fur took on a golden cast, its eyes turned blue and its face, legs and tail became the colour of the earth. However, the cat's paws, having touched the priest, remained white as a symbol of purity.

The Birman temple cat used as a model here is true to this distinctive colouring. It has been painted from two different photos as well as from life. The photo of the cat sitting on the wooden floor shows the better pose, but the more interesting background in terms of colour is the one with the cat on the sofa, so the artist combined the two in her painting.

Blending with gouache

A small palette of gouache colours is used for this exciting project. Gouache works equally well for delicate areas such as the cat's fur and for the strong, bold background. Used wet-on-wet, the paint creates areas of colour that blend softly together.

FIRST STEPS

1 ▼ Make a pencil sketch Using the photograph showing the cat in a sitting pose as a guide, make a sketch with a 2B pencil. This species is characteristically fluffy, so the front body, back body and head form roughly circular shapes.

EXPERT ADVICE
Get the proportions right

Use your pencil to gauge the proportions of the cat. Align the tip with the top of the head and note where the bottom of the paws fall on the pencil. Use this measurement to check the breadth of the body. You'll find that, ignoring the tail, the two are roughly the same, so make sure your drawn cat is about as tall as it is broad.

2 ▲ Establish the darkest areas Make a mix of ivory black with just a touch of Van Dyke brown. Using a No. 4 round brush, start painting the darkest tones – the face (apart from the cheeks) and the bottom of the legs and tail.

3 ▲ Vary the tones Add a little zinc white to your brown mix and finish off the tail and front legs. Use this lighter tone for the cheeks, too, taking special care around the eyes.

4 ▼ **Work on the light tones** Change to a No. 10 round brush and make a thin, pale mix of zinc white with a hint of raw umber. Use this to paint the cat's body. For the darker tones, add a little more of the raw umber to the mix.

5 ▼ **Paint wet-on-wet** Referring to the photograph, build up tonal variations within the fur. Work wet-on-wet with various dilute mixes of white and raw umber, adding darker browns over lighter ones. The colours will bleed into each other, giving the fur a sense of softness so that the cat looks suitably fluffy.

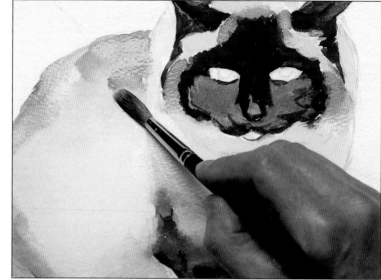

6 ▼ **Change the background** Allow about 15 minutes for the cat to dry. Now put your photo aside and look at the other one, where the cat is surrounded by colourful cushions. Use this as reference for the background. Still using the No. 10 brush, add slashes of strong cobalt blue both above and below the cat.

7 ▶ **Add some red** The blue changes the composition entirely, framing your subject and throwing it into relief. Add an equally strong red to the right of the blue, using scarlet lake with a touch of Van Dyke brown. Paint carefully around the fur so as to not disturb any of the creamy body colour.

8 ◀ **Paint the final cushion** On the left is a cushion patterned with browns, gold and blue. Use yellow ochre mixed with a little white for the gold areas and, while this is still wet, add a thick band of cobalt blue. Paint the darker areas wet-on-wet with various mixes of raw umber, white and black.

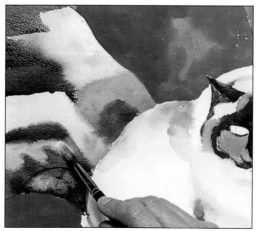

DEVELOPING THE PICTURE

The completed background forms a striking contrast to the shape and colouring of the cat. Now turn your attention back to the cat itself and start to develop its features and the texture of its fluffy, silky fur.

9 ◄ **Paint the eyes** Use the No. 4 brush for finer details such as the eyes. Birman cats have pale blue eyes, so mix up a dilute cobalt blue for these. Use pure black for the pupils to make them really stand out.

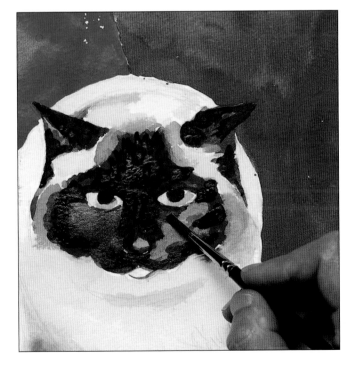

10 ▲ **Strengthen the face** Make a very dark mix of black and Van Dyke brown. Using the No. 4 brush, accentuate the darkness of the face, particularly around the eyes.

11 ▲ **Define the fur** With the No. 4 brush, paint a pale gold ruff around the cat's face with a mix of yellow ochre and white. To give the fur a more downy appearance, apply the pale mix from step 4 with the very tip of the brush to paint individual hairs along the right-hand side of the body.

12 ▶ **Add tonal variation to the blue** Continue defining individual hairs above the cat's head and along the contour of its back, varying the tones by using some of the mixes from step 5. Finally, add shadows to the blue cushion with a mix of cobalt blue and black to make it appear softer and more luxurious.

Express yourself
Change of scenery

The original background of wooden floorboards was used for this interpretation of the Birman temple cat. The brown tones harmonize well with the neutral colours of the cat's fur, but the more colourful background of the step-by-step project complements the character of the cat.

A FEW STEPS FURTHER

The picture is almost complete. As a finishing touch, add a few highlights to the cat's facial features to help liven it up and make it stand out more against the richly coloured background.

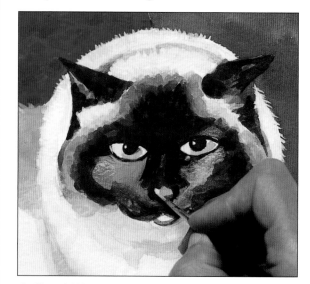

13 ▲ **Add highlights** Add a spot of white to each pupil to show reflected light. Make a pale grey mix from white plus touches of black and cobalt blue, and paint the highlights on the fur under the eyes. For the tip of the nose, add more white to the mix.

14 ▼ **Create shadows** As the composition is built up from a combination of two photos, you'll need to use your imagination to create cast shadows on the cushions. Paint some dark shadows around the cat's paws and lower body,

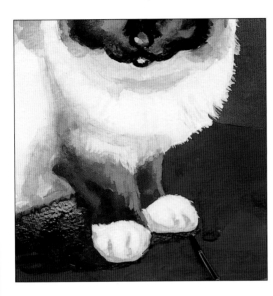

15 ▲ **Draw the whiskers** Finally, use a No. 1 round brush and the pale grey mix from step 13 to draw in the delicate, sensitive hairs of the whiskers.

THE FINISHED PICTURE

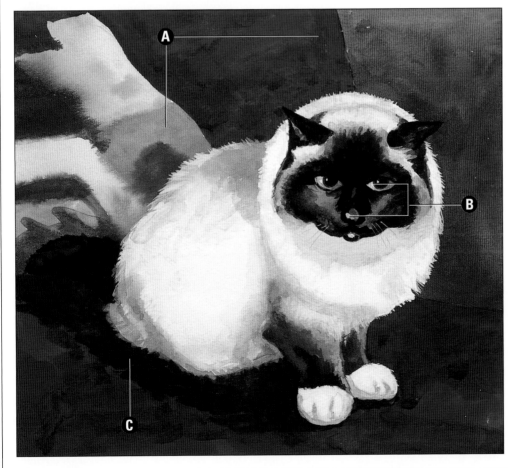

A Bold background
The bold swathes of colour in the background are left largely undefined, so as not to distract from the cat — the focus of the picture.

B White highlights
Dots of pure white on the eyes and pale grey on the tip of the nose suggest moistness and add an important touch of realism.

C Areas of shadow
The dark shadows around the cat's hindquarters prevent it from appearing to float above the surface of the cushion.

Birds in flight

Arctic terns give structure and scale to this energetic study of the churning seas off the remote Farne Islands in the North Sea.

You don't have to be a dedicated ornithologist to enjoy watching, drawing and painting birds. Apart from their variety and grace, they enliven a composition, leading the eye into or around a picture. They are especially useful in seascapes, where there are no sight lines and few other spatial clues. Birds wheeling over the sea inject a sense of scale into a marine study.

Emphatic shapes

There are other ways in which birds can contribute to a composition. In flight,

birds create a series of emphatic shapes. The fully extended wingspan provides a strong horizontal which becomes a dynamic diagonal when tilted, while the beating wings make a series of V-shapes. These forms can become an important element within a composition, especially when the birds are placed to the front of the picture space.

Broad characteristics

When you are painting birds as part of a landscape, you won't need the same degree of detail as an artist dedicated to

bird studies. It is more appropriate to capture their broad characteristics and sense of movement in a simple way. The birds depicted in this painting are Arctic terns, which are closely related to gulls, but are smaller and more slender in build with narrow, tapering wings, a forked tail and long bills. Most have whitish plumage with black caps.

The terns in the foreground were first sketched in silhouette, using light-

▼ This image captures the graceful flight of Arctic terns as they dip and wheel above the surging waters of the North Sea.

coloured pastels. Simple tonal shading built up the birds' forms, which were then refined by adding the characteristic markings and bright orange bills and legs. The bird in the background was more simply drawn.

Find the right approach

When you are working on your painting, avoid the temptation to give more attention to the birds than to their surroundings – if they become more resolved than the rest of the painting, then the picture will jar.

For example, if your style is loose and impressionistic, render the birds in the same way. If you tend to work in a tighter, more closely focused way, then apply that approach over the entire support, depicting the birds in more detail.

YOU WILL NEED

Piece of 300gsm (140lb) Not watercolour paper 56 x 76cm (22 x 30in)

Brushes: No.20 flat; 75mm (3in) hake; No.20 filbert; Nos.4 and 8 rounds

9 gouache paints: Prussian blue; Burnt sienna; Marine blue; Winsor green; Naples yellow; Ultramarine; Permanent white; Ivory black; Indian red

Piece of thin plastic for scraping

16 soft pastels: White; Sky blue; Putty grey; Light grey; Lemon yellow; Off-white; Light blue; Yellow ochre (light tint); Raw umber; Dark grey; Burnt orange; Pale yellow; Cobalt blue; Cerulean blue; Pale blue; Ultramarine (light tint)

Paper tissue and cotton cloth

Putty rubber

Strips of card to crop the image

PICK AND CHOOSE

Don't feel you have to take all your information from a single photograph or sketch. The photo above helped with the drawing of the far left tern, while the photo on the right was used for the sea and spray. Reference books can also be invaluable for establishing bird shapes.

FIRST STEPS

1 ▶ Block in the rocks
Mix Prussian blue and burnt sienna gouache to create a deep blue colour for the rocky promontory. Use a No.20 flat brush and big gestures to apply the colour. Work broadly and try to 'feel' your way around the looming bulk of the rocks.

2▲ **Block in the sea** Using the same brush and a wet wash of marine blue, apply broad strokes of colour to the sea. Do the same with a thin wash of Winsor green. This transparent blue-green provides an effective base for the heaving sea.

4▲ **Add dark tones** Mix ultramarine and burnt sienna to make a deep, almost black tone. Returning to the No.20 flat brush, apply this colour over the surface of the rocks, using broad, sweeping strokes.

EXPERT ADVICE
Scraping back

By scraping paint from the support, you can create light tones and interesting textures and reveal underlying paint layers. This technique is very effective with gouache, which has more body than watercolour. The best scraping tools are slightly springy – a piece of scrap plastic, an old credit card or a plastic painting knife.

3◀ **Apply base colour to the sky** Mix a wash of Naples yellow and block in the sky, using a 75mm (3in) hake to give broad coverage. The creamy yellow hue captures the sense of sunlight. Mix in a little marine blue on the right.

5▲ **Scratch through the paint** Use a piece of thin plastic to scrape through the dark paint at the base of the rock (see Expert Advice, above). This lightens the area and restores the transparency of the paint layer. Work into the rock forms, using your scraping tool to reveal the planes of the rock surface.

DEVELOPING THE PICTURE

As both soft pastel and gouache are opaque and slightly chalky, they complement each other very well. Alternating one with the other as the painting develops gives a range of effects.

6 ▼ **Apply soft pastel** Start to work into the rocks with pastel sticks which allow you to make more precise marks. Apply highlights in white, sky blue, putty grey and light grey. Use the tip of the stick to make narrow lines and the side of the stick for broader swathes of colour.

7 ▼ **Add highlights on the water** Change to a No.20 filbert brush and apply washes of permanent white gouache at the base of the rocks, where the sea swells against them and breaks up into spray. Brush on the paint with a series of energetic marks.

8 ▼ **Develop the rocks** Take white gouache over the sky. Refine the silhouette of the rocks and apply brushy marks over their surface. While the paint is still wet, soften the marks with your fingertips to create a thin veil of scumbled colour. Where the paint covers the pastel marks, it becomes tinted with the pigments.

9 ▼ **Apply pale pastel across the sky** With the stick held on its side, work lemon yellow pastel into the sky. Then use the tip of the pastel to draw back into the rocks, highlighting some of the edges.

10 ▶ **Block in the tern** Sketch the silhouette of the tern in the centre of the composition, using a combination of off-white, light grey and light blue pastels. Look only for the main shapes at this stage – leave the details for later.

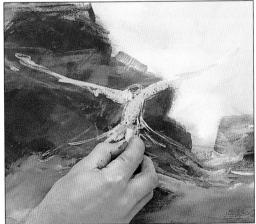

11 ▶ **Add details to the bird** Using a yellow ochre (light tint) pastel with a few touches of raw umber, add warm tones under the tern's body. Put in some dark grey shadow and white highlights. Use a No.4 round brush and ivory black gouache for the bird's characteristic black cap, the long curving beak and the legs.

12 ▼ **Work colour details** The Arctic tern has a distinctive orange bill and legs. Use a burnt orange pastel to apply colour to them.

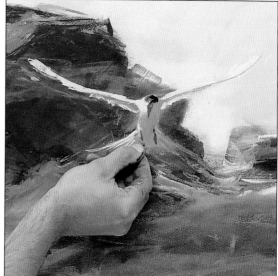

Master Strokes
_—∽—_

Winifred Nicholson (1893–1981)
Sandpipers, Alnmouth

In this simple, semi-abstract composition, the flock of birds together with the curved shapes of the seascape form a simple, graphic image. Note how the birds echo the curve of the inlet. The colours in the painting are restricted to shades of blue and honey brown, with a few emphatic strokes of dark grey and white for contrast. This gives an overall effect that is light, airy and harmonious.

Thickly applied oil paint leaves brush marks visible on the sea, giving an impression of its rippling surface.

A glaze of light brown applied over the water in the shallow inlet suggests reflections of the sandy banks.

Scattered over wet paint in the foreground, a sprinkling of sand creates a granular texture on the beach.

13 ▼ **Develop the sea** Add pale yellow pastel highlights on the tern's bill and legs. Apply dark grey pastel to the tern's head and to the rock behind the bird. Develop the sea, using cobalt blue and cerulean blue pastels, then soften the marks with your fingers or a tissue to create a film of colour.

14 ▼ **Add dark tones in the sea** Mix Prussian blue gouache with a touch of Indian red to make a deep blue tone. Using the No.20 filbert brush fairly dry, make a succession of vigorous, sweeping marks that follow the undulations of the waves around the rocks.

15 ▼ **Indicate spray** Scumble cobalt blue pastel over the sea and rocks, using the side of the stick. Make a pad from a piece of cotton cloth and work this over the surface of the pastel, spreading it thinly to produce a veil of pigment that suggests spray.

16 ▲ **Add a second tern** Outline the second tern with white pastel. Block in the shadows under the body and wings with light grey, dark grey, yellow ochre and raw umber pastel. Work broadly, looking for light and dark areas and warm and cool tones rather than details such as the feathers.

17 ◄ **Build up layers on the sea** Finish the second tern by indicating the black cap and burnt orange bill and legs. Add touches of pale blue to enliven the shadows on the bird. The sea in the foreground needs more texture and detail to pull it forward in the picture plane. Using the No.20 filbert and a wash of permanent white gouache, start to apply the colour with sweeping gestural marks that follow the shapes of the waves. Note that the white paint picks up the cobalt blue pigment from step 15 and tints the white to a very pale blue in places.

18 ▲ **Add more blue** Skim an ultramarine (light tint) pastel over the surface of the sea on the left. Blend and soften the pigment with your fingertips to add a further glaze of colour to the sea.

Express yourself
Solo flight

If you are interested in birds, devote some time to making studies of different species in their natural habitat. Here, a gannet is depicted in mid-flight against an impressionistic sky. Seen in profile, the shape of the head and the characteristic long, pointed beak are clearly discernible, while the upstretched wings, poised for a down beat, give a sense of imminent movement. As in the main step-by-step painting, a combination of gouache and pastel provides soft passages of layered colour.

19 ▲ **Paint a third bird** Use off-white, white and light grey pastels to draw a third tern in the distance. With a No.4 brush, paint the bill and legs with burnt sienna gouache and the cap and wingtips in pale grey mixed from permanent white and ivory black. By showing birds at different sizes, you create a sense of recession in the painting.

20 ▲ **Create more texture** Load a No.8 round brush with a thinned wash of permanent white paint and describe a few foam-tipped waves in the centre ground with linear marks. Draw more swirling lines with the white pastel. Using the tip of the brush, flick white paint across the sea and rocks to suggest spray.

A FEW STEPS FURTHER

Before continuing, tape strips of card over the painting to crop it to a wide format known as a 'marine' format (see The Finished Picture, below). This emphasises the birds in the composition, but makes the left-hand rock look too dominant. Correct this by adjusting the rock's silhouette to fall below the bird.

21 ▼ **Overpaint the rock** Apply light grey pastel over the rock behind the left-hand tern, working carefully around the bird. Work freely over the rock to suggest waves breaking over it.

22 ▲ **Soften the pastel** Use a putty rubber to soften and smear the light grey pastel – this enhances the effect of water streaming off the rocky surfaces.

THE FINISHED PICTURE

A Layered colour
The shifting mass of the sea was suggested with layers of scumbled and dry-brushed gouache, and with pastel applied as blended veils of thin colour.

B Selective editing
The left-hand tern creates a dark shape against the light background of the sky. This is in contrast to the other tern, which appears light against dark.

C Warm sky
An underwash of Naples yellow worked across the sky glows through subsequent layers, suggesting sunlight glimpsed through scudding clouds.

D Bright lights
Touches of opaque white pastel and gouache above the rocks capture the misty effect created by spray and foam thrown up by the crashing waves.

Brilliant anemones

Use alizarin crimson and brilliant violet gouache paints to bring out the vivid colours of these anemones.

▼ **The unusual textural effects in this floral still life are achieved with a wax-resist technique and by overdrawing with water-soluble painting crayons.** around the whole of the display. Note also how the glass vase with its sharp verticals pleasingly offsets the natural shapes of the flowers.

Anemones, with their beautiful and vivid colours, look wonderful arranged casually in a vase and simply cry out to be painted. This still life, with its mixed-media approach, is a particularly unusual interpretation of these well-loved flowers.

Unusual approach

The artist began this gouache study in the conventional way, laying down colours from lights to darks. However, she didn't stop there – instead, she chose to give the picture more character with different methods and materials.

The mottled texture seen on the vase and background was created by rubbing a household candle over these areas to act as a resist. The picture was given a lift by adding bold lines of water-soluble crayon in white and pale blue. The result is a dense, richly textured work.

As she painted, the artist decided to alter the composition she had initially set up (left). The red flowers were still painted at the centre of the display – with the bold colour pulling the eye into the composition – but the other flowers were more widely spaced, so they create a roughly elliptical shape around the red ones. This encourages the eye to travel

YOU WILL NEED

Piece of rough 300gsm (140lb) watercolour paper 46 x 38cm (18 x 15in)

Green water-soluble coloured pencil

9 gouache paints: lemon yellow; cerulean blue; ultramarine; cadmium red; cadmium red pale hue; brilliant violet; alizarin crimson; indigo; Winsor green

Brushes: No. 16 wash brush; No. 8 round; No. 2 rigger

Mixing palette or dish

White household candle

2 water-soluble painting crayons: white; pale blue

FIRST STEPS

1 ▼ Rough in the flowers Water-soluble pencils are good drawing tools as they wash out as soon as you paint over them. Use a green one to plot the position of the vase, the flowers and the tablecloth.

2 ▼ Wash in the background Load a No. 16 wash brush with clean water and 'paint' over the lightest areas of the composition – around the vase and the tops of the flowers. Then go over these wetted areas with lemon yellow gouache. Painting in this way, rather than simply diluting the yellow in the palette, creates a lovely pale hue.

3 ▶ Pick out some leaves With the same brush, put in some green accents with mixes of lemon yellow and cerulean blue to start suggesting particular stems and leaves. Let the leaves bleed into the yellow for a softer, more naturalistic effect.

4 ▶ Outline the flower-heads Select a No. 8 round brush for the more delicate details and, as before, work first with just water, then paint over the moistened areas with your colour. Use cerulean blue to outline the vase and form the shapes of the flowers, including their dark centres.

5 ▲ Switch to a cooler blue Change back to the No. 16 wash brush to put in some of the shadows with ultramarine. Apply directional brush strokes, painting a shadow to the left of the vase and adding a few darker touches to the tablecloth.

6 ▲ Start with the reds Using the No. 8 round brush, paint the red flowers with cadmium red and cadmium red pale hue. Vary the colour strengths to give the petals form.

DEVELOPING THE PICTURE

Continue adding vivid mixes of gouache to the anemones to bring out the intense colours of their petals. Define their outlines and add details such as the flower centres with a No. 2 rigger brush.

8 ◄ **Mix mauve tones** The blue flowers have touches of mauve in them. To create these tones, mix brilliant violet with ultramarine, and apply in varying strengths to the petals with the No. 8 round. Paint the flower to the right of the arrangement first.

7 ▲ **Paint a pinkish-purple flower** Use brilliant violet and the wash brush for the dark tones on the central flower, working inwards from a dark outline. Wash in a little alizarin crimson for the pinker touches on the top petals.

EXPERT ADVICE
Soften the colours

Create softer tones on the anemones by first painting the petals in your chosen colour, then brushing over them with water. Quickly blot the loosened pigment with paper tissue or kitchen paper to lift some of the colour away.

9 ▼ **Define the edges of the petals** Paint the blue flower to the right of the pinkish-purple one, using the mix from step 8. Now, with the tip of the No. 2 rigger brush, paint tiny dots of indigo paint around the centre of the blue flower. With the same brush and indigo, define the edges of the pinkish-purple flower petals.

10 ▼ **Continue painting the flowers** Move from one flower head to the next, painting and defining the petals as before. To strengthen the white flowers, add touches of the mauve mix from step 8 (applying water first). Outline the petals of the lower white flower in cerulean blue.

11 ▶ **Work on the vase** There is a suggestion of water in the vase, but it needs to be strengthened. With the No. 16 wash brush, paint a slash of cerulean blue inside the right-hand corner to suggest a shadow. Add a few lines of Winsor green for the stems, then accentuate the base of the vase with a strong line of cerulean blue.

12 ▼ **Create a sense of space** Add a shadow at the base of the vase with a broad slash of cerulean. Darken the fabric folds with a cerulean/ultramarine mix. Strengthen the background with vertical strokes of Winsor green and ultramarine.

Express yourself
A square format

Experiment with different formats and viewpoints. Here the flowers take centre stage, radiating upwards and outwards. The view is more stylized than realistic – the anemones are framed by a square within a square, rather than sitting firmly and palpably on a table. The smaller square could be read as a window or simply as an artistic device.

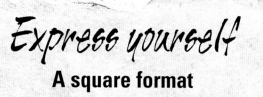

13 ▼ **Strengthen the background** To add warmth and energy to the painting, strengthen the background with a wash of lemon yellow. Work carefully around the flower-heads.

14 ▼ **Paint over wax** Rub a white household candle over the vase and lower right-hand corner to form a resist. Mix indigo with a touch of ultramarine and apply this thickly over the waxed surface. Notice the grainy effect that results from the wax repelling the paint.

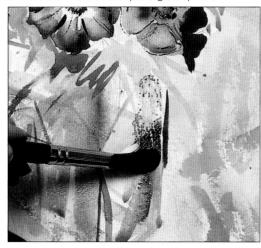

WAX-RESIST EFFECTS

You can achieve richly textured effects by painting gouache over a resist of candle wax. Experiment with washes of different strengths.

▲ **An indigo/ultramarine mix applied over white candle wax (see step 14).**

▲ **Candle wax over a dried yellow wash, overlaid with an indigo/ultramarine wash (see step 15).**

15 ▼ **Apply a second layer of wax** Continue applying wax to sections of the still life. Work your way all around the arrangement from the top left-hand corner to the right of the vase and below it. Now paint a dark indigo/ultramarine glaze over the wax.

16 ◄ **Strengthen the background** The dark tones provide depth and solidity. Continue building up shadows on the right and around the edges with a stronger indigo/ultramarine wash.

A FEW STEPS FURTHER

Having built up the area to the right of the flowers, it now appears somewhat dark and lacking in texture. The surface of the table could be improved, too, by putting in some creases and points of visual interest.

17 ◄ **Draw a white line** Using a white water-soluble painting crayon, draw a strong vertical line behind the top right-hand flowers to highlight the background.

18 ◀ **Add more highlights** Still using the white painting crayon, add a few short strokes along the edge of the vase. Then rub the crayon over the table top to the left of the vase and wash over it with clean water to make the area appear lighter.

19 ▲ **Use a blue crayon** Add more dramatic lines in white, both on and around the vase, then switch to a pale blue painting crayon. Put a strong blue accent on the edge of the vase, and softer ones in the shadows.

THE FINISHED PICTURE

A Focal point
The tall white anemone, reaching up above the others and silhouetted by the dark background, forms a focal point in the composition.

B Light and dark
Exaggerating the dark shadows on the right gives the picture punch and helps to make the petals stand forward.

C Illusion of water
Two lines of crayon – one blue, one white – suggest the surface of the water seen through glass.

Introducing mixed media

Some of the most exciting and unexpected effects in painting can be created by combining media. Begin here by exploring watercolour paints and pencils.

The most important (and most familiar) quality of watercolour paint is the clear, translucent colour it produces. Most early watercolour painters were unwilling to combine it with any other media, in case this quality should be lost, but many contemporary artists have experimented with watercolour and revealed its versatility. With watercolour pencils and crayons, used with paint from tubes, pans or concentrate, you can create an enormous variety of unique effects.

Wet and dry

Apply watercolour paints in thin layers or washes, so that they dry without affecting the texture of the paper (making the fibres fluff up, for example). When the colour is dry, you will be able to work on the painted surface with many other materials, including crayons and drawing pencils.

▲ Watercolour paints were combined with soluble pencils and crayons to create the many textures in this rural landscape. Several different techniques were used; the distant trees, for example, were loosely worked in crayon and partly softened with water, and the foreground tree is a mixture of wash and lightly worked crayon.

By using water-soluble pencils and crayons (instead of the more usual non-soluble ones), you have yet another advantage: when you have finished the picture – or any one area of the picture – you can then use water or watercolour paint to dissolve and blend the soluble lines into the painted colour.

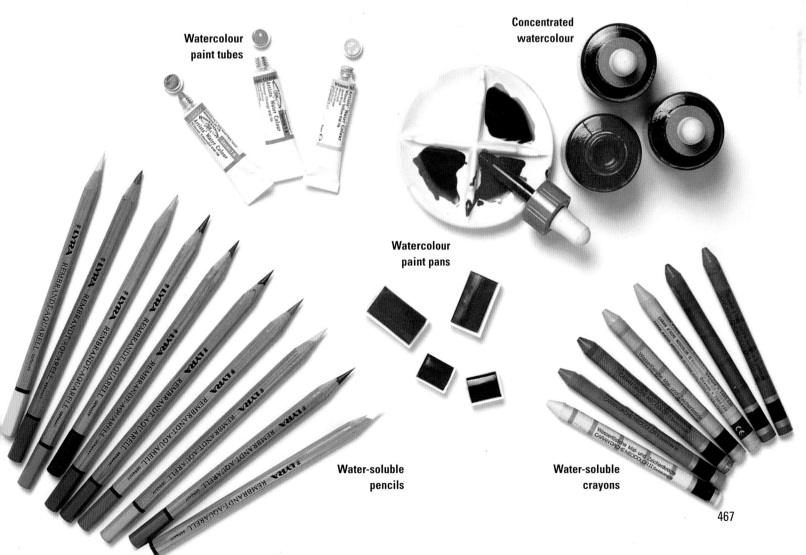

Watercolour paint tubes

Concentrated watercolour

Watercolour paint pans

Water-soluble pencils

Water-soluble crayons

Combining colour and water

◄ Blending with water Make rough pencil marks in two colours, then wash them with water, causing them to run together and form a third colour.

► Drawing on damp paint Draw water-soluble pencil on to a wash of damp watercolour paint to produce fine, slightly

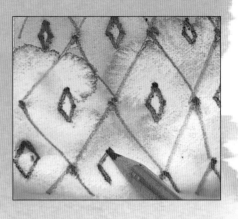

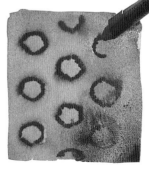

▲ **Crayon washing** Wash graded crayon marks with water, creating an effect similar to a graded watercolour wash.

▲ **Washed patches** Dissolve roughly worked pencil marks with water to form contrasting textured patches.

▲ **Self-colour washing** Overpaint a rough crayon pattern with a similar colour, creating a pattern of softly blended shapes.

Lines and washes

A combination of watercolour paint and water-soluble drawing materials allows you to include fine lines, rugged texture, flat wash and blended colour all in the same painting. Try using water-soluble pencils or crayons to draw directly into areas of wet paint. The resulting lines will be blurred and soft, merging gently into the background colour.

In the landscape painting illustrated on the previous page, much of the drawing was done in this way, by drawing directly on to wet watercolour washes. Further blending and softening was achieved later using clean water and a soft brush.

When dampened, water-soluble pencils and crayons are brighter and bolder than non-soluble products. Many artists appreciate and exploit this quality. It does mean that the results

from soluble drawing materials can be more unpredictable than those you expect from the non-soluble varieties, but this is part of the excitement of experimenting. Also, if the strokes are very heavy, no amount of water will be able to dissolve the lines completely, so the marks will show through the wet colour.

Experiment and discover

Always choose a sturdy, good-quality watercolour paper for mixed media work. The support should be heavy enough to withstand wet watercolour washes without buckling. It should also be tough enough to allow the pencil colours to be blended with a brush – on coarse, poor quality papers, the fibres may be raised by the water.

Mixed media work allows you great scope to experiment and create exciting and unusual effects. As you try out

different materials – either singly or in combination – you will become more familiar with their special qualities and the way they behave when combined with other materials.

The water-based materials illustrated here are just the beginning. As you gain more experience, you will be able to add other materials and techniques to your repertoire; always bear in mind that individual taste and originality are all-important when using mixed media.

► Here, water-soluble crayon was applied to wet colour, forming broad, soft lines that run into the background.

Pen and wash

You don't need expensive materials to create effective pictures. Even the humble fibre-tipped pen will produce lively line drawings, which you can enhance with a coloured wash.

The next time you write out a shopping list, or do a crossword puzzle with a black fibre-tipped pen, take a second look at it. Even an inexpensive, throw-away pen such as this, readily available from stationers and art shops, can be a perfect medium for creating art. These pens are not only extremely portable, they can produce an amazing variety of strokes.

Take this group of vegetables (above), for example. Depending on whether you press the nib hard or quite lightly, you can portray the leafy veins of the cabbage, the solidity of the onion, or the smooth skin of the pepper. Other good subjects to practise drawing with a fibre-tipped pen are small objects like shells, eggs, feathers, pebbles or stones.

Creating texture and form

Dots, dashes and lines of different lengths and intensities can have a very potent effect. The closer together the marks, the darker the area will appear. Very dark areas can be defined by first drawing one set of lines and then adding another set in a different direction across the top of them. This is known as cross-hatching.

A sense of roundness is achieved by making

▲ **Thin washes of watercolour allow the light tone of the paper to show through, while the water soluble line ink seeps into the colour wash, creating a soft effect.**

objects darker in the dips of their curves and lighter as they curve out, because this is where they catch the most light.

Adding a wash

Once a pen drawing is complete, a coloured wash can be applied on top of it. The washes used in this project are made from block watercolour paints diluted with water.

These washes have to be kept thin, so as not to hide the contours of the drawing and the 'light' that reflects from the white paper beneath. The artist used a water soluble pen for the line drawing, to encourage the pen lines to dissolve slightly and to seep into the washes, creating an interesting effect.

The first part of this exercise shows you how to draw the vegetables in considerable detail, using the fibre-tipped pen. Then, as washes work best on simple drawings, 'A Few Steps Further' asks you to start afresh and draw the vegetables once more – this time without using so many intricate lines.

1 ▲ **Make a rough outline sketch** Pressing lightly with the 2B pencil, draw the main vegetable shapes. Make them quite large and bold. No detail is necessary yet, just draw a circle for the main part of the red cabbage and an oval for the lemon. It is more important to try and sketch the correct positions and relationships of the vegetable shapes. Don't worry if you have to go over the outlines more than once to achieve the correct size.

EXPERT ADVICE
Using different papers

Pen and wash works well with various types of paper. Those with smooth, shiny surfaces allow the pen to move unhindered over the page, making line drawing easier. Heavier, grainy papers look especially good with washes brushed over; however, a surface that is too rough can mean that pen marks fall into the crevices. This can make drafting an image unnecessarily complicated for anyone other than an expert. The softer nature of highly grained paper also means that the pen might sometimes catch on it and clog up.

2 ► **Begin to add detail in pen**
Having completed your rough pencil sketch, use the fibre-tipped pen to trace over the delicate frayed edges of the green cabbage leaves. Follow the outlines of the leaves. The veins in these leaves are thick, so press hard with the pen and go over them more than once if

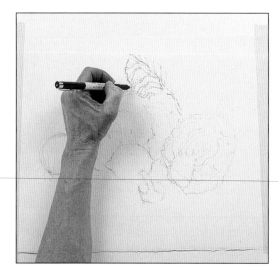

3 ► **Create the first shadows** Draw a series of short pen lines close together at the bottom of each of the cabbage leaves, behind the main ball of the red cabbage and the lemon. This will create the shadows that silhouette the shapes of the vegetables in front.

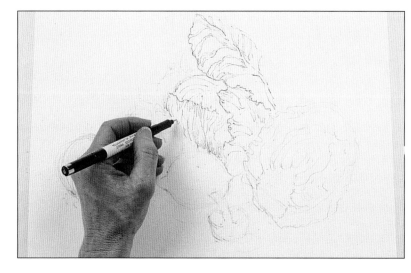

DEVELOPING THE PICTURE

Depending on how hard you press with your pen, objects can look close to, or further away. Vibrantly-coloured vegetables nearer the front of the still life need to have stronger lines.

4 ▶ **Draw in the contours of the red cabbage** The lines of the red cabbage are dramatic and very thick in places. They have an irregular, twisting pattern, so it doesn't matter if you make an error. Make the outside, purple part of the cabbage darker by drawing the pen lines close together.

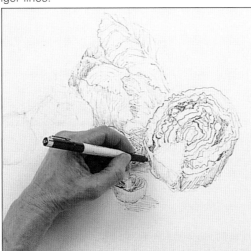

5 ▲ **Work on the outline and surface of the lemon** Press quite hard with the pen to draw a heavy outline around the lemon. The lemon has a dotted surface. Draw your dots close together near the bottom of the lemon, but put fewer dots at the top, where the light hits it.

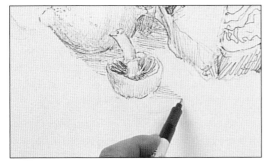

6 ▲ **Shape and shade the mushroom** Draw the outline of the mushroom. Make some strong lines under the mushroom umbrella, starting from the central stem outwards. The dark shadows under the mushroom are created by drawing lines close together.

7 ▲ **Build up the pepper** To define the pepper, go over its outline and stem more than once. Outline the highlighted areas around the top. Draw small, tightly-packed lines in the dips of the pepper curves, but allow these to thin out as you approach the more bulbous parts that catch the light. Draw more small, tightly-packed lines in the shady area behind the lemon to create the shade.

Master Strokes

Floris van Schooten (1605–55)
Still Life with Brass Pot

The Dutch masters of the 17th century were famed for their still life studies, which were meticulous in every detail. The Dutch, with their Calvinist beliefs, were keen moralists, and their still life paintings often show the simple things in life – the message being that these are more important than sensual pleasures.

The fruit in the foreground of this painting by Floris van Schooten glows with vitality, while the cabbage and artichoke behind them are painted in heavier colours, to give an impression of solidity. The neutral earth-coloured wall is a perfect backdrop to this skilfully arranged composition.

The earthy tones of the backdrop to this composition have the effect of thrusting forward the timeless objects chosen as the centrepiece.

The exquisite use of tone, colour and shade on the polished fruit and gleaming brass pot bring an unusual degree of reality to the painting.

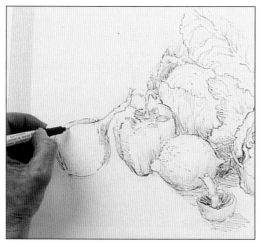

8 ▲ **Add detail to the onion** Follow the curved lines of the skin segments around the onion. Thicken up the lines at each end, not forgetting the root and stem. Now continue to darken and reinforce the lines and shapes of the vegetables where you think it necessary.

9 ▲ **Complete the pen drawing** The finished drawing should clearly show the differences in the subjects' size, shape, solidity and shadow. Keep practising your pen strokes until creating depth becomes easier.

A FEW STEPS FURTHER

Once you are satisfied with your pen drawing, put it aside and start with a clean sheet of paper. Draw the vegetables again, but without such detailed lines and shade. Then the colour washes can be applied. These can be very loose – the main thing is to enjoy moving the colours over the surface of the page. Washes don't need to be terribly accurate – if a colour runs from one vegetable to the next, so much the better. This kind of 'accident' often looks terrific. Use a saucer or palette to mix the combination and consistency of colours before applying them.

EXPERT ADVICE
Watercolour blocks

Watercolour comes in two varieties – blocks and tubes – and blocks have many plus points. First they can be bought separately and slotted into a suitably sized palette, like this one for square blocks. The beauty of this is that, when one block is used up, it can be replaced by another of the same or a different colour. Such palettes are ideal for a technique like pen and wash, where you are required to work fairly quickly, with all the paints to hand.

10 ▲ **Begin adding the wash** Draw the rough outlines of the vegetables. Load your brush with monestial green then dip just the end into some clean water. Trace it over the green cabbage. The paint does not have to be all one consistency – it will actually work better with thick and thin patches. Mix more monestial green with cobalt violet. Use this darker blue-green to define the cabbage with a few dark lines.

11 ▶ Colour the lemon and mushroom Clean the brush. Mix together cadmium yellow and monestial green. This will make a lime green colour. Then dip the brush in water and wash it over the top part of the lemon. Without cleaning the brush, dip the end of it into the cadmium red. Use this deeper yellow tone to colour the bottom part of the lemon. Add more water to the colour so that it looks very light and wash it over the mushroom.

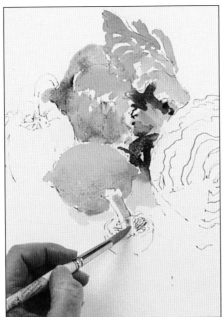

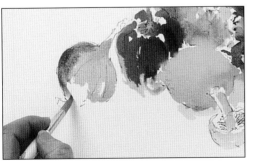

13 ▲ Mix a wash for the onion Clean the brush. Mix together cadmium red and cadmium yellow, then add enough water to make a fine orange wash to cover the onion. Load the brush with burnt sienna and put a line of this along the right edge of the onion, blending it into the rest of the colour.

Express yourself
Monochrome effect

Pen and wash are again used in this alternative version of a vegetable still life, but the overall effect is completely different. The line work is done in sepia coloured ink, which gives a softer effect than the black fibre-tipped pen used for the main exercise. The ink was applied with a water soluble cartridge art pen, which runs in water.

To create the wash effect, a brush was simply dipped in pure water (no added colour) and run over the top of the line work. The water splits the sepia into pink and green and spreads, creating contrast.

12 ◀ Add a red wash to the pepper Clean the brush with water, then load it with lots of cadmium red and just a dab of water. Wash it over the pepper, leaving white gaps at the top for the highlights. Then, without cleaning it, dip the tip of your brush into the monestial green. Apply this darker red tone to the most bulbous areas of the pepper.

USING AN INK RUBBER

TROUBLE SHOOTER

Mistakes made with pen and wash are difficult to hide. The paint is translucent, so you cannot cover up errors by putting new layers of paint on top. Some mistakes, however, can be remedied with a grainy-textured ink rubber, so long as it is used correctly. It is important to wait until the paint is dry first. Then just rub over the problem area as lightly and evenly as possible. A heavy hand will take away the surface of the paper along with the ink and paint and create an area that does not blend in.

14 ▶ **Paint the contours of the red cabbage** Clean the brush and dab dry. Mix cadmium yellow with water to paint in the lighter areas of the red cabbage. Clean the brush, then load it with a mixture of cobalt violet and cadmium red with just a little water. Use this vivid colour to follow the general line pattern of the red cabbage.

15 ▲ **Fill in the background shadow** Clean the brush and mix cobalt blue with cobalt violet for the shadowed area in the background. Make this deep violet tone strongest directly behind the vegetables, then fade it out as you move away from the group by continually adding more water.

THE FINISHED PICTURE

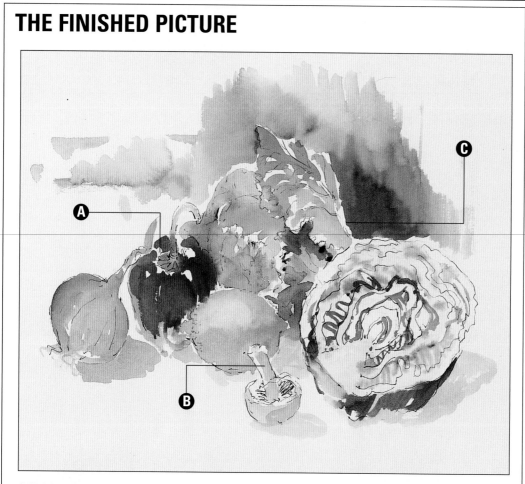

A Bright colours
Less water is added to the more densely coloured objects, like the red pepper, to make the colour stronger and brighter.

B Line and wash contrast
The sharpness of the lines complements the flowing, loose applications of paint that overlap the edges.

C Unpainted areas
White unpainted areas are left, allowing the paper to show through. This gives a neutral contrast to the paint.

Hand-tinting photographs

Give a black-and-white photograph a suggestion of delicate colour by tinting it with watercolour inks.

Hand-tinting can completely alter the look of a black-and-white photo. You need to choose an image with a high proportion of pale tones as tints do not show up against dark areas. And matt, rather than glossy, prints generally accept the tints best.

As for subject matter, virtually anything goes. You might want to use pale, delicate tints on more ornate subjects – such as flowers or contemplative portraits – while bolder, brasher colours might be more suitable for happy family snapshots. Try experimenting with different colour mixes by ordering reprints of your photo and tinting them in different ways.

Tinting techniques

When applying the tints, make sure you rinse your brush in water and dry it with cotton wool each time you change to a new colour. Remember also to change your water regularly to prevent tainting the subtle tints.

To check you've got the right mix of water and ink, test out your colours on a scrap of paper before starting on the actual print. You can use a piece of cotton wool to absorb excess ink. If you make a serious mistake, soaking the photo should remove the colour.

◀ **The delicate tints on these flowers create a beautiful, muted image.**

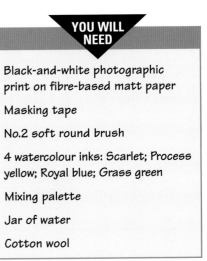

YOU WILL NEED

Black-and-white photographic print on fibre-based matt paper

Masking tape

No.2 soft round brush

4 watercolour inks: Scarlet; Process yellow; Royal blue; Grass green

Mixing palette

Jar of water

Cotton wool

1 ▼ **Fixing down the photograph** Attach the print securely to your work surface, using masking tape. When the diluted ink is applied, the paper is likely to wrinkle, so taping it down will keep the print as flat as possible.

2 ▲ **Colour the first flower** Dilute some scarlet ink in your palette to a very light pink – a single drop of ink is all you need to create the right shade. Using a No.2 brush, apply a first layer of scarlet to the flower on the left, filling in the colour within the outlines of the petals. Be careful not to make the brush too wet.

3 ▼ **Tint the water in the vase** Clean your brush, then apply diluted process yellow ink to the flower on the right. Leave the middle flower for the moment to prevent colours running between the two flowers. Clean your brush once more, then add a very faint hint of diluted royal blue to indicate the water in the vase.

EXPERT ADVICE
Diluting coloured inks

To create a diluted mix of a colour, first place a single drop of ink on your palette. Then soak a piece of cotton wool in water and gently and slowly squeeze it over the ink. This gives you greater control over the precise amount of water you use to dilute the ink, and enables you to judge more easily the exact shade of ink you require.

4 ▶ **Add a second wash** Once the ink has dried, paint on a second layer of each colour. Rinse and dry your brush, then add a wash of royal blue ink to the flower in the centre of the picture. Be careful not to let this colour overlap the ink on the flowers on each side.

5 ◄ Colour in the flower stems
Dilute a drop of grass green ink and apply it carefully to the flower stems. When this has dried, add a third layer of royal blue to the water in the vase to build up the depth of colour.

6 ▲ Deepen the shade of water Add a drop of process yellow to the diluted royal blue ink already on your palette. Mix the colours with your brush to create a greenish blue shade. Use this to deepen the shade of the water in the vase.

THE FINISHED PICTURE

7 ▲ Fill in the details Make up a very diluted shade of blue and fill in the centres of the flowers on the left and right. Then mix and apply an equally diluted shade of process yellow for the centre of the middle flower.

A Subtle colours
The watercolour ink was thoroughly diluted to produce soft, pastel colours for the flower petals and stalks.

B Crisp edges
To prevent two shades of ink running together, each colour was allowed to dry thoroughly before a new one was applied.

C Tinting in stages
Deeper tones, such as the dark blue of the water, were built up by painting on more than one layer of ink.

Underwater swimmer

Full of life and movement, this unusual picture of a swimmer gliding through the water is a combination of watercolour and collage.

▼ Paint and torn paper complement each other in this graphic representation of a streamlined figure in the water.

Swimming pools are full of colour and pattern. Ripples play across the water and light catches the splashes, producing a sparkling effect. This makes for an interesting painting subject.

This composition focuses on a single swimmer gliding just below the surface of the water. The movement of the water distorts the appearance of the tiled pool floor and the swimmer's body, giving rise to unexpected, fluid shapes. The light hitting and reflecting off both the water and the figure creates a distinctive patterned effect that lends itself to being reproduced in blocks of colour.

Paint and paper

Watercolour and collage have been combined in this step-by-step to create an interesting textured painting. The paint is applied in stages wet-on-dry, each layer building up the strength of colour.

Once you have mixed a wash, add a little more of one or other of the colours as you paint to avoid a uniform look. In addition, you could add a little gum arabic to the mixes to intensify the colour, but this is up to you.

Apply the collage once the painting is complete, using painted watercolour papers. When tearing shapes, try to capture the general movement of the water and the patterns on the swimmer. Due to the weave of the paper, tearing in one direction will produce a white edge, whereas if you tear the other way you'll get a coloured edge. Use this to your advantage by letting the white edges represent ripples catching the light.

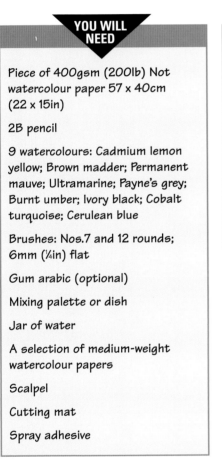

YOU WILL NEED

Piece of 400gsm (200lb) Not watercolour paper 57 x 40cm (22 x 15in)

2B pencil

9 watercolours: Cadmium lemon yellow; Brown madder; Permanent mauve; Ultramarine; Payne's grey; Burnt umber; Ivory black; Cobalt turquoise; Cerulean blue

Brushes: Nos.7 and 12 rounds; 6mm (¼in) flat

Gum arabic (optional)

Mixing palette or dish

Jar of water

A selection of medium-weight watercolour papers

Scalpel

Cutting mat

Spray adhesive

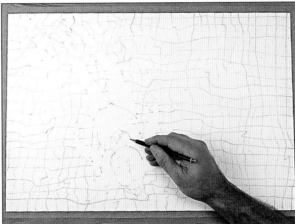

FIRST STEPS

1 ▲ **Draw the main elements** Using a 2B pencil, outline the figure of the swimmer and draw the tiles on the base of the swimming pool. Notice how the rippling water distorts the tiles into a pattern of undulating lines.

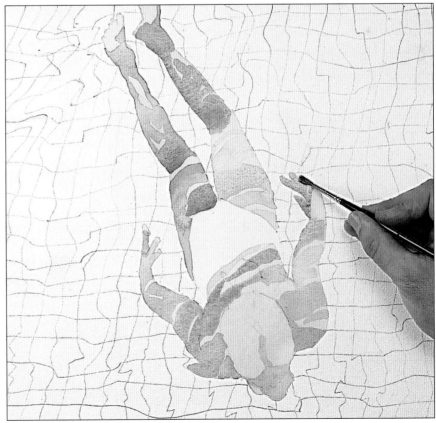

2 ▲ **Begin painting** Mix cadmium lemon yellow and brown madder watercolour. Using a No.7 round brush, wash this over the figure. Darken the mix with brown madder and permanent mauve and paint mid tones on the body, leaving bands of pale tone showing through.

3 ▶ Add dark tones
Add ultramarine to the brown mix to make a purplish-brown for the hair; dilute for the pattern of dark tones on the figure. Extend the fingers to give an impression of movement. Block in the swimsuit with the cadmium lemon; add brown madder for the shadow. Mix Payne's grey and burnt umber to make a dark tone for the hair and the right eye.

4 ▼ Block in the water Mix Payne's grey and ivory black. Changing to a 6mm (¼in) flat brush, paint stripes on the swimsuit. Make a dilute wash of cobalt turquoise and cerulean blue. Wash over the pool with a No.12 round.

Express yourself
A change of format

Combining paint with collage is fun, so why not try another composition in the same vein? Here, the swimmer glides down the paper, creating a vertical line that leads to a circle of ripples. Her shadow on the tiles is a distorted version of her body shape and gives depth to the water. Texture is built up with collage shapes, as in the step-by-step, but the watercolour is more subdued.

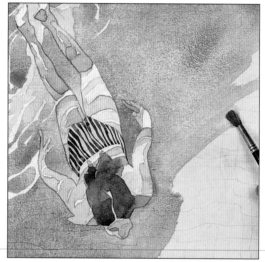

5 ◀ Paint the water pattern Make a stronger mix of the two blues and paint the pattern made by the moving water on the left, leaving some of the undercolour showing. On the right, completely cover the undercolour.

DEVELOPING THE PICTURE
You have now laid the foundation for the collage. Before you begin, paint papers with colours that correspond to those of the swimmer and water: a dark and a pale blue, a dark and a pale flesh tone, and a dark hair colour.

6 ▶ Arrange pale blue shapes Tear a piece of pale blue painted paper (see Expert Advice, p.481) into a variety of strips and patches that correspond with the pattern of light and ripples on the water. Arrange the torn paper shapes on the painting – some pieces can overlap the swimmer's body.

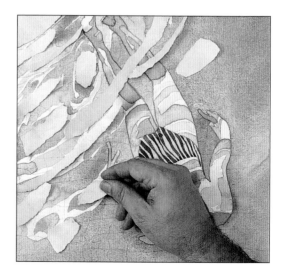

© Private Collection/Courtesy Fischbach Gallery, New York

Master Strokes
Alice Dalton Brown (b. 1939)
Pool, Tropical Reflection

Dalton Brown has used oils to produce a wonderfully detailed rendition of a swimming pool – quite a contrast to the more abstract shapes of the step-by-step project. The artist has divided the canvas broadly into two halves – the green of the foliage against the blue of the water. Look closely at the green foliage and you begin to see other beautiful colours – yellows for the sunlit leaves, browns for the branches and even the odd shade of purple.

The wall helps guide the eye around the picture – from the red flowered plant in the corner to the trunk of the palm tree on the right.

The swimming pool holds a wonderful array of reflections, from the spiky palm leaves to the bold linear shape of the trunk.

7 ▶ Glue the ripples
Spray adhesive on to the back of the pale blue shapes and stick them in position. You can butt shapes up to the body by cutting long strips with a scalpel. Either cut them directly on the paper, or if you prefer, mark a line with the pencil and then use the scalpel on a cutting mat.

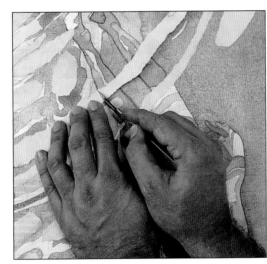

EXPERT ADVICE
Prepare collage papers

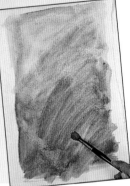

Choose a variety of papers for the collage – firm, slightly textured ones are best. Using a No.12 round brush, paint the papers loosely, working in all directions and allowing the brush marks to show so that you create an interesting surface (as shown right).

8 ▼ Add to the collage Tear some dark blue paper into curved bands and glue them on the right. Now tear small patches and strips of paper in dark flesh and hair shades; place them on the legs, shoulders and hair. Make some fit the body contours, but extend others to suggest the distorting effect of the water.

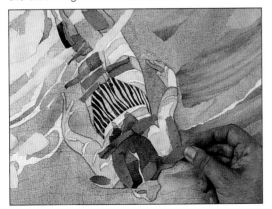

9 ▼ Stick on pale colours Stick small strips of pale, flesh-coloured paper on the legs, feet, shoulders and back to add highlights. Finally, glue tiny scraps of white paper in the top left of the picture to represent dappled light.

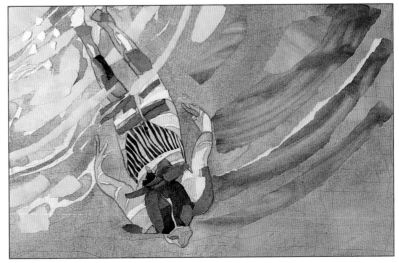

A FEW STEPS FURTHER

The collage is now complete and cleverly plays up the textural and patterned elements in the picture. To blend the collage into the painting a little, add some more touches of watercolour here and there.

10 ▶ Work on the water Using the stronger blue wash from step 5, paint some ripples in the water, taking the brush marks right across the arms and legs. Splatter drops of dark blue to the left of the swimmer.

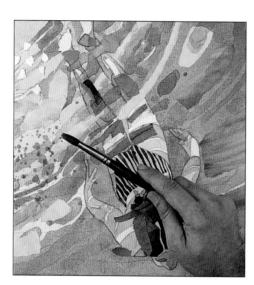

11 ▲ Add definition With stronger mixes of the hair and flesh colours from the palette, paint shadows on the hair and limbs. Define the right eye, and the fingers, heels and toes.

THE FINISHED PICTURE

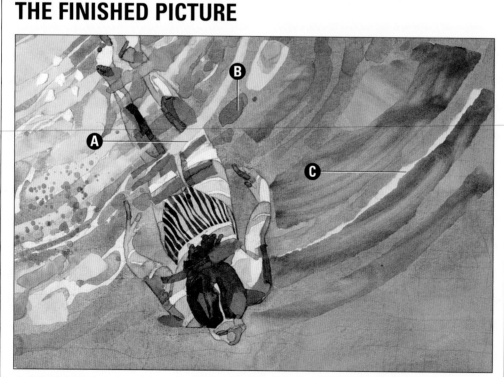

A Raised texture
Torn from a range of medium-weight watercolour papers, the stuck-down shapes add texture to the smooth, flat surface of the underpainting.

B Wet-on-dry
Each layer of paint was left to dry before the next was applied, so the blocks of colours have well-defined edges that complement the patterns made by the collage.

C Torn edge
The uneven white edge of one of the torn pieces of collage paper is left unpainted to suggest a ripple catching the light in the swimming pool.

Still life of peppers

Red and green peppers create a visually striking image that is ideally suited to watercolour washes and water-soluble pencils.

One way of creating a sense of depth in a still life is to work over a watercolour wash. To achieve the highly effective drawing of these peppers, for example, the artist first painted thin washes of red and green watercolour over the initial sketch to give a coloured surface on which to continue the drawing with water-soluble pencils.

Practical points

As you are using water with the paints and the coloured pencils, you will need to work on sturdy watercolour paper. Blocks of watercolour paper are useful for this kind of exercise, where you are not intending to wet the paper very much. You can paint directly on to the top sheet, which is still secured to the block, thus avoiding having to stretch the paper first.

When you lay down the washes, change your water frequently in order to keep the paint as clean as possible. If your wash spreads too far outside the lines of the sketch, you can easily mop it up with a piece of kitchen paper. Remember, though, that as a large part of the wash will eventually be covered by coloured pencil, you do not need to be too accurate.

Using water-soluble pencils

Water-soluble pencils are ideal to use in conjunction with watercolours, as they can be handled like ordinary coloured pencils, but can also be dampened with a wet brush to blend and intensify their colours. You can build up the shapes of the peppers with shading, leaving the underlayer of paint showing where you want the tones to be light.

◀ The peppers are built up layer by layer, starting with an underwash of watercolour and progressing to water-soluble pencils, which are themselves wetted selectively to show form and tone.

483

FIRST STROKES

1 ▼ Draw the outlines Using a 4B pencil, draw the outlines of the peppers with loose strokes. Try not to make the pencil marks too strong, as you don't want them to show through the watercolour in the final picture. On the cut pepper, indicate the shape of the seed area and the pith.

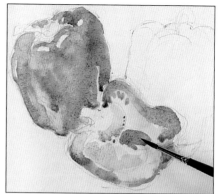

2 ▲ Apply a wet-on-wet wash Using a No. 5 brush, first wash clear water over the parts of the peppers that you are going to paint. Avoid wetting the paper where the highlights will be, as you want to leave these white. Make a thin wash of alizarin crimson with a little cadmium red and paint over the wetted parts of the red peppers. Mix a little Payne's grey into the wash for the darker areas, and some sap green for the brown hollow in the cut pepper.

3 ▶ Begin the green pepper Wet the green pepper again if the paper has dried out, as you need to apply the washes wet-on-wet. Leave the highlights dry, as before. Make a thin sap green wash and add a little of the previous red wash to make an olive-green colour. Paint the left side of the green pepper, then deepen the wash with more of the previous red to paint the right-hand side and the shaded part of the stalk.

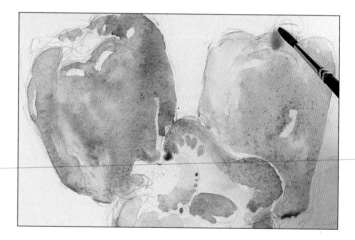

4 ▶ Wash over the shadows Wet the shadow areas on the right of the green pepper and under the red peppers with clear water. Avoid the edges of the previous washes so that the colours won't run together. Then brush on a dilute wash of neutral tint, mixed from all the colours on the palette, to show the grey shadows.

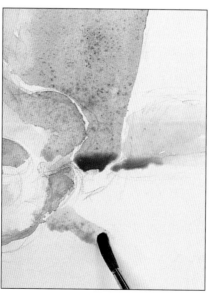

5 ▶ Add a few details Leave the paint to dry. Change to a No. 3 brush to add some detail. Paint the stalks on the red peppers with sap green. Then add sap green to the original red wash to make brown. Darken the hollow in the cut pepper, dab on more seeds and paint the stalk on the green pepper. Emphasize the edges and centre of the cut pepper with a strong mix of alizarin crimson and cadmium red.

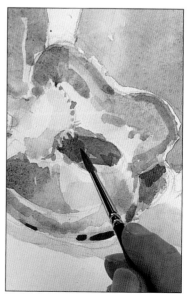

DEVELOPING THE PICTURE

Now that the main shapes and tones of the peppers have been indicated with washes of watercolour, you can begin to define their forms more clearly with water-soluble pencils. Make sure the washes are dry before you begin – you can use a hair-dryer to speed up the process if you wish.

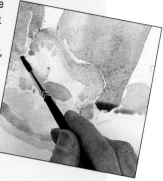

TROUBLE SHOOTER

SMOOTHING OUT PUDDLES

As you are laying down the washes, you might notice that an earlier wash has gathered in a small puddle on the paper, forming a dark patch like the one at the base of the green pepper shown here. To remove this, tip your drawing board up so that the paint runs back into the main part of the wash. In this way, the colour will be evened out.

6▲ Shade the red and green peppers Using a rose carmine water-soluble pencil, shade over the wash on the red pepper with hatching marks until most of it is covered. Leave the highlights and some bands of lighter tone to create the pepper's ridges and curves. Change to a moss green water-soluble pencil to begin shading the green pepper. In the same way as for the red pepper, leave the pale wash showing where the tone is lighter.

7▲ Work on the cut pepper Complete the shading on the green pepper, then shade the stalks with the moss green pencil. Darken the top corner of the cut pepper with a patch of rose carmine. Using a dark orange water-soluble pencil, colour across the lighter areas of the flesh and pith of this pepper with free strokes.

8▲ Darken the shadows Warm up the shaded side of the red pepper with hatched lines made with an Indian red pencil. Use a medium grey pencil to deepen the colours of the cast shadows, keeping within their outlines.

9◄ Begin to wash over the pencil marks Deepen the colour in the hollow of the cut pepper with the Indian red and dark orange pencils. Then, using the No. 3 brush, wet this area to diffuse the colour.

10 ▼ **Add more lines and wash** Continue diffusing the colours of the pencils by washing clear water over the darker areas of the green pepper. Liven up the red pepper with the dark orange pencil, and again add a wash over these areas to intensify their colour. Add hard lines to the curves of the red pepper with the Indian red pencil, then soften them slightly with water.

A FEW STEPS FURTHER

The picture is now a pleasing combination of watercolour washes and pencil shading softened with added water. With additional colour, you can enhance the tones and make the peppers even more realistic.

11 ▶ **Add depth to the darkest areas** Using the medium grey pencil, deepen the darkest tones on the red pepper with just a little colour. The darker colour helps to throw the lighter colours forward in the picture.

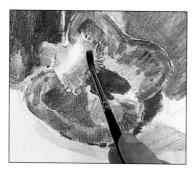

12 ◀ **Give the picture a final wash of water** Colour in the seed area and the tops of the stalks with ochre pencil. Outline some of the seeds with the Indian red pencil, and put in some lines of texture on the edge of the cut pepper. With the rose carmine pencil, deepen the outer edge of the cut pepper. Smooth out the colours once more with the No. 3 brush.

THE FINISHED PICTURE

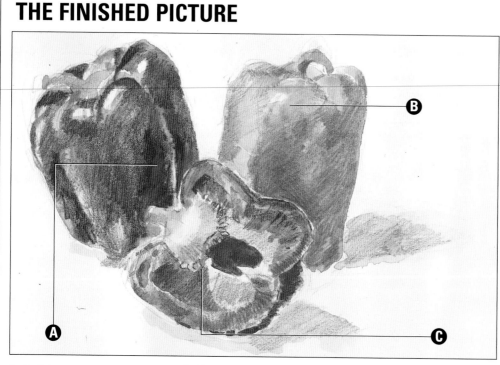

A Dark tones
Deeper tones were created with water-soluble pencil marks, which were then washed over to intensify the colour.

B Light tones
The initial pale watercolour wash shows through in places to form the light tones in the picture.

C Sharp details
The seeds in the cut pepper were drawn over the underlying washes with a well-sharpened water-soluble pencil.

The drama of the sky

Watercolours aren't usually associated with textural marks. However, by mixing them with ordinary paper glue, you can create thick, exciting brush strokes.

Two hundred years ago, J. M. W. Turner (1775–1851) mixed flour paste with watercolour to paint atmospheric clouds and mists. The landscape below has a similar drama, but here the watercolours are mixed with

▼ Using watercolour with glue allows you to emphasise the brush strokes – as if you were working in oils or acrylics.

YOU WILL NEED

Piece of 400gsm (200lb) Not watercolour paper 41 x 51cm (16 x 20in)

7 watercolour paints: Cerulean blue; Mauve; Ultramarine; Prussian blue; Lemon yellow; Sap green; Cadmium red

Brushes: No.4 soft round; 25mm (1in) decorator's brush; Nos.12, 4 and 6 stiff flats

Mixing palette or dish and a jar of water

Paste-type paper glue (eg Gloy) and tissue

1 ◄ Paint the basic outlines Make a well-diluted wash of cerulean blue and water. Using a No.4 soft round brush, mark the position of the horizon and paint in the main cloud formations.

2 ► Start painting the sky Mix mauve and ultramarine with plenty of glue – the ratio here is about one part colour to four parts glue – then add enough water to make the mixture easy to spread. Using a 25mm (1in) decorator's brush, establish the cloudy sky in free sweeps.

paper glue to make the colour thick and viscous. Glue delays the drying time of the paint, allowing you to move the colour around on the paper. The thickened paint also retains the brush marks to give a good texture. Alternatively, by adding water to the mixture, the colour can be spread thinly and flatly.

Which glue?

For this technique, use the paste-type, liquid paper glues available at stationers – Gloy is a well-known brand. Water-soluble glues are particularly good – if you make a mistake, you can simply wet the area and wipe the colour away.

For pale colours, use only a touch of paint with the glue – about 5% watercolour is a good starting point. Increase the paint-to-glue ratio for stronger colours. Most of the colours in this image were about 20% paint and 80% glue. However, this is by no means an exact recipe. The best method is to pour some glue next to the colours on your palette and mix the two until you get the desired result.

As creative expression is the name of the game when using glue, the artist took a few liberties with his reference photo, including adding some bright red flowers.

EXPERT ADVICE
Mixing glue and paint

Mix the watercolour paint and glue on a white palette or dish. Against a white background, you can control the strength and transparency of the mixture more easily and assess how dark or pale the colour will appear on the white paper. Note that using glue and watercolour on their own produces a stiff mix, suitable for highly textured work. For general brushwork and washes, dilute the mix with water.

3 ▼ **Add pure blue** Still working with lively strokes, dip the brush in water and spread the sky colour unevenly across the paper. Mix ultramarine with glue and water and add diagonal streaks across the centre of the sky.

4 ▲ **Establish the horizon** Start to build up the colour in the lower part of the sky by painting a strong mixture of Prussian blue and glue along the horizon line.

5 ◄ **Develop the sky** Put a large blob of the Prussian blue and glue mixture in the middle of the sky. Use a crumpled paper tissue to smear the paint upwards and outwards to create an eruption of colour spreading from the centre of the picture.

6 ▲ **Use a dry brush** Start to manipulate the wet, viscous colour to give a turbulent, windswept effect. Use a dry decorating brush and drag it across the sky to create shafts of diffused sunlight.

7 ◄ **Define the clouds** Using a clean, dry No.12 stiff flat brush, work further into the wet colour with short, stubby strokes. This reveals the white paper to suggest light on the clouds. If the colour has already begun to dry, simply wet the area with a little clean water before using the dry brush.

TROUBLE SHOOTER

CORRECTING MISTAKES

By using water-soluble glue, you can dissolve and remove mistakes even after the painted surface has dried. Here, clean water is applied to dissolve the dry colour before removing it with a brush or tissue.

DEVELOP THE PICTURE

Now that the sky is complete, move on to the landscape, painting it in clear, bright colours with lively, textural strokes.

8 ▲ Remove colour Wet the top right-hand sky area and use the dry bristles of the No.12 flat brush to wipe off the colour, creating a large white cloud.

9 ▲ Add the distant landscape Mix pale green from lemon yellow and a little sap green. Add glue and paint this along the horizon with a No.4 stiff flat brush. Mix a deeper green from ultramarine and lemon yellow and add a few trees.

Master Strokes

Nicolas Roerich (1874–1947)
Skyscape

While Roerich paints the receding hills with flattish colours, he makes the clouds into fully modelled, sculptural forms. Indeed they seem to be more solid than the land. The resulting effect is rather menacing – almost as if we are looking at an alien world.

The brown clouds in the distance take on the appearance of upturned hills – almost as if the landscape is reflected in the sky.

To convey distance, aerial perspective is used – the hills get progressively bluer in the distance.

10 ▶ **Paint the foreground grass**
Make a dilute mix of lemon yellow with a touch of ultramarine to create a light lime green. Using long, sweeping horizontal strokes, paint the grass right across the foreground.

A FEW STEPS FURTHER

As it stands, the painting could be considered complete – a dramatic landscape with a turbulent sky and windswept fields. However, you might wish to add a little more colour, giving an indication of the yellow flowers in the field and perhaps also adding some red ones for variety.

11 ◀ **Scratch in some texture**
Paint long vertical streaks of grass, using the deep green tree mixture from step 9. While the colour is still wet, use the tip of the brush handle to scratch bold, scribbled texture into the grass.

Express yourself
Washes of watercolour

This sketch shows how different sky effects can be achieved by using watercolours without glue. The loose, stretched-out washes of paint capture the blustery atmosphere in a very immediate way. The dark grey shapes in the distance have been applied wet-in-wet and give the impression of distant trees.

12 ▲ **Finish the foreground** Complete scratching back the grass, and allow the painting to dry before moving on to the next stage.

491

13▼ **Paint sunlit fields** Using the No.6 stiff flat brush, mix lemon yellow with a little glue and apply this in broad horizontal strokes to depict light on the fields. Add a few

14▲ **Add red flowers** Finally, mix cadmium red with a little glue and dot in clusters of poppies to show up against the yellow and green grass.

THE FINISHED PICTURE

A Revealed white
A dry brush was used to wipe back wet colour in the sky, revealing pale clouds and creating a sense of movement.

B Sgraffiti
Long grasses were scratched into the viscous colour with the tip of the brush handle, creating lively texture in the foreground.

C Pure colour
Many of the colours are used unmixed. For example, the flowers are painted in pure lemon yellow and cadmium red.

Glossary

Absorbency
The degree to which a paper absorbs paint or water. Absorbency is governed by the amount of "size" built into the paper. Waterleaf paper contains no size and is highly absorbent. Papers with very little size are referred to as "soft." A paper's absorbency has a major effect on the way a medium behaves on it, especially in watercolour painting: a highly absorbent paper will soak up brushstrokes immediately, while a well-sized one allows more time for manipulation.

Acid-free paper
Paper with a neutral pH. An acidic paper, such as one made from untreated wood pulp, will yellow as the acid breaks down the fibres. Chemically treated wood pulp papers are generally neutral. Artist's rag papers, made from cotton fibres, have a much higher standard of purity. Acid-free paper is recommended for any drawing that you wish to preserve in good condition.

Adjacent colours
Colours close to each other on the colour wheel; also used to describe colours that lie next to each other in a painting.

Advancing colour
Effect where colours toward the warm (red) end of the spectrum appear to move toward the viewer. Compare *Receding colour*.

Afterimage
The phenomenon of staring intently at a strong colour and then looking away and seeing a 'ghost' image in its complementary. Also called 'colour irradiation'.

Anamorphosis
The distortion of an image by transferring it from a regular rectangular grid to a stretched perspective grid, so that when it is seen from an oblique angle, it reverts to its original appearance.

Art board
Artist's quality paper mounted on card. Its stiffness reduces the risk of pigment loss caused by flexing.

Artist's quality paints
Premium-quality paints with a high pigment strength and content.

Artist's quality paper
Paper with a neutral pH balance and a high rag content which, unlike wood pulp paper, does not yellow or become brittle with age.

Ascending vanishing point
Point above the horizon line at which two or more parallel lines in the same plane and receding away from the viewer appear to converge – for example, on a pitched roof.

Atmospheric perspective
Effect of the Earth's atmosphere on the way we perceive tones and colours as they recede towards the horizon. Tones lighten and decrease in contrast; colours drift to the cool (blue) end of the spectrum. Also known as 'aerial perspective'.

Axonometric projection
A system where a plane is set up at a fixed angle to the horizontal, such as 45 degrees, and verticals are drawn true to scale to show the sides of the object.

Binder
A substance that holds particles of pigment together and enables them to adhere to the support. In watercolours, the binder is water-soluble gum.

Bleeding
The tendency of some organic pigments to migrate through a covering layer of paint.

Blending
Creating a gradual transition from one colour or tone to another. This can be done with physical or optical mixing of pigments, or with shading techniques such as cross-hatching.

Broken colour
An application of colour that allows the underlying colour to show through in an irregular pattern. Often achieved using dry brush or scumbling techniques.

Burnisher
A polished stone used to smooth down paper fibres.

Canvas
Fabric used as a support for painting. There are two main types of canvas: artist's linen (made from flax) and cotton duck. You can purchase pre-primed canvases or prepare your own. See also *Support*.

Carborundum pastel board
A board coated in powdered carborundum which creates an exceptional degree of tooth that can hold a thick application of pastel.

Centre of vision
Point at which the line of vision intersects the horizon line. In one-point perspective, it forms the one and only vanishing point.

Chromatic
Drawn or painted in a range of colours.

Collage
An art form in which an image is built up out of pieces of cloth, paper, photographs, card, or other materials pasted onto a board or similar support.

Collagraph print
A print taken by pressing a sheet of paper onto the inked surface of a low-relief surface constructed in the same way as a collage.

Colour wheel
A method of depicting natural and artificial spectrums as circles to show the relationships between colours.

Complementary colours
Colours of maximum contrast that oppose each other on a colour wheel. The complementary of a primary colour is the combination of the other two primaries; for example, the complementary of blue is orange (red plus yellow).

Cone of vision
A cone of up to 60 degrees, within which a subject can be comfortably represented without perceived distortion.

Contour shading
A form of shading in which curved parallel lines are used to show the rounded forms of the human body. Contour shading echoes the natural curves of the human figure and is useful for defining musculature.

Convergence
The apparent coming together of parallel lines that recede from the viewer toward a fixed point.

Cool colours
Colours toward the blue end of the spectrum.

Cross-hatching
Parallel marks overlaid roughly at right angles to another set of parallel marks. This process can be repeated until the desired depth of tone is achieved.

Darks
Dark tones; the parts of a painting that are in shadow.

Descending vanishing point
A point below the horizon line to which two or more parallel lines in the same plane and receding away from the viewer appear to converge – such as a street sloping downhill.

Diagonal vanishing point
The vanishing point for lines receding at 45 degrees from the picture plane.

Distance point
A point on the horizon line from which a line is drawn to establish the intersection points of transversals with orthogonals. In one-point perspective, it corresponds to a diagonal vanishing point.

Dragged brushstrokes
Brushstrokes made across the textured surface of canvas or paint, or at a shallow angle into wet paint.

Drawing grid
A grid made for transferring a sketch proportionately onto a large-scale support.

Dry brush
A method of painting in which paint of a stiff consistency is stroked or rubbed across the canvas. The paint is picked up by the ridges of the canvas, leaving the underlying colour still visible to produce a broken colour effect.

Easel
A frame for holding a drawing while the artist works on it. Artists working outdoors tend to use easels of light construction. A good sketching easel allows the drawing to be held securely in any position.

Elevation
A two-dimensional scale drawing of the side of a building.

GLOSSARY

Ellipse
A regular oval shape formed when a circle is put into perspective.

Eye-level
The plane of vision from the viewer to the horizon, i.e. the horizon line.

Feathering
Laying roughly parallel marks, often over a previous area of colour, to modify the strength of colour or tone.

Ferrule
The metal part of a brush that surrounds and retains the hairs.

Finder
A cardboard viewer in which the shape of the paper or canvas is cut out to scale. The viewer is held up at arm's length by the artist, who views the scene through it in order to establish what will be drawn or painted and roughly where it will be on the canvas.

Flat colour
An area of colour of uniform tone and hue.

Flat wash
A wash of uniform tone and colour.

Focal point
The main area of visual interest in a painting.

Foreshortening
An effect of perspective in which uniformly spaced, parallel horizontal lines appear to get closer together as they recede into the distance. It also causes the part of an object closest to the viewer to appear proportionately larger than the rest of the object. The degree of foreshortening depends on the angle at which you view the scene.

Form
The shape of a three-dimensional object, usually represented by line or tone in a two-dimensional drawing.

Fugitive
Colours that are not lightfast and will fade over a period of time.

Glycerin
The syrupy ingredient of watercolor paints used to keep them moist.

Gouache
Opaque watercolour paint. Also known as 'bodycolour'.

Gouache resist
Application of gouache paint to protect areas of paper or paint film from additional applications of watercolour. The gouache is subsequently washed off.

Graded wash
A wash in which the tones move smoothly from dark to light or from light to dark.

Granulation
The mottled effect made by coarse pigments as they settle into the hollows of a textured paper.

Graphite pencil
A more accurate name for the 'lead' pencil. Standard pencils are made from a mixture of graphite and clay encased in wood. The proportion of graphite to clay varies, and it is this proportion that determines the hardness or softness of the pencil. Graphite has a silvery sheen if used densely.

Graphite stick
A thick graphite pencil, used for large-scale work. Graphite sticks are usually fixed in a graphite holder rather than encased in wood.

Grid system
A method of superimposing a grid over an image or view, and then copying the image square by square into a corresponding grid on the support.

Ground
Surface coating of the support on which the paint is applied. A coloured ground is often used in low-key paintings, where it provides the halftones and unifies the other colours. A coloured ground can also be applied as an imprimatura.

Ground line
The bottom edge of the picture plane, where it cuts the ground plane. Parallel to the horizon line.

Ground plane
Level at which the viewer is imagined to be standing in order to view a scene. Stretches to the horizon.

Gum arabic
Gum from the acacia tree, used as a binding material in watercolour paints.

Gum arabic resist
A gum arabic solution used to protect the paper or paint film from more applications of paint. The gum arabic is subsequently washed off.

Gum solution
A dilution of gum in water, used as a binder to hold the pastel pigment in stick form.

Gum tragacanth
The gum used as a binder for soft pastel.

Halftones
Transitional tones between highlights and darks.

Hard watercolours
Blocks of straight pigment-and-gum mixes with no added humectant.

Hatching
In drawing, making tonal gradations by shading with parallel marks. In painting, making tonal gradations by shading with long, thin brushstrokes; often used in underpainting.

Heel
The base of the hairs of a brush.

Height line
Vertical line on the picture plane with heights marked to scale of objects that are behind or in front of it. Also known as 'measure line'.

High-key colour
Brilliant and saturated colour. High-key paintings are usually painted on white or near-white grounds.

Highlight
The lightest tone in a drawing or painting; usually white or near-white. In transparent watercolour techniques on white paper, highlights are represented by the white of the paper; in opaque watercolour techniques, highlights are represented with opaque white gouache.

Horizon line
The location of all horizontal vanishing points. It is the line at which land and sky appear to meet and is always at eye-level.

Hot-Pressed paper
Paper with a very smooth surface; the smoothest of the three main surface types for artist's-quality paper. Also called 'HP'.

Hue
The basic name or description of an object's colour, such as red, yellow, or blue. The term does not describe how light or dark the colour is or how saturated or intense it is.

Humectant
A moisture-absorbing additive, such as glycerin, which keeps watercolour paints moist.

Imprimatura
A thin overall film of translucent colour that is applied over a white primer before painting. This film does not affect the reflective qualities of the ground, but provides a useful background colour and makes it easier to paint between the lights and the darks.

Isometric projection
A form of axonometric projection that denies the apparent convergence of receding lines. Height lines are true and to scale. The angle of receding lines relates to the angles where the planes of the cube meet.

Laminating
A process of gluing thin sheets of tissue paper over each other between layers of glue; the glue transforms the tissue paper into transparent sheets of colour. An extension of Collage.

Laying in
Initial painting stage in which broad areas of flat colour are applied over a preliminary drawing. Also known as 'blocking in.'

Lifting out
Modifying a colour or creating highlights by removing paint with a wet brush, or a sponge or kitchen paper. Also called 'lifting off'.

Lightfastness
The permanence or durability of a colour; its resistance to fading.

Line drawing
A drawing technique where the subject is defined through an outline rather than with tonal shading.

Line of vision
Imaginary line from the viewer to the horizon, bisecting the angle of the cone of vision and at 90 degrees to the picture plane. It intersects the horizon line on the picture plane at the centre of vision. Also called 'centre line of vision'.

Linear perspective
System of representing three-dimensional space on a two-dimensional surface by recording the intersection on the picture plane of rays of light from the scene as they converge on the viewer. Also known as "artificial perspective."

Loomstate canvas
A canvas which has not been 'finished'.

Low-key colour
Subdued, unsaturated colour that tends toward brown and gray.

Mahl stick
A pole about 1.25 m (4 ft.) long with a ball-shaped end that is used to support the painting arm when working on a very large canvas.

Masking fluid
A peel-off rubber solution that can be applied with a brush or dip pen to mask out areas of an artwork before applying a wash. Available in white or pale yellow (for use on white paper).

Masking out
A technique for leaving areas of paper unpainted when applying washes by first covering them with paper or masking fluid.

Masking tape
Pressure-sensitive tape used to protect areas of paint.

Medium
A substance that alters the consistency of paint, such as for glazing.

Metamerism
Where two colour matches can appear to differ under different illumination. This is actually caused by the varying compositions of each colour.

Modelling
Describing the form of a solid object using solid shading or linear marks.

Monochromatic
Made with a single colour. A monochromatic drawing can still show a full range of tones.

Monoprint
A technique that results in a single print.

Mortar and pestle
A bowl and grinding tool used to reduce pastel sticks to a powder for dry wash techniques and for reconstituting pastel fragments into new pastels.

Muller
A glass grinding tool used to grind and mix pigments on a glass slab.

Negative shape (space)
The shape created between objects or parts of objects. If a figure is standing with one hand on his or her hip, the triangular space between the arm and the body forms a negative shape.

NOT paper
As in not hot-pressed paper, it is paper with a medium or fine grained surface, midway between HP (smooth) and rough. Also known as 'cold-pressed paper'.

Oblique projection
In oblique projection, an elevation is drawn and receding lines are added all at the same angle, for example 45 degrees to the horizontal. The length of these receding lines is reduced by the same ratio of the 90 degree angle to the angle of the elevation that the receding line represents.

One-point perspective
Simplest form of linear perspective in which all parallel lines at 90 degrees to the picture plane and parallel with the ground plane appear to converge at the same vanishing point on the horizon.

Optical mixing
Colour mixing by laying one colour over, or next to, another, rather than mixing the colours in a palette.

Orthogonals
Lines that recede at right angles from the picture plane to a vanishing point on the horizon.

Orthographic projection
The standard method of showing a plan and elevation.

Physical mixing
Creating colours by mixing them on the palette or, wet-in-wet and wet-on-dry, on support.

Picture plane
Plane on which the image of a scene lies. Optically, the point at which rays of light from the scene meet in the viewer's eye. Normally at 90 degrees to the ground plane but this angle changes if you look up at, or down on, a scene.

Pigment
Solid-coloured material in the form of discrete particles that form the basic component of all types of paint; colour in its raw state.

Plan
A two-dimensional scale drawing of a horizontal section of an object, such as a building.

Plein air
Painting in the open air.

Primary colours
The three colours – red, blue, and yellow – that cannot be produced by mixing other colours.

Primer
Preliminary coating, usually made from a white pigment and extender in a binding medium, to prepare a support for painting. Stops the support from being damaged by the paint and provides a surface with the right key, absorbency level and colour.

Projection
In linear perspective, carrying lines from the station point to points on the plan and thereafter to the picture plane where the points of intersection are marked.

Quill
A bird's feather that has been made into a pen.

Rag paper
Artist's quality paper made from cotton fibres to a high standard of purity.

Receding colour
Effect where colours toward the cool (blue) end of the spectrum appear to move away from the viewer.

Resist
A method of preventing paint from coming into contact with the paper, or other paint layers, by interposing a paint-resistant coating such as wax or gum. Often used to preserve highlights, or for specific textural effects.

Rough paper
The most heavily textured of the three main surface types of artist's paper.

Sgraffito
A technique in which dried paint or pastel is scratched or scraped off to reveal the colour below. Often used for textural effects.

Sable
Mink tail hair used to make fine watercolour brushes.

Saturation
The intensity of a colour. Saturated colours are vivid and intense; unsaturated colours are dull and muted. Also known as 'chroma'.

Scratching out
A technique similar to Sgraffito, in which wet or dry paint is scratched to reveal the paint or paper beneath.

Scumbling
A painting technique in which semiopaque or thin opaque colours are loosely brushed over an underpainted area so that patches of the underlying colour show through.

Secondary colours
Colours that contain a mixture of two primaries.

Section
A scale drawing showing a two-dimensional slice through an object, such as a building, in the vertical or horizontal plane.

Sight size
The measurement of the size of a distant object as you see it, which is then transferred exactly to the paper.

Size
The surface coating, built-in or brushed on, of paper. Ready-made size generally contains a mixture of gelatine, water, and preservative. Sizing affects the hardness and absorbency of the paper, which in turn affects how the paint behaves.

Soft-hair brushes
Brushes with soft, flexible bristles of sable or synthetic material. They are mainly used for watercolours.

Spattering
Flicking paint off the hairs of a bristle brush or a toothbrush to create irregular patterns.

Spectrum
The band of frequencies at which light is visible, running from low (red) through to high (blue).

GLOSSARY

Sponging out
Soaking up paint with a sponge or paper towel so that areas of pigment are lightened or removed from the paper. Can be used to correct mistakes or to create particular effects.

Squaring up
A grid system used to transfer a sketch or other image accurately to the painting surface.

Staining power
The degree to which a pigment stains the paper and resists being washed off or scrubbed out.

Station point
Point on the ground plane from which a subject is viewed.

Stenciling
The application of designs, shapes or characters to a surface using a plastic, metal or card sheet in which the image has been cut out. Ink or paint is applied to the surface through the cutout areas.

Stippling
A method of painting or drawing that involves the application of tiny spots of colour to create an area of tone, for example by stabbing and dotting with the tip of a brush or pastel.

Stretcher
The wooden frame on which a canvas is supported.

Stretching
In watercolour, preparing lighter weights of paper so that they will not buckle when wet. Normally done by taping the paper to a flat surface with masking tape, coating it with water and leaving it to dry.

Subdivision
Method of putting images into perspective by subdividing them into simple shapes, then putting the outlines of these shapes into perspective.

Support
Material on which a painting or drawing is made, such as paper, pastel board or, canvas.

Surface
The three standard grades of surface are HP (hot-pressed), NOT (cold-pressed), and Rough.

Surface sizing
Decreasing the absorbency of a paper by sizing.

Tertiary colours
Colours with a mixture of all three primaries.

Three-point perspective
System in which the subject is angled vertically, as well as horizontally, to the picture plane; requires an extra vanishing point for the third (vertical) plane.

Tint
Colour mixed with white. Thinning the paint with water and allowing more of the white surface of the paper to reflect through it.

Tinting strength
The strength of a particular colour or pigment.

Toe
The tip of the hairs on a brush.

Tonal key
The degree of light that dominates a subject. For example, a very bright subject such as a beach in full sunlight would have a high tonal key.

Tonal value
The extent to which a colour reflects light.

Tone
Degree of darkness or lightness of a colour.

Toned ground
An opaque layer of coloured paint of uniform tone applied over the priming before starting the painting. Also known as "coloured ground."

Tooth
The grain of the paper that holds the pigment. The coarser the texture of the paper, the more the more medium is retained by the paper surface.

Torchon
A pencil-shaped tool made of tightly rolled paper and used to soften or blend tones during drawing. Also known as 'tortillon'.

Transparent painting
A painting technique that relies on the transparency of the paints used.

Transversals
Receding horizontal lines parallel to the picture plane.

Two-point perspective
Perspective in which an object or scene has its vertical edges parallel to the picture plane, but its horizontal sides set at an angle. Needs two vanishing points, both of which will be on the horizon line.

Underpainting
Preliminary painting, often in flat colour, that gives the final painting more reflectivity or density.

Unsaturated colour
A pure, saturated colour becomes unsaturated when mixed with another colour into a tint (lighter) or shade (darker).

Value
The extent to which a colour reflects or transmits light; how light or dark a colour is.

Vanishing axis
A vertical axis at right angles to the horizon line. Descending or ascending parallel lines in the same plane have their vanishing points on this axis.

Vanishing line
A line that converges on a vanishing point.

Vanishing point
The point at which any two or more parallel lines that are in the same plane and receding from the viewer appear to converge.

Variegated wash
A wash in which different colours have been applied so that they run into one another.

Viewfinder
Two L-shaped pieces of card that form a framing device. This tool is usually held at arm's length and the scene to be drawn is seen through it.

Viewpoint
The point, particularly the height, from which a scene is viewed. Determines the height of the horizon line.

Warm colours
Colours toward the red end of the spectrum.

Wash
An application of well-diluted paint or ink. Washes of water-soluble colours are made by diluting the colours with water in a mixing dish before application.

Washing off
Dislodging an area of water-soluble paint, usually with a bristle brush dipped in water or a damp sponge.

Watercolour
Paint made by mixing pigments with a water-soluble binding material such as gum arabic.

Waterleaf
A highly absorbent paper with no built-in size.

Weight
Watercolour paper is measured in pounds per ream (lb) or grams per square metre (gsm). Watercolour paper comes in a wide range of weights, but standard machine-made papers are 90 lb. (190 gsm), 140 lb. (300 gsm), 260 lb. (356 gsm) and 300 lb. (638 gsm). Heavier papers – 60 lb. and over – generally do not need stretching.

Wet-in-wet
Working with wet paint into wet paint directly on the support.

Wet-on-dry
Applying a layer of wet paint onto a dry surface.

Wove paper
Paper that retains the pattern of the wire mold on which it was made, giving it a woven appearance.